GW00569950

TONKIN GULF YACHT CLUB

TONKIN GULF YACHT CLUB

US Carrier Operations off Vietnam

René J Francillon

First published in Great Britain in 1988 by
Conway Maritime Press Ltd
24 Bride Lane, Fleet Street
LONDON EC4Y 8DR

ISBN 0 85177 484 9

Designed by John Mitchell
Maps by Denys Baker
Typeset by Lasertext Ltd, Stretford, Manchester
Printed and bound in Great Britain by
Richard Clay Ltd, Chichester

Contents

Tables

Maps

Preface and Acknowledgments

Work on this book began as a personal research project to compile the listing of carriers and Air Wings deployed to the Gulf of Tonkin during the Southeast Asia War which I needed for other writing projects. When I later showed it to several Naval Aviators and aviation enthusiasts, their reactions convinced me to seek a publisher prepared to take a risk in producing a reference book of this type. I am grateful to Robert Gardiner for supporting me in this venture.

The selection of USS *Coral Sea* (CVA-43) as the subject of the carrier monograph was based on sound reasoning as she spent more days on the line than any other Task Force 77 carrier and made the longest war cruise. Admittedly, however, I had reasons of my own for making this selection. As early as July 1948, *Coral Sea* had made a great impression on my mind; as a young boy I had come aboard while she was riding at anchor in Golfe Juan during her first cruise to the Mediterranean Sea. Twenty-eight years later, it was aboard *Coral Sea* that I first experienced the thrills of carrier operations when, as a guest of COMNAVAIRPAC and her skipper, Capt Joseph F Frick, I spent three days on board during a training cycle in the SoCal OpArea in October 1976. Later on, I often saw her from my office in San Francisco before her departure from Alameda in March 1983. I make no apologies for being partial to *Coral Sea* and her crew.

The principal source documents used in the preparation of this book, and notably the listing of carrier deployments appearing in Appendix 1, include the following:

- *United States Naval Aviation, 1910–1980*, NAVAIR 00-80P-1, US Government Printing Office, Washington, DC, 1981
- *Line Periods for Carriers Deployed to Southeast Asia, May 1964—December 1973*, Doreen K Wolownik, Center for Naval Analyses, Arlington, Va, 1974
- *Allowances and Location of Naval Aircraft*, OPNAV Notice C3110, Office of the Chief of Naval Operations, Washington, DC, various issues between 1964 and 1973
- *CNA Loss/Damage Data Base*, Office of the Chief of Naval Operations, Washington, DC, undated
- Cruise books for the twenty-one carriers deployed to Southeast Asia

I wish to express my most sincere gratitude to the following organizations and individuals for their valuable assistance:

- CHINFO (Capt M T Sherman, Special Assistant to the Secretary of the Navy, and LCdr R J Donovan, Head, Media Services Branch)
- Naval Air Systems Command (Dr William J Armstrong)
- Naval Historical Center (Dr Dean C Allard, Head, Operational Archives Branch; Roy Grossnick, C I Rakestraw, and Gwendolyn Rich, Naval Aviation History and Archives; and John C Reilly, Jr, Ships' Histories Branch)
- the PAO staff aboard the USS *Coral Sea* (CV-43) and USS *Kitty Hawk* (CV-63)

I am also greatly indebted to Pete Clayton for his 'Thirty-Five Years of *Coral Sea*' which he compiled for the CV-43 WestPac 81-82 cruise book and to Jerry Edwards, Norman Friedman, Michael J Grove, William T Larkins, Robert L Lawson, Peter B Lewis, Peter Mersky, Jay Miller, Mark Morgan, Rick Morgan, Douglas D Olson, Mick Roth, Larry Smalley, Richard K Smith, and Don J Willis for loaning documents and photographs, providing guidance or suggesting new approaches, or reviewing my manuscript. Without them I could not have completed my task.

The photographic help provided by the News Photo Branch, Department of the Navy, and by several manufacturers of naval aircraft—notably Grumman Corporation, Kaman Aerospace, LTV Aerospace and Defense Company, McDonnell Douglas Corporation, Rockwell International Corporation's North American Aircraft Operations, and Sikorsky Aircraft—is gratefully acknowledged.

Vallejo, California
October 1988

Glossary and Abbreviations

AAA	Anti-Aircraft Artillery
AAM	Air-to-Air Missile
ABCCC	Airborne Command and Control Center
AF	Air Force
AEW	Airborne Early Warning (or Airborne Electronic Warfare)
AOC	Aviation Officer Candidate
ARM	Anti-Radiation (or -Radar) Missile
ARVN	Army of the Republic of Vietnam
ASW	Antisubmarine Warfare
AW	Automatic Weapons
BarCAP	Barrier Combat Air Patrol
BDA	Bomb (or Battle) Damage Assessment
BEQ	Bachelor Enlisted Quarters
BIS	Board of Inspection and Survey
BN	Bombardier Navigator
Bolt	To go around after failing to trap
Bolter	Missed carrier landing (balked landing in the Royal Navy terminology) when the hook fails to engage an arresting cable and the aircraft must go around
BOQ	Bachelor Officers' Quarters
CAG	Commander Air Group (Commander of a Carrier Air Wing)
CAP	Combat Air Patrol
CarQuals	Carrier Qualification Landings
ChiCom	Chinese Communist
CINCPAC	Commander in Chief, Pacific Command
CO	Commanding Officer
COD	Carrier Onboard Delivery
COMINT	Communications Intelligence
COMNAVAIRLANT	Commander Naval Air Force, Atlantic
COMNAVAIRPAC	Commander Naval Air Force, Pacific
CONUS	Continental United States
CRC	Control and Reporting Center
Cross-deck pendant	(*See* Pendant)
CRP	Control and Reporting Post
CTF	Carrier Task Force
CV	Aircraft Carrier, or Multi-purpose Aircraft Carrier
CVA	Attack Carrier
CVAN	Attack Carrier Nuclear
CVB	Aircraft Carrier, Large
CVG	Carrier Air Group
CVS	Antisubmarine Warfare Support Carrier
CVSG	Carrier Antisubmarine Warfare Air Group
CVT	Training Carrier
CVW	Carrier Air Wing
DD	Destroyer
DECM	Defensive (or Deception) Electronic Countermeasures
DMZ	Demilitarized Zone
ECM	Electronic Countermeasures
ELINT	Electronic Intelligence
EW	Electronic Warfare
FAC	Forward Air Controller
FLDO	Flying Limited Duty Officer
FLIR	Forward Looking Infrared
ForCAP	Force Combat Air Patrol
FRAM	Fleet Rehabilitation and Modernization
GCI	Ground-Controlled Intercept
HATRON	Heavy Attack Squadron
HC	Helicopter Combat Support Squadron
HRU	Hose Refueling Unit
HS	Helicopter Antisubmarine Squadron
HU	Helicopter Utility Squadron
INS	Inertial Navigation System
IOIC	Integrated Operational Intelligence Center
IRS	Internal Revenue Service
JBD	Jet Blast Deflector
JCS	Joint Chiefs of Staff
JMSDF	Japanese Self-Defense Maritime Force
KIA	Killed in Action
LANTFLT	Atlantic Fleet
LOC	Lines of Communications
LLLTV	Low Light Level Television
LSO	Landing Signal Officer

LTV	Ling-Temco-Vought, Inc
MAAG	Military Assistance Advisory Group
MACV	Military Assistance Command, Vietnam
MIA	Missing in Action
MiGCAP	MiG Combat Air Patrol
NARF	Naval Air Rework Facility
NAS	Naval Air Station
NATRACOM	Naval Air Training Command
NFO	Naval Flight Officer
NROTC	Naval Reserve Officer Training Corps
NSC	National Security Council
NSY	Naval Shipyard
NTDS	Naval Tactical Data System
NVA	North Vietnamese Army
NVAF	North Vietnamese Air Force
NVN	North Vietnamese Navy
OpArea	Operations Area
ORE	Operational Readiness Exercise
ORI	Operational Readiness Inspection
OSS	Office of Strategic Services
PACAF	Pacific Air Forces
PACFLT	Pacific Fleet
Pendant	The portion of the arresting cable stretching across the deck
PIRAZ	Positive Identification Radar Advisory Zone
PLAT	Pilot Landing Aid Television
POW	Prisoner of War
PRC	People's Republic of China
PT	Patrol Torpedo (boat)
RAV	Reduced Availability
RCVSG	Replacement Carrier Antisubmarine Warfare Air Group
RCVW	Replacement Carrier Air Wing
RefTra	Refresher Training
ResCAP	Rescue Combat Air Patrol
RHAW	Radar-Homing and Warning
RIO	Radar Intercept Officer
ROE	Rules of Engagement
ROKAF	Republic of Korea Air Force
ROKN	Republic of Korea Navy
RP	Route Package
R&R	Rest and Recuperation (or Rehabilitation, or Relaxation)
RTAF	Royal Thai Air Force
RTARCC	Rolling Thunder Armed Reconnaissance Coordinating Committee
RTCC	Rolling Thunder Coordinating Committee
RVAH	Reconnaissance Heavy Attack Squadron

SAM	Surface-to-Air Missile
SAC	Strategic Air Command
SAR	Search and Rescue (or Sea-Air Rescue)
SARH	Semi-active Radar Homing
SCB	Ship Characteristics Board
SecDef	Secretary of Defense
SIGINT	Signals Intelligence
SLEP	Service Life Extension Program
SoCal	Southern California
TACOS	Tactical and Countermeasure Strike Support
TarCAP	Target Combat Air Patrol
TCN	Third Country National
TF	Task Force
TFS	Tactical Fighter Squadron
TFW	Tactical Fighter Wing
Trap (noun)	Carrier arrested landing
Trap (verb)	To land aboard carrier
Unrep	Underway replenishment
USA	United States Army
USAF	United States Air Force
USMC	United States Marine Corps
USN	United States Navy
USNR	United States Naval Reserve
USS	United States Ship
VA	Attack Squadron
VAH	Heavy Attack Squadron
VAW	Carrier Airborne Early Warning Squadron
VC	Composite Squadron (or Viet Cong)
Vertrep	Vertical replenishment
VF	Fighter Squadron
VFP	Light Photographic Squadron
VFR	Visual Flight Rules
VNAF	Vietnamese Air Force
VR	Fleet Logistics Support Squadron (or Transport Squadron)
VRC	Fleet Logistics Support Carrier Onboard Delivery Squadron
VS	Air Antisubmarine Squadron
VT	Training Squadron
WestPac	Western Pacific
WSO	Weapon Systems Officer
XO	Executive Officer

First aircraft specially developed as a carrier-based nuclear bomber, the North American Savage entered service in 1949. This AJ-1 is seen landing on the wooden plank-covered straight deck of USS Kearsarge *(CVA-33). Note the eleven cross-deck pendants of the Mk 5 arresting gear and the LSO platform on the port side.* (US Navy/National Archives)

Below: The starboard side of the forward deck as seen from the bridge of USS Enterprise *(CVAN-65) on 29 January 1963. Coded AF, the aircraft belong to CVG-6 and include six A-5As from VAH-7, one A-4C from VA-76, and one F-4B from VF-102. This photograph was taken eight days before the nuclear carrier left Norfolk for her second cruise to the Mediterranean.* (US Navy)

US Carrier Aviation in the Early Sixties

Until November 1944, when Marianas-based Boeing B-29s began regularly hammering Japanese cities and industries, the primary offensive weapon in the Pacific War had been carrier aviation. Carriers and their aircraft dominated operations in this theater, from the Battle of the Coral Sea in May 1942, when they stopped Japan's offensive, until the Battle of Leyte Gulf in October 1944, when they effectively finished the Japanese fleet. Consequently, at the end of World War II, many strategists considered carriers of primary importance and the US Navy then had twenty-seven fleet carriers and seventy-one escort carriers in commission (plus thirty-two under construction)—a force to be reckoned with.

Postwar disarmament, however, saw the construction of twenty-seven carriers cancelled and that of five delayed while two were stricken (the prewar USS *Enterprise* (CV-6) and USS *Saratoga* (CV-3)) and several placed in mothballs. Moreover, with the size of early nuclear bombs requiring large aircraft for their delivery, the US Navy lost the internecine conflict within the newly created Department of Defense. Thus, in spite of the development of the first carrier-based nuclear bomber (the North American AJ Savage), the construction of the first super carrier (USS *United States* (CVB-58)) was cancelled in April 1949 and the Strategic Air Command (SAC) became the primary keeper of America's nuclear deterrence. In the space of less than four years, carriers had lost their pre-eminent position in the arsenal of the free world and suddenly were considered by many to be weapons of the past.

The Korean War, during which aircraft operating from fifteen carriers flew 275,910 combat sorties (versus 720,980 Air Force sorties), proved once again the flexibility of employment of carrier-based aircraft. In addition, during the same period, three developments—reduction in the dimension and weight of nuclear weapons, the ordering into production of the Douglas A3D Skywarrior in February 1951, and the laying down of USS *Forrestal* (CVA-59) in July 1952—gave naval aviation a genuine role in strategic operations. However, the US Navy was still prevented by budgetary considerations from operating the number of carriers deemed necessary to cope with all requirements, notwithstanding their demonstrated capabilities during localized wars, their effectiveness in projecting power—as was done so successfully during Operation Blue Bat off Lebanon in July 1958 and in the Quemoy Straight off China one month later—and their newly-found nuclear deterrence potential. Consequently, from its zenith at the end of World War II, the US carrier fleet had dwindled to twenty-one operational carriers, one training carrier and four carriers in reserve when, in 1964, it found itself at war.

The Carriers

On 31 July 1964, two days before carriers went back to war in Asia, the Atlantic Fleet (LANTFLT) had four large attack (CVA) carriers (CVA-59, CVA-60, CVA-62, and CVAN-65), two older attack carriers (CVA-38 and CVA-42), and five antisubmarine warfare (ASW) carriers (CVS-9, CVS-11, CVS-15, CVS-18, and CVS-39). The Pacific Fleet (PACFLT), with a greater geographical area to cover, had two more carriers for a total of thirteen, including three large CVAs (CVA-61, CVA-63, and CVA-64), six older CVAs (CVA-14, CVA-19, CVA-31, CVA-34, CVA-41, and CVA-43), and four antisubmarine warfare support (CVS) carriers (CVS-10, CVS-12, CVS-20, and CVS-33). (See details in Table 1. In addition, the Navy had two more conventional-powered attack carriers under construction (the USS *America* (CVA-66), which had been launched on 1 February 1964, and the USS *John F. Kennedy* (CVA-67), which was about to be laid down at the Newport News Shipbuilding yard) and four ASW carriers laid up in reserve (USS *Franklin* (CVS-13), *Bunker Hill* (CVS-17), *Leyte* (CVS-32), and *Antietam* (CVS-36)). Moreover, USS *Lexington* (CVS-16), based in Pensacola, Florida, which was used for training operations in the Caribbean and the Gulf of Mexico could, in time of national emergency, be returned to service as an ASW carrier.

With the exception of CVA-67, all of the CVAs listed above, as well as five of the ASW carriers, made at least one combat cruise to the Gulf of Tonkin. Of recent construction, these carriers included four *Forrestal* class ships, three *Kitty Hawk* class ships, and the nuclear-powered *Enterprise*. With full load displacements ranging from 78,509 tons (71,222 tonnes) for the *Forrestal* to 89,804 tons (81,469 tonnes) for the *Enterprise*, all were built with an angled deck, four steam catapults (two forward and two on the angled deck), Mark 7 arresting gear with four cross-deck pendants, and four deck-edge elevators.[1] The length of their flight decks ranged from 1018ft (310.29m) to 1079ft (328.88m). In 1964, these carriers typically embarked ninety aircraft and helicopters. Ship complements ranged from 2765 (CVA-59) to 3325 (CVAN-65) and air wing personnel from 1300 to 1900.

Completed too late to see service during World War II, the three *Midway* class carriers had been the only carriers during the late forties and early fifties capable of launching

[1] The four oldest—CVA-59, CVA-60, CVA-61, and CVA-62—had three elevators on the starboard side, one forward and two aft of the island, and one on the port side at the forward end of the angled deck. As this arrangement proved partially unsatisfactory (ie, if the port elevator was stuck in the down position it was not possible to launch or recover off the waist), starting with CVA-63, all large carriers have been completed with two of the starboard elevators forward of the island and one aft, while the port elevator has been relocated aft to serve the two waist catapults.

Lockheed P2V-3C Neptunes and North American AJ-1 and AJ-2 Savages, the Navy's first atomic bombers. As such, they had been of great import to the development of strategic naval deterrence. Moreover, their effectiveness was greatly increased between 1954 and 1960 when they were fitted with an angled deck, C-11 steam catapults (two in the bow and one on the angled deck), and relocated and enlarged aircraft elevators. The first two, CVA-41 and CVA-42, were modernized under Project SCB 110 and had one forward elevator between the bow catapults, a deck-edge elevator aft of the island, and one at the forward edge of the angled deck, whereas CVA-43, modernized under Project SCB 110A, had three deck-edge elevators[2] (one forward and one aft of the island, and one aft on the port side to clear the waist catapult). After the incorporation of SCB 110 modifications, *Midway* had a full displacement of 62,614 tons (56,802 tonnes) and normally embarked eighty aircraft.

[2] Before her second deployment to the Gulf of Tonkin, *Midway* (CVA-41) had acquired a similar elevator arrangement as she was reconstructed in 1966–70 under Project SCB 101-66. At that time, the two C-11 bow catapults were replaced by C-13 units and the angled deck catapult was removed.

The lengths of her flight deck and angled deck respectively were 977ft (297.79m) and 531ft (161.85m). Her complements were 4060 (ship) and 1700 (wing).

The remaining ten carriers which operated in the Gulf of Tonkin during the Southeast Asia War belonged to the *Hancock* class and were the survivors of twenty-four *Essex* class short-hull and long-hull ships which had been built during World War II (with the exception of *Oriskany* which had been launched in October 1945 but was only completed five years later and commissioned in September 1950) and progressively modernized. Notably, by the time of their deployment to the Gulf of Tonkin, all had been fitted with angled decks and enclosed ('hurricane') bows but only six had been retrofitted to operate modern jet aircraft through installation of steam catapults, mechanical positioning of aircraft at the catapults, JBDs (jet blast deflectors), deck cooling, and nylon barricades.

Five of the six fully jet capable *Hancock* class carriers—USS *Bon Homme Richard* (CVA-31), *Hancock* (CVA-19), *Intrepid* (CVS-11), *Shangri-La* (CVS-38), and *Ticonderoga* (CVA-14)—had been brought up to Ship Characteristics Board (SCB) 27C standards. The sixth, USS *Oriskany* (CVA-

An A3D-2 from VAH-8 is seen just forward of the bow after a port catapult shot during WestPac operations aboard USS Midway *(CVA-41)on 12 February 1960. This was* Midway's *second deployment since being fitted with an angled deck. Between August 1958 and November 1965, VAH-8 deployed six times aboard CVA-41; the* Fireballers *only flew combat operations during the last of these cruises.* (US Navy)

This view shows well the revised island and radar arrangement adopted when USS Oriskany *(CVA-34) received an SCB 125A refit. In this photograph taken in the late fifties or early sixties, three Grumman WF-2 Tracers and two McDonnell F3H-2 Demons are seen parked on deck. Only the former, by then redesignated E-1Bs, saw wartime service in Southeast Asia.* (Grumman History Center)

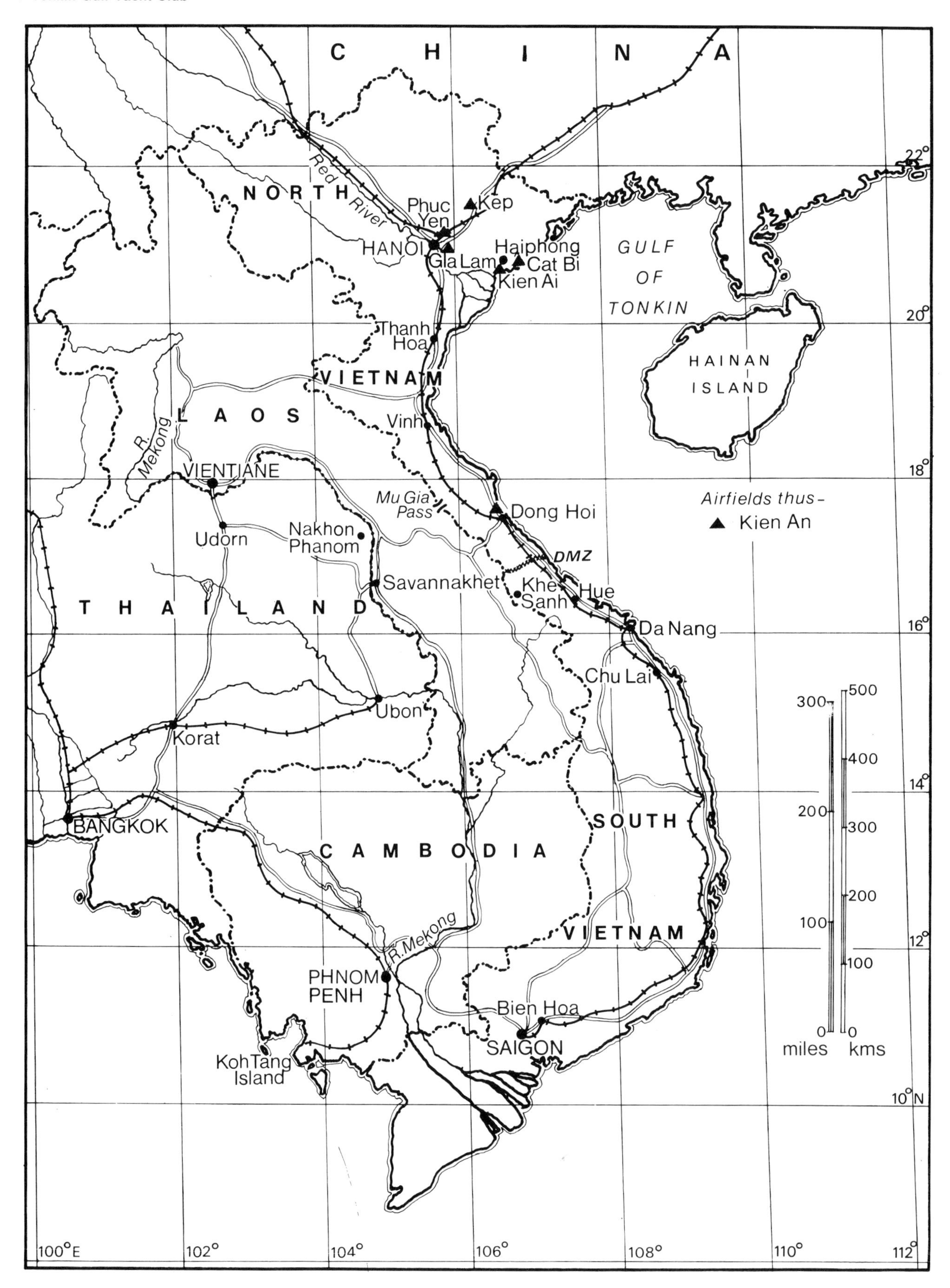

Map 1: The Southeast Asia war zone

34), had been modified to generally similar SCB 125A standards. Typical of these long-serving carriers, *Bon Homme Richard* had a full displacement of 44,700 tons (40,550 tonnes), an overall length of 894ft 6in (272.64m), a flight deck length of 861ft (262.43m), and an angled deck length of 520ft (158.50m). She had two C-11 bow steam catapults, four-pendant Mark 5 arresting gear, and three aircraft elevators (one on the centerline between the catapults, one on the starboard deck edge aft of the island, and one on the port side at the forward edge of the angled deck). Her air wing was comprised of five squadrons and five detachments, with a total of seventy aircraft, and her complements were 2585 (ship) and 960 (air wing).

The four carriers which could not operate jets[3]—USS *Bennington* (CVS-20), *Hornet* (CVS-12), *Kearsarge* (CVS-33), and *Yorktown* (CVS-10)—were used exclusively in the ASW role. Modernized to SCB 27A standards during the fifties and further upgraded during the Fleet Rehabilitation and Modernization (FRAM) program in the early sixties, they had a full load displacement of 41,200 tons (37,375 tonnes), an overall length of 890ft (271.27m), a flight deck length of 861ft (262.43m), and an angled deck length of 520ft (158.50m). They had two H-8 bow catapults, five-pendant Mark 5 arresting gear, and three aircraft elevators. For ASW operations, they embarked forty-five aircraft and helicopters.

The Aircraft

Two days before the Gulf of Tonkin Incident, 10,598 fixed-wing and rotary-wing aircraft were in US naval service. This impressive total was broken down into the following categories:

Fleet Combat	3552
Direct and Indirect Fleet Support	1265
Training Command	1411
USNR	770
Rework and Pipeline	1384
Reserve Stock	970
Sub-total (program aircraft)[4]	9352
Non-program aircraft[5]	1246
TOTAL	10,598

However, only the 2888 aircraft listed in Table 2—barely 27 per cent of the total inventory—were carrier-capable aircraft assigned to operational and fleet replacement squadrons of the Navy and Marine Corps. With the exception of a handful of McDonnell F-3B Demon fighters, which still equipped VF-161 while this squadron was converting to McDonnell F-4B Phantom IIs (a process scheduled to be completed by the end of 1964) and the piston-powered Douglas A-1 Skyraider attack aircraft and its EA-1E airborne early warning and EA-1F electronic warfare versions, which were phased out before war's end, all of these aircraft were of recent design and went on to be flown from carriers operating in the Gulf of Tonkin during the Southeast Asia War. During the war years, they were joined in service by a new type of attack aircraft, the LTV A-7 Corsair II, and a new fighter, the Grumman F-14 Tomcat. However, only the A-7 saw combat service in Vietnam as the F-14 had just been assigned to operational squadrons when Congress mandated an end to US combat operations in Southeast Asia. (Brief details and technical data for all the types of aircraft which flew from carriers during the war are provided in Appendix 2.)

A Douglas AD-6 Skyraider of Attack Squadron Eighty-Five (VA-85) in flight over the Mediterranean while operating from USS Forrestal *(CVA-59) on 18 July 1961. This squadron completed its conversion from A-1Hs (formerly AD-6s) to A-6As prior to the Gulf of Tonkin Incident and, equipped with Intruders, then made four deployments to Southeast Asia between October 1965 and May 1970.* (US Navy)

The Carrier Air Wings

On 31 July 1964, three of the Carrier Air Wings (CVWs) assigned to the Commander Naval Air Force, Atlantic (COMNAVAIRLANT) and two of its Carrier Antisubmarine Warfare Air Groups (CVSGs) were deployed aboard carriers while three CVWs and three CVSGs, as well as Replacement Carrier Air Wing Four (RCVW-4) and Replacement Carrier Antisubmarine Warfare Air Group Fifty (RCVSG-50), were land-based. Three of the CVWs and two of the CVSGs assigned to the Commander Naval Air Force, Pacific (COMNAVAIRPAC) were aboard carriers, and six of its CVWs, two of its CVSGs, and its

[3] Even though these carriers only had conventional H-8 catapults, they eventually acquired limited self-defense capability by embarking small detachments of lightly-loaded LTV F-8 Crusaders or Douglas A-4 Skyhawks.

[4] Program aircraft were then defined by the US Navy as 'all production aircraft in the physical custody of Navy and Marine units for which current or future operation within an authorized allowance is intended or can reasonably be expected.'

[5] Non-program aircraft were defined as 'all aircraft of project development and service test (BIS) configuration, target drones (man-carrying), aircraft retired but not yet stricken (including contingency reserve), and aircraft on loan or on bailment contracts.'

Photographed aboard USS Saratoga *(CVA-60) in July 1959, these Douglas A4D-2 Skyhawks of Attack Squadron Thirty-Four (VA-34) each carry a Bullpup A air-to-surface guided missile on the centerline station. Bullpup guided missiles were first used in Vietnam in 1965.* (US Navy)

RCVW-12 and RCVSG-51 were on the beach. The location, composition, and equipment of the deployed air wings and air groups and of shore-based squadrons are detailed in Table 3 and Table 4.

Typically, when deploying aboard large carriers, CVWs were composed of two fighter squadrons (VFs), one with twelve F-4Bs for all-weather operations and one with twelve F-8D/Es, two light attack squadrons (VAs), each with fourteen A-4C/Es, a medium attack squadron (VA) with twelve A-1H/Js, and either one heavy attack squadron (VAH) with twelve A-3Bs or a reconnaissance heavy attack squadron (RVAH) with six RA-5Cs and a VAH detachment with six A-3Bs. In addition, the air wings' combat capability was increased by the habitual inclusion of a detachment from a carrier airborne early warning squadron (VAW) with three to four E-1B or E-2A AEW aircraft, a detachment from a utility helicopter squadron (HU) with three to four UH-2 plane guard helicopters, and, when no RA-5Cs were embarked, a detachment from a light photographic squadron (VFP) with two to three RF-8A photo-reconnaissance aircraft.[6] Moreover, when required, a small detachment of EA-1Fs was added to provide electronic countermeasures. With the exception of the propeller-driven aircraft and helicopters, all of the CVW aircraft could be air refueled either by tanker-configured A-3Bs or A-1s and A-4s fitted with buddy refueling pods. Not included among the CVW aircraft was the single Grumman C-1A Trader COD aircraft which was assigned directly to the carrier.

For deployment aboard *Hancock* class carriers, the air wing composition was generally similar to that adopted for deployment aboard the large carriers; however, the F-4 squadron was replaced by a second F-8 squadron while a detachment of four A-3Bs and a detachment of three to six RF-8As were substituted for both the VAH squadron and RF-8A detachment or for the RVAH squadron and the detachment of tanker-configured A-3Bs. Altogether, CVWs embarked aboard these smaller carriers operated from eight to twenty fewer aircraft than those aboard *Kitty Hawk* class carriers.

[6] There was at least one exception to this practice. For its August 1964 to May 1965 cruise aboard *Ranger*, CVW-9 had both an RA-5C squadron (RVAH-5) and an RF-8A detachment (VFP-63 Det M), apparently since the photo-reconnaissance Vigilantes were only making their first deployment and still had some teething problems.

Although during the early sixties Marine squadrons seldom deployed as part of a normal Carrier Air Wing complement, most Marine pilots were carrier qualified. These two F8U-2 Crusaders from VMF-333 were photographed in 1961 during CarQuals aboard USS Forrestal *(CVA-59).* (US Marine Corps)

The Air Groups operating from the ASW carriers were comprised of two air antisubmarine (VS) squadrons equipped with Grumman S-2 Tracker piston-engined ASW aircraft, a helicopter antisubmarine squadron (HS) with Sikorsky SH-3A ASW helicopters, and detachments of Kaman UH-2 plane guard helicopters and Douglas EA-1E or Grumman E-1B AEW aircraft. Occasionally, a detachment of Douglas A-4 Skyhawks was also embarked, thus endowing the CVSs with limited self-defense capability.

Whether deployed aboard large carriers or older attack carriers, squadrons and detachments assigned to CVWs were usually Navy units. However, whenever required, Marine Corps squadrons and detachments could be substituted as most Marine aircrews were carrier-qualified and flew the same types of aircraft as their Navy brethren. Similarly, the Marine Corps occasionally provided A-4 detachments for deployment aboard ASW carriers.

Aircrew Training

Most carrier aviators were officers who had entered basic flight training after being commissioned either at the Naval Academy or through the AOC (Aviation Officer Candidate) or NROTC (Naval Reserve Officer Training Corps) programs, or who came from the ranks through the FLDO (Flying Limited Duty Officer) program. (Exceptions were the third crewman in A-3Bs, the antisubmarine warfare specialists in S-2s and SH-3s, the electronic warfare (EW) and airborne electronic warfare (AEW) specialists in a variety of aircraft (E-1Bs, E-2As, EA-1Es, EA-1Fs, and EA-3Bs), the photo technicians in RA-3Bs, and rescue personnel in UH-2s.) Basic and advanced pilot and NFO (Naval Flight Officer) training was provided by two Naval Air Training Command (NATRACOM) components, while training in a particular type of aircraft was provided by RCVW or RCVSG squadrons. Enlisted personnel selected to become aircrewmen received non-flying orientation and indoctrination at the naval aircrew candidate school at Pensacola and specialized AEW, ASW, and EW classroom and flight training in RCVW or RCVSG squadrons.

The Naval Air Basic Training Command was then comprised of four squadrons with piston-engined trainers (VT-

Closely monitored by the LSO who, to get an unobstructed view, has stepped from his platform onto the deck of USS Lexington *(CVT-16), a naval cadet practises carrier landing in a North American T-28C Trojan of Training Squadron Five (VT-5), one of nine squadrons assigned to the Naval Air Basic Training Command during the early sixties.* (US Navy)

1 with Beech T-34Bs, VT-2 and VT-3 with North American T-28B/Cs, and VT-5 with T-28Cs), one multi-engined aircraft squadron (VT-6 with Beech TC-45Js), three jet training squadrons (VT-4, VT-7, and VT-9 with North American T-2A/Bs), a helicopter training squadron (HT-8 with a variety of aircraft—T-28Bs, T-34Bs, and TC-45Js—and helicopters—Sikorsky UH-19Fs and UH-34D/Gs), and the training aircraft carrier USS *Lexington*. The Naval Air Advanced Training Command possessed six squadrons equipped with jet trainers and/or obsolescent jet fighters (VT-21, VT-22, VT-24, and VT-25 with Grumman AF-9Js and TF-9Js; and VT-23 and VT-26 with Grumman F-11As), one squadron with a variety of piston-engined aircraft (VT-30 with Beech T-34Bs, Douglas A-1Hs, and North American T-28Bs), and four multi-engined aircraft squadrons (VT-27, VT-28, and VT-31 with Grumman TS-2As; and VT-29 with Convair T-29Bs and Douglas TC-117Ds). Including aircraft assigned to the Naval Air Technical Training Command, NATRACOM had 1411 operational aircraft on 31 July 1964.

On completion of flight training and upon receiving their wings, pilots and NFOs were sent to a replacement squadron for training on operational aircraft prior to going to their first permanent squadron. Depending on the type of aircraft they had been selected to fly, aircrews assigned to LANTFLT either went to VA-42, VA-43, VA-44, VA-45, VF-101, VF-174 or RVAH-3 in RCVW-4 or to HS-1 or VS-30 in RCVSG-50. Those in PACFLT went to VA-122, VA-125, VA-126, VA-127, VF-121, VF-124 or VAH-123 in RCVW-12 or to HS-10 or VS-41 in RCVSG-51. The types of aircraft flown by these replacement squadrons and their stations are provided in Table 3 and Table 4.

Table 1: Operational Carriers (Homeports and Assigned Air Wings/Air Groups) 31 July 1964

Carrier	Homeport	Air Wing/Group
COMNAVAIRLANT, Norfolk, Virginia		
Attack Carriers		
USS *Shangri-La* (CVA-38)	Mayport, Florida	CVW-10
USS *Franklin D. Roosevelt* (CVA-42)	Mayport, Florida	CVW-1
USS *Forrestal* (CVA-59)	Norfolk, Virginia	CVW-8
USS *Saratoga* (CVA-60)	Mayport, Florida	CVW-3
USS *Independence* (CVA-62)	Norfolk, Virginia	CVW-7
USS *Enterprise* (CVAN-65)	Norfolk, Virginia	CVW-6
Antisubmarine Warfare Support Carriers		
USS *Essex* (CVS-9)	Quonset Point, Rhode Island	CVSG-60
USS *Intrepid* (CVS-11)	Norfolk, Virginia	CVSG-56
USS *Randolph* (CVS-15)	Norfolk, Virginia	CVSG-58
USS *Wasp* (CVS-18)	Boston, Massachusetts	CVSG-52
USS *Lake Champlain* (CVS-39)	Newport, Virginia	CVSG-54
COMNAVAIRPAC, San Diego, California		
Attack Carriers		
USS *Ticonderoga* (CVA-14)	Alameda, California	CVW-5
USS *Hancock* (CVA-19)	North Island, California	CVW-21
USS *Bon Homme Richard* (CVA-31)	Alameda, California	CVW-19
USS *Oriskany* (CVA-34)	Alameda, California	CVW-16
USS *Midway* (CVA-41)	Alameda, California	CVW-2
USS *Coral Sea* (CVA-43)	Alameda, California	CVW-15
USS *Ranger* (CVA-61)	Alameda, California	CVW-9
USS *Kitty Hawk* (CVA-63)	Alameda, California	CVW-11
USS *Constellation* (CVA-64)	Alameda, California	CVW-14
Antisubmarine Warfare Support Carriers		
USS *Yorktown* (CVS-10)	Bremerton, Washington	CVSG-55
USS *Hornet* (CVS-12)	Bremerton, Washington	CVSG-57
USS *Bennington* (CVS-20)	North Island, California	CVSG-59
USS *Kearsarge* (CVS-33)	Long Beach, California	CVSG-53

***Table 2*: Fleet Combat Units (Carrier Aircraft Inventory) 31 July 1964**

	COMNAVAIRLANT USN + USMC	COMNAVAIRPAC USN + USMC	TOTAL
Fighters			
F-4A/B/G	101 + 28	136 + 55	320
F-8C/D/E	142 + 32	215 + 73	482
Attack aircraft			
A-1H/J	51 + 0	147 + 0	198
A-3B	15 + 0	90 + 0	105
A-4B/C/E	265 + 108	366 + 128	867
A-6A	28 + 7	0 + 0	35
Photo-reconnaissance aircraft			
RF-8A	27 + 6	36 + 18	87
RA-3B*	11 + 0	12 + 0	23
RA-5C	21 + 0	0 + 0	21
ECM aircraft			
EA-1F*	11 + 0	19 + 0	30
EA-3B*	11 + 0	11 + 0	22

	COMNAVAIRLANT USN + USMC	COMNAVAIRPAC USN + USMC	TOTAL
AEW aircraft			
E-1B	39 + 0	41 + 0	80
E-2A	0 + 0	12 + 0	12
EA-1E	15 + 0	16 + 0	31
ASW aircraft			
S-2D/E/F	145 + 0	113 + 0	258
COD aircraft			
C-1A	36 + 0	36 + 0	72
Helicopters			
UH-2A/B	41 + 0	45 + 0	86
SH-3A	91 + 0	68 + 0	159
TOTAL	1050 + 201	1363 + 274	2888

* Usually land-based but deployed aboard carriers when required

Bearing the tail code AC identifying aircraft assigned to Carrier Air Wing Three (CVW-3), this North American RA-5C Vigilante of RVAH-7 is taking on fuel from a tanker-configured Douglas A-3B Skywarrior of VAH-2. The latter carries the tail code ZA identifying aircraft belonging to the lowest numbered squadron of Heavy Attack Wing Two. (US Navy)

A Grumman S-2F Tracer of VS-23 photographed during a training flight off the coast of San Diego, California. The Black Cats of Air Antisubmarine Squadron Twenty-Three made three wartime deployments to the Gulf of Tonkin aboard USS Yorktown *(CVS-10).* (US Navy)

Below: For her round-the-world cruise between 8 February and 3 October 1964, USS Enterprise *(CVAN-65) still had a squadron of Crusaders as part of her CVW-6. However, shortly after the end of that cruise, the* Tarsiers *of VF-33 traded their F-8Es for F-4Bs.* (US Navy)

***Table 3*: COMNAVAIRLANT Carrier Units 31 July 1964**

Unit	Aircraft	Notes
CVW-1 aboard USS *Franklin D. Roosevelt* (CVA-42)		
VF-11	12 × F-8E	
VF-14	14 × F-4B	
VA-12	12 × A-4C	(due to convert to A-4E by December 1964)
VA-172	12 × A-4C	
VA-15	12 × A-1H	(due to convert to A-6A by March 1965 but actually converting to A-4B in mid-1965)
VAH-11	6 × A-3B	
VFP-62 Det 42	3 × RF-8A	
VAW-12 Det 42	3 × E-1B	
HU-2 Det 42	3 × UH-2A	
COD	1 × C-1A	
CVW-6 aboard USS *Enterprise* (CVAN-65)		
VF-33	14 × F-8E	(due to convert to F-4B by December 1964)
VF-102	12 × F-4B	
VA-64	12 × A-4C	
VA-66	13 × A-4C	
VA-76	13 × A-4C	
VA-65	12 × A-1H	(due to convert to A-6A by September 1964)
VAH-7	12 × A-3B	
VFP-62 Det 65	3 × RF-8A	
VAW-12 Det 65	4 × E-1B	
VAW-33 Det 65	3 × EA-1F	
HU-2 Det 65	3 × UH-2A	
VRC-40 Det 65	2 × C-1A	
COD	1 × C-1A	
CVW-8 aboard USS *Forrestal* (CVA-59)		
VF-74	12 × F-4B	
VF-103	12 × F-8E	
VA-81	13 × A-4E	
VA-83	13 × A-4E	
VA-85	9 × A-6A	
VAH-6	11 × A-3B	
VFP-62 Det 59	3 × RF-8A	
VAW-12 Det 59	4 × E-1B	
VAW-33 Det 59	3 × EA-1F	
HU-2 Det 59	3 × UH-2A	
COD	1 × C-1A	

CVSG-52 aboard USS *Wasp* (CVS-18)

VS-28	12 × S-2E	
VS-32/CVSG-54	13 × S-2F	(temporarily replacing VS-31)
HS-11	16 × SH-3A	
VAW-33 Det 18	4 × EA-1F	
COD	1 × C-1A	

CVSG-60 aboard USS *Essex* (CVS-9)

VS-34	12 × S-2D
VS-39	13 × S-2D
HS-9	16 × SH-3A
COD	1 × C-1A

CVW-3, CVW-7, CVW-10, CVSG-54, CVSG-56, CVSG-58, RCVW-4, and RCVSG-50 then were shore-based. As noted below, their squadrons were distributed among the following Naval Air Stations.

A Blue Blasters A-4C over the Mediterranean during operations from USS Saratoga *(CVA-60) as part of CVW-3. When not aboard* Saratoga*, VA-34 was based at NAS Cecil Field, Florida. While equipped with A-4Cs, VA-34 made only one wartime cruise. On that occasion, the squadron was assigned to CVW-10 and embarked aboard USS* Intrepid *(CVS-11).* (US Navy)

NAS Cecil Field, Florida

VA-34/CVW-3	15 × A-4C	
VA-36/CVW-3	15 × A-4C	
VA-44/RCVW-4	30 × A-4B/C/E	
VA-45/RCVW-4	29 × TF-9J, A-1E and T-28B	
VA-46/CVW-10	16 × A-4C	
VA-106/CVW-10	14 × A-4C	
VF-13/CVW-10	1 × F-8E	
VF-31/CVW-3	15 × F-4B	
VF-32/CVW-3	16 × F-8D	
VF-62/CVW-10	15 × F-8E	
VF-174/RCVW-4	37 × F-8B/C/D/E	
VFP-62	13 × RF-8A	(plus carrier detachments as noted)

NAS Jacksonville, Florida

VA-35/CVW-3	14 × A-1H	(due to convert to A-6A by December 1964)
VA-176/CVW-10	13 × A-1H	
VAP-62	8 × RA-3B	(with Det 19 at NS Rota, Spain)

NAS Key West, Florida

Unit	Aircraft	Notes
HS-1/RCVSG-50	11 × SH-3A	
VF-101/RCVW-4	26 × F-4A/B	
VS-30/RCVSG-50	25 × S-2D/E/F	

NAS Lakehurst, New Jersey

Unit	Aircraft	Notes
HU-2	14 × UH-2A/B	(plus carrier detachments as noted and a temporary detachment aboard *Independence*, CVA-62)

NAS Norfolk, Virginia

Unit	Aircraft	Notes
HS-3/CVSG-56	13 × SH-3A	
HS-7/CVSG-58	17 × SH-3A	
VAW-12	28 × E-1B	(plus carrier detachments as noted)
VS-24/CVSG-56	12 × S-2F	(due to convert to S-2E by December 1964)
VS-26/CVSG-58	11 × S-2D	
VS-27/CVSG-56	11 × S-2F	(due to convert to S-2E by December 1964)
VS-36/CVSG-58	11 × S-2D	

NAS Oceana, Virginia

Unit	Aircraft	Notes
VA-42/RCVW-4	8 × A-6A	
VA-43/RCVW-4	50 × A-4C/E and TF-9J	
VA-72/CVW-7	14 × A-4E	
VA-75/CVW-7	11 × A-6A	
VA-86/CVW-7	14 × A-4E	
VF-41/CVW-7	15 × F-4B	
VF-84/CVW-7	9 × F-4B	

During the summer of 1964, VAW-33 was based at NAS Quonset Point, Rhode Island, and also had detachments aboard USS Enterprise *(CVAN-65), USS* Forrestal *(CVA-59), USS* Independence *(CVA-62), USS* Intrepid *(CVS-11), and USS* Wasp *(CVS-18). The* Knight Hawks *of VAW-33 were among the last users of the EA-1E, the AEW version of the Douglas Skyraider.* (US Navy)

Right: Carrying a 300-gallon buddy refueling store on the centerline station, this A-4C of VA-146 is being readied on the port bow catapult of USS Constellation *(CVA-64). Two weeks after this photograph was taken on 23 July 1964,* Constellation *and her Carrier Air Wing Fourteen (CVW-14) took part in Operation Pierce Arrow, the opening phase of the naval air war in Southeast Asia.* (US Navy)

NAS Quonset Point, Rhode Island

Unit	Aircraft	Notes
HS-5/CVSG-54	15 × SH-3A	
VAW-33	14 × EA-1E/F and EC-1A	(plus carrier detachments as noted and temporary detachments aboard *Independence*, CVA-62, and *Intrepid*, CVS-11)
VS-22/CVSG-54	12 × S-2F	
VS-31/CVSG-52	12 × S-2E	

NAS Sanford, Florida

Unit	Aircraft	Notes
VAH-1	3 × A-3B	(temporarily aboard *Independence*, CVA-62)
VAH-11 Det 8/CVW-1	7 × A-3B	
RVAH-3/RCVW-4	34 × RA-5C, TA-3B, TF-9J and TC-47K	
RVAH-5/CVW-8	6 × RA-5C	(temporarily shore-based)
RVAH-7	none	(converting to RA-5C)
RVAH-9/CVW-3	8 × RA-5C	

NS Rota, Spain

Unit	Aircraft	Notes
VQ-2	9 × EA-3B	(normally shore-based and also equipped with land-based EC-121Ms, VQ-2 sent temporary EA-3B detachments to carriers whenever required)

***Table 4*: COMNAVAIRPAC Carrier Units 31 July 1964**

CVW-5 aboard USS *Ticonderoga* (CVA-14)	
VF-51	13 × F-8E
VF-53	13 × F-8E
VA-55	13 × A-4E
VA-56	12 × A-4E
VA-52	12 × A-1H/J
VFP-63 Det B	5 × RF-8A
VAW-11 Det B	3 × E-1B
HU-1 Det 1 Unit B	2 × UH-2A
COD	1 × C-1A
CVW-14 aboard USS *Constellation* (CVA-64)	
VF-142	12 × F-4B
VF-143	12 × F-4B
VA-144	13 × A-4C
VA-146	13 × A-4C
VA-145	12 × A-1H/J
VAH-10	11 × A-3B
VFP-63 Det F	2 × RF-8A
VAW-11 Det F	4 × E-1B
HU-1 Det 1 Unit F	2 × UH-2A
COD	1 × C-1A

Back at NAS Lemoore on 26 May 1964, after completing its last peacetime deployment aboard USS Midway *(CVA-41), VA-25 then prepared for its first war cruise aboard the same carrier. Two Fist of the Fleet A-1Hs are seen here during RefTra (Refresher Training) off the Californian coast on 5 November 1964.* (US Navy)

CVW-19 aboard USS *Bon Homme Richard* (CVA-31)

VF-191	14 × F-8E
VF-194	14 × F-8C
VA-192	13 × A-4C
VA-195	13 × A-4C
VA-196	12 × A-1H/J
VAH-4 Det E	4 × A-3B
VAW-11 Det E	3 × E-1B
HU-1 Det 1 Unit E	2 × UH-2A
COD	1 × C-1A

CVSG-53 aboard USS *Kearsarge* (CVS-33)

VS-21	10 × S-2F	(to convert to S-2E by March 1965)
VS-29	10 × S-2F	(to convert to S-2E by March 1965)
HS-6	14 × SH-3A	
VA-153 Det R	4 × A-4B	
VAW-11 Det R	5 × EA-1E	
HU-1 Det 1 Unit R	2 × UH-2A	
COD	1 × C-1A	

CVSG-59 aboard USS *Bennington* (CVS-20)

VS-33	10 × S-2E
VS-38	9 × S-2E
HS-8	15 × SH-3A
VA-93 Det Q	4 × A-4B
VAW-11 Det Q	5 × EA-1E
HU-1 Det 1 Unit Q	1 × UH-2A
COD	1 × C-1A

CVW-2, CVW-9, CVW-11, CVW-15, CVW-16, CVW-21, CVSG-55, CVSG-57, RCVW-12, and RCVSG-51 then were shore-based. As noted below, their squadrons were distributed among the following Naval Air Stations.

NAS Agana, Guam		
VAP-61	14 × RA-3B	
NAS Alameda, California		
VA-152/CVW-15	6 × A-1H/J	
VA-165/CVW-16	12 × A-1H/J	
VA-215/CVW-21	12 × A-1H/J	
VAW-13	15 × EA-1F, A-1G and EC-1A	
NS Atsugi, Japan		
VQ-1	11 × EA-3B and A-3B	(normally shore-based and also equipped with land-based EC-121Ms, VQ-1 sent temporary EA-3B detachments to carriers whenever required)
NAS Cubi Point, the Philippines		
VAW-13 Det 1	7 × EA-1F	
NAS Lemoore, California		
VA-22/CVW-2	14 × A-4C	
VA-23/CVW-2	12 × A-4E	
VA-25/CVW-2	19 × A-1H/J	
VA-93/CVW-9	12 × A-4C	
VA-94/CVW-9	13 × A-4C	
VA-95/CVW-9	12 × A-1H/J	
VA-112/CVW-11	10 × A-4C	
VA-113/CVW-11	10 × A-4C	
VA-115/CVW-11	14 × A-1H/J	
VA-122/RCVW-12	40 × A-1E/H/J and T-28B	
VA-125/RCVW-12	78 × A-4B/C/E and A-1E	
VA-127/RCVW-12	21 × TF-9J	
VA-153/CVW-15	15 × A-4C	
VA-155/CVW-15	13 × A-4E	
VA-164/CVW-16	15 × A-4E	
VA-212/CVW-21	12 × A-4E	
VA-216/CVW-21	14 × A-4C	

Photographed at NAS Whidbey Island, Washington, this A-3B of VAH-13 bears the NH tail code of Carrier Air Wing Eleven (CVW-11). In August 1964, the squadron was transferred to NAS Sanford, Florida, for conversion to the RA-5C. The Bats were redesignated RVAH-13 on 1 November 1964 and then made four wartime deployments with their RA-5Cs. (US Navy)

NAS Miramar, California		
VA-126/RCVW-12	26 × TF-9J	
VA-163/CVW-16	15 × A-4C/E	(converting to A-4E)
VF-21/CVW-2	15 × F-4B	
VF-26/CVW-2	14 × F-8D	(temporarily aboard *Midway*, CVA-41)
VF-92/CVW-9	12 × F-4B	
VF-96/CVW-9	12 × F-4B	
VF-111/CVW-11	15 × F-8D	
VF-114/CVW-11	11 × F-4B	
VF-121/RCVW-12	34 × F-4A/B and TF-10B	
VF-124/RCVW-12	40 × F-8C/D/E	
VF-151/CVW-15	13 × F-4B	
VF-154/CVW-15	15 × F-8D	
VF-161/CVW-16	6 × F-3B	(due to convert to F-4B by December 1964)
VF-162/CVW-16	16 × F-8E	
VF-211/CVW-21	18 × F-8E	
VF-213/CVW-21	17 × F-4B/G	
VF-214/CVW-21	17 × F-8C	
VFP-63	20 × RF-8A	(plus carrier detachments as noted)
NAS North Island, California		
VAW-11	39 × E-1B, E-2A and A/EA-1E	(plus carrier detachments as noted)
VS-23/CVSG-55	12 × S-2E	
VS-25/CVSG-55	13 × S-2E	
VS-35/CVSG-57	12 × S-2D	
VS-37/CVSG-57	12 × S-2D	
VS-41/RCVSG-51	17 × S-2D/E/F	
NAAS Ream Field, California		
HS-2/CVSG-57	17 × SH-3A and SH-34J	
HS-4/CVSG-55	18 × SH-3A and SH-34J	
HS-10/RCVSG-51	11 × SH-3A	
HU-1	31 × UH-2A/B, UH-13P, TH-13N, CH-19E, UH-34D/E/G and UH-46A	(plus Det 1 units aboard carriers as noted)
NAS Whidbey Island, Washington		
VAH-2/CVW-15	12 × A-3B	(aboard *Coral Sea*, CVA-43, for CarQuals)
VAH-4/CVW-5	8 × A-3B	
VAH-8/CVW-2	11 × A-3B	
VAH-13/CVW-11	9 × A-3B	
VAH-123/RCVW-12	21 × A-3B and TA-3B	

Task Force 77 at War

Preceded by skirmishes, the most protracted, bitter, and costly war fought by US Naval Aviators began on 2 August 1964, when F-8E Crusaders from USS *Ticonderoga* (CVA-14) struck North Vietnamese patrol torpedo (PT) boats which threatened USS *Maddox* (DD-731) during operations off Hon Me Island. It ended on 15 August 1973, in compliance with a Congressional mandate terminating US combat involvement in Southeast Asia, after 21 carriers had made 86 war cruises and spent a total of 9178 days on the line in the Gulf of Tonkin. In the process, 377 Naval Aviators had been killed in action or operational accidents, 64 reported missing in action, and 179 taken prisoner of war. In addition, 205 officers and men had been lost during major fires aboard three carriers. Equipment losses included 530 fixed-wing aircraft and helicopters lost in combat and 329 lost in operational accidents while the carriers were on the line. Tragically, these grievous losses had been in vain as political vagaries had, from the onset, precluded all possibility of an American victory.

The number and length of deployments made by each carrier assigned to Task Force 77 (TF 77)—the operating command which became known to sailors and Naval Aviators as the 'Tonkin Gulf Yacht Club'—and the losses incurred by these carriers are summarized in Table 5. These deployments are listed chronologically in Table 6. Monthly

A loss luckily avoided. In spite of the apparent hopelessness of this scene aboard USS Shangri-La *(CVS-38) on 2 July 1970 during operations on Yankee Station, neither pilot nor aircraft was lost. When his A-4E began rolling toward the port edge of the deck as the result of a starboard brake failure, the VA-152 pilot ejected. Lt (jg) Wiliam E Belden was recovered and his Skyhawk was pulled out of the catwalk with only minor damage.* (US Navy)

Nicknamed 'Willy Fudd' because of its pre-1962 WF-2 designation, the Grumman Tracer operated on Yankee Station from seventeen carriers. Although this photograph was taken on 8 February 1963, five months after the type had been redesignated E-1B, this VAW-11 Tracer still had the WF-2 designation painted above its Bureau Number on the rear fuselage. The large radome atop the fuselage housed the 17ft 6in (5.33m) antenna for the Hazeltine AN/APS-82 search radar. (US Navy)

figures for the number of carriers in the Gulf of Tonkin between August 1964 and 1973, the total number of days they spent on the line, the air combat victories credited to their air wings, and their combat and operational aircraft losses are given in Table 7. The story behind these statistics is recounted below.

Rough Sailing: From Dien Bien Phu to the Gulf of Tonkin

Following five years of Japanese occupation, Indochina was reoccupied by French troops in September 1945 in an attempt by France to restore control over its five Indochinese colonies (Annam, Cambodia, Cochinchina, Laos and Tonkin). This endeavor met with little enthusiasm on the part of most of the local population and was strongly opposed by the Communist-led Viet Minh.[1] Moreover, the French move was initially frowned upon by the United States which, through certain elements in the Office of Strategic Services (OSS), had established cordial relations with Ho Chi Minh and did not favor a return to pre-war colonialism. The North Korean onslaught across the 38th parallel in June 1950 brought about a rapid change in American opinion and thereafter French operations in Indochina were regarded in Washington as being part of a common fight against Communism in Southeast Asia.

For the US Navy, the revised policy toward France quickly led to transfer of obsolete aircraft to shore up both the Armée de l'Air, with Grumman F6F-5 Hellcats being first flown in combat in Indochina at the end of December 1950 and Grumman F8F-1 Bearcats doing so three months later, and the Aéronautique Navale which received four-engined Convair PB4Y-2S Privateers in late 1950. In addition, previously imposed restrictions, which up to then had prevented the Aéronautique Navale from using its carrier-based Grumman F6F-5 Hellcats and Curtiss SB2C-5 Helldivers in Indochina, were lifted and two light carriers—USS *Langley* (CVL-27) and USS *Belleau Wood* (CVL-24)—were loaned to the Marine Nationale in June 1951 and September 1953 respectively and were operated off Indochina as the *Lafayette* and *Bois Belleau*.

Notwithstanding USN material assistance and training of French naval aviators, and similar transfers of equipment and ordnance by the USAF and USA, the military situation in Indochina steadily worsened for the French while at home (much as was later the case in the United States during the Southeast Asia War) popular support for the war effort waned rapidly. By the fall of 1953, Communist insurgents controlled most of the countryside in Tonkin and Annam and the Viet Minh leadership was preparing a major offensive in Laos. It was then that the French military made their fateful decision to try to entice the Viet Minh to

[1] Viet Minh was the abbreviation of the Viet Nam Doc Lap Dong Minh, the League for the Independence of Vietnam, which since 1941 had been controlled by Ho Chi Minh ('the one who enlightens'). In December 1960, North Vietnam announced the formation of the National Front for the Liberation of Vietnam. Thereafter the name Viet Cong (VC) was used to identify Communist forces in South Vietnam for which the Hanoi-based Viet Minh provided political leadership, cadres and weapons.

With the afterburner of its J57-P-20 turbojet glowing and its variable incidence wing in the up position, an F-8E of Fighter Squadron 211 (VF-211) has just cleared the deck of USS Bon Homme Richard *(CVA-31) at the start of a sortie on 24 May 1967. This aircraft, BuNo 150352, was shot down by heavy aimed AAA during a Rolling Thunder mission against the Hanoi thermal power plant on 10 June 1967. The pilot, Lt (jg) T R Hall, Jr, was taken prisoner of war.* (US Navy)

Apparently taken during a training sortie over the South China Sea on 25 August 1964, this photograph spectacularly illustrates the flames and smoke occurring when 5in (127mm) Zuni rockets are fired. The aircraft is an F-4B of VF-143 then based aboard USS Constellation *(CVA-64).* (US Navy)

fight in the open by setting up a major defensive base at Dien Bien Phu. As is well known, the Viet Minh military commander, Vo Nguyen Giap, outmaneuvered his French opponents. Soon, in spite of sustained air support by the Armée de l'Air and the Aéronautique Navale and logistic support gallantly provided in adverse weather and against heavy hostile ground fire by French military and civilian aircrews, and by American civilian crews from Civil Air Transport, the defenders were surrounded by four infantry divisions and one artillery division.

In March 1954, realizing that a defeat at Dien Bien Phu would spell an end to the French struggle against Communist insurgents, the US government quickly stepped up delivery of aircraft, weapons, and supplies. The USN contribution consisted primarily of the emergency transfer of twenty-five Chance Vought AU-1 Corsairs and twelve Sikorsky HRS helicopters by Marine Corps units in the Far East. In addition, the USAF undertook to fly French troop reinforcements from France to Indochina. Moreover, President Dwight Eisenhower and his cabinet initially received favorably a request on 4 April from French Premier Joseph Laniel for either US naval air strikes against Viet Minh artillery positions around Dien Bien Phu or the loan of Boeing B-29 heavy bombers which were to be flown by French crews and maintained by USAF personnel. The B-29 loan, however, was rejected as the French did not have the required crews and as the USAF feared that unescorted bombers would come under attack from Chinese MiGs. Conversely, the Chairman of the Joint Chiefs of Staff, Adm Arthur W Radford, indicated that the Navy had in the area the necessary units for the strikes against the Viet Minh.

Three fleet carriers—USS *Essex* (CV-9), USS *Wasp* (CV-18), and USS *Boxer* (CV-21) which embarked a mix of jet fighters (Grumman Panthers and Cougars, and McDonnell Banshees) and piston-engined Douglas Skyraiders—were operating in Philippine waters and ready to intervene in support of the beleaguered Dien Bien Phu defenders. In the end, British political opposition to direct US intervention in Indochina and French unwillingness to accept an overall American commander in the event of joint operations delayed the decision to proceed with the planned naval air strikes until it was too late. Dien Bien Phu fell on 7 May 1954. The next day delegates from France, the Democratic Republic of Vietnam, the State of Vietnam, Cambodia, Laos, the United States, Great Britain, the People's Republic of

In addition to seeing much use in Vietnam as the standard Marine medium lift helicopter, the Boeing-Vertol Sea Knight also proved most valuable in the Gulf of Tonkin where the Navy used it extensively in the Vertical Replenishment (VERTREP) role to airlift supplies between logistic ships and warships as demonstrated by this CH-46A of HC-1. (US Navy)

China, and the Soviet Union began meeting in Geneva to find means of ending the Indochina War.

On 20 July 1954, French and Viet Minh representatives signed a cease-fire agreement granting full independence to Cambodia, Laos, and Vietnam (the former French colonies of Annam, Cochinchina, and Tonkin) and providing for (1) the division of Vietnam at the 17th parallel along the Ben Hai River, (2) the creation of a demilitarized zone (DMZ) on each side of the line, and (3) the withdrawal of French troops from the North and of Viet Minh forces from the South. Elections to unify the two Vietnams were to be held by July 1956. The United States, however, refused to endorse the Geneva Agreement and the State of Vietnam (South Vietnam) immediately protested the agreement and claimed not to be bound by France's decision to accept a date for the unification election. Furthermore, 880,000 Vietnamese fled from the North to the South and 130,000 Viet Minh sympathizers went North during the year following the Geneva Conference. The seeds for troubles had been planted.

While steadfastly refusing to hold the election for the reunification of the country, President Ngo Dinh Diem[2] repressed rebellion by various politico-religious groups in the State of Vietnam, now called the Republic of Vietnam, and attempted to consolidate his power. Diem succeeded in besting his non-Communist opponents. However, in spite of the Communist assassination and propaganda campaign against local government officials, he failed to gain the support needed to prevent the Viet Cong (VC) from initiating the struggle to carry out Chairman Ho's vows of reunifying the country under Communist rule. With North Vietnam opening the first sections of the Ho Chi Minh Trail across the DMZ in early 1959 and utilizing its first three transport aircraft to support the planned extension of the trail system through Laos and Cambodia, the steady infiltration of men and supplies began. In September 1959 the Communist insurgents fought their first battle when they ambushed two Army of the Republic of Vietnam (ARVN) companies in the Plain of Reeds, southwest of Saigon. Unfortunately for the Republic of Vietnam, at this time structural fatigue finally grounded its only combat aircraft, the survivors of a batch

[2] Following disagreements with Emperor Bao Dai, who then resided in France, Prime Minister Ngo Dinh Diem repudiated the Emperor's authority. A referendum on 23 October 1955 settled the issue of national authority and Diem became the first president of the Republic of Vietnam.

A Douglas A-1H Skyraider of VA-145 makes an unassisted take-off from the deck of USS Constellation *(CVA-64) at the start of a training sortie during WestPac operations on 8 July 1963. The two-edged sword on the forward fuselage of the A-3Bs parked on the starboard deck edge identifies these Skywarriors as belonging to the* Vikings *of VAH-10.* (US Navy)

of 25 Bearcats left behind by the French to equip the Vietnamese 1er Groupe de Chasse (1st Fighter Squadron) which had been activated at Bien Hoa on 1 June 1956.

As the Geneva Agreement prohibited the introduction of jet aircraft, the Commander in Chief, Pacific Command (CINCPAC) and the Air section of the US Military Assistance Advisory Group (MAAG) in Saigon selected two types of US naval aircraft to fill the void, Douglas AD-6 Skyraider attack aircraft to replace the Bearcats of the 1st Fighter Squadron and North American T-28B Trojan trainers to equip the soon to be organized 2nd Fighter Squadron. As a result of this decision, and following initial training of Vietnamese Air Force (VNAF) Skyraider pilots by Advanced Training Unit 301 at NAS Corpus Christi, Texas, Lt Ken Moranville and six petty and chief petty officers were sent to Bien Hoa in September 1960 to oversee the introduction of the AD-6 in the VNAF inventory. Acting strictly as advisors, with Lt Moranville flying only training and demonstration sorties, they were the first of many Naval Aviators to serve in Vietnam.

During the following eighteen months, the United States was drawn progressively into the fray as South Vietnamese forces were unable to contain the Viet Cong insurgency. Between 20 October and 21 November 1961, the USAF deployed four McDonnell RF-101C reconnaissance aircraft to Tan Son Nhut Air Base, to fly Pipe Stem reconnaissance sorties over South Vietnam and Laos. On 11 November 1961, the first direct support contingent of US military forces, 400 Army troops and two helicopter companies, arrived in Vietnam; three days later the first Air Force Farm Gate aircraft arrived at Bien Hoa.[3] On 21 March 1962, four Convair F-102A interceptors were sent on temporary duty to Tan Son Nhut to initiate the joint Air Force/Navy Operation Water Glass, an unsuccessful attempt to intercept North Vietnamese transport aircraft flying Tha Vo (Free Drop) missions over the Central Highlands of South Vietnam. On 15 April 1962, it was the turn of the Marines to deploy to Vietnam. Marine Medium Helicopter Squadron 362 (HMM-362)—a specially reinforced Marine squadron under the command of Lt-Col Archie J Clapp and equipped with twenty-four Sikorsky HUS-1 helicopters, three Cessna

[3]As an example of bureaucratic nonsense, it may be pointed out that the Internal Revenue Service (IRS) considered neither the arrival of US military forces nor the Gulf of Tonkin Incident as the start of the war. For the purpose of federal income tax exemptions, as authorized by law, the IRS eventually designated Vietnam and contiguous zones as combat zones retroactive to 1 January 1964

OE-1 observation aircraft, and one Douglas R4D-8 transport—arrived at Soc Trang to become the first US naval aviation unit[4] to begin operations in direct support of South Vietnamese ground forces.

The first carrier-qualified aviators assigned operational duty in Vietnam were those crewing the Douglas AD-5Qs sent in July 1962 by Carrier Airborne Early Warning Squadron Thirteen (VAW-13) Detachment One to relieve the Water Glass F-102 interceptors at Tan Son Nhut. Although the AD-5Q was a radar reconnaissance and radar countermeasures aircraft not a fighter, it was armed with four 20mm cannon, could use its AN/APS-31C surface search radar to locate low-flying aircraft, and was in a way better suited than jets to attempt intercepting low-and-slow aircraft such as the Soviet-built Antonov An-2 Colt and Lisunov Li-2 Cab used by the North Vietnamese for Tha Vo resupply missions into Laos and South Vietnam. Nevertheless, the AD-5Qs (redesignated EA-1Fs in September 1962) proved just as unsuccessful as the F-102s in finding enemy aircraft and the Water Glass and Candy Machine rotational deployments to Tan Son Nhut were terminated in December 1963.

If the Communists could claim that the South Vietnamese refusal to hold reunification elections (as provided by the 1954 Geneva Agreement) justified their support of the Viet Cong, their backing of Pathet Lao insurgents and the intervention of regular North Vietnamese Army (NVA) troops to drive the Laotian military from the border between Laos and South Vietnam when construction of the Ho Chi Minh Trail began in mid-1959 constituted an interference in the internal affairs of an independent nation and a clear breach of the sovereignty of the Kingdom of Laos. This distinction, however, did not seem to bother leaders in Hanoi, Moscow, or Peking.

Concerned by increased Communist activities in the Kingdom of Laos and the mid-December 1960 shelling of the US Embassy, the US air attaché in Vientiane regularly used the embassy's Douglas VC-47 transport for observation flights in Laos. In the process, on 21 and 27 December Soviet-registered Ilyushin Il-14 Crate transport aircraft were photographed dropping supplies to Pathet Lao rebels. To replace the VC-47, which had been damaged by ground fire during the 27 December flight, the Air Force provided a camera-equipped SC-47. When this modified transport was shot down on 24 March 1961, the Air Force sent to Royal Thai Air Force (RTAF) Base Udorn a Lockheed RT-33A borrowed from the Philippine Air Force as a replacement. This jet-engined aircraft flew Field Goal

[4] On 1 August 1962 HMM-163 replaced HMM-362 as the operational squadron assigned to Marine Task Unit 79.3.5 (Shufly). The copilot and crew chief of an HUS-1 from HMM-162 were the first Naval Aviators killed in action when their helicopter crashed on 6 October 1962.

Primarily operating from Da Nang Air Base in South Vietnam, where they arrived in April 1965 and where these Skyknights were photographed, Douglas EF-10Bs of Marine Composite Reconnaissance Squadron One (VMCJ-1) provided much needed electronic reconnaissance and ECM support for Task Force 77 during early Rolling Thunder phases. (David W Menard)

reconnaissance sorties over Laos until 10 May when a cease-fire was proclaimed. Three weeks later, during a summit meeting in Vienna with President John Kennedy, Premier Nikita Khrushchev agreed to have 'a neutral and independent Laos under a government chosen by the Laotians'. Notwithstanding this declaration, President Kennedy still found it necessary during the fall of 1961 to authorize stepped-up reconnaissance activities over Laos by Air Force RF-101s of the Pipe Stem and Able Mable detachments operating from Tan Son Nhut in South Vietnam and Don Muang in Thailand respectively.

Communist advances in Laos increased markedly during the spring of 1962 and the United States came close to intervening in May when 5,000 troops and a squadron of North American F-100 fighters were sent to Thailand for possible operations across the Mekong River. Shortly afterwards, on 12 June, the Neutralists, Rightists, and Pathet Lao factions formed a new coalition government headed by Prime Minister Souvanna Phouma, and on 23 July, the Declaration and Protocol on the Neutrality of Laos was signed by 14 nations in Geneva. United States forces withdrew from Thailand, the Able Mable detachment was pulled back to Tan Son Nhut for operations over South Vietnam, and the 660 officers and men assigned to MAAG left Laos in accordance with the Protocol; North Vietnamese forces, however, stayed in Pathet Lao territory.

When Pathet Lao and NVA forces attacked government troops in the Plain of Jars during the early spring of 1964, the coalition government failed and Prime Minister Souvanna Phouma, now leading a government without Pathet Lao participation, authorized the US-requested resumption of reconnaissance flights over Laos. This time, the Navy took the lead in providing the Yankee Team reconnaissance missions which were initiated on 19 May 1964. Carrier aviators immediately came under fire for the first time during the Southeast Asia War.

The First Skirmishes: Yankee Team, Pierce Arrow, and Barrel Roll

In the spring of 1964, four attack carriers—USS *Bon Homme Richard* (CVA-31) with CVW-19 on board, *Constellation* (CVA-64) with CVW-14, *Kitty Hawk* (CVA-63) with CVW-11, and *Ticonderoga* (CVA-14)[5] with CVW-5—and one CVS—USS *Bennington* (CVS-20) with CVSG-20—were deployed to the Western Pacific (WestPac) and responsibility for the first Yankee Team Navy missions fell to *Kitty Hawk* and the RF-8A Crusaders of her VFP-63 Detachment Charlie. On 21 May, one of these Det C RF-8As was hit by ground fire but its pilot, Lt Charles F Klusmann, succeeded in returning safely to CVA-63. A little over two weeks later, however, on 6 June, he was less fortunate. Flying at 525 knots (970kmh) and 1500ft (460m) over Muong Soui in the Plain of Jars, he was forced to eject after his RF-8A was hit by 37mm fire in the utility hydraulic system. Lt Klusmann was immediately captured by Pathet Lao troops but his good fortune was not totally gone. Eighty-three days later, on 28 August, he and several Laotian prisoners escaped into the jungle, from which he was picked up by an Air America helicopter on 1 September.

After Lt Klusmann was shot down, the US ambassador in Vientiane requested and immediately obtained authorization from Prime Minister Souvanna to use fighters to escort the unarmed reconnaissance aircraft. However, this move proved ill-fated, and on 7 June an F-8D from VF-111 escorting an RF-8A from VFP-63 Det C over the Plain of Jars was hit by automatic weapons. The pilot, LCdr D W Lynn, ejected and was recovered by an Air America helicopter. For *Kitty Hawk*, this had been a most inauspicious start to combat operations in Southeast Asia. In retaliation, Air Force F-100D fighter-bombers, supported by RF-101C reconnaissance aircraft and KB-50J tankers, flew a strike against antiaircraft sites in Laos.

This did not deter Pathet Lao gunners from interfering again with Yankee Team operations, and the 'blue suiters' lost three fighters and one reconnaissance aircraft between 14 August and the end of 1964. During that same period, RF-8As of VFP-63 Det F from *Constellation*, escorted by F-8Es from a six-plane F-8E detachment from VF-51 (cross-decking from *Ticonderoga* to *Constellation* until the F-4Bs from VF-142 and VF-143 were authorized to fly over Laos), also flew Yankee Team sorties; fortunately, none of the Navy aircraft was lost.

Laos was not at the time the only country in Indochina to be the recipient of US reconnaissance activities. In January 1964, within two months of taking office, President Lyndon Johnson authorized a twelve-month program to pressure North Vietnam into ceasing its logistic support of the Viet Cong and Pathet Lao. This program, which was detailed in OPLAN 34-A, provided both US support for South Vietnamese clandestine actions against North Vietnam and US gathering of photographic and electronic intelligence in and around North Vietnam. Thus, during most of the first seven months of 1964, Lockheed U-2Cs from the 4080th Strategic Reconnaissance Wing went on Lucky Dragon high-altitude reconnaissance sorties from Bien Hoa over Laos and North Vietnam, Lockheed C-130B-IIs from the 6091st Reconnaissance Squadron flew from Bangkok's Don Muang Airport to intercept communications during Queen Bee missions off the North Vietnamese coast, and Navy destroyers sailed in international waters close to the North Vietnamese coast to gather Signal Intelligence (SIGINT) during De Soto patrols for which carrier-based aircraft provided air cover. Moreover, operating under US guidance, the South Vietnamese were increasingly aggressive in their covert operations against the North. With all these activities being perceived by the North Vietnamese as a threat to their sovereignty and interfering with their logistic support of the Viet Cong in the South, a major incident was almost inevitable.

In the afternoon of 2 August 1964, after the North

[5] *Ticonderoga* was not new to the South China Sea. In January 1945, she had been part of TF 38 which had roamed along a 420-mile stretch of the Indochina coast, from Saigon northward, to inflict heavy losses on Japanese shipping and port facilities.

With the exception of the RF-8Gs of a VFP-62 detachment aboard USS Franklin D. Roosevelt *(CVA-42) in 1966-67 and infrequent short-term detachments by Marine RF-8As, all photo-reconnaissance Crusaders operating in the Gulf of Tonkin came from VFP-63. Taken early during the war, this photograph shows deck personnel wearing simple 'Mickey Mouse' ear protection equipment. Later on, the wearing of 'cranials' became mandatory.* (US Navy via Rick Morgan)

Trailed closely by two A-4Es from VA-55, this Skywarrior from VAH-4 Det Bravo lacks both the refueling probe on the port forward fuselage side and the HRU unit protruding beneath the rear of the bomb bay, items which later in the war were always fitted to A-3Bs and KA-3Bs. Attack Squadron Fifty-Six (VA-56) and Heavy Attack Squadron Four (VAH-4) Det Bravo were two of the units assigned to Carrier Air Wing Five (CVW-5) for the first war cruise of USS Ticonderoga *(CVA-14) in 1964.* (US Navy)

Vietnamese possibly confused the USS *Maddox* (DD-731) with one of the South Vietnamese patrol boats which had shelled a radar station on Hon Me Island and a radio transmitter on Hon Ngu Island, three P-4 PT boats approached at high speed the US destroyer, steaming on De Soto SIGINT patrol some 28 miles off the coast. *Maddox* first fired three warning shots and, after the North Vietnamese craft launched torpedoes, she returned fire. The destroyer hit at least one of the PT boats and avoided the torpedoes but was machine gunned before breaking off the engagement and calling for support by CVW-5 aircraft from *Ticonderoga*, the only attack carrier then in the Gulf of Tonkin.

Led by Cdr R F Mohrhardt, four *Iron Angels* F-8Es, which were already airborne on a training sortie some 300 miles south of DD-731, quickly came to the rescue and probably sank one of the P-4 boats with gunfire and 5in Zuni rockets. Although the air war had not yet openly started, Naval Aviators had had their first direct encounter with the North Vietnamese.

After her brief engagement in the afternoon of 2 August, *Maddox* had been pulled back further out to sea for the night, but the next day, now accompanied by *Turner Joy* (DD-951), she was back on her De Soto station as ordered by President Johnson. Furthermore, anticipating a possible North Vietnamese reaction, the Navy ordered *Constellation* to leave Hong Kong and head for the Gulf of Tonkin while the President and his advisors evaluated whether or not to launch punitive air strikes on North Vietnam as requested by CINCPAC, Adm Ulysses S Grant Sharp, Jr.

During the night of 4–5 August, while CINCPAC's request was under consideration in Washington, South Vietnamese raiders struck a radar station on Cape Vinh Son and a security station near Cua Ron. On patrol further north, *Maddox* and *Turner Joy* identified radar contacts as probable torpedo boats and soon reported that they were taking evasive action to avoid torpedoes. However, weather was bad and visibility very poor when two Skyraiders from VA-52 arrived on the scene to lend assistance. Although the presence of enemy patrol craft could not be confirmed, the apparent North Vietnamese hostile action against the destroyers on patrol in international waters was enough for President Johnson to order military forces to retaliate.

As authorized by the President, Operation Pierce Arrow,

a 'limited and fitting' response, consisted of air strikes against 'gun boats and certain facilities in North Vietnam'. It was launched in the early afternoon of 5 August as soon as *Constellation* joined *Ticonderoga* in the Gulf of Tonkin. Operating from *Constellation*, CVW-14 struck the PT boat bases at Hon Gai and Loc Chao—twenty Skyraiders, Skyhawks, and Phantom IIs going against the former and twelve aircraft of the same types attacking the latter. *Ticonderoga*'s CVW-5 sent six Crusaders to strike the PT boat base at Quang Khe and twenty-six Skyraiders, Skyhawks, and Crusaders to bomb petroleum storage facilities at Vinh. Damage assessments indicated that eight North Vietnamese boats had been sunk and twenty-one damaged and that facilities at Vinh had been left burning with 90 per cent of the oil tanks out of commission. Tragically, in achieving these results Naval Aviators paid a higher price than anticipated. The North Vietnamese, forewarned of the impending attack by President Johnson's premature announcement of his decision to order the retaliatory strike, put up a heavy automatic weapons and AAA barrage over the targets. Lt (jg) R C Sather was killed during the strike against Loc Chao when his *Swordsmen* A-1H was hit by AAA and Lt (jg) E Alvarez was taken prisoner of war after ejecting from a *Roadrunners* A–4C during his second run against PT boats at Hon Gai. Two other CVW-14 aircraft were hit but were able to recover aboard *Constellation*.

Initially, popular reaction in the United States to the swift strike by naval aircraft in retaliation for the North Vietnamese attack against Navy ships was highly favorable and led the US Congress to pass the Gulf of Tonkin Resolution on 10 August giving the President power to 'take all necessary measures to repel any armed attack against the forces of the United States and to prevent further aggression'. Both sides, sensing the inevitability of war, beefed up their forces. The Navy ordered the USS *Ranger*

When USS Maddox *(DD-731) and USS* Turner Joy *(DD-951) came under apparent North Vietnamese hostile action during the night of 4-5 August 1964, two Skyraiders from VA-52 came to the assistance of the destroyers. This* Knightriders *A-1H was photographed at NAS Alameda, California, after USS* Ticonderoga *(CVA-14) and her Carrier Air Wing Five (CVW-5) had returned to the States.*

With the Director and Cat Offficer in light (yellow) shirts providing guidance, deck personnel secure an A-4C of VA-146 on one of the four steam catapults of USS Constellation *(CVA-64). On 5 August 1964, two weeks after this photograph was taken, the* Blue Diamonds *were at war.* (US Navy)

Throughout the war, attack carriers embarked either a detachment of RF-8As or RF-8Gs or a squadron of RA-5Cs. The one exception was USS Ranger *(CVA-61) which for its August 1964-May 1965 cruise had both VFP-63 Det Mike and RVAH-5. Crusaders and Vigilantes of these two units flew reconnaissance sorties over Laos in support of Barrel Roll.* (US Navy)

(CVA-61) and USS *Kearsarge* (CVS-33) to join TF 77 and resumed De Soto patrols, while the Communists transferred thirty-nine MiG-15 and MiG-17 fighters from China to Phuc Yen Air Base. Tension rose. During the night of 17 September the destroyers *Morton* (DD-948) and *Edwards* (DD-619) reported firing on unidentified naval targets, prompting the USAF and the USN to propose retaliatory air strikes against the air base northeast of Hanoi to destroy the MiGs. However, the necessary authorization was not granted and, to reduce the risk of confrontation at sea, De Soto naval patrols were replaced by weekly Box Top COMINT/SIGINT flights flown by RB-47H of the 55th Strategic Reconnaissance Wing. Thereafter both sides warily watched each other's moves and refrained from directly antagonizing their opponents. In outlying areas, they were less careful and Laos became the scene of the next skirmishes.

Increased North Vietnamese infiltration through Laos into South Vietnam and the arguable, but perceived, need to shore up the South Vietnamese government by demonstrating US resolve prompted President Johnson to approve, on 2 December 1964, a multi-phase military action plan. According to this plan, during the first phase US air strikes along infiltration routes in Laos and stepped-up covert maritime operations would warn Hanoi of the risks it was taking in supporting the Viet Cong. In the event that this proved to be an insufficient intimidation—the second phase would see air strikes extended to lines of communications (LOCs) just north of the DMZ. Finally, if need be, the third phase would encompass unrestricted air strikes against North Vietnamese airfields and petroleum, oil, and lubricants (POL) storage as well as naval mining and blockading operations. The plan was sound; however, when it later became necessary to implement the third phase, the political will was missing and the full might of US air power was not unleashed until it was too late.

On 14 December 1964, twelve days after presidential approval of the first phase had been granted and after the required acquiescence of the Laotian government had been obtained, USAF tactical aircraft flew the first of the very restricted Barrel Roll armed reconnaissance missions over Laos. The second of these missions was undertaken on 17 December by CVW-9 from *Ranger*; four A-1Hs escorted by eight F-4Bs flew armed reconnaissance over Routes 12 and

The Grumman C-1A Trader was the main COD aircraft shuttling personnel, mail, and urgently needed parts from shore bases to TF 77 carriers. It had a crew of two and could carry either up to 3500lb (1590kg) of cargo or nine pasengers in spartan accommodations. Bearing the modex 000 'artistically' arranged to appear as 'triple nut', this C-1A was the COD aircraft assigned to USS Constellation *(CVA-64).* (Grumman History Center)

121 but failed to damage the Ban Boung Bau bridge. Thereafter, a National Security Council (NSC) committee each week designated two road segments over which armed reconnaissance sorties could be flown and a fixed target over which unused ordnance could be expended. At the same time, aviators were enjoined to attack only targets which evidenced 'unmistakingly military activity of a transient or mobile nature' and local commanders were given no leeway regarding tactics, ordnance, or other tactical considerations. These were the first ROEs, the infamous Rules of Engagement.

Although the limited nature of the Pierce Arrow retaliatory strike in early August 1964 had somewhat justified politically-motivated restrictions, when Barrel Roll started, the imposition of more hindering ROEs was not. Unfortunately, the air war in Southeast Asia went on to be fought under a stringent set of controls and restrictions as ROEs were extended and expanded for Rolling Thunder, and most remained in force until Linebacker II in December 1972. President Johnson, determined to avoid a larger conflict with the People's Republic of China (PRC) and the Soviet Union, initially kept a firm control over the air campaign and personally approved targets and target areas. In addition, political considerations injected by the US ambassadors in Saigon, Vientiane, and Bangkok carried much weight and were usually paramount to military considerations. Sanctuary areas and buffer zones were established, and aircrews were strictly forbidden from hitting non-military targets or inflicting civilian casualties. The politicians were no longer content to be armchair strategists; they wanted to be tacticians from the safety of their offices near the Potomac.

On the Line: Flaming Dart and Rolling Thunder I

Air strikes against the North, which had been programmed as the contingent second and third phases of the plan approved by President Johnson on 2 December 1964 and which had long been advocated by many military commanders as well as by several presidential advisors, almost became a reality after seventy-three US personnel

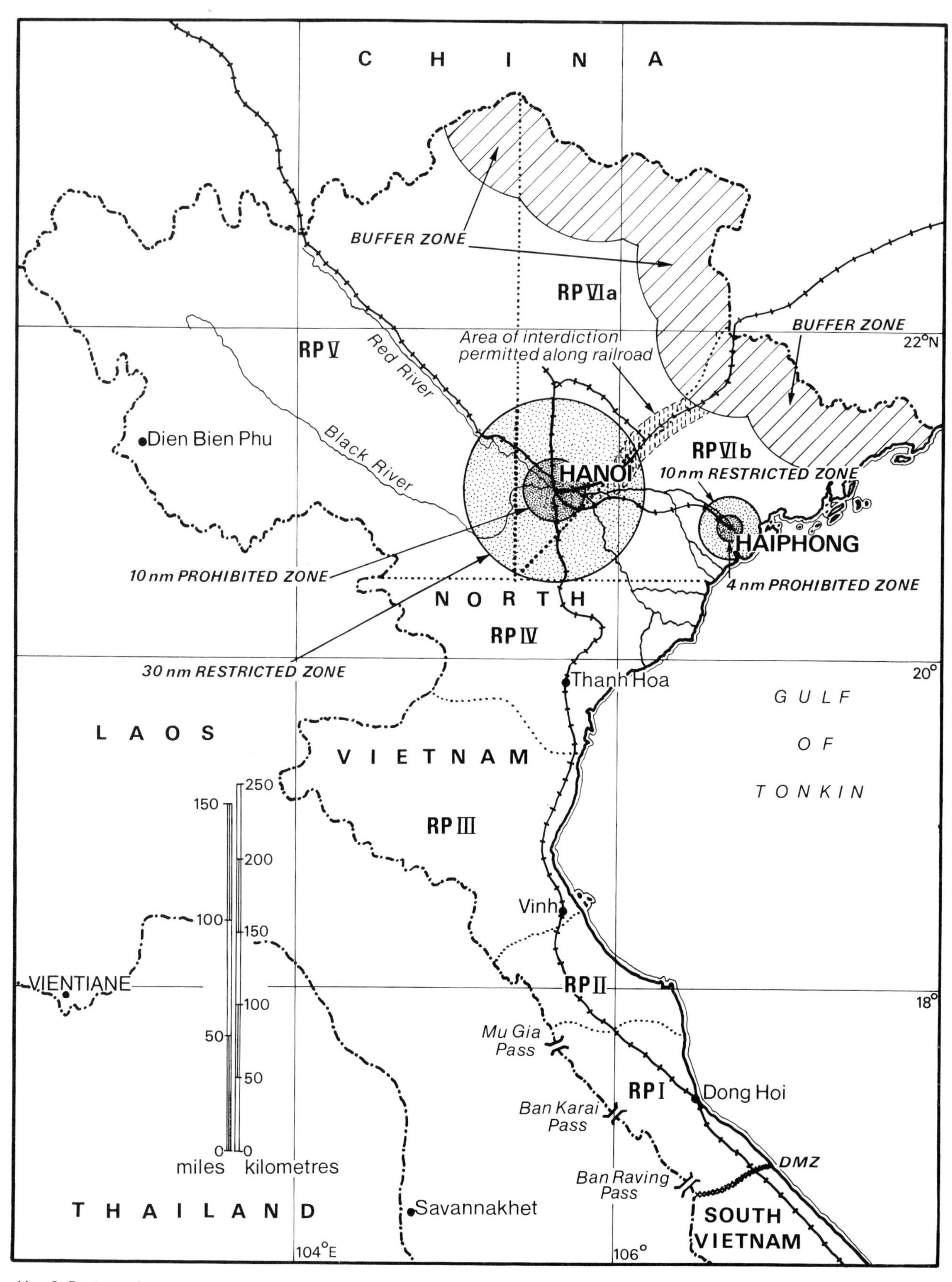

Map 2: Route packages

Decks are always crowded when a full Carrier Air Wing is aboard. The use of a telephoto lens magnifies this situation as shown in this 1964 view of the aft deck of USS Ranger *(CVA-61). The aircraft are an RA-5C of RVAH-5 (modex 102), an A-4C of VA-93 (modex 309), and A-1Hs of VA-95 (modexes 511, 509, 508 and 512). Modex 512 was hit by AAA during a Rolling Thunder sortie against the ammunition dump in Phu Qhi on 15 March 1965. The pilot, Lt (jg) C F Clydesdale, was killed when his aircraft crashed into the sea as he tried to reach the carrier.* (US Navy via Rick Morgan)

were killed or injured in the bombing of the Brink Hotel Bachelor Officers' Quarter (BOQ) in Saigon on Christmas Eve. However, the President held back his approval until 7 February 1965 when he authorized the first Flaming Dart retaliatory strikes in response to new Viet Cong attacks against USA facilities near Pleiku and Camp Holloway during which eight Americans were killed and 109 were wounded. Once again, the Navy led the way as aircraft from USS *Coral Sea* (CVA-43) and USS *Hancock* (CVA-19)[6] hit their assigned targets north of the DMZ in the afternoon of the 7th. Other targets were struck by VNAF aircraft, but those designated for aircraft from the USS *Ranger* (CVA-61) and Air Force units in South Vietnam could not be hit due to poor visibility.

Appropriately, as they were selected in retaliation for Viet Cong attacks against US military quarters in South Vietnam, the targets for Flaming Dart One were barracks at Dong Hoi and Vit Thu Lu. While the latter could not be struck as monsoon weather hid them from the *Ranger*'s 34-aircraft strike force, those at Dong Hoi were extensively damaged by twenty aircraft from *Coral Sea* and twenty-nine aircraft from *Hancock*. The Communists, however, also knew how to play tit-for-tat and the Viet Cong blew up the Bachelor Enlisted Quarters (BEQ) at Qhi Nhon on 10 February, killing or wounding forty-four US servicemen. The US responded the following day with Flaming Dart Two, an attack against the Chanh Hoa barracks for which planners in Washington specified both the number of strike and support aircraft (ninety-nine from *Coral Sea*, *Hancock*, and *Ranger*) and the type of ordnance to be delivered.

Unfortunately, the price paid was already disproportionate to the target value. During the two Flaming Dart strikes, one pilot was killed, one was taken prisoner of war, and four aircraft were lost. The lesson, however, was not learned in Washington; for most of the war, targets assigned to Naval Aviators and their Air Force brethren were seldom worth the price paid in terms of ordnance expended and aircraft lost. The human toll was even more tragic.

Whereas Pierce Arrow had been undertaken against North Vietnam in retaliation for a direct action by its forces, Flaming Dart One and Two were launched against North

[6] Like *Ticonderoga*, *Hancock* was no stranger to the South China Sea, having also been part of TF 38 during operations off Indochina in January 1945.

Vietnam in alleged retaliation for attacks in South Vietnam by the Viet Cong. However, following President Johnson's decision on 13 February 1965 to authorize the initiation of Rolling Thunder, a sustained program of bombing targets in North Vietnam, there was no more pretense at disguising operations over the North as retaliatory strikes. The air war in Southeast Asia had openly started.

Initially scheduled to commence on 20 February but postponed four times, Rolling Thunder began on 2 March 1965 when USAF aircraft bombed preplanned targets, an ammunition depot at Xom Bang and a naval base at Quang Khe. As TF 77 carriers were busy providing air cover for the Marine landing at Da Nang on 8 March, the next Rolling Thunder mission was also flown by the USAF. Naval Aviators only joined the fray on 15 March when CVW-9 from *Ranger* lost a pilot and an aircraft during a mission against the Phu Qhi ammunition dump. The Navy's next Rolling Thunder mission was flown on 26 March by aircraft from *Coral Sea* and *Hancock*. The pilots of three aircraft shot down during strikes against radar sites at Bach Long Vi, Ha Tinh, and Vinh Son were recovered. In addition, on 3 March the Navy began flying sustained Blue Tree photo-reconnaissance missions over the North.

Arriving on the line two weeks after the Gulf of Tonkin incident, USS Ranger *(CVA-41) remained in the area until after the start of Rolling Thunder. Like other aircraft from her Carrier Air Wing Nine (CVW-9), the A-1Hs of VA-95 flew Barrel Roll missions over Laos and Flaming Dart and Rolling Thunder sorties over the North. Heavily loaded with fuel and bombs, this Skyraider roars off* Ranger*'s angled deck in early April 1965. This is believed to be the aircraft lost by VA-95 on 11 April 1965 during a sortie over Laos.* (US Navy)

As Rolling Thunder gradually evolved into a sustained strategic air campaign, CINCPAC set up a Rolling Thunder Armed Reconnaissance Coordinating Committee (RTARCC, later RTCC when Armed Reconnaissance was deleted from the committee's full title) to assign targets to TF 77 and to Seventh Air Force (7th AF). These targets, released by the Joint Chiefs of Staff (JCS) from the preapproved list under authority directly delegated by the President and the Secretary of Defense (SecDef), were specifically authorized first for armed reconnaissance sorties over assigned areas and then for preplanned strikes against fixed points (the first of these so-called Alpha strikes was flown by Navy aircraft on 5 March 1966). However, once targets had been assigned, commanders of air wings (CAGs) and aviators were precluded by ROEs from planning their missions in a manner consistent with sound tactical and weather considerations.

To avoid duplications and to coordinate Air Force and Navy Rolling Thunder operations over the North, RTARCC first established a time-sharing arrangement whereby TF 77 and 7th AF were given discrete three-hour periods during which to execute their respective strikes in a given area. As this method proved cumbersome, RTARCC briefly considered replacing it with an arbitrary division of North Vietnam along a north-south axis, whereby carrier-based aircraft would concentrate their efforts against targets east of that line while Thailand-based Air Force aircraft would operate west of the line. In the end, the solution retained was a division of North Vietnam into six sectors (officially designated 'Route Packages' and commonly abbreviated 'RPs'), with the Air Force and the Navy alternating responsibility for operations over the seven sectors every week. Route Package I was the sector just north of the DMZ and included the main passes feeding into the Ho Chi Minh Trail from North Vietnam to Laos (Ban Karing, Ban Karai, and Mu Gia); RP II, RP III, and RP IV were coastal sectors further north; RP V was in the northwestern corner and bordered China; and RP VI, which also bordered China, included the heart of North Vietnam and was subdivided into RP VIA with the capital city of Hanoi and RP VIB with the port city of Haiphong. In Route Packages V, VIA, and VIB, additional restrictions or prohibitions applied. Operations over a 25- to 30-nautical mile buffer zone along the Chinese border, a 30-nautical mile radius area around Hanoi, and a 10-nautical mile radius area around Haiphong were permitted only on special occasions. Operations were normally prohibited over the 10-nautical mile and 4-nautical mile zones respectively centered on downtown Hanoi and downtown Haiphong.

Regardless of the Route Package over which a mission took place, local commanders could not select new targets based on the changing tactical situation and all requests to add new targets had to be sent to CINCPAC in Hawaii and then forwarded to the JCS and SecDef at the Pentagon. If the Pentagon considered a request to have merit, a recommendation was sent to the White House. Only the President could add targets to the approved list. Likewise, the number of sorties and the type of ordnance were dictated by Washington. Unexpended ordnance had to be jettisoned at sea rather than dropped on targets of opportunity. Clearly military targets on civilian sites, such as trucks parked in villages or AAA batteries on irrigation and flood control dikes, could not be attacked, as US politicians went out of their way to ensure that North Vietnamese civilians would not be hurt. Enemy aircraft, which made their combat début

The Xom Ca Trang highway bridge was situated on Route 12 on the way to the Mu Gia Pass. One of the four spans of this steel truss highway bridge was destroyed on 16 April 1965 during an early Rolling Thunder strike. Unfortunately, the interdiction campaign proved costly and of limited effectiveness as the North Vietnamese quickly became experts at making emergency repairs and devising bypass routes. (US Navy)

Even when tanker configured as is this VAH-8 aircraft, the Skywarrior retained the ability to carry bombs as demonstrated by this Fireballer *A-3B making a dive bombing attack on a target just in-shore of the North Vietnamese coast on 19 August 1965. After this deployment aboard USS* Midway *(CVA-41), VAH-8 was transferred out of CVW-2 and returned twice to Yankee Station aboard USS* Constellation *(CVA-64), once as part of CVW-15 and then as part of CVW-14.* (US Navy)

on 4 April 1965, had to be positively identified before missiles could be launched. The list of restrictions went on and on. Conversely, the North Vietnamese did not have to contend with similar restrictions on their operations as both the Soviet Union and the PRC supported them diplomatically and materially. The latter form of support soon consisted of a seemingly inexhaustible supply of radar-directed AAA batteries, surface-to-air missiles, combat and transport aircraft, ammunition, training, and advisors.

After a relatively slow start, the first phase of Rolling Thunder gained tempo as the United States sought to destroy North Vietnam's logistical system and thus curtail its ability to infiltrate men and supplies into South Vietnam. With the previously mentioned *Coral Sea*, *Hancock*, and *Ranger*, the latter leaving the line on 12 April, and the USS *Midway* (CVA-41) arriving in the Gulf of Tonkin on 10 April, TF 77 attack carriers and their escorts remained on Yankee Station[7] for up to five weeks at a time to conduct offensive operations against military and transportation targets in the panhandle of North Vietnam below the 20th parallel. Lasting until 11 May 1965, this first phase resulted in the loss of twenty Navy aircraft without achieving the desired results.

An Enduring Air War: Rolling Thunder II

Seeking to induce the North Vietnamese to begin peace talks, the US government ordered air operations suspended on 12 May. Six days later, when it became evident that Hanoi was not yet prepared to talk, armed reconnaissance and strike missions were resumed and operations against some targets above 20 degrees north latitude began. Thereafter, new targets were progressively added during this

[7] Yankee Station, initially known as Point Yankee, was in the Gulf of Tonkin southwest of Hainan, north of the DMZ, and east of the North Vietnamese coast. In April 1966, it was moved northward, thus reducing the distance aircraft had to fly to reach their targets and then return to their carrier. After Rolling Thunder ended in 1968, it was moved back south. In 1972, after the resumption of operations over the North, Yankee Station returned to its northernmost location.

second phase of Rolling Thunder. Strikes against bridges along the northwestern rail line between Hanoi and Lao Cai on the Chinese border were first authorized in July and strikes against bridges along the shorter Hanoi-China northeastern rail line were allowed two months later.

During the first two phases of Rolling Thunder in 1965, North Vietnamese defenses became more sophisticated with a simultaneous build-up in fighter, missile and AAA strength. The Vietnam People's Air Force (more usually referred to as the North Vietnamese Air Force or NVAF), which had brought its Soviet-built fighters to Phuc Yen in August 1964, had not attempted to interfere with the initial Flaming Dart and Rolling Thunder activities as its pilots and ground-controlled intercept (GCI) personnel were not yet sufficiently trained. At last, when the Hanoi leadership realized that the United States was no longer relying on occasional retaliatory strikes and had initiated a major air offensive, the NVAF was ordered to enter the fray. On 3 April 1965, three MiG-17s made an unconclusive pass at aircraft from *Coral Sea* and *Hancock*, who were attacking a bridge at Dong Phuong Thong in RP IV some 70 miles south of Hanoi. The only aircraft lost on that date was an A-4C from VA-216 which was hit by small arms fire during its bombing run on the bridge. The next day, however, the MiGs downed two F-105D fighter-bombers from the 355th Tactical Fighter Wing, USAF, to claim the first air combat victories of the war.

For Naval Aviators who, unlike Air Force crews, operated regularly over the Gulf of Tonkin and close to the Chinese island of Hainan, NVAF MiGs were not the only hostile fighters with which they had to contend. This was clearly demonstrated on 9 April, when VF-96 Phantoms flying barrier combat air patrol (BarCAP) from *Ranger* were jumped south of Hainan by four MiG-17s belonging to China's Air Force of the People's Liberation Army (and designated ChiCom by US aviators). At the end of the confusing engagement, the score was even; the loss of an F-4B and its *Fighting Falcons* crew, Lt (jg) Terence Murphy and Ens Ron Fegan, was offset by this crew's probable destruction of a ChiCom MiG. However, for fear of publicly antagonizing the PRC, this kill was never officially confirmed and, to this day, remains shrouded in mystery. Likewise, the probable cause of the F-4B loss is unclear, the Navy believing that the aircraft was gunned down by one of the MiG-17s while at the time PRC sources claimed that the F-4B had been downed by another friendly aircraft.

The next aerial engagement between F-4s and MiGs, on 17 June, resulted in clear-cut victories for two *Freelancers* crews flying BarCAP from *Midway*. Cdr Lou Page, the executive officer (XO) of VF-21, and his radar intercept officer (RIO), Lt John Smith, downed a MiG-17 with an AIM-7 Sparrow air-to-air missile and were credited with the first confirmed US air victory in Vietnam, while another crew, Lt Jack Batson and LCdr Robert Doremus[8], almost simultaneously shot down another NVAF MiG-17. Three

The first officially confirmed victory over a North Vietnamese fighter was credited to Cdr Louis C Page, Jr, and Lt John Smith, Jr, from Fighter Squadron Twenty-One (VF-21) on 17 June 1965. The victorious Freelancers *later posed aboard USS* Midway *(CVA-41) for this publicity shot. Neither, however, took the trouble of donning harness, g-suit, and other flight paraphernalia prior to striking a dashing pose.* (US Navy)

days later, on 20 June, a more unusual victory was shared by two VA-25 pilots, Lt Clint Johnson and Lt (jg) Charlie Hartman. Flying propeller-driven A-1H attack aircraft as part of a four-aircraft division assigned rescue combat air patrol (ResCAP) duty to cover the recovery of an Air Force F-4C crew from the 45th TFS, the *Fist of the Fleet* pilots were surprised at low-altitude by a pair of MiG-17s. Taking violent evasive action and dropping external tanks and bombs, Lt Johnson and Lt (jg) Hartman finally maneuvered their aircraft into favorable positions and succeeded in 'bagging' one of the MiGs with their 20mm cannon. Another victory was obtained, on 6 October, by a VF-151 crew from *Coral Sea* but, again because of diplomatic niceties which certainly did not fool the PRC, it was not officially acknowledged that the victim was a ChiCom MiG. No other victories or air combat losses were recorded by the Navy during the remainder of 1965, thus resulting in an official

[8] A little over two months later, on 24 August, LCdr Doremus was taken prisoner of war after he and his pilot, Cdr F A Franke, ejected from their F-4B which had been hit by an SA-2 missile while flying BarCAP during a strike against the Thanh Hoa Bridge.

Vigilantes, Phantoms, and a Tracer on the deck of USS Ranger *(CVA-61).*

3:0 kill ratio in favor of Naval Aviators and an unofficial but more realistic 5:1 ratio[9], when including air combat against ChiCom aircraft.

On 5 April 1965, two days after MiGs had first been met in combat, an RF-8A from VFP-63 Det Delta returned to *Coral Sea* from a Blue Tree reconnaissance sortie with the first photographs of a surface-to-air missile (SAM) site under construction, some 15 miles southeast of Hanoi. The rear admiral commanding TF 77, Edward C Outlaw, and his staff wanted the site struck without delay. However, in accordance with established ROEs, they could not order the strike and had to request approval through the chain of command. Although the commander of the 7th AF, the ranking USAF officer in the theater, and CINCPAC concurred with Adm Outlaw, approval was not obtained from Washington. As could be expected, the North Vietnamese lost no time in taking advantage of this respite and kept building more sites to disperse their SAMs (the Soviet-built SA-2s could be redeployed to prepared sites in two to three hours). Finally, on 24 July 1965, when their Soviet advisors considered construction and training to have reached a satisfactory level, the North Vietnamese used their first SA-2 Guideline surface-to-air missiles to bring down an F-4C from the 47th TFS, USAF, flying target combat air patrol (TarCAP) during a Rolling Thunder strike against the Lang Chi munitions factory. The loss of this aircraft and its crew (the aircraft commander was killed and the backseater taken prisoner of war) finally convinced the President and his advisers that SAMs indeed represented a new and serious threat and that something ought to be done to neutralize them. Their response, however, was timid. At first the Air Force was only authorized a single retaliatory strike against SAM Site Nos 6 and 7, near Hanoi. Flown on 27 July, this retaliatory strike resulted in the destruction of one of the sites, but the AAA protecting them claimed four Air Force F-105Ds and an RF-101C sent on a BDA reconnaissance sortie two days later.

After a second Air Force retaliatory strike proved less successful (the SAMs having previously been moved to other sites) and after the first loss to a SAM during the night of 11–12 August of a Navy aircraft—an A-4E from VA-23 off *Midway*—both the Air Force and the Navy quickly developed appropriate active and passive tactics to limit the effectiveness of the SAMs and to seek and destroy them. Notably, mission profiles were altered, the use of specialized electronic countermeasures (ECM) aircraft was stepped up, strike aircraft were fitted with self-protection jamming pods and chaff dispensers, and Iron Hand and Wild Weasel defense suppression flights were included in major strike forces. The first of these measures, the adoption of new mission profiles, saw strike pilots attempt to fly below the effective ceiling of the SA-2 missiles. However, this tactic exposed aircraft for too long to heavy small arms fire and heavily-laden strike aircraft lost too much maneuvering energy and speed in popping up to dive altitude. Therefore, pilots switched to approaching their targets at medium altitude where the use of warning devices enabled them to take evasive action as soon as SAMs were launched. However, once over the target, aircraft had to dive down into concentrated AAA and small arms fire and their only defensive tactic consisted in jinking violently.

Whereas during the early sixties the Air Force and the Marine Corps had not neglected their electronic reconnaissance and countermeasure tactical capabilities, the former relying on various versions of the Douglas RB-66 for these tasks and the latter operating Douglas EF-10Bs, the Navy did not then assign ECM aircraft as part of the normal complement of its carrier air wings. Whenever necessary, however, detachments of Douglas EA-3Bs from VQ-1 (then shore-based at NAS Atsugi, Japan) and of Douglas EA-1Fs from VAW-13 Detachment One (then on six-month deployment to NAS Cubi Point, the Philippines) were temporarily deployed aboard carriers operating in WestPac. Thus, at the time of the Gulf of Tonkin Incident and from the onset of Rolling Thunder, detachments of EA-3Bs and EA-1Fs were aboard TF 77 carriers[10]; 'queer'[11] Skywarriors collected electronic intelligence and 'Electric Spads'[12] jammed North Vietnamese radar in support of strike aircraft. In addition, ECM support for TF 77 was often provided by Marine detachments of Douglas EF-10Bs from VMCJ-1 which were temporarily embarked aboard *Constellation*, *Coral Sea*, *Oriskany*, and *Ticonderoga* in late 1964 and early 1965. Beginning in late April 1965, VMCJ-1 substituted a permanent EF-10B detachment operating from Da Nang Air Base in South Vietnam for its carrier detachments, as maintenance of the EF-10Bs old electronic equipment was easier at a centralized location.

Whereas the Marine EF-10B detachments temporarily operating at sea had not been part of the CVWs with which they had operated, VMF(AW)-212 became an integral part of CVW-16 when it replaced VF-161 as one of the two Crusader squadrons embarked aboard *Oriskany* in April 1965. Spending 141 days on the line along with the other squadrons of CVW-16, VMF(AW)-212 had two of its F-8Es shot down by the North Vietnamese AAA (one on 5 November 1965 and one on 17 November) and lost two others in operational accidents. Three of the Marine pilots were recovered but Capt H P Chapman was taken prisoner

[9] During that year the Air Force did not fare as well as its loss of three F-105s was only partially offset by the downing of two MiG-17s by F-4Cs.

[10] VQ-1 detachments are known to have operated EA-3Bs aboard all CVAs assigned to TF 77 during 1964 and 1965: *Bon Homme Richard*, *Constellation*, *Coral Sea*, *Enterprise*, *Hancock*, *Independence*, *Kitty Hawk*, *Midway*, *Oriskany*, *Ranger*, and *Ticonderoga*. During that period, VAW-13 detachments flew EA-1Fs from *Bon Homme Richard*, *Coral Sea*, *Independence*, *Midway*, *Oriskany*, and *Ticonderoga*.

[11] Electronic reconnaissance and countermeasure aircraft have been known in the US Navy as 'queers' since the mission suffix 'Q' was first used in the designation of the radar countermeasure versions of the Grumman Avenger and Martin Mercator, the TBM-3Q and P4M-1Q.

[12] The nickname Spad was derived from the Skyraider's pre-1962 designation, AD-1 through AD-7, and was given in witty respect to all versions of the superannuated propeller-driven aircraft. Indeed to many of the young jet-era flyers, Skyraiders almost looked to be contemporary to World War I Spad fighters. In September 1962, the AD-5Q version, which was known in the Fleet as the 'queer' Skyraider, was redesignated EA-1F and became known as the 'Electric Spad'.

of war after being forced to eject during his bombing run against the Hai Duong bridge.

Although EA-3Bs detached aboard carriers or to Da Nang Air Base did furnish invaluable MiG and SAM warning services, the 'Electric Spads' were the aircraft providing the bulk of electronic countermeasure support from 1965 until 1967. The hard-working *Zappers* of VAW-13 Det 1, organized in two-aircraft teams with eight aircrewmen and a dozen maintenance personnel, deployed from Cubi Point for twenty to thirty days at a time and cross-decked frequently to operate from whichever carrier was on the line. Typically, a pair of EA-1Fs—configured with two ALT-2 noise jammer pods, two chaff dispensers, a podded APS-31 radar, and a centerline tank—was launched long before strike aircraft as, cruising at 110 to 140 knots when fully loaded, they required time to get in position three to four miles off the coast of North Vietnam. On station, they cruised at 5000ft to monitor enemy electronic activity until an active radar was identified. The 'Electric Spads' then slowly descended while flying directly toward the emission source, jamming the appropriate frequency and dispensing chaff. In the process, flying slow and along a predictable path, EA-1Fs came within AAA range. Luckily, in more than two years of intensive operations, only one 'Electric Spad' was lost; however, the four-man crew operating from *Midway* was killed in action on 2 June 1965 while providing ECM support for a search and rescue (SAR) mission in RP IV.

Surprisingly, as the Navy pioneered the use of self-protection jamming devices and chaff dispensers and flew its first Iron Hand missions more than $3\frac{1}{2}$ months before the Air Force flew its Wild Weasel sorties[13], the role played by Naval Aviators in the war against SAMs has not received the recognition it deserves. Reacting swiftly to the new threat, the Navy initiated Project Shoehorn in August 1965 to fit self-protection equipment in the Douglas A-4E, which

Whether operating from land bases or temporarily deployed aboard TF 77 carriers, Douglas EA-3Bs of VQ-1 proved most valuable in the war against SAMs by collecting electronic intelligence and providing SAM warning. Caught trapping aboard USS Hancock *(CVA-19) on 6 May 1966, this 'electronic snooper' carries the appropriate 007 modex.* (US Navy)

was then its primary attack aircraft. Working with engineers from Douglas Aircraft and Sanders Associates, the Navy team approved the design and installation of a humped fairing to house the receiver/transmitter for the Sanders AN/ALQ-51A ECM deception system and the receiver for the Magnavox AN/APR-27 SAM launch system. Pulse and receiving antennas for these systems were located in the nose, beneath the fuselage, and in the tail of the aircraft. To further improve the Skyhawk's ability to locate, identify, and neutralize enemy radar and SAM control systems, wiring for wing-mounted Sanders AN/ALQ-81 ECM jamming pods and the Itek AN/APR-25 RHAW system was added soon thereafter. Moreover, two 30-cartridge Goodyear/Tracor AN/ALE-29A chaff dispensers were installed in the rear of the fuselage and a number of A-4s were fitted to carry and launch AGM-45 Shrike anti-radiation missiles. Still later, A-4Es and A-4Fs had their anti-SAM capability improved through the installation of the Bendix AN/APS-107 RHAW system, this modification being easily identified by the installation of a canted refueling probe to avoid interfering with RHAW emission. Skyhawks, however, were

[13] Instead of rushing radar-homing and warning (RHAW) sets for installation on aircraft already in the war zone and assigning anti-SAM missions to regular squadron crews as the Navy did, the Air Force elected to proceed with a more ambitious program with specially modified aircraft—initially North American F-100Fs and then Republic EF-105Fs and F-105Gs—and specially trained Wild Weasel crews. The 6234th TFW (Wild Weasel Detachment) flew its first sorties on 1 December 1965, lost its first F-100F on 20 December, was credited with the destruction of its first SAM site on 22 December, and launched its first AGM-45 Shrike anti-radiation missile on 18 April 1966.

As carriers moved on and off the line, the hard-working Zappers *of VAW-13 Detachment One kept cross-decking as their EA-1Fs were in great demand. Even though their mission required that they fly along a well defined path taking them slowly and predictably toward the North Vietnamese coast, only one 'Electric Spads' was lost in combat. In this view, the underwing stores are an AN/ALT-2 noise jammer (port) and an AN/APS-31 radar (starboard).* (Jerry Edwards)

not the only carrier-based aircraft modified for Iron Hand operations as the Navy went on to use F-8 Crusaders, A-7 Corsair IIs, and A-6B Intruders in the defense suppression role.

Following the loss of its first aircraft to a SAM during the night of 11–12 August 1965, TF 77 was immediately authorized to find and destroy the enemy missile batteries. However, as strike aircraft were not yet equipped with specialized electronic equipment to locate the missiles' guidance radar, the first anti-SAM sorties—not yet called Iron Hand—had to be flown at low levels when aircraft from *Coral Sea* and *Midway* sought out the sites visually on 12 and 13 August. No SAMs were found, but the two air wings lost six aircraft (three A-4s, one A-1, one F-8, and one RF-8) to AAA. Two pilots were killed and four recovered. Although neither fired nor found, surface-to-air missiles were already taking a heavy toll.

Over the next two months, SAMs shot down two Navy

With North Vietnamese SAM crews and their Soviet advisors devising increasingly effective methods to defeat Iron Hand tactics, the US electronic industry had to develop ever more sophisticated systems to provide ample warning of a missile launch and to break its tracking. This photograph, taken at Davis-Monthan Air Force Base, Arizona, after the Warhorses *of VA-55 came back from their last war cruise aboard the USS* Hancock *(CVA-19) in 1973-74, shows the canted refueling probe adopted to avoid interference with the AN/APS-107 RHAW system fitted to late model Skyhawks used in the Iron Hand defense suppression role. The cannon in the starboard wing root has been removed, apparently to make room for additional electronic equipment.* (Ben Knowles by courtesy of Fred Harl)

Prior to departing the East Coast for the Gulf of Tonkin, USS Independence *(CVA-62) and her Carrier Air Wing Seven (CVW-7) worked up in the Caribbean where this launch scene was photographed on 2 March 1965. The aircraft are A-4Es of VA-72 and VA-86, F-4Bs of VF-41 and VF-84, and an A-6A of VA-75. Seven and a half months later, VA-72 and VA-75 teamed up for the first successful Iron Hand strike.* (US Navy)

aircraft, an F-4B from USS *Midway* (CVA-41) on 24 August and an F-8E from USS *Oriskany* (CVA-34) on 5 October, and an Air Force F-105D. To fight this growing threat, air wings began to include one or two Iron Hand sections in each major strike force. At that time, an Iron Hand section was normally comprised of a Skyhawk carrying conventional or cluster bombs and a cannon-armed Crusader to 'hose down' the site and its defensive AAA batteries with 20mm fire. The tactic first paid off on 17 October when four Iron Hand A-4Es from VA-72, led by an A-6A from VA-75 flying from USS *Independence* (CVA-62), destroyed a site near Kep Air Base. Thereafter, Iron Hand operations steadily gained in importance and became even more effective in March 1966 when Shrike anti-radiation missiles were first used operationally.

During the late fifties, and even more so during the early sixties after high-flying Lockheed U-2s were brought down in the Soviet Union (May 1960), China (September 1962), and Cuba (October 1962) by surface-to-air missiles, defense planners in the United States and Europe had become convinced that SAMs would now be the most effective defense against high performance combat aircraft. However, in spite of North Vietnam's initial success with SA-2s, this contention proved erroneous. It was conventional barrage and radar-directed AAA and automatic weapons which accounted for the destruction of the greatest number of US aircraft in North Vietnam. In 1965, 158 of the 173 aircraft and helicopters lost by the Air Force, Navy, and Marine Corps during operations over the North were shot down by AAA or automatic weapons fire whereas MiGs and SAMs respectively claimed four and eleven aircraft.

Already formidable and ubiquitous when Rolling Thunder began (according to a February 1965 US estimate, the North Vietnamese possessed between 1400 and 2100 automatic weapons and anti-aircraft artillery (AW/AAA) guns and four AAA fire control radars), conventional defenses were steadily built up. By the summer of 1967, the estimated number of AW/AAA guns had risen to over 8500 and the number of fire control radars had zoomed to 250. Moreover, integrated tactics linking SAMs, AAA and MiGs were developed and backed up by a fast-increasing number of early warning radars (the estimated number of Moon Cone radars rising from 22 in August 1964 to 47 at the end of 1965, and to 144 one year later) and by liaison links with ChiCom radars on Hainan Island. While standoff jamming and the use of ECM jamming pods and chaff limited the efficiency of Fire Can fire control radars, the sheer number of guns resulted in rising losses, with automatic weapons and 37/57mm AAA proving particularly lethal. In 1966, 239 of the 285 US fixed- and rotary-wing aircraft lost over North Vietnam were shown down by AW/AAA; in 1967, the worst year for losses to SAMs and MiGs (60 and 72 aircraft respectively), AAA claims rose to 250 out of a total of 337. Altogether, AW/AAA accounted for 93.2 per cent (4513 out of 4843) of the US aircraft and helicopters lost in combat in all Southeast Asian theaters between 1962 and 1973. Obviously, the whiz kids advising Secretary of Defense McNamara had not properly programmed their computers. The price of this midjudgment was paid not by these then much admired proclaimers of a new age but by Naval Aviators and Air Force, Army, and Marine flyers long vilified by an ungrateful nation for doing their duty during an unpopular war.

Notwithstanding stiffening North Vietnamese defenses, Rolling Thunder operations continued unabated throughout 1965 until Christmas Eve when the United States declared a truce unilaterally. With TF 77 carriers and their escort steaming on Yankee Station, offensive operations of two clearly distinct types—cyclic operations and maximum effort strikes—had been flown during the year by carrier-based aircraft. The former included armed reconnaissance missions and strikes against relatively minor targets and were flown around the clock by small formations of attack aircraft (mainly Douglas A-1s and A-4s during the early phases of Rolling Thunder) and bomb-carrying McDonnell F-4s and LTV F-8s. In addition, fighters flew MiGCAPs to position themselves between the strike aircraft and the direction from which MiGs were expected to arrive, TarCAPs to protect the strike aircraft in the immediate target area, ResCAPs to provide fire support during rescue missions just offshore or deep into North Vietnam, and BarCAPs and force combat air patrols (ForCAPs) to protect the battle group by positioning themselves between TF 77 and the threat or by flying in the immediate vicinity of TF 77 respectively.

Operating in a support role, other CVW aircraft played less glamorous but equally vital roles. Grumman E-1Bs flew long AEW missions to protect TF 77 and its aircraft by supplementing Red Crown cruisers and destroyers, which provided Positive Identification Radar Advisory Zone (PIRAZ) services, and other Air Force and Navy assets which monitored enemy communications and electronic emissions and by giving MiG and SAM warnings to aircraft operating over North Vietnam. With their crews often flying in the reconnaissance community's 'alone and unafraid' tradition, the North American RA-5Cs and LTV RF-8As performed Blue Tree medium-level photo-reconnaissance sorties and brought back valuable pre-strike target information and post-strike bomb damage assessments (BDAs). The Douglas EA-1F jammers provided ECM support for the strike aircraft while the tanker-configured Douglas A-3Bs gave sterling services not only in extending the endurance of fighters and strike aircraft but, even more importantly, in providing unscheduled refueling for battle-damaged aircraft or those running out of fuel after taking evasive action to avoid North Vietnamese defenses.[14] When demand for refueling services exceeded the capacity of available tanker-

[14] The Navy credited tanker-configured A-3Bs with saving some 380 carrier-based aircraft valued at over $450 million during an 18-month period in 1966-67. The success of these bomber/tanker convertible aircraft led to the development by NARF Alameda of a permanently tanker-configured Skywarrior, the KA-3Bs, and a dual role ECM/tanker aircraft, the EKA-3B Tactical and Countermeasure Strike Support Aircraft (TACOS).

Carrying a pair of Sidewinder training rounds, this F-8E of VF-211 was photographed prior to going aboard USS Hancock *(CVA-19) for that carrier's second war cruise in 1965-66. This Crusader was lost in a carrier landing accident on 24 December 1965 when it was returning from a CAP sortie. The pilot was recovered.*

configured A-3Bs, buddy refueling stores were fitted to A-1s and A-4s, and later to A-7s. Finally, the Kaman UH-2 helicopters flew plane-guard duty from the carriers and SAR from cruisers and destroyers.

Maximum effort strikes, which soon became known as Alpha strikes after the addendum to a JCS Rolling Thunder plan in which these targets were identified, saw one or more carriers send large formations against major fixed targets, with groups of aircraft being assigned specific roles. Most were attack or fighter aircraft carrying bombs but others were assigned flak suppression duty, for which cluster bombs were favored, Iron Hand anti-SAM duty, or TarCAP. In addition, even more frequently than for armed reconnaissance missions, EA-1Fs and tanker-configured A-3Bs flew offshore to provide ECM and tanking support.

During 1965, while concentrating its efforts on Rolling Thunder operations over North Vietnam, TF 77 continued flying missions over Laos and began providing air support to friendly troops in South Vietnam. In Laos, where Yankee Team reconnaissance missions were flown over most of the country as they had been during the previous year, offensive operations were divided, after 3 April 1965, into Barrel Roll strikes against fixed targets in northern Laos, along the border with North Vietnam and including the Plain of Jars, and Steel Tiger interdiction missions along the Ho Chi Minh Trail in the panhandle along both the North and South Vietnamese borders.[15] Barrel Roll strikes against any given target had to be specifically requested and approved in advance by the US Embassy in Vientiane. LOC targets identified by Air Force forward air controllers (FACs) within 200 yards from roads in the Steel Tiger area could be attacked on the authority of Laotian officers flying aboard Airborne Command and Control Center (ABCCC) aircraft;[16] those further away from roads could not be struck unless the US Embassy approved.

Primary responsibility for Barrel Roll and Steel Tiger operations rested with the Air Force and, under normal conditions, TF 77 aircraft were diverted to targets in Laos only when weather conditions prevented operations over North Vietnam. In such cases, they crossed the Vietnamese coast near the DMZ and, after reporting to *Panama*—the Air Force-operated Control and Reporting Center (CRC) at Da Nang — checked with the duty ABCCC and were assigned targets by Air Force forward air controllers (FACs). Another factor limiting the use of carrier-based aircraft over Laos was the distance between the carriers and the targets (via a detour south from Yankee Station to the DMZ and back) which made reliance on air refueling absolutely vital for jets; conversely, propeller-driven Skyraiders were ideal due to their long endurance. Eight carrier-based aircraft were lost over Laos to AW and AAA in both 1966 and 1967, when Air Force losses were respectively eleven and forty-eight aircraft, but this number dropped to one in 1968 versus sixty-four for the USAF.

TF 77 first provided air support for ground forces in South Vietnam on 15 April 1965 when aircraft from *Coral Sea* and *Midway* struck VC positions near the Black Virgin Mountains. As not enough airfields were yet available in-country to accommodate the fast increasing number of Air Force and Marine Corps aircraft required to support stepped-up US ground operations in Vietnam, General William C Westmoreland, Commander, US Military Assistance Command, Vietnam (MACV), requested the permanent assignment of a carrier to support his troops. CINCPACFLT approved the request on 16 May and four days later *Oriskany* became the first carrier to be assigned

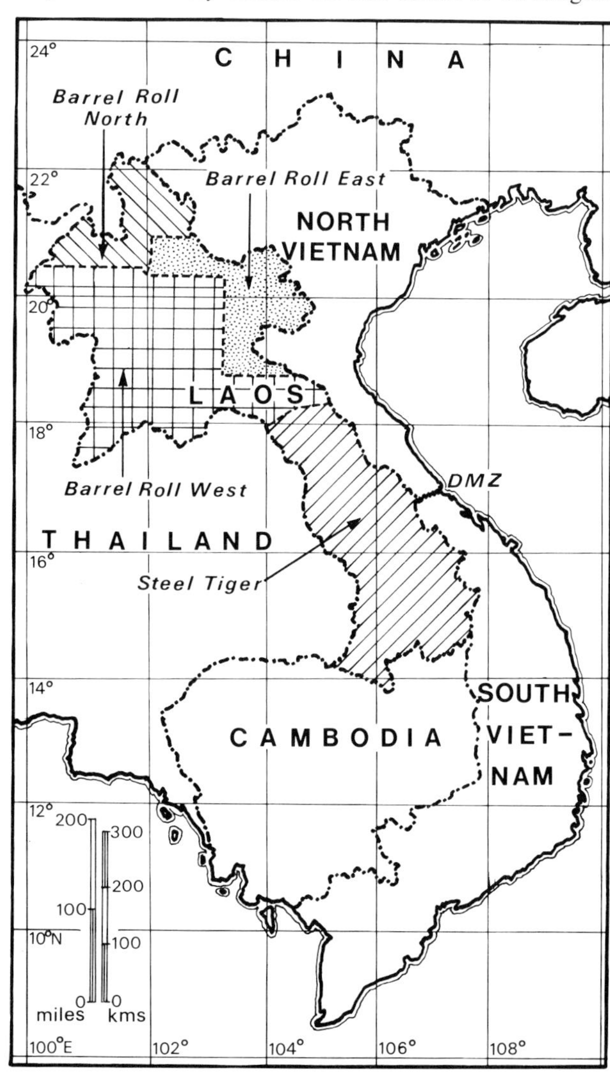

Map 3: Areas of operation in Laos

[15] The area over which Steel Tiger operations were authorized changed several times. From December 1965 until October 1966, only operations south of the Mu Gia Pass and north of Tchepone were designated Steel Tiger missions, those further south being Tiger Hound missions; thereafter, all were again called Steel Tiger missions. By 1969, Steel Tiger missions were flown over the entire width of the Laotian panhandle south of the 17th parallel. North of that latitude, the whole of Laos was included in the Barrel Roll area and subdivided into three areas. The largest and least active, Barrel Roll West, was located next to the Thai border; Barrel Roll North next to the Chinese border, and Barrel Roll East, over which most missions were flown, along the North Vietnamese border.

[16] For this role, Air Force Lockheed C-130s carried air-conditioned capsules containing electronic gear and data processing equipment to enable a crew of specialists to direct air strikes, relay friendly radio communications, and record enemy signals. The ABCCC operating over the Barrel Roll area used the call signs *Cricket* during the day and *Alley Cat* during the night. The corresponding call signs for the ABCCC over the Steel Tiger area were *Hillsboro* and *Moonbeam*.

Above: The use of buddy refueling stores, as demonstrated in this prewar photograph by a pair of aircraft from USS Oriskany *(CVA-34) — an A-4B of VA-164 and an RF-8A of VFP-63, was extensively used during Gulf of Tonkin operations. Both these squadrons made several deployments aboard* Oriskany, *VA-164 operating A-4Es during three cruises and VFP-63 detachments flying RF-8As for one war cruise before switching to RF-8Gs for the next six.* (US Navy)

Below: The Douglas RA-3B lacked the performance required for target reconnaissance in heavily defended areas. Conversely, it had several features not found in the faster RA-5C and RF-8G. Notably, it was the only Navy aircraft equipped for cartography and night photography. Both features were used extensively during operations over the Ho Chi Minh Trail and other parts of Laos from land bases and from carriers. (US Navy)

to Dixie Station in the South China Sea, about 100 miles southeast of Cam Ranh Bay, for temporary operations over the South before returning to Yankee Station. From then until 4 August 1966, when the air base construction program in Vietnam began to have positive results and the tempo of operations against the North required a maximum concentration of force, one carrier and her escorts operated on Dixie Station while two or three were on Yankee Station. During 1965, attack carriers thus spent 215 days on the line at Dixie Station[17]—from which their aircraft operated under Air Force FAC control to provide support to troops in the I Corps area south of the DMZ— and 732 at Yankee Station. During 1966, these numbers were respectively 200 and 882 days. After 1966, the carriers remained on Yankee Station, primarily for operations over North Vietnam and Laos, but occasionally their aircraft were diverted to provide indirect support for the troops in South Vietnam by bombing NVA artillery positions just north of the DMZ. Moreover, during the 1968 Tet Offensive and 1972 Spring Offensive, TF 77 aircraft were again called to provide extensive air

[17] The first carrier-based aircraft lost during operations over South Vietnam was an F-8E from VF-194 (CVW-19 aboard *Bon Homme Richard*) which went down during a strafing run against a VC position on 30 June 1965; the pilot, LCdr R E Weedon, was recovered by an Army helicopter. The first Naval Aviator killed during combat operations from Dixie Station was another *Bon Homme Richard* fighter pilot, Lt (jg) E D Brown from VF-191, who died in the crash of his F-8E on 29 July 1965.

After the summer of 1965, the A-3B was used almost exclusively as a tanker, a role for which it proved exceptionally well suited. This Skywarrior from VAH-2 Det Mike refuels a Phantom from VF-96 during CVW-9's deployment aboard the USS Enterprise *(CVAN-65) in 1966-67. The Fighting Falcons' F-4B, BuNo 152219, ran into the water on 12 February 1967 while flying a CAP sortie. Pilot and RIO were killed.* (US Navy by courtesy of Cloud 9 Photography)

Below: On 15 April 1965, aircraft from USS Midway *(CVA-41), including this A-1J from VA-25, joined those from USS* Coral Sea *(CVA-43) in flying the Navy's first air support sorties for ground forces in South Vietnam. Subsequently,* Midway *spent 35 days on Dixie Station during her 1965 deployment.* (US Navy)

support for ground forces battling Communist invaders in South Vietnam.

Concurrent operations in Laos and North and South Vietnam, combined with the effects of budgetary restrictions in existence prior to America's involvement in Southeast Asia, soon strained not only the resources of TF 77 but also those of PACFLT and the entire Navy. By early 1966, serious shortages in personnel, ordnance, aircraft, and carriers were in evidence as the result of the high level of sustained effort. Short-term relief was provided by depleting other commands of aircrews, ordnance[18] and aircraft to

[18] Shortage of bombs even led on one occasion to using depth charges against targets under deep jungle foliage. In that case, however, depth charges proved ineffective.

make up shortages in the line squadrons, while long-term improvements were expected to result from stepped-up aircrew training at the various NATRACOM bases and massive increases in aircraft and munition production.

The carrier shortage was more serious. The time required from budget approval for the construction of a new carrier to her first deployment typically exceeded four years. Thus, the only carriers commissioned during the Southeast Asia War were those laid down before the war: USS *America* (CVA-66) in January 1965 and USS *John F. Kennedy* (CVA-67) in September 1968. Those laid down during the war, USS *Nimitz* (CVN-68) and USS *Dwight D. Eisenhower* (CVN-69) were commissioned after the war had ended, in May 1975 and in October 1977 respectively. Moreover, several PACFLT carriers were reaching the end of their useful lives or had to undergo major refit.[19] Consequently, to offset the carrier shortage and keep as many carriers as possible in the Gulf of Tonkin, the Navy extended the duration of on-line periods beyond the normal three weeks (the longest on-line period during 1965, 59 consecutive days, was recorded by *Ranger* in January–March) and the length of deployments beyond the normal six months (the record was set by *Coral Sea* which spent 331 days away from home from 7 December 1964 until 1 November 1965). Turn-around time between deployments was also reduced (*Hancock*, for example, left her homeport on 10 November 1965, only 164 days after returning from her first war cruise; this already fast turn-around was shortened several times, with *Kitty Hawk* setting up the wartime record of 145 days in 1966).

Damaged during combat operations over North Vietnam, this A-4B of VSF-3 was on board USS Intrepid *(CVS-11) when the carrier came back to Norfolk on 30 December 1967 at the end of her second war cruise. It was photographed at the Military Aircraft Storage and Disposition Center, Davis-Monthan Air Force Base, Arizona on 10 February 1968. Antisubmarine Fighter Squadron Three (VSF-3) was the only VSF which deployed to Southeast Asia.* (Peter B. Lewis)

To make up the shortage of carriers experienced by PACFLT, it also became necessary for some LANTFLT carriers to join the Tonkin Gulf Yacht Club. The first to do so, *Independence*, left Norfolk on 10 May 1965. After going around the Cape of Good Hope, she arrived at Subic Bay on 17 June to bring the number of attack carriers assigned to TF 77 to five for the first time. Ten days later, her CVW-7, which included VA-75 with the first Grumman A-6A Intruder all-weather attack aircraft, began flying combat sorties over South Vietnam while she was on Dixie Station; on 2 July, operations from Yankee Station began.

[19] During the Southeast Asia War, the longest such refit was that given to *Midway* which entered the San Francisco Naval Shipyard after returning from the Gulf of Tonkin in November 1965 and was not recommissioned until January 1970. Other carriers underwent less comprehensive overhaul on one or more occasions and were then out of the war for one to two years instead of being turned around in six months or less. Typical was *Constellation* which did not operate on Yankee Station between November 1964 and June 1966 as she underwent major overhaul at the Puget Sound Naval Shipyard, was fitted with newer systems including an Inertial Navigation System (INS) and an Integrated Operational Intelligence Center (IOIC), and received the necessary support installations to operate A-6s, E-2s, and RA-5s. *Constellation* was again overhauled four years later when she was kept out of the Gulf of Tonkin between April 1970 and November 1971.

Grumman E-2A Hawkeye AEW aircraft were first deployed to the Gulf of Tonkin by VAW-11 Det Charlie which arrived on Yankee Station aboard USS Kitty Hawk *(CVA-63) on 26 November 1965. This Det Charlie aircraft is about to trap aboard* Kitty Hawk, *a task made easy by the Hawkeye's good approach characteristics and the smooth sea state. The radome atop the fuselage, which houses the antenna for the AN/APS-96 radar, rotates six times per minute.* (Grumman History Center)

Remaining in the Gulf of Tonkin until mid-November, *Independence* spent 100 days on the line during which she lost thirteen aircraft in combat and four in operational accidents. She subsequently returned to LANTFLT and did not deploy again to Southeast Asia. Later, four other LANTFLT carriers, USS *America* (CVA-66), *Forrestal* (CVA-59), *Franklin D. Roosevelt* (CVA-42), and *Saratoga* (CV-60), and two CVSs operating in a limited CVA capability, USS *Intrepid* (CVS-11) and *Shangri-La* (CVS-38), made ten deployments to the war zone between May 1966 and March 1973 and spent 1075 days on the line.

LANTFLT also made a more durable contribution to PACFLT by permanently transferring USS *Enterprise* (CVAN-65), then the world's only nuclear carrier. CVAN-65 left Norfolk for the last time on 26 October 1965, spent 131 days on the line between December 1965 and June 1966, and then proceeded to Alameda, her new homeport on the West Coast. From there she made five more war cruises to Southeast Asia to spend a total of 669 days on the line.

As mentioned above, Intruders made their combat début with the *Sunday Punchers* at the end of June 1965 while operating from *Independence*. Results were initially disappointing as three aircraft were lost during Barrel Roll and Rolling Thunder operations, one each on 14, 18, and 24 July. The four crew members who ejected over Laos were recovered, but the pilot and bombardier-navigator of the aircraft lost over North Vietnam were taken prisoner of war. Subsequent investigations revealed that the three aircraft were all lost due to premature detonation of their Mk 82 bombs. The substitution of ejector bomb racks for the original racks and a switch from electrical to mechanical fusing corrected the problem, and during the remainder of this cruise CVW-7 lost only one more Intruder, that in which Cdr L F Vogt and Lt R F Barber were killed on 17 September after being hit by AW fire during a night attack against PT boats off Bach Long Vi Island. Thereafter, A-6s made thirty-three war deployments aboard nine carriers to bring back an enviable war record. In particular, A-6s were highly praised for their ability to hit targets regardless of weather conditions, their long unrefueled combat radius, and their ability to carry a heavier load than any other carrier-based aircraft—a maximum of 18,000lbs being carried externally.[20]

Another Grumman aircraft, the E-2A Hawkeye, was first deployed in 1965 when VAW-11 Detachment Charlie arrived on the line on 26 November aboard *Kitty Hawk*. Since her pre-Tonkin Gulf Incident cruise in 1964, during which her aircraft had taken part in the first Yankee Team operations over Laos, *Kitty Hawk* had become the first carrier to be fitted with a state-of-the-art Naval Tactical

[20] On 18 April 1966, ten months after the A-6 combat début, its heavy load carrying capability even fooled the North Vietnamese into believing that the night bombing of the Uong Bi thermal power plant by a pair of Intruders from VA-85 had been the work of Air Force B-52s!

Four months later, the A-6's ability to strike precisely under the cover of darkness or bad weather was conclusively demonstrated when, during the night of 12 August 1966, a single VA-85 Intruder destroyed the center span of the highly defended Hai Duong bridge between Hanoi and Haiphong.

After the tailhook of his A-4C was ripped when he first tried to recover aboard USS Yorktown *(CVS-10) on 14 December 1964, the pilot of this A-4C of VMA-223 Det Tango made a successful barricade engagement. Skyhawks provided limited self-defense capability to all four Antisubmarine Warfare Support Carriers during their first deployment to the Gulf of Tonkin. Those aboard USS* Bennington *(CVS-20) were A-4Bs from VA-113 Det Q, those aboard USS* Hornet *(CVS-12) were A-4Cs from H&MS-15 Det N, and those aboard USS* Kearsarge *(CVS-33) were A-4Bs from VA-153 Det R.* (US Navy)

Data System (NTDS) designed to take full advantage of the Hawkeye advanced AEW features. However, both the E-2A and the carrier's NTDS suffered more than their fair share of teething troubles, thus slowing the planned E-1B phase-out, with Hawkeyes not fully replacing Tracers until after the end of the Southeast Asia War.

Carrier Air Wings operating from attack carriers or from *Intrepid* were not alone on the line as four Carrier Antisubmarine Warfare Air Groups—CVSG-53, -55, -57, and -59—also deployed to the Gulf of Tonkin between 1964 and 1969. Although Trackers and Sea Kings embarked aboard Antisubmarine Warfare Support Carriers flew ASW and sea control patrols in support of TF 77 until August 1969 and (as detailed below) SH-3 helicopters from these carriers flew most of the inland rescue missions until Helicopter Combat Support Squadron Seven (HC-7) was commissioned in September 1967 as the first specialized combat rescue squadron in the Navy, CVS deployments to the Gulf of Tonkin have not been adequately chronicled. In 1964, no submarines were known to be operated by the North Vietnamese Navy (NVN) but, as it was feared that the Soviet Union or the PRC would transfer submarines to North Vietnam or that the PRC would use its thirteen submarines to run interference with TF 77 operations, the Navy found it necessary to deploy a CVS to Yankee Station whenever possible. Thus, *Kearsarge* (CVS-33) first operated with TF 77 during the summer of 1964 and was followed on the line by *Yorktown* (CVS-10) beginning in February 1965, *Bennington* (CVS-20) from July 1965, and *Hornet* (CVS-12) from October 1965. Altogether, these four carriers made thirteen wartime cruises to the Gulf of Tonkin, *Kearsarge* being the last to depart the line on 14 August 1969 and returning to her homeport, Long Beach, on 4 September. For their assigned ASW role, each of these antisubmarine carriers embarked a CVSG comprised of two fixed-wing ASW squadrons equipped with Grumman S-2Ds, S-2Es, or S-2Fs, an ASW helicopter squadron with Sikorsky SH-3As, and an AEW detachment with Douglas EA-1Es or Grumman E-1Bs. In addition, CVS carriers were initially assigned a detachment of four Douglas A-4s endowing them with a limited self-defense capability.

Whereas most of their Sea King combat SARs were all but routine, the main portion of the CVS deployments were fairly mundane. Representative of these deployments was that made by *Hornet* in 1967. Embarking CVSG-57, with the S-2Es from VS-35 and VS-37, the SH-3As from HS-

2, and the E-1Bs from VAW-11 Detachment November (redesignated VAW-111 Det 12 on 20 April), *Hornet* departed Bremerton on 27 March. On her way to Hawaii, where she was scheduled for an Operational Readiness Exercise (ORE), CVS-12 located an Echo-class Soviet submarine 700 miles west of San Francisco and kept it under surveillance for six days. After an in-port period in Pearl Harbor, she proceeded to Japan and Korea for ASW exercises with the Japanese Self-Defense Maritime Force (JMSDF), the Republic of Korea Navy (ROKN) and the Republic of Korea Air Force (ROKAF) prior to proceeding to the Gulf of Tonkin. *Hornet* joined TF 77 on 22 May and went on to spend seventy-seven days on the line during three different periods on Yankee Station. During the on-station periods, her S-2Es flew ASW patrols, provided sea surveillance, and performed Sea Dragon naval gunfire spotting duty while her Tracers were utilized for radar surveillance and communications relay. Busiest of all were her Sea Kings which not only flew ASW sorties and transferred 2742 passengers and 170 tons of cargo and mail while operating in the Gulf of Tonkin but also rescued a total of 15 personnel during the deployment. HS-2 made eight SAR penetrations overland into North Vietnam and three of the aviators it rescued were retrieved while under hostile fire. Three of the helicopters were lost during rescue missions over North Vietnam and three in operational accidents. Moreover, a C-1A and a US-2C from VC-5 were lost in operational accidents while operating from *Hornet*. Nine crew members were killed in these eight combat and operational losses. With *Hornet* last leaving the line on 5 October, CVSG-57 arrived back at NAS North Island on 28 October.

Even though helicopters had conclusively demonstrated their worth during combat rescue operations in Korea and the Kaman HU2K-1 (redesignated UH-2A in September 1962) had been developed to meet 1956 Navy requirements for a long-range, all-weather rescue helicopter, the Navy did not have specialized helicopter combat rescue units until 1967. At the start of the Southeast Asia War, plane guard duty aboard carriers was assigned to detachments from Helicopter Utility Squadrons One and Two (HU-1, with PACFLT, and HU-2, with LANTFLT, became HC-1 and HC-2 respectively when these units were redesignated Helicopter Combat Support Squadrons on 1 July 1965). Equipped with UH-2As and UH-2Bs, they were given the collateral duty of combat rescue. In this role, they were soon supplemented by other HC-1 detachments operating from the aft deck of cruisers and destroyers and by SH-3As from Helicopter Antisubmarine Squadrons operating both from their ASW carriers and from escort vessels.

Unmodified Seasprites and Sea Kings, however, had neither armor nor self-sealing fuel tanks to withstand withering hostile fire, and they lacked armament to keep enemy troops at bay while hovering to pick up downed airmen. Moreover, their range was insufficient for rescue missions deep into North Vietnam. To correct these deficiencies, field modifications were improvised, with crews carrying a variety of hand-held or pintle-mounted weapons, fitting sundry pieces of armor plating, and jury rigging auxiliary tanks, while long-term modifications were developed by the manufacturers and the Navy. Foremost among early modifications was that enabling Sea Kings to be refueled while hovering above specially fitted destroyers. This Hover In-Flight Refueling or High Drink technique

Assigned to Carrier Antisubmarine Warfare Air Group Fifty-Seven, HS-2 made three war cruises aboard USS Hornet *(CVS-12) and lost four of its Sikorsky SH-3A Sea Kings during combat SAR missions. Operational losses claimed four more HS-2 Sea Kings.* (Peter B Lewis)

was first used operationally in the fall of 1965 by HS-2.

To avoid capture, pilots whose aircraft had been hit over North Vietnam or Laos or who experienced mechanical difficulties over enemy territory tried whenever possible to get 'feet wet'—crossing the coast back toward the sea—before ejecting. Obviously, when able to do so they greatly eased the task of the rescue helicopter crews and also furthered their own chances of recovery by coming within reach of Navy ships and of Air Force Albatross SAR flying-boats and rescue helicopters operating out of Da Nang. On 11 February 1965, Lt W T Majors, an A-4C pilot from VA-153, became the first Naval Aviator to be recovered by a USAF helicopter after ejecting feet wet, and on 29 March Cdr J H Harris, an A-4E pilot from VA-155, was the first to be recovered by a USN ship in the Gulf of Tonkin. Whether from the sea or in Laos or South Vietnam, fourteen more TF 77 pilots and RIOs were recovered by naval vessels and by Air Force, Army, and Air America helicopters prior to the first combat rescue at sea by a Navy helicopter, that of Lt W J Fidelibus from VA-155 on 12 August. From then until the end of 1965, helicopters from HC-1, HC-2, HS-2,

Belonging to VA-113, these two Douglas A-4C Skyhawks were photographed in the United States prior to the first war cruise of USS Kitty Hawk *(CVA-63). Departing North Island on 19 October 1965,* Kitty Hawk *first went on the line on 26 November. Less than five months later, on 20 April 1966, BuNo 149495 was hit by 37mm fire while flying an armed reconnaissance sortie over Route Package III. After reaching the relative safety of the sea, Lt (jg) H G Welch ejected. He was almost immediately recovered by a SAR helicopter.* (US Navy)

HS-4, and HS-8 made up for lost time and were credited with saving an Air Force pilot and eight Naval Aviators. One of the latter, Lt (jg) J R Harris from VA-72, became on 20 September the first Navy pilot to be recovered in North Vietnam while under enemy fire. Forced to eject twenty miles east of Hanoi almost immediately after his Skyhawk had been hit by AAA while dive bombing the Cao Hung railroad bridge in RP VIB, Lt (jg) Harris was saved by LCdr W Wetzel and his HC-1 Det A crew in a Seasprite operating from the cruiser USS *Galveston* (CLG-3). On this occasion, suppressive fire was provided by a pair of Skyraiders, whose long endurance, heavy load of ammunition and ordnance, and ability to stay with the slow-flying helicopters were already recognized as ideal attributes for SAR support.

Throughout most of 1965, Rolling Thunder operations either were directed against LOCs, ammunition depots or NVA barracks, or were undertaken to take out SAM, AAA, and radar sites. However, intending to order a truce beginning on Christmas Eve, President Johnson wanted to forewarn the North Vietnamese of the risks they would be taking by not responding to his invitation to negotiate an end to the conflict. To that effect, he authorized, for the first time, the bombing of a significant industrial target, the Uong Bi thermal power plant located in RP VIB, fifteen miles northeast of Haiphong. Preceded on 20 December by a pre-strike reconnaissance mission during which an RVAH-13 pilot and his navigator were killed in the crash of their RA-5C while on their way to photograph the power plant, the bombing took place in the afternoon of 22 December. Aircraft from CVW-5, -9, and -11, embarked aboard *Ticonderoga*, *Enterprise* and *Kitty Hawk* respectively, succeeded in putting the power plant out of commission at the cost of two A-4s. One of the pilots was killed and the other taken prisoner of war.

The bombing halt in the North went into effect on 24 December but not before *Kitty Hawk* had lost two more aircraft during operations against the Hai Duong railroad bridge. In South Vietnam and Laos, however, where only brief truce periods were observed by the US for Christmas and New Year's Day, operations continued virtually unabated and *Enterprise* lost an F-4B and its VF-92 crew during a Steel Tiger night armed reconnaissance mission on 28 December. This was the last Navy aircraft lost during 1965, bringing the year's total to 102 combat and 35 operational losses.

Even though air operations were limited during the first thirty days of 1966 to in-country air support missions, Steel Tiger interdiction sorties and routine activities in the Gulf of Tonkin, two aircraft were lost in South Vietnam, one in Laos, and one in North Vietnam. The latter, in which the four VS-35 aircrewmen were killed, was unusual as the aircraft was a Grumman S-2D from *Hornet* flying a night coastal surveillance sortie off the RP IV coast.

More Sticks and Carrots: Rolling Thunder III and Rolling Thunder IV

As the North Vietnamese apparently were not ready to respond to the US call for negotiations, President Johnson ordered the third phase of Rolling Thunder to commence on 31 January. However, still hoping to entice Hanoi to sit at the conference table, the President once again excluded most significant targets from the authorized list, restricted operations to lower North Vietnam, and limited the daily number of sorties to a combined total of 300 for the Air

Above: Heat, noise, wind blast, and crowded space combined to make life miserable for the crew on deck as shown by this scene aboard USS Constellation *(CVA-64) during Rolling Thunder IV. Below deck crowding reached unprecedented levels during wartime operations when carriers stayed on the line for up to fifty days at a time as peacetime ship and Carrier Air Wing complements were boosted to incorporate new specialists and room had to be made available for the personnel of various dctachmcnts.* (US Navy)

Left: A Grumman S-2E Tracker of VS-37 being launched from the deck of USS Hornet *(CVS-12) during operations in the Gulf of Tonkin on 22 January 1969. The only Tracker lost in combat during the war was an S-2D from* Hornet's *other Air Antisubmarine Squadron, VS-35, which failed to return from a night coastal surveillance sortie on 21 January 1966.* (US Navy)

Force and Navy. Notwithstanding these restraints and the fact that operations took place over the least defended portions of North Vietnam, losses rose. Having lost two aircraft on the very first day of Rolling Thunder III, TF 77 lost seven more over the North in February[21] and nine in March. One of the February losses, an F-4B which was brought down by a SAM on the 18th, is noteworthy as it occurred while the VF-92 Phantom was flying BarCAP for a Lockheed EC-121M from VQ-1 flying a Big Look

[21] In February 1966, the Navy also lost three aircraft during Steel Tiger sorties. Two of the pilots were recovered but the third, Lt (jg) Dieter Dengler, was captured after crashlanding in Laos on 2 February. In an incredible display of courage and faith, Dieter Dengler succeeded in escaping on 29 June and was finally recovered by a USAF helicopter on 20 July.

intelligence-gathering sortie.

During the second and third months of 1966, Air Force losses were also high while military results were negligible and diplomatic achievements nonexistent; this, at last, prompted the President to clear most of North Vietnam, aside from specific sanctuary areas, for Rolling Thunder IV operations beginning on 1 April. At that time, the time-sharing arrangement through which Air Force and Navy operations in the various Routes Packages had so far been coordinated was replaced by assignment to the Air Force of exclusive responsibility for operations in RP I, RP V, and RP VIA, whereas the Navy was given the responsibility for operations over the four coastal sectors (RPs II, III, IV, and VIB).

When Rolling Thunder IV got underway, however, authorization to hit significant military or industrial targets was still granted piecemeal. Naval Aviators and Air Force crews were again expended in futile attacks against insignificant targets and those which were easily repaired, such as bridges which the North Vietnamese had become experts at bypassing or repairing quickly. Typical of the former were wooden bridges, such as that which caused the death of Cdr J C Mape on 13 April, and junks and sampans, such as those which resulted in the loss of a VF-114 F-4B on 26 April. On other occasions, however, losses were offset by damage inflicted to the enemy. This was notably the case on 19 April when the loss of an RF-8A and an F-8E came after *Ticonderoga* aircraft destroyed a span from the important Haiphong highway bridge.

All in all, TF 77 losses rose alarmingly during that month and for the first time exceeded twenty aircraft in a single month. Seventeen aircraft failed to return from sorties over North Vietnam, two were lost over Laos, one went down during operations in South Vietnam, and four were lost in operational accidents. Another aircraft, a tanker-configured A-3B from VAH-4 Det C, was shot down by a ChiCom MiG after it strayed off course during a ferry flight from Cubi Point to the *Kitty Hawk*. Altogether, fifteen aircrewmen were lost in combat and four in operational accidents during April 1966. Fortunately, combat losses dropped to nine aircraft in May and eight in June.

In June, the pressure against North Vietnam increased when attacks against its oil storage facilities (approval of which had long and strenuously been advocated by CINCPAC and the JCS) were finally authorized. After *Hancock*'s aircraft bombed a petroleum depot west of Thanh Hoa on the 16th in what initially appeared to be an isolated incident, the POL offensive got fully underway. On the 29th, Air Force F-105Ds hit the Hanoi POL facilities while CVW-14 and CVW-15 aircraft inflicted very heavy damage respectively to the Haiphong and Do Son petroleum storage facilities. The next day the Air Force struck POL storage at Nguyen Khe, and the Navy went after those at Bac Giang. Thereafter, the pressure was maintained with frequent attacks on virtually all POL storage facilities and against tank barges and railroad tank cars. Unfortunately, this limited strategic bombing campaign came too late to be effective. The North Vietnamese, who had anticipated it, quickly switched to storing fuel drums in caves, transporting fuel by rail across the Chinese border, and building an underground pipeline.

Not unexpectedly, the US offensive against these POL storage facilities prompted the Communists to stiffen their defenses. On 1 July, three of their PT boats were sent against USN destroyers on SAR station, some forty miles off the North Vietnamese coast. Spotted by F-4s from *Constellation*, the PT boats were sunk with bombs, rockets, and 20mm cannon fire by aircraft from *Constellation* and *Hancock* before getting into effective torpedo range of USS *Coontz* (DLG-9), *King* (DLG-10), and *Rogers* (DD-876).

In the air, MiGs soon also rose to the challenge in spite of their poor showing earlier in the year. Indeed, during the first six months of 1966, NVAF fighters had been rather ineffective, and were credited only with shooting down an Air Force A-1E on 29 April and finishing off an AAA-damaged F-8E from VF-211 on 21 June. During the same six months, they were outfought by the Air Force, which claimed seven MiG-17s and one MiG-21 between 23 April and 29 June, and by Navy Crusaders. Unsuccessful until that time, the superb F-8 first came into its own in June when three VF-211 pilots scored. On the 12th, Cdr Hal Marr shot down a MiG-17 and probably destroyed another one. Nine days later Lt (jg) Phil Vampatella and Lt Gene Chancy were each credited with the destruction of an enemy fighter. For Gene Chancy, who had been recovered at sea on 2 May by a Navy helicopter after having been forced to eject from his AAA-damaged Crusader, the victory was bitter sweet as it was obtained while flying during an ill-planned rescue mission for a VFP-63 pilot downed by AAA over the northeast railroad line.

Before the Naval Aviators' luck temporarily ran out, the next air combat victory was claimed on 13 July by a Phantom crew from VF-161, Lt William McGuigan and Lt (jg) Robert Fowler, who bagged a MiG-17. Then, on 14 July, a MiG-17 badly damaged an F-8E from VF-162, forcing Cdr Dick Bellinger to bail out before reaching Da Nang on a divert, and on 5 September another 'Fresco' (as the MiG-17 was nicknamed) shot down an F-8E from VF-111, sending Capt W K Abbott to the 'Hanoi Hilton', the infamous prisoner of war camp. On 10 September, Naval Aviators got it right again as Dick Bellinger avenged himself by shooting down a MiG-21, the first 'Fishbed' claimed by a Navy pilot, while Lt (jg) William Patton, an A-1H pilot from VA-176, caused envy in the fighter community by shooting down the second MiG-17 to fall to the guns of the Skyraider. After being outshone during the early part of the year not only by the older F-8 but also by the 322mph Spad, the Mach 2.5 F-4 claimed two victories on 20 December. Unfortunately for the egos of the VF-114 and

Lt Ronald F Ball of VFP-63 Det Bravo, Carrier Air Wing Five (CVW-5), USS Ticonderoga *(CVA-14), is being hoisted aboard a Sea King of HS-4 as North Vietnamese junks move into the area. Lt Ball's RF-8A had been hit by automatic weapons fire while flying at 2000ft (600m) over Cac Ba Island on 19 April 1966.* (US Navy)

VF-213 crews who claimed these kills, their victims were a pair of 157mph, unarmed Antonov An-2 biplanes! Including these less glamorous 'kills' in the Navy's count and the A-3 loss to a Chinese MiG and the AAA-damaged F-8 in that of the enemy, the final 1966 air-to-air tally was 8 to 4, a marked drop from the previous year's achievement.

Although during 1965, the MiG threat never fully materialized, many Naval Aviators felt that the standard non-specular light gull gray and gloss white US aircraft color scheme was not appropriate for operations over the lush green terrain generally encountered in North Vietnam. Accordingly, early during their 1966 deployments, CVW-11, aboard *Kitty Hawk*, and CVW-15, aboard *Constellation*, participated in a camouflage evaluation under combat conditions. For that purpose, one half of their aircraft had camouflaged upper surfaces while other aircraft, acting as control group, retained the normal scheme. Evaluation results were mixed as the reduced detectability in air-to-air operations of camouflaged aircraft was apparently offset by greater AAA losses. Moreover, camouflaged aircraft rendered 'spotting the deck' (moving aircraft to their desired location) more difficult during night operations. Consequently, as MiGs still did not prove too serious a threat, the use of camouflage was discontinued during the summer of 1966.

Navy aircraft losses to SAMs fluctuated markedly during 1966. After claiming two aircraft in February and one each in March and April, SAMs lost some of their effectiveness as Iron Hand and Wild Weasel operations became increasingly effective. However, the North Vietnamese continued to build SAM sites, the number of which increased from 59 at the end of 1965 to 139 one year later. Furthermore, with much help from their Soviet advisors, they devised effective defensive measures, notably reducing the length of time during which the missiles' Fan Song guidance radars were on. Consequently, SAMs regained much of their effectiveness as 1966 went on and claimed two Navy aircraft each in July, September, and October, and five in December.

While Rolling Thunder IV had been speeding up during the spring and summer of 1966, two new players had taken up station in the South China Sea and the Gulf of Tonkin as LANTFLT committed more carriers to allow TF 77 strength to be kept at the desired five-carrier level. Thus, following the arrival of *Intrepid* and *Franklin D. Roosevelt*, respectively on 15 May and 10 August, and the termination of operations at Dixie Station, TF 77 began keeping three or four of its carriers on Yankee Station at all times. Although still classified as a CVS, *Intrepid* had exchanged her CVSG-56 for CVW-10 prior to departing Norfolk for the Gulf of Tonkin where she was to operate in the limited attack role with two squadrons of A-4Bs (VA-15 and VA-95) and two of A-1Hs (VA-165 and VA-176). During 103 days on the line, *Intrepid* had three of her A-1Hs shot down by North Vietnamese AAA and lost both an A-4B and one of her two UH-2As in operational accidents. Her human losses totalled five aircrewmen. She was back in Norfolk on 21 November 1966, and later returned twice to the Gulf of Tonkin prior to resuming her ASW duty with the Atlantic Fleet in 1969.

Lt (jg) William T Patton of VA-176 shot down a MiG-17 on 9 October 1966 during a sortie from USS Intrepid *(CVS-11). Officially this victory is said to have been acquired while Bill Patton was flying an A-1H wearing the modex 409. However, the aircraft used for this publicity photograph, complete with kill marking beneath the pilot's left elbow, appears to have the modex 404 painted on its cowling.* (US Navy)

Quite remarkably in view of the frantic pace of day and night activities aboard carriers during line periods, TF 77 operations had been commendably safe and, during the 26-month period following the Gulf of Tonkin Incident, had only been marred by aircraft accidents and relatively minor ship accidents. This fortunate situation, however, came to an end on 26 October 1966 when mishandled magnesium flares ignited in a storage locker and started an inferno aboard *Oriskany*. Before the fire could be controlled, 44 officers and men died[22], including 25 pilots, and 38 were injured. Valiant efforts by the crew, heroism on the part of many, and the prompt jettisoning overboard of bombs and other explosives prevented greater human losses. *Oriskany*, however, was badly damaged and, after receiving temporary repairs at Subic Bay, she sailed back home. Less than nine

[22] In a macabre coincidence, less than six weeks earlier *Oriskany*'s helicopters had rescued the same number of British sailors from a merchant vessel which on 16 September was breaking up in heavy seas southeast of Hong Kong.

Above: The Tigers *of VA-65 flew camouflaged A-6As as part of the CVW-15's experiment. Upper surface camouflage, however, proved of little value over North Vietnam where the main threats were the AAA and the SAMs. Neither North Vietnamese gunners nor Fan Song radar operators were much disturbed by coats of paint whereas the task of Navy deck handling crews and maintenance personnel was negatively affected by the use of camouflage.* (Grumman History Center)

Below: During the spring and summer of 1966, several camouflage schemes were evaluated under combat conditions by CVW-11 and CVW-15. This VA-155 A-4E was photographed in a hangar at NAS Lemoore, California, on 1 May 1966, less than two weeks before it was embarked aboard USS Constellation *(CVA-64) to take part in the second war cruise of that carrier. By then, CVW-15 was already reporting that camouflaged aircraft required more maintenance manhours.* (Peter B. Lewis)

Photographs of the first North Vietnamese SAM site were obtained on 5 April 1965 by an RF-8A from VFP-63 Det Delta. The number of sites then increased rapidly with surface-to-air missiles eventually accounting for the destruction of more than two and a half times as many US aircraft and helicopters as did MiGs. However, this represented barely more than 7.5 per cent of US fixed-wing aircraft combat losses in Southeast Asia. This site was photographed near Haiphong during a Blue Tree sortie on 22 June 1967. Arrows indicate launch pads with SA-2s in position. (US Navy)

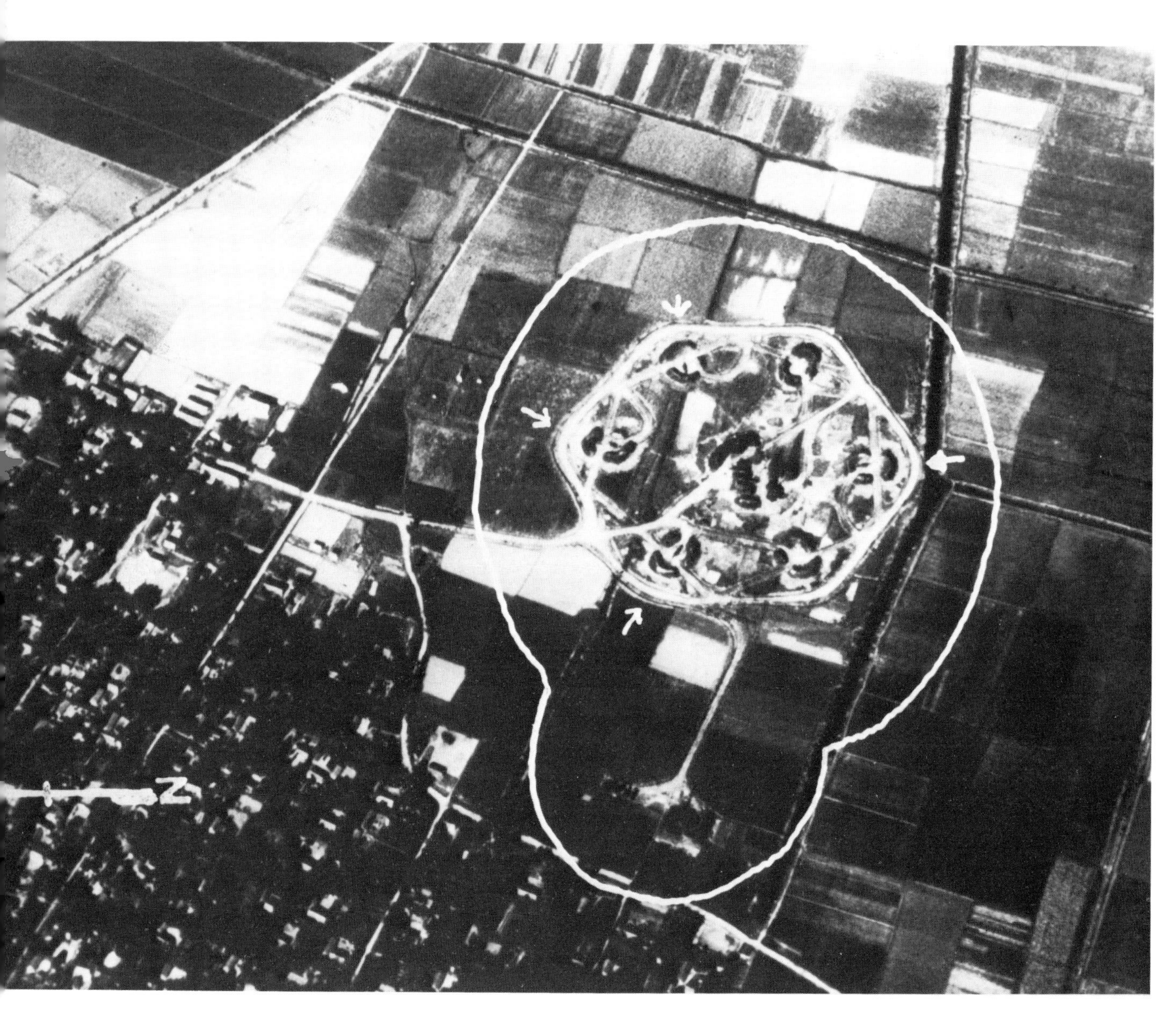

months later she was back on the line for what became the costliest carrier deployment of the war in terms of the number of aviators killed in combat or operational accidents.

During 1966, nine attack carriers, the hybrid *Intrepid*, and four ASW carriers spent a total of 1253 days on the line, a 17 per cent increase over 1965, during which they lost 126 aircraft in combat and forty-nine in accidents. Happily, and even though the Navy still did not have dedicated SAR helicopter units, human losses were minimized as specialized HC and HS detachments did a superb job in recovering more flyers than in any prior or later years. Showing much courage, these 'Clementine' and 'Big Mother' SAR crews, respectively flying Seasprites and Sea Kings, rescued sixty-four downed aircrewmen during the year, fifty from the Navy, one from the Marine Corps, and thirteen from the Air Force, from the Gulf of Tonkin or in North Vietnam.

After 48-hour standdown periods for the Christmas and New Year holidays, Rolling Thunder IV operations resumed and immediately proved costly for the NVAF as Air Force Phantoms went on the offensive. Seven MiG-21s were shot down on 2 January 1967 during Operation Bolo and two more were destroyed four days later. With the threat of enemy fighters temporarily removed, TF 77 aviators kept on 'pounding the dirt' and concentrated their efforts on LOC targets in RP III and RP IV. Eight carrier aircraft

were shot down by AW/AAA and one crashed on a rocket run during the first six weeks of the year. Then, on 7 February, the United States again suspended operations over the North for seven days in observance of Tet, the lunar New Year as celebrated in Southeast Asia.

Strike camera view of an attack against the Hai Dong Army barracks on 4 October 1967 by aircraft from CVW-14 flying from USS Constellation *(CVA-64). A Skyhawk diving almost straight down toward the target can be seen to the right of the explosion.* (US Navy)

The Pressure is On: Rolling Thunder V

Rolling Thunder V, which began on 14 February 1967, marked a new phase in the air war and was characterized by a major escalation as President Johnson authorized attacks against an ever increasing number of new targets. The North Vietnamese were given a taste of things to come on 26 February when six VA-35 Intruders from *Enterprise* sowed mines in the estuaries of the Song Ca and Song Giang rivers to interdict coastal waters to barge traffic. Although military commanders had long advocated the mining of these river mouths and small harbors in the panhandle area as well as that of the deep water ports of Haiphong, Cam Pha, and Hon Gai where North Vietnam received most of its oil and war supplies, the mining of the latter had not been authorized for fear that Soviet bloc or neutral merchant vessels would be sunk. Conversely during March, the mining campaign was extended to include the Cua Sot, Kien Giang, and Song Ma rivers, soon forcing the North Vietnamese to give up using coastal barges and suspend fishing in the five mined estuaries.

At last, the air war against the North Vietnamese transportation system was beginning to be waged against the right targets and with the right weapons as efforts to deprive the Viet Cong of its war supplies were no longer limited to the conventional interdiction campaign in the North Vietnamese panhandle and along the Ho Chi Minh Trail. New targets were added every month and the use of AGM-62A Walleye guided bombs was authorized to increase bombing accuracy in attacks against both new and old targets. First launched by VA-212 A-4Fs from *Bon Homme Richard*, AGM-62As proved effective against the Sam Son military barracks and the Phu Dien Chau highway bridge, both hit on 11 March, and the Hanoi thermal power plant, a new industrial target first attacked on 19 May. Unfortunately the new weapon's 850lb warhead was not powerful enough to fell the infamous Ham Rung (Dragon's Jaw) bridge[23] in spite of direct hits by three VA-212 pilots on 12 March.

As the United States sought to coerce North Vietnam to the negotiating table, significant new targets came under attack. In addition to the Hanoi thermal power plant and the river estuaries mentioned above, these new targets included harbor dredges and shipyard installations in Haiphong, coal loading facilities at Cam Pha, and MiG bases at Kep and Hoa Lac. While all of these targets were militarily significant, none had been more sought after than the Kep air base which the Air Force and the Navy had wanted to attack ever since it had first been used by MiG-15s and MiG-17s in August 1964. Finally, after remaining out of bounds for twenty months, the main MiG base at Kep was hit by the Air Force on 23 April 1967 and by TF 77 on the following day.

All in all, however, it was the sustained campaign to isolate Haiphong from the rest of the country and, to a lesser degree, that to interdict rail transportation between China and North Vietnam which appeared to have the most telling effects on the North Vietnamese war effort. Although still not prepared to risk a direct confrontation with the Soviet Union which might have resulted from blockading Haiphong or bombing vessels unloading war material in that harbor, the President and the Secretary of Defense had finally been convinced by the JCS during the summer of 1967 of the need for decisive action to prevent those supplies from reaching Hanoi or from being transhipped for use by the Viet Cong in South Vietnam. Accordingly, the four main bridges between Hanoi and Haiphong were first bombed in September to isolate the main port from the capital city. Almost simultaneously several restrictions on strikes along the northeast and northwest rail lines near the Chinese border were lifted in an effort to prevent supplies from being transported by rail from China to Hanoi. In addition, Navy and Air Force aircraft kept hitting previously approved rail and road targets in the panhandle.

The North Vietnamese, increasingly feeling the pressure applied against their war industry and transportation facilities, put up a stiff resistance. Diplomatically, they stepped up their propaganda campaign to gain further support both in the United States, where the antiwar movement was getting stronger, and among non-belligerent nations. Logistically, they did everything in their power to repair quickly damage to bridges and other fixed installations and, with considerable use of manpower, indeed proved to be experts at so doing. Militarily they were also able to do quite well as their Soviet and Chinese allies more than made up their losses in aircraft and surface-to-air missiles and supplied them lavishly with AAA weapons and ammunition.

MiGs which, after being mauled by the Air Force in early January had virtually disappeared from the scene for two months, timidly returned to the fray in March and were back in force in April. On the 25th of that month, a VA-76 A-4C from *Bon Homme Richard* became the first Navy aircraft to be shot down by enemy aircraft during 1967; its pilot Lt C D Stackhouse, was taken prisoner of war. Eight days later, however, on 1 May VA-76 got its revenge when LCdr Ted Swartz turned his Skyhawk to face an aggressive MiG-17 and shot it down with Zuni air-to-ground unguided rockets!

In a series of quirks of fate, the two VF-114 crews who obtained the first Navy victories of the year, when they shot down a pair of MiG-17s on 24 April, ran into trouble. While flying TarCAP during the Navy's first strike against Kep airfield, Lt Charles Southwick and Ens Jim Laing, the pilot and RIO of an *Aardvarks* F-4B, were hit by North Vietnamese AAA. Nevertheless, they then shot down a MiG-17 before being forced to eject after getting feet wet. Both were recovered by Navy SAR helicopters. The second victory was obtained by Lt Dennis Wisely—one of the pilots credited with the destruction of an Antonov An-2 transport on 20 December 1966—and Lt (jg) Gareth Anderson. However, unpleasant surprises awaited the two VF-114 pilots and one of their RIOs. On 14 May Lt Southwick and his RIO on that mission, Lt D J Rollins, were taken prisoner-of-war after ejecting from their F-4B while flying flak support during a strike against the Thanh Hoa bridge. One week later Lt Wisely and Lt Southwick's RIO on the 24 April mission, Ens Laing, were recovered by a USAF helicopter after ejecting from their F-4B which had

[23] Better known as the Thanh Hoa bridge, this Chinese-engineered railroad and highway bridge was built between 1957 and 1964 to span the Song Ma River near Thanh Hoa. It was first struck on 3 April 1965 by forty-six Air Force F-105Ds carrying Bullpup missiles and 750lb bombs. Two and one half months later, on 17 June, TF 77 aircraft flew their first mission against it. Repeatedly hit throughout the duration of Rolling Thunder (the last attack being made by Navy and Air Force fighter-bombers on 28 January 1968), the bridge was badly damaged on several occasions but could not be destroyed before the 1968 bombing halt came into effect. Then on 10 May 1972, after operations against the North were resumed, Air Force Phantoms from the 8th TFW destroyed the bridge's western span with laser-guided 3000lb bombs. Repaired once again, the Ham Rung bridge was finally put out of commission during the fall of 1972.

been hit by AW fire during a mission against the Van Dien vehicle depot in North Vietnam.

Fate was not any kinder to LCdr Eugene P Lund and Lt (jg) James R Borst, a VF-142 crew from *Constellation*, who shot down two aircraft on 30 October 1967, a MiG-17 and their own F-4B! The latter had an engine damaged and lost its hydraulic and pneumatic systems after running into debris from an AIM-7E missile which exploded prematurely when fired at another enemy aircraft. 'Gino' Lund and 'Bif' Borst ejected feet wet and were recovered by a Navy helicopter.

Although Phantom crews were credited with destroying four more enemy aircraft (three MiG-21s and one MiG-17) during 1967, they were outshone by Crusader pilots who claimed ten MiG-17s (nine confirmed kills and one probable) between 1 May and 14 December. Overall, however, the years ended for TF 77 with an unsatisfactory 3.2:1 kill ratio as two VA-196 Intruders had been shot down by Chinese MiGs on 21 August when they strayed over the PRC after bombing the Duc Noi railroad yard and two VF-151 F-4Bs had been claimed by the NVAF on 19 November. (One of these F-4Bs, that flown by LCdr C D Clower and Lt (jg) W O Estes II, was the first US aircraft shot down by a Soviet-made air-to-air missile.)

Losses to SAMs were more than six times heavier than those to MiGs despite the good results obtained during the sustained Iron Hand campaign waged by the Navy and the

Even though their F-4B had been hit by heavy flak while flying TarCAP during a strike against the MiG base at Kep on 24 April 1967, Lt Charles E Southwick and Ens James W Laing succeeded in shooting down a MiG-17 and in avoiding an Atoll air-to-air missile fired by another enemy fighter. However, AAA damage subsequently prevented them from transferring fuel from wing tanks. After their engines flamed-out before they could reach a tanker, Lt Southwick and Ens Laing were forced to eject over water. On this occasion the two Aardvarks *were recovered by SAR helicopters.* (US Navy)

Air Force. The price was high: thirty-three TF 77 aircraft were directly lost to SA-2s between 11 March, when a *Ticonderoga* A-4C failed to return from an Iron Hand mission, and 31 December, when a *Kitty Hawk* A-6A was shot down during a strike against storage caves near Vinh, and at least three more were shot down by AW/AAA during anti-SAM operations. Aircrew losses during these risky missions were particularly high as, after their aircraft were hit, few could keep them flying until reaching the relative safety of the Gulf of Tonkin. Thus, during 1967 ten pilots and NFOs were killed in action (among whom was Cdr Michael J Estocin who was awarded the Medal of Honor posthumously for his gallantry during missions on 20 and 26 April), one reported missing, and twenty-seven taken prisoner of war.

The most grievous loss of the year, however, came as the

result of an operational accident aboard *Forrestal*, the fourth LANTFLT carrier to deploy to Vietnam, which occurred five days after she had commenced operations on Yankee Station. In the morning of 29 July, as aircraft were readied for the second strike of the day, a Zuni rocket shot across the deck and ignited the drop tank of another aircraft. The fire spread quickly and bombs and aircraft fuel tanks exploded in quick succession. In spite of immense and courageous efforts on the part of the crew and help from other TF 77 ships, seventeen hours were required to extinguish the fire. Casualties were 134 officers and men dead and sixty-two injured; twenty-one aircraft were destroyed and forty-three damaged. Too badly damaged to be repaired locally, *Forrestal* was forced to return home after temporary repairs were made in the Philippines.

Other significant developments during 1967 were the activation in August of HC-7, the Navy's first combat SAR helicopter squadron, and the début in December of the newest light attack aircraft, the LTV A-7A Corsair II, and of the Douglas EKA-3B, the tanker/ECM modification of the Skywarrior. Both arrived on Yankee Station aboard *Ranger*, the A-7As being assigned to the *Argonauts* of VA-147 and the EKA-3Bs to the *Zappers* of VAW-13 Det 61.

Rolling Thunder V ended on 31 December 1967 and with it the costliest year of the war for TF 77 came to an end. No fewer than ten attack carriers and four antisubmarine capacity, had spent a total of 1,197 days on the line during which 133 aircraft and helicopters had been lost in combat and forty-eight more in operational accidents.[24] Not counting those lost in the *Forrestal* fire, seventy-eight aircrewmen had been killed or died in captivity and nine were reported missing in action. On the positive side, fifty-five flyers, forty-five from the Navy and ten from the Air Force, had been recovered by Navy SAR helicopters during combat operations.

[24] Nearly 19 per cent of the aircraft lost by TF 77 during 1967 belonged to CVW-16. Altogether, during 122 days on the line aboard *Oriskany* between 14 July 1967 and 11 January 1968, CVW-16 lost more aircraft, 29 in combat and 10 in accidents, in a single cruise than any other air wing.

Relaxing in the VF-211 ready room aboard USS Bon Homme Richard *(CVA-31) Cdr Paul H Speer and Lt (jg) Joseph M Shea compare experiences following their almost simultaneous victories over MiG-17s on 19 May 1967. On that day, two other MiG kills were obtained by Crusader pilots from VF-24, the other CVW-21's F-8 squadron.* (US Navy)

After a major fire broke out on the deck of USS Forrestal *(CVA-59) in the morning of 29 July 1967, other ships came to the rescue. Here, a Kaman UH-2A of HC-1 Det Golf from USS* Oriskany *(CVA-34) is about to land on the* Forrestal *to pick up wounded personnel for transfer to the medical wards of other TF 77 ships.* (US Navy)

War and Rumors of Peace: Rolling Thunder VI and Peace Talks in Paris

When the sixth and final phase of Rolling Thunder was initiated on 3 January 1968, it had been intended that operations would follow the pattern established during Rolling Thunder V in 1967. However, meteorological conditions, a confrontation with North Korea, and a Communist offensive in South Vietnam led to a sharp reduction in the level of operations over the North during the first quarter of 1968.

In January, weather conditions over the North were appalling as the winter northeast monsoon brought heavier precipitation and more constant cloud cover than in previous years. Only the all-weather A-6s could consistently fly their assigned missions and reach their targets and thus the North Vietnamese were given a respite to repair some of the damage which had been inflicted during the second half of 1967. Meanwhile, in spite of the weather-induced reduction in its level of activities, TF 77 lost seven aircraft over North Vietnam (three each to SAMs and AAA and one to an unknown cause) and two over Laos during January 1968.

With its resources already over-extended—with three carriers on the line (*Coral Sea*, *Kitty Hawk* and *Oriskany*), *Ranger* on rest and recuperation (R&R), and two others (*Enterprise* and *Ticonderoga*) on their way to relieve *Oriskany* and *Coral Sea*—the Seventh Fleet suddenly had to face a new crisis. On 23 January, the North Koreans seized USS *Pueblo* (AGER-2) in international waters. *Ranger* and her escort were ordered to the Sea of Japan, where they were soon joined by *Enterprise* and supporting vessels, to provide a show of strength and stand ready for possible operations against North Korea. This was the moment chosen by the Communists to launch their Tet Offensive in South Vietnam.

Caught by surprise when the VC and supporting elements from the NVA launched their offensive on 30 January, American and South Vietnamese troops took heavy casualties and were in danger of being routed if not given massive air support. Accordingly, to enable TF 77 to double the number of sorties flown by its aircraft over South Vietnam to a daily average of 300 while, weather permitting, keeping up the pressure over the North and along the Laotian side of the Ho Chi Minh Trail, *Kitty Hawk* was retained on the line instead of departing for a previously scheduled R&R and *Coral Sea*'s deployment was extended into February. Furthermore, by the end of February both *Enterprise* and *Ranger* were released from operations off Korea with TF 71, and on the 21st of that month *Bon Homme Richard* began operations on Yankee Station.

As this photograph is credited by the US Navy to a Vigilante of RVAH-11 and shows the door over the starboard AN/ALE-29A chaff/flare dispenser in the open position and the dispenser to be empty, it is likely to have been taken when this F-4B of VF-114 was returning to USS Kitty Hawk *(CVA-63) at the end of a Blue Tree escort mission over the North in March 1968.* (US Navy)

Although operations against the North were primarily directed against LOCs to stem the supply flow on which the VC and NVA depended to continue their offensive, at least one new major target, port facilities in Hanoi, was added, to the authorized list and was first hit by VA-75 Intruders during the night of 24 February. At about the same time, the VC offensive was finally broken, with the South Vietnamese Army regaining control of Hue's walled city on 24 February and NVA troops being forced to pull out from around Khe Sanh starting in mid-March. For TF 77, this period of intense activity resulted in the loss of eight aircraft: an A-1H from VA-25, making the last combat deployment of the Skyraider in the attack role, was shot down by a ChiCom MiG during a ferry flight from Cubi Point to the *Coral Sea* on 14 February; five aircraft were lost to SAMs and AAA over North Vietnam in February and March, and two failed to return from Steel Tiger sorties in March.

Once the enemy offensive was halted, President Johnson, who was starting to feel intense pressure from antiwar protesters at home, announced on 31 March that he was ordering an end to US aerial and naval bombardment of North Vietnam 'except in the area where the continuing enemy buildup directly threatens allied forward positions and where the movement of their troops and supplies are clearly related to that threat.' The President also called upon North Vietnam to respond by agreeing to negotiate an end to the hostilities.

Following the President's order to halt bombing north of the 20th parallel (this arbitrary boundary was almost immediately moved further south to the 19th parallel) operations over North Vietnam were limited to armed reconnaissance missions against truck convoys, barges, bridges, and storage areas and to occasional strikes against more significant targets such as POL storage and the recently upgraded airfield in Vinh. Moreover, as Steel Tiger sorties were then only flown intermittently and as the number of air support sorties in South Vietnam also decreased from the high level reached during the first quarter, aircraft losses dropped from ninety-seven between April and October 1967 to forty-two during the same seven-month period in 1968.

USS *America* (CVA-66), which LANTFLT sent as a replacement for the unlucky *Forrestal*, and its CVW-6 arrived on Yankee Station at the end of May, bringing with them new models of the Phantom, the F-4J with AWG-10 fire-control radar and more powerful engines, and the Intruder, the A-6B equipped to launch AGM-78A Standard ARM anti-radiation missiles. Both the new Phantom and the new Intruder obtained a mixed record during their first deployment: VF-33 and VF-102 lost four F-4Js and VA-85 one of its A-6Bs. Nevertheless, F-4Js progressively replaced F-4Bs in service with squadrons aboard the large carriers, and A-6Bs were dispersed among several A-6A squadrons for use in the Iron Hand defense suppression role.

Even though in April the focus of operations had moved south, away from their bases, MiGs remained a threat as North Vietnam started to reap benefits from the training of pilots and GCI controllers in the Soviet Union and China. Venturing south of the 19th parallel, NVAF MiGs scored kills on 7 May and 16 June against Phantoms from VF-92 and VF-102 and did not themselves incur losses until 26 June when Cdr 'Moose' Meyers, an F-8H pilot from VF-51, evened the score for the Naval Aviators by shooting

Right: Carrying a hefty load — ten 560lb (254kg) Mk 82 Snakeye low-drag general-purpose bombs — this A-7A of VA-97 is ready to be catapulted off the bow of USS Constellation *(CVA-64) for a Rolling Thunder VI sortie in August 1968. The black cross painted on the radome is intended to help LSOs differentiate the A-7 from the similarly configured F-8.* (US Navy)

down a MiG-21.[25] No other naval aircraft were lost to enemy aircraft during 1968, but Crusader pilots shot down four more MiGs between 9 July and 19 September and a Phantom crew got one on 7 October. Including the Skyraider shot down by the Chinese and the unidentified MiG-21 shot down by the VF-96 crew, the year ended with a 2.33:1 kill ratio which was even less satisfactory than that achieved the previous year. Thus the USN was prompted to emphasize air combat training once again and to establish the Navy Fighter Weapons School, the now-famous Top Gun.

During the spring of 1968, all indications were that the reduced level of air operations was having little effect on North Vietnam's ability to keep on fighting. Nevertheless, encouraged by the increased effectiveness of the antiwar movement in the United States, which had already succeeded in forcing President Johnson not to seek re-election, the Hanoi government decided that this was an opportune time to negotiate a favorable settlement of the war. Peace talks began in Paris on 13 May 1968, but in five months little progress was made. However, President Johnson unwittingly proved Hanoi's confidence in the war protesters to be well founded when he ordered a halt to all bombing of North Vietnam on 31 October.

In the futile hope that a peaceful settlement of the war could be negotiated in Paris, air operations over North Vietnam were thereafter limited to Blue Tree reconnaissance missions and Laos became the principal area of operations for TF 77 aircraft. Reflecting this reduced level of activity and the new operational priorities, the only losses during the last two months of the year were an RA-5C from RVAH-5 which failed to return from a Blue Tree sortie on 25 November and two A-6As from VA-196 which were shot down over Laos on 18 and 19 December respectively. Altogether during 1968, TF 77 lost sixty aircraft in combat, a substantial reduction over the 133 aircraft lost during the

[25] An earlier victory had been obtained by a VF-96 crew—Maj John Hefferman, an Air Force exchange pilot, and Lt (jg) Frank Schumacher, his Navy RIO—against another MiG-21. However, whether because the victim was shot down over China or was identified by Intelligence as being flown by a foreign 'adviser', details of this 26 June victory have still not been released.

Even earlier, on 23 May, another MiG-21 had been shot down by a Talos guided missile after it ventured too close to TF 77. Before the war ended at least six other MiGs were claimed by missiles fired from TF 77 ships.

previous year. Operational accidents, on the other hand, had risen from forty-eight to fifty-one. Worth noting is the fact that even though there were fewer A-6s than other attack aircraft or fighters, Intruders accounted for a disproportionate number of combat losses; thirteen were shot down during the year.

Withdrawal on Land, War in the Air

For Naval Aviation, the year 1969 started badly in spite of the reduced level of activities: on 3 January an A-4C from VA-216 was shot down over Laos (the pilot being recovered) and on 14 January *Enterprise* became the third carrier to suffer a major accident and fire while on a war deployment. The nuclear carrier was engaged in an Operational Readiness Inspection (ORI) off Hawaii, having left her homeport on 6 January, when a Zuni rocket overheated and exploded. Closely packed aircraft ignited and their fuel and ordnance created an inferno in which twenty-seven men died, 344 were injured, and fifteen aircraft were lost. Notwithstanding the extent of material damage, her crew and personnel from the Pearl Harbor shipyard succeeded in having *Enterprise* ready again for operations in barely two months. She was back on the line on 31 March. Two weeks later, after tensions had risen following the shooting down by North Korean MiGs of a VQ-1 Lockheed EC-121M on a routine reconnaissance patrol over the Sea of Japan, *Enterprise* was sent to Defender Station off Korea to operate temporarily with *Ranger*, *Ticonderoga*, the CVS *Hornet*, and their cruiser and destroyer screens.

President Nixon, upon taking office in January 1969, confirmed the bombing halt ordered by his predecessor and ordered the progressive withdrawal of American forces from South Vietnam. During the remainder of the year, the level of activities dropped progressively; the number of attack carriers assigned to the Seventh Fleet was reduced to four in July, and *Kearsarge* completed the last CVS wartime deployment in August. Also down were combat losses. Only nine aircraft were lost during the first seven months of the year and then, for the first time since January 1965, TF 77 lost no aircraft in combat in August, September, or December. (One aircraft was shot down over Laos in October and three did not return from Steel Tiger sorties in November.) These downward trends continued during 1970, when carriers spent 755 days on the line and lost only eleven aircraft over Laos, and during 1971, when the number of days on the line decreased to 587 and the number of aircraft lost to four, two each in Laos and North Vietnam.

For more than three years after the 1 November 1968 bombing halt, carrier aircraft operations followed a predict-

Left: BuNo 155553, the Tarsiers' aircraft in which Lt Roy Cash, Jr, and Lt Joseph E Kain, Jr, shot down a Mig-21 on 10 July 1968, comes aboard USS America *(CVA-66) during the first F-4J deployment to the Gulf of Tonkin in 1968. The empty triple ejector rack on the inboard wing pylon and the absence of Sparrows from the forward fuselage stations indicate that the aircraft is returning from an attack sortie. In addition to the MiG kill, the tally painted on the starboard splitter plate include 16 'baseball caps' for CAP sorties and five 'bombs' for prior attack sorties.* (Bud Joyce)

Below: On 4 July 1968, two CVW-19 aircraft—an A-4F of VA-192 and an F-8E of VF-194—collided in mid-air during a strike. Both pilots ejected and were recovered. One of the lucky pilots is being placed on a stretcher after being brought back aboard USS Ticonderoga *(CVA-14) by an UH-2B of HC-1 Det 14.* (Kaman Aerospace)

Photographed at NAS North Island, its shore base in California, this S-2E belongs to VS-21, one of the two Tracker squadrons which deployed four times to the Gulf of Tonkin with CVSG-53 aboard USS Kearsarge *(CVS-33). The last war cruise of CVSG-53 and* Kearsarge *ended with their return to CONUS on 4 September 1969.* (Peter B Lewis)

able pattern. In Laos, the interdiction campaign along the Ho Chi Minh Trail saw bombing and strafing attacks supplemented by night sorties during which A-6s and A-7s sowed land mines. In South Vietnam, air support for allied ground forces was provided on an irregular basis depending upon tactical requirements. In North Vietnam, Blue Tree reconnaissance activities continued unabated but offensive operations were limited to occasional protective reaction strikes against SAM and AAA sites which had fired on Blue Tree reconnaissance aircraft or their escorting fighters. This routine, however, was broken on a few occasions such as on 28 March 1970, when Lt Jerry Beaulier and Lt Steve Barkley, flying an F-4J of VF-142 off *Constellation*, shot down a MiG-21 while escorting a Vigilante from RVAH-7 during a Blue Tree mission in the vicinity of Tanh Hoa, and on 21 November 1970, when TF 77 aircraft flew diversionary sorties along the coast to confuse North Vietnamese radar defenses while Air Force helicopters were attempting to rescue US prisoners of war from the Song Tay camp, twenty miles west of Hanoi.

Two Intruder versions were first deployed during these lull years, VA-145 first taking A-6Cs aboard *America* beginning in April 1970 and VA-115 first deploying with KA-6Ds aboard *Midway* one year later. These A-6Cs, which were fitted with a forward-looking infrared (FLIR) and low light level television (LLLTV) sensor package in a ventral fairing, had been especially developed for night interdiction operations but proved only moderately successful and were only deployed once more with VA-145 aboard *Ranger*. The KA-6D tankers, with a hose refueling unit (HRU) in and beneath their aft fuselage, performed well and quickly began replacing KA-3Bs. Also making its début in April 1970 when VA-146 and VA-147 deployed aboard *America*, the A-7E (an improved version of the Corsair II with, notably, TF41 turbofan and head-up display) became the new standard light attack aircraft aboard US carriers.

The Line is Taut: Linebacker and Endsweep

Imperceptibly at first, the lull in the air war over the North came to a progressive end during the last two months of 1971 and the first quarter of 1972. The North Vietnamese, seeking to hide preparations for their new offensive against South Vietnam, began firing more frequently at reconnaissance aircraft and their escorts flying Blue Tree missions, and the US responded with more and heavier protective reaction strikes. Thus, during the last week of December, aircraft from *Constellation* and *Coral Sea* flew over 400 Proud Deep strike sorties against targets from Dong Hoi to Vinh. Additional protective reaction strikes were flown during the first three months of 1972 and resulted in the destruction of a MiG-21 on 19 January and a MiG-17 on

This bridge near Duong Phuong Thuong was hit by A-4Fs of VA-212 aircraft from USS Hancock *(CVA-19) during a Freedom Train strike on 27 April 1972. As shown by this photograph, the main span of this truss bridge was dropped into the river.* (US Navy)

Left: An A-6B Mod 1 aircraft photographed during evaluation in the United States. This SAM suppression version of the Intruder is seen carrying a pair of AGM-78A Standard ARM anti-radiation missiles on wing racks and an AN/APS-118 target identification and acquisition pod beneath the fuselage. Numerous 'warts' on the radome are warning system receivers. (Grumman History Center)

6 March by Phantom crews from VF-96 and VF-111. Meanwhile, TF 77 aircraft not only continued to operate primarily over Laos but also temporarily increased the number of air support sorties flown over South Vietnam to counter the expected enemy offensive.

As increased evidence of an incipient North Vietnamese offensive was being gathered and as the Paris Talks were stalemated, the United States broke off the negotiations on 23 March. Furthermore, not wanting to be caught unprepared as they had been four years earlier when the Communists launched their 1968 Tet Offensive, South Vietnamese and American forces went on full alert. Thus, when three NVA divisions, including tanks and heavy artillery supported by a large number of shoulder-fired SA-

7 surface-to-air missiles, crossed into South Vietnam on 30 March to initiate the 1972 Spring Offensive, the defenders were ready on the ground and a schedule to bring air reinforcements had been detailed. For TF 77, this meant that its aircraft were immediately thrown into the battle to provide much needed air support to the South Vietnamese defenders (680 sorties were flown during the first week of April as opposed to an average of sixty-six weekly sorties during the previous quarter) while plans were made for a new air offensive against the North.

Designated Freedom Train and initiated on 5 April, this new offensive was aimed at destroying North Vietnamese offensive resources, harassing and disrupting enemy military operations, and reducing and impeding movements of men and materials in the panhandle area. Initially strikes were limited to targets below the 19th parallel, but by the end of April the northern limit had been moved to 20° 25'N. Special strikes further north were also authorized on several occasions, such as on 16 April when aircraft from *Constellation*, *Coral Sea*, and *Kitty Hawk* flew diversionary sorties in the Haiphong area in support of Freedom Porch B-52 strikes against POL storage facilities. Moreover, TF 77 aircraft continued providing much air support in South Vietnam, not only in Military Region I south of the DMZ area (as had been most often the case in the past) but also in Military Region III within a few miles of Saigon.

Already intense, the pace of activity increased even further in May as the scope of US air operations over the North was broadened with the launching of Operations Pocket Money and Linebacker. On 10 May, restrictions on sustained air operations above the 20th parallel were lifted as Freedom Train gave place to Linebacker I. On 18 May, bombing of several industrial targets in the Haiphong restricted zone were first authorized. From the Naval Aviation point of view, however, the most significant event was Pocket Money, the mining campaign against all major North Vietnamese harbors and waterways, which was announced by President Nixon on 9 May. Simultaneously with this announcement, in which a three-day warning was given to enable Soviet and neutral merchant vessels to leave North Vietnamese waters before the mines were armed, A-6As and A-7Es from CVW-15 sowed the first thirty-six mines (with 72-hour arming delays) in the outer approaches of Haiphong Harbor. Two days later, six other harbors

Left: Four beaming Chargers *photographed in the VF-161 ready room aboard USS* Midway *(CVA-41) after downing two MiG-19s 30 miles northeast of Hanoi on 18 May 1972. From left to right, they are: Lt Oran R Brown, RIO and his pilot Lt Henry A 'Bart' Bartholomay, and Lt Patrick E 'Pat' Arwood, pilot, and his RIO, Lt James M 'Mike' Bell.* (US Navy)

Seen here during a training sortie on 29 March 1972 when USS Constellation *(CVA-64) was off the line, this F-4J of VF-96 is the aircraft in which Lt Randall H Cunningham and Lt (jg) William P Driscoll shot down three MiG-17s on 10 May and from which they were forced to eject after the aircraft was damaged by the nearby explosion of a SAM.* (US Navy)

against the Navy than against the Air Force. The Navy lost a VF-51 Phantom on 27 April after having obtained one victory in both January and March, whereas through the end of April the Air Force claimed six MiGs without taking a single loss. May, however, saw a reversal of luck and during that month, when air combat opportunities abounded, the Navy's faith in its Topgun program was amply rewarded. Without losing a single aircraft to enemy fighters during May, Navy Phantom crews shot down three MiGs on 6 May, one on the 8th, eight on the 10th (including the last three kills by the Navy aces, Lt Randall H Cunningham and Lt (jg) William P Driscoll), and two each on the 18th

were mined and soon thereafter mining operations were extended to include most coastal and inland waterways. Eventually, over an eight-month period, more than 11,000 mines were planted, effectively blockading maritime transport to and from North Vietnam.

With activities almost evenly divided between offensive missions over the North and defensive sorties over the South (3949 Linebacker I and Freedom Train sorties were flown in May versus 3290 air support sorties in South Vietnam), TF 77 operations peaked toward the end of May when six carriers were on the line for the first time. In June, the number of in-country sorties flown by Navy aircraft began dropping when the Communist offensive in the South was broken. Nevertheless, TF 77 offensive operations over the North continued virtually unabated throughout the summer and into the fall, with a monthly record of 4819 sorties being set in August. Finally, however, as a result of perceived progress in diplomatic talks, President Nixon decided to have Linebacker I operations north of the 20th parallel ended on 22 October 1972. Once again, the Hanoi government had been saved by the political gong.

During the first four months of 1972, MiGs fared better and 23rd. Naval Aviators scored nine more confirmed victories during the remainder of Linebacker I, a period when the only aircraft shot down by a MiG was a VF-103 F-4J which was downed on 10 July. The success achieved by TF 77 fighters was even more remarkable considering that it was obtained while preventing enemy fighters from shooting down a single attack or reconnaissance aircraft. Furthermore, as Air Force fighters also shot down thirty-nine enemy aircraft between May and October while losing sixteen F-4s and two F-105s to the MiGs, the whole Freedom Train/Linebacker I period proved extremely costly for the NVAF.

Not surprisingly, however, US losses to AAA, SAMs, and other factors rose steadily from the start of the year until May, when TF 77 lost fourteen aircraft in combat (more than in any other month since October 1967). Losses then dropped slightly during the next three months but rose to eleven in September prior to falling to two in October, thus bringing to sixty-one the total number of aircraft lost in combat by the Navy from the beginning of 1972 until the end of Linebacker I operations. Quite significantly, nearly 30 per cent of these losses were due to SAMs, thus indicating that the Communists had taken advantage of the lull years to improve their missile operations in the face of increased US defense suppression activities. Among the victims claimed by SAMs were the aforementioned Navy fighter aces as well as the crew credited with the only all-Marine air combat victory of the Southeast Asia War.[26] The aces, Lt Cunningham and Lt (jg) Driscoll, ejected feet wet after their F-4J was damaged by the nearby explosion of a SAM as they were flying back toward *Constellation* after shooting down their third, fourth, and fifth MiGs on 10 May. They were quickly recovered by a pair of HH-3A from HC-7 Det 110 operating from USS *Okinawa* (LPH-3). The Marines, Maj Lee T Lasseter and Capt John D Cummings, were assigned to VMFA-333, one of the two Phantom squadrons embarked aboard *America* for that carrier's third deployment to the Gulf of Tonkin. On 11 September, five minutes after shooting down a MiG-21, the two Marines were forced to eject after their F-4J was hit by a SAM while crossing the coast back toward the carrier; both were recovered by a Navy helicopter.

During November and the first two weeks of December, although operations against the North were limited to the panhandle area and fewer sorties were flown in the South, TF 77 still lost six aircraft, one to an SA-2 missile and five to AAA. The North Vietnamese took advantage of this respite to repair damage and bring in new supplies by rail from China. Moreover, this time the Hanoi government miscalculated the strength of the US antiwar movement. The Vietnamese negotiating team at the Paris Talks first stiffened demands and sought better terms on previously agreed items, then finally broke off negotiations on 13 December. Faced with this new situation, the US government surprised Hanoi by ordering the resumption of bombing of North Vietnam on a scale previously unseen. Designated Linebacker II and initiated on 18 December, this decisive phase of the war saw Strategic Air Command B-52s bomb for the first time major military and industrial targets in the heavily defended Hanoi and Haiphong areas while Air Force, Marine, and Navy tactical aircraft flew support missions and attacked other targets.

During eleven days of intense operations, with recesses for Christmas and New Year's Day, aircraft from *America*, *Enterprise*, *Midway*, *Oriskany*, *Ranger*, and *Saratoga* flew 505 day and night sorties during which they attacked SAM batteries, AAA emplacements, POL storage areas, rail and road targets, shipyards, port facilities, and enemy army barracks. Then, on 3 January 1973, bombing north of the 20th parallel was again suspended. This time, however, the message had been heard, and rapid progress was made by the negotiators in Paris while limited operations continued for three weeks in Vietnam.

Six Navy aircraft, including an RA-5C from RVAH-13 which was shot down by a MiG-21 on 28 December, were lost during Linebacker II, and one MiG-21 was brought down on the same date by a VF-142 crew. Naval Aviators obtained one more victory and lost two more aircraft over North Vietnam after Linebacker II operations ended. The two aircrewmen of a VA-115 Intruder brought down by a SAM during the night of 9 January were the last Naval Aviators lost in combat during the war; the pilot, Lt M T McCormick, and the bombardier navigator (BN), Lt (jg) R A Clark, were killed in action and reported missing in action respectively. In an odd coincidence, a VF-161 pilot, Lt Victor T Kovaleski, claimed the last victory and flew the last aircraft to be shot down over the North. On 12 January 1973, he and his RIO, Lt (jg) James A Wise, shot down a MiG-21 while flying BarCAP off *Midway*. Two days later, while he was teamed with Ens D H Plautz, his Phantom was hit by AAA while flying escort during a Blue Tree sortie in the Thanh Hoa area; fortunately, pilot and RIO ejected safely and were recovered at sea by a Navy helicopter.

At last, on 23 January 1973, the hollow but grandiloquently titled 'Agreement on Ending the War and Restoring the Peace in Vietnam' was signed in Paris. In accordance with the Agreement, preparations for the return of the prisoners of war (Operation Homecoming) were made, the removal of mines from Haiphong harbor (Operation Endsweep) was scheduled to commence within a month, and all air operations over both North and South Vietnam were to end. Offensive operations against the North had been suspended on 15 January, and all other air activities over North Vietnam ceased on 23 January. The last sorties over South Vietnam were flown on 27 January but not before two more aircraft were lost. The pilot and BN of a VA-35 A-6A from *America* were recovered by a Navy helicopter on 24 January, thus becoming the last of 161 Naval Aviators saved by Navy SAR helicopters. Cdr H H Hall and LCdr P A Kientzler, the pilot and RIO of a VF-143 F-4J from *Enterprise*, the last Navy aircraft to be lost in combat during the Southeast Asia War, were taken prisoner of war after ejecting on 27 January but were soon released.

Whereas air operations in Vietnam ended immediately after the Vietnam ceasefire, those over Laos and Cambodia continued for a while, with TF 77 aircraft joining Air Force tactical aircraft and B-52s in hitting North Vietnamese-supported guerrillas. In Laos, the last tactical sorties were flown on 22 February and B-52s flew their last sorties on 17 April. In Cambodia, where all US combat operations ended on 15 August 1973 in accordance with a congressional mandate, the final sortie of the war was flown by an Air Force A-7D from the 354th Tactical Fighter Wing.

Planning for Operation Endsweep had begun before the conclusion of the Peace Talks as, knowing that the mining of Haiphong was having telling effects on the North Vietnamese economy, the US negotiating team had used an offer of removing the mines as a bargaining point to obtain from Hanoi the release of American prisoners of war. Accordingly, as soon as the negotiations were concluded, the Navy set up Task Force 78 (TF 78) to conduct minesweeping operations in North Vietnamese waters using surface mine-

[26] Nearly five years earlier, on 17 December 1967, Capt Doyle Baker, a Marine pilot on exchange duty with the 432nd Tactical Reconnaissance Wing, shot down a MiG-17 while flying an F-4D. However, on that occasion his backseater was not another Marine but an Air Force Weapon Systems Officer (WSO), 1st Lt John D Ryan, Jr.

When air operations over North and South Vietnam ended in January 1973, TF 77 had five carriers on the line, USS America *(CVA-66), USS* Enterprise *(CVAN-65), USS* Midway *(CVA-41), USS* Oriskany *(CVA-34), and USS* Ranger *(CVA-61). In addition, USS* Constellation *(CVA-64) had chopped in with Seventh Fleet but had not yet been sent on the line. This is an A-7B of VA-215 which at that time was one of the CVW-19 squadrons aboard* Oriskany. (By courtesy of Cloud 9 Photography)

Below: Bearing a MiG silhouette and the name 'THE MIG KILLERS' on its port splitter plate, this VF-161 F-4J is the Phantom in which Lt Victor T Kovaleski and Lt (jg) James A Wise shot down a MiG-21 on 12 January 1973 to claim the war's last victory. BuNo 153405 was photographed at NAS Miramar on 16 March 1973, thirteen days after VF-161 had returned to California at the completion of the third war cruise of USS Midway *(CVA-41).* (Peter B. Lewis)

sweepers and specially configured CH-53 helicopters from one Navy and two Marine squadrons (HM-12, HMH-463, and HMM-165) which operated from the deck of two amphibious assault ships, USS *Inchon* (LPH-12) and USS *New Orleans* (LPH-11). Mine removal operations began on 6 February and ended on 27 July 1973. During that time, *Coral Sea*, *Enterprise*, *Oriskany*, and *Ranger* were sent at various times to the Mine Logistics Carrier Station to provide air cover for TF 78. However, the most important contribution made by Naval Aviators during the Operation Endsweep was that made by the crews from the three helicopter squadrons, which flew over 1100 hours on mine removal duty.

On 20 June 1973, five weeks before Operation Endsweep was completed, Congress ordered the cessation of all combat operations in Southeast Asia on 15 August. Although this congressional action effectively ended US participation in the Southeast Asia War, fighting continued in Vietnam and Cambodia. For US military personnel, the relief brought by this unconclusive end to their fighting was bittersweet as nothing could be shown for the sacrifices and suffering of so many. While serving with TF 77, 377 Naval Aviators had been killed in action, 144 of the 179 aircrewmen known to have been taken prisoner of war were returned by the North Vietnamese, and at least 99 others were still reported as missing in action.

The End of the Line: US Carrier Aviation at War's End

Matériel losses, including over 850 carrier aircraft, and the high cost of the war left Naval Aviation in worse shape at war's end than it had been nine years earlier. In terms of multi-purpose carriers and attack carriers, of which fourteen were in service in September 1973 as shown in Table 8, the Navy's strength had held nearly constant. However, the retirement of the nine antisubmarine carriers which had been in service when the war started in 1964 was only partially offset by adding fixed-wing ASW aircraft and ASW helicopters to air wings assigned to multi-purpose carriers. In terms of aircraft, the situation was worse. Total Navy

inventory had dropped from 10,598 fixed-wing and rotary-wing aircraft in service on 31 July 1964, to 7681 in service on 30 September 1973. Fortunately, as shown below, the greatest drop, both in actual numbers and as a percentage, had been in non-program aircraft.

	Aircraft Inventory	
	31 July 1964	*30 September 1973*
Fleet Combat	3552	2961
Direct and Indirect Fleet Support	1265	741
Training Command	1411	1165
USNR	770	623
Rework and Pipeline	1384	998
Reserve Stock	970	650
Sub-total (Program aircraft)	9352	7138
Non-program aircraft	1246	543
TOTAL	10,598	7681

Although the number of carrier-capable aircraft assigned to operational and fleet replacement squadrons of the Navy and the Marine Corps (see Table 9) had decreased to 1822, or less than 24 per cent of the total inventory as opposed to 27 per cent in July 1964, Naval Aviation was still strong as the reduction in numbers had been made up by improvements in quality. The level of aircrew training was far superior to that of nine years earlier and the Fleet now had some of the world's most advanced combat aircraft. Particularly outstanding were its F-14As, which were just entering service, and its A-6Es, A-7Es, E-2Cs, and EA-6Bs.

After the war ended, the causes of aircraft losses and the experience gained in air combat became the subjects of countless official analyses and simulation studies, most of which remain classified. The following analysis, therefore, is only a modest attempt to put into perspective the relative loss rates of the most important carrier-based aircraft of the Southeast Asia War and to summarize air combat data.

Ships of Task Force 78 during Operation Endsweep, the removal of mines from Haiphong and other North Vietnamese harbors and coastal waterways. CH-53 helicopters can be seen on the deck of USS Inchon *(LPH-12).* (US Navy)

An A-7E of VA-146 being readied on the port bow catapult of USS Constellation *(CVA-64) at the start of an Alpha Strike on 25 April 1972. Four Mk 82 low-drag general-purpose bombs are carried on multiple ejection racks attached to the outboard wing pylons. No Sidewinders are carried on the fuselage pylons as protection will be provided by F-4Js from VF-92, including NG 212 being positioned on the starboard catapult. This Phantom was shot down by North Vietnamese AAA on 10 May 1972 while flying TarCAP for a strike against POL drum storage at Hai Duong. Cdr H L Blackburn and Lt S A Rudloff were taken prisoner of war.* (US Navy)

In the absence of data regarding the number of sorties flown by each type of aircraft, an estimate of the number of days each spent on the line was substituted as a common denominator for evaluating the combat loss rates of the eight major types of combat and reconnaissance aircraft. Admittedly, the number of aircraft-days on the line does not reflect several operational factors affecting the risk factor of each type, such as whether it operated over enemy territory or flew over the relative safety of the Gulf of Tonkin, whether or not it flew more than one mission per day, and the type of targets against which it operated. Be that as it may, this analysis yielded the following results:

Aircraft Type	*Number of Aircraft Lost in Combat*[27]	*Number of Days on the Line*	*Number of Days on the Line per Aircraft Loss*
A-1H/J Skyraider	48	30,648	639
A-4B/C/E/F Skyhawk	195	140,940	723
A-6A/B Intruder	51	48,324	948
A-7A/B/C/E Corsair II	55	82,596	1502
F-4B/G/J Phantom II	75	118,860	1585
F-8C/D/E/H/J Crusader	57	75,816	1330
RA-5C Vigilante	18	21,894	1216
RF-8A/G	19	18,700	984

On this basis, the Skyraider and Skyhawk had the worst combat loss rates whereas the Phantom had the best record. In the case of the latter, this relatively low combat loss rate

[27] In addition to the 518 aircraft in this tabulation, TF 77 combat losses included one EA-1F, one S-2D, two A-3Bs, and eight SH-3As.

can be partly explained by the fact that F-4s, unlike F-8s and all attack aircraft, were not initially used for the more dangerous attack and defense suppression missions. Quite remarkably, in view of the fact that they flew exclusively in the attack role, the A-7 experienced a combat loss rate almost as low as that of the F-4. More than likely this was due to the fact that the Corsair II entered service after better tactics had been developed and after the use of ECM and chaff had been standardized. Somewhat surprisingly in view of the commonly held belief that photo-reconnaissance aircraft were facing greater risks as they flew predictably over previously struck targets when collecting BDA data, the North American RA-5C had one of the lowest combat loss rates and that of the LTV RF-8A/G was just below average.

As shown in the following tabulations, the bulk of the losses were due to AAA and small arms fire and the great majority of losses occurred during operations over North Vietnam.

Causes	*Number of Losses*	*Percentage*
AAA	345	65.1
SAM	91	17.2
MiG	15	2.8
Other causes	79	14.9

Fifty-five A-7s and fifty-one A-6s were lost during combat operations in Southeast Asia. As Corsair IIs spent nearly twice as much time on the line as did Intruders, A-7 pilots appear to have had a much better chance of coming back unscathed than did A-6 crews. These bomb-laden aircraft, an A-7E of VA-147 and an A-6A of VA-165 from USS Constellation *(CVA-64), are on their way to a North Vietnamese target during Freedom Train operations in the spring of 1972.* (US Navy)

Locations	*Number of Losses*	*Percentage*
North Vietnam	451	85.1
Laos	54	10.2
South Vietnam	20	3.8
China (PRC)	2	0.9

The sixty-two confirmed victories, including two not officially released, credited to TF 77 pilots and crews were obtained against four types of aircraft as follows:

	An-2	*MiG-17*	*MiG-19*	*MiG-21*	*Total*
A-1	—	2	—	—	2
A-4	—	1	—	—	1
F-4	2	23	2	14	41
F-8	—	14	—	4	18
TOTAL	2	40	2	18	62

These victories were obtained by twenty-three squadrons. The largest number of kills, ten, was achieved by the *Fighting Falcons* of VF-96 which flew F-4Bs and F-4Js successively from *Ranger* (one deployment and one victory), *Enterprise* (five deployments and one victory), *America* (one deployment and no victory), and *Constellation* (two deployments and eight victories). The next best squadron score, seven confirmed victories and one probable, was achieved by the *Checkmates* of VF-211 flying F-8Es, F-8Hs, and F-8Js from *Hancock* (two deployments, three confirmed victories and one probable), *Bon Homme Richard* (one deployment and four victories), and again *Hancock* (five deployments and no victory).

The only Navy aces were Lt Randall H Cunningham and Lt (jg) William P Driscoll, a VF-96 pilot/RIO team, with five confirmed victories. Two other F-4 crews, Lt Michael J Connelly and Lt Thomas J J Blonski of VF-96, and LCdr Ronald E McKeown and Lt John C Ensch of VF-161, and an F-4 pilot, Lt Dennis Wisely of VF-114, were each credited with two victories.

The Phantom, which initially trailed the Crusader (at the end of 1968, F-8 pilots had already claimed eighteen confirmed victories whereas F-4 crews had destroyed only fifteen enemy aircraft), came into its own in 1972 when it obtained twenty-four confirmed kills. It is highly probable that the poor initial showing of the F-4s was due to the fact that their crews received only minimal air combat training in the mid-sixties as their primary task then was long-range fleet air defense using missiles, whereas F-8 pilots were still trained to dogfight against enemy fighters. Clearly, Topgun and a renewed emphasis on air combat maneuvering produced the desired results as during the last thirteen months of operations against the NVAF (whose pilots had by then also received much additional training), the F-4 crews destroyed twenty-five MiGs while enemy fighters could only claim the destruction of one F-4 and one A-4.

By far the greatest number of these victories was obtained with simple but effective AIM-9 Sidewinder air-to-air (AAM) short-range missiles. Phantom crews used AIM-9s for thirty-one of their forty-one kills and AIM-7 Sparrow medium-range AAMs for their other victories. (Apparently the small number of kills obtained with Sparrows resulted to a large extent from the ROE mandating that pilots identify their targets positively before firing. In poor visibility, as often prevailed over North Vietnam, this could only be done by

Sterling work by crews from AEW aircraft did much to reduce losses to enemy aircraft by providing timely warning of air interceptions and to boost the score of the fighters by vectoring them toward MiGs. This E-2B Hawkeye of VAW-116 is being directed onto a catapult aboard USS Constellation *(CVA-64) during operations in the Gulf of Tonkin on 25 April 1972.*
(US Navy)

An F-8J Crusader of Fighter Squadron Fifty-Three (VF-53) is at marshall prior to recovering aboard USS Bon Homme Richard *(CVA-31) during operations on the line in June 1970. This was the last war cruise for 'Bonnie Dick' as this attack carrier was decommissioned on 2 July 1971 and placed in reserve at Bremerton, Washington.* (US Navy)

coming in so close that the AIM-7's semi-active radar homing (SARH) guidance system could not lock on the target.) Crusader pilots shot down fifteen of their eighteen MiGs with AIM-9s and used these missiles to damage two other MiG-17s which they went on to destroy with cannon fire. Zuni air-to-ground rockets were used to finish off a MiG-17 which had been damaged by F-8 cannon fire. (It is worth noting again that, notwithstanding the F-8 pilots' pride in being the 'last of the gunfighters', none of their victories resulted from gunfire alone.) Finally, the three victories not credited to fighter crews were obtained by Skyraider pilots with their 20mm cannon and by a Skyhawk pilot with Zuni rockets.

Eagle Pull, Frequent Wind, and the *Mayaguez* Incident

Barely four months after Congress voted on 20 June 1973 to stop all spending on US combat activities in or over Southeast Asia, the North Vietnamese Central Committee adopted a resolution during its 21st Plenum stating that the path of revolution in the South left no alternative but to conduct a revolutionary war to destroy the enemy and liberate the South. Accordingly, the NVA began a series of raids against selected targets during the first week of November 1973. As there was no US military reaction[28], the Communists felt safe to increase their pressure progressively not only against South Vietnam but also against Cambodia. By the beginning of 1975, when it was becoming clear that North Vietnam would soon win the war, President Ford had no choice but to order US Armed Forces to implement plans to evacuate US citizens, key South Vietnamese and Cambodian officials, and third country nationals (TCNs) from the two beleaguered countries. For Naval Aviators, this meant returning on the line in the South China Sea.

PACFLT had three carriers in the Western Pacific at the

[28] On 7 November 1973, both chambers of Congress had overridden President Nixon's veto and passed the War Powers Resolution Act, making it illegal to commit US forces for more than sixty days without congressional approval.

beginning of 1975, after *Oriskany*, *Kitty Hawk*, *Ranger*, and *Constellation* had completed their 1974 deployments. *Enterprise* had departed Alameda on 17 September 1974 and her CVW-14 had on board the first two squadrons equipped with Grumman F-14As (VF-1 and VF-2), *Coral Sea* and her CVW-15 had left Californian shores on 5 December and *Midway*, which had been permanently home-ported in Yokosuka since September 1973, operated out of Japan with CVW-5. In addition, to be able to provide effective support for the anticipated evacuation of Phnom Penh (Operation Eagle Pull) and Saigon (Operation Frequent Wind), COMNAVAIRPAC ordered *Hancock* and her CVW-21 to leave the Continental United States (CONUS) on 18 March 1975 to bring the number of available carriers in the South China Sea back to four.

Five days before the Khmer government surrendered to Communist insurgents on 17 April 1975, 275 Americans, TCNs, and selected Cambodians were air evacuated from Phnom Penh. However, in the end direct Navy support was not required during Eagle Pull. On the other hand, more than 5000 evacuees were flown out of Saigon through the four aircraft carriers during Frequent Wind. During the last two days of the evacuation, on 29 and 30 April, aircraft from *Coral Sea* and *Enterprise* flew 173 sorties to provide air support. Although no ordnance was expended during these sorties, an A-7E from *Enterprise* was lost due to an undetermined cause. Meanwhile *Hancock* and *Midway*, which had left some of their aircraft at Cubi Point in order to receive Air Force and Marine helicopters, served as platforms for these helicopters and those from Air America which carried out the evacuation of Americans, South Vietnamese, and TCNs as Saigon was being overrun by the VC and NVA. In addition, large numbers of VNAF helicopters, as well as a Cessna O-1 observation aircraft, landed on *Midway* as South Vietnamese pilots sought to save themselves and their families from being captured by the Communists. Most of the VNAF helicopters, however, had to be pushed overboard to make room for more arrivals. Once these sad tasks were accomplished, *Enterprise* began her return voyage and *Midway* ferried out of Thailand some 100 VNAF aircraft which had been flown there during the final days of the Republic of Vietnam. It appeared that, at last, the war was over.

However, as related in the next chapter, Naval Aviators had not quite ended their participation in combat operations in Southeast Asia. On 15 May 1975, barely two weeks after taking part in Frequent Wind, *Coral Sea* was called on to take part in the *Mayaguez* rescue operations. This civilian

Right: The KA-6D tanker version of the Grumman Intruder was first deployed to the Gulf of Tonkin in the spring of 1971 when VA-115 arrived on the line aboard USS Midway *(CVA-41) with its twelve A-6A medium attack aircraft supplemented with five KA-6D tankers. The KA-6B in this photograph belongs to VA-165, a CVW-9 squadron which made two war cruises aboard USS* Constellation *(CVA-64) and was still aboard CVA-64 when this carrier made her first postwar deployment to WestPac in 1974.* (Grumman History Center)

Below right: Clean and not yet soiled by combat operation, this A-4F from VA-144 was photographed on 13 April 1970 during a training flight over the Western Pacific. Its carrier, USS Bon Homme Richard *(CVA-31), was then in transit from Alameda to the Gulf of Tonkin at the start of her sixth and final war cruise.* (US Navy)

Left: SH-3As from Helicopter Combat Support Squadron Seven (HC-7) coming on board USS Constellation *(CVA-64) on 17 January 1970. The aircraft on deck are an EKA-3B of VAQ-133 and F-4Js of VF-142 and VF-143.* (US Navy)

container ship and her thirty-nine crewmen were rescued but, in fourteen hours of intense fighting against the Khmer Rouge on the small Cambodian island of Koh Tang, fifteen Americans were killed, three were reported missing in action, and fifty were wounded. In this last American action of the war, Naval aviators were more fortunate than Air Force rescue helicopter crews and Marine 'grunts' as none of these casualties were from *Coral Sea* or her CVW-15.

***Table 5*: Carrier Deployments to Southeast Asia (activities per carrier) 2 August 1964 to 15 August 1973**

			AIRCREW LOSSES			AIRCRAFT LOSSES	
CARRIER	NO OF DAYS ON THE LINE	NO OF CRUISES	KIA	MIA	POW	COMBAT	OPS
USS *America* (CVA-66)	370	3	9	2	7	21	11
USS *Bennington* (CVS-20)[1]	176	3	5	0	0	1	3
USS *Bon Homme Richard* (CVA-31)	620	6	21	2	13	43	24
USS *Constellation* (CVA-64)	824	7	34	4	18	45	22
USS *Coral Sea* (CVA-43)	875	7	41	16	26	69	26
USS *Enterprise* (CVAN-65)[2]	669	6	30	2	24	39	18
USS *Forrestal* (CVA-59)[3]	5	1	0	0	0	0	0
USS *Hancock* (CVA-19)	843	8	26	2	14	46	41
USS *Hornet* (CVS-12)[1]	233	3	13	0	0	5	6
USS *Independence* (CVA-62)	100	1	7	0	9	13	4
USS *Intrepid* (CVS-11)[4]	312	3	8	3	3	17	7
USS *Kearsarge* (CVS-33)[1]	258	4	11	0	0	2	3
USS *Kitty Hawk* (CVA-63)	806	6	42	11	20	55	23
USS *Midway* (CVA-41)[5]	426	3	22	3	12	32	12
USS *Oriskany* (CVA-34)[6]	800	7	35	5	18	64	45
USS *Ranger* (CVA-61)	765	7	41	8	4	30	34
USS *Franklin D. Roosevelt* (CVA-42)	95	1	7	2	2	7	8
USS *Saratoga* (CV-60)	173	1	5	3	5	13	4
USS *Shangri-La* (CVS-38)[4]	120	1	2	0	0	1	8
USS *Ticonderoga* (CVA-14)	516	5	14	1	4	27	26
USS *Yorktown* (CVS-10)[1]	192	3	4	0	0	0	4
	9178	86	377	64	179	530	329

[1] ASW carriers operating in the anti-submarine and ocean surveillance roles
[2] CVAN-65 also lost 27 men and 15 aircraft in an accidental fire on 14 January 1969
[3] CVA-59 also lost 134 men and 21 aircraft in an accidental fire on 29 July 1967
[4] ASW carriers operating in a limited attack carrier capacity
[5] CVA-41 spent the most days on the line during a single cruise: 208 days between April 1972 and February 1973
[6] CVA-34 also lost 44 men and three aircraft in an accidental fire on 26 October 1966

Grumman E-1B Tracers of VAW-11 Det Golf were aboard USS Oriskany *(CVA-34) during two war cruises in 1965 and 1966.* (Grumman History Center)

Carrying neither Sidewinder nor Sparrows, this F-4J of Fighter Squadron Ninety-Two (VF-92) is seen just after leaving the angled deck of USS Enterprise *(CVAN-65) at the start of a training flight. This photograph was taken as CVAN-65 was steaming off the Californian coast in August 1969 between her fourth and fifth war cruises.* (US Navy)

***Table 6:* Carrier Deployments to Southeast Asia (chronological listing by date of arrival on the line) 2 August 1964 to 15 August 1973**

CARRIER	FIRST DAY ON THE LINE	LAST DAY ON THE LINE
Line periods starting in 1964		
USS *Ticonderoga* (CVA-14)	2 August 1964	27 November 1964
USS *Constellation* (CVA-64)	5 August 1964	21 November 1964
USS *Kearsarge* (CVS-33)	11 August 1964	8 November 1964
USS *Bon Homme Richard* (CVA-31)	31 August 1964	8 October 1964
USS *Ranger* (CVA-61)	18 September 1964	12 April 1965
USS *Hancock* (CVA-19)	28 December 1964	2 May 1965
Line periods starting in 1965		
USS *Coral Sea* (CVA-43)	1 February 1965	14 October 1965
USS *Yorktown* (CVS-10)	9 February 1965	28 April 1965
USS *Midway* (CVA-41)	10 April 1965	4 November 1965
USS *Oriskany* (CVA-34)	8 May 1965	25 November 1965
USS *Bon Homme Richard* (CVA-31)	28 May 1965	16 December 1965
USS *Independence* (CVA-62)	27 June 1965	11 November 1965
USS *Bennington* (CVS-20)	28 July 1965	11 September 1965
USS *Hornet* (CVS-12)	11 October 1965	3 February 1966
USS *Ticonderoga* (CVA-14)	5 November 1965	20 April 1966
USS *Kitty Hawk* (CVA-63)	26 November 1965	22 May 1966
USS *Enterprise* (CVAN-65)	2 December 1965	5 June 1966
USS *Hancock* (CVA-19)	17 December 1965	10 July 1966

CARRIER	FIRST DAY ON THE LINE	LAST DAY ON THE LINE
Line periods starting in 1966		
USS *Ranger* (CVA-61)	15 January 1966	5 August 1966
USS *Yorktown* (CVS-10)	25 February 1966	3 July 1966
USS *Intrepid* (CVS-11)	15 May 1966	17 October 1966
USS *Constellation* (CVA-64)	14 June 1966	9 November 1966
USS *Oriskany* (CVA-34)	30 June 1966	26 October 1966
USS *Franklin D. Roosevelt* (CVA-42)	10 August 1966	27 December 1966
USS *Kearsarge* (CVS-33)	12 August 1966	24 November 1966
USS *Coral Sea* (CVA-43)	12 September 1966	31 January 1967
USS *Ticonderoga* (CVA-14)	13 November 1966	28 April 1967
USS *Kitty Hawk* (CVA-63)	4 December 1966	22 May 1967
USS *Enterprise* (CVAN-65)	18 December 1966	20 June 1967
USS *Bennington* (CVS-20)	21 December 1966	15 April 1967
Line periods starting in 1967		
USS *Hancock* (CVA-19)	5 February 1967	27 June 1967
USS *Bon Homme Richard* (CVA-31)	26 February 1967	30 July 1967
USS *Hornet* (CVS-12)	22 May 1967	5 October 1967
USS *Constellation* (CVA-64)	28 May 1967	11 November 1967
USS *Intrepid* (CVS-11)	21 June 1967	23 November 1967
USS *Oriskany* (CVA-34)	14 July 1967	11 January 1968

CARRIER	FIRST DAY ON THE LINE	LAST DAY ON THE LINE
USS *Forrestal* (CVA-59)	25 July 1967	29 July 1967
USS *Coral Sea* (CVA-43)	28 August 1967	20 February 1968
USS *Kearsarge* (CVS-33)	23 October 1967	19 February 1968
USS *Ranger* (CVA-61)	3 December 1967	9 May 1968
USS *Kitty Hawk* (CVA-63)	23 December 1967	1 June 1968
Line periods starting in 1968		
USS *Ticonderoga* (CVA-14)	26 January 1968	23 July 1968
USS *Bon Homme Richard* (CVA-31)	21 February 1968	13 September 1968
USS *Enterprise* (CVAN-65)	22 February 1968	26 June 1968
USS *Yorktown* (CVS-10)	13 March 1968	16 June 1968
USS *America* (CVA-66)	31 May 1968	29 October 1968
USS *Bennington* (CVS-20)	25 June 1968	20 October 1968
USS *Constellation* (CVA-64)	28 June 1968	7 January 1969
USS *Intrepid* (CVS-11)	24 July 1968	27 December 1968
USS *Hancock* (CVA-19)	23 August 1968	9 February 1969
USS *Coral Sea* (CVA-43)	10 October 1968	30 March 1969
USS *Hornet* (CVS-12)	3 November 1968	17 April 1969
USS *Ranger* (CVA-61)	29 November 1968	16 April 1969
Line periods starting in 1969		
USS *Kitty Hawk* (CVA-63)	28 January 1969	16 August 1969
USS *Ticonderoga* (CVA-14)	4 March 1969	1 August 1969
USS *Enterprise* (CVAN-65)	31 March 1969	16 June 1969
USS *Bon Homme Richard* (CVA-31)	18 April 1969	8 October 1969
USS *Kearsarge* (CVS-33)	4 May 1969	14 August 1969
USS *Oriskany* (CVA-34)	16 May 1969	31 October 1969
USS *Hancock* (CVA-19)	1 September 1969	26 March 1970
USS *Constellation* (CVA-64)	12 September 1969	17 April 1970
USS *Coral Sea* (CVA-43)	27 October 1969	1 June 1970
USS *Ranger* (CVA-61)	17 November 1969	12 May 1970
Line periods starting in 1970		
USS *Shangri-La* (CVS-38)	12 April 1970	5 November 1970
USS *Bon Homme Richard* (CVA-31)	2 May 1970	20 October 1970
USS *America* (CVA-66)	26 May 1970	8 November 1970
USS *Oriskany* (CVA-34)	14 June 1970	22 November 1970
USS *Hancock* (CVA-19)	20 November 1970	3 May 1971
USS *Ranger* (CVA-61)	21 November 1970	17 May 1971
USS *Kitty Hawk* (CVA-63)	8 December 1970	23 June 1971
Line periods starting in 1971		
USS *Midway* (CVA-41)	18 May 1971	10 October 1971
USS *Oriskany* (CVA-34)	16 June 1971	19 November 1971
USS *Enterprise* (CVAN-65)	16 July 1971	24 January 1972
USS *Constellation* (CVA-64)	4 November 1971	13 June 1972
USS *Coral Sea* (CVA-43)	14 December 1971	30 June 1972
Line periods starting in 1972		
USS *Hancock* (CVA-19)	7 February 1972	14 September 1972
USS *Kitty Hawk* (CVA-63)	8 March 1972	4 November 1972
USS *Midway* (CVA-41)	30 April 1972	12 February 1973
USS *Saratoga* (CV-60)	18 May 1972	8 January 1973
USS *Oriskany* (CVA-34)	29 June 1972	5 March 1973
USS *America* (CVA-66)	14 July 1972	28 February 1973
USS *Enterprise* (CVAN-65)	3 October 1972	28 May 1973
USS *Ranger* (CVA-61)	9 December 1972	31 May 1973
Line periods starting in 1973		
USS *Constellation* (CVA-64)	31 January 1973	15 August 1973
USS *Coral Sea* (CVA-43)	31 March 1973	8 August 1973
USS *Hancock* (CVA-19)	1 June 1973	6 August 1973

Although the Thunderbolts *of VA-176 made only one war cruise while flying Douglas Skyraiders, when they were on the line aboard USS* Intrepid *(CVS-11) between April and November 1966, the colorful markings applied to their A-1Hs became well known. After converting to Grumman Intruders and getting a new nickname,* Main Battery, *VA-176 was a member of the Tonkin Gulf Yacht Club five more times.* (McDonnell Douglas Corporation by courtesy of Harry S Gann, Jr)

***Table 7*: Carrier Deployments to Southeast Asia (monthly activity levels) 2 August 1964 to 15 August 1973**

	NO OF CARRIERS CVA + CVS	TOTAL	NO OF DAYS ON THE LINE (YANKEE + DIXIE + CVS)	AIR COMBAT VICTORIES	AIRCRAFT LOSSES COMBAT	OPS
1964						
August	3 + 1	75	(54 + 0 + 21)	0	2	2
September	3 + 1	74	(50 + 0 + 24)	0	0	1
October	3 + 1	41	(36 + 0 + 5)	0	0	0
November	3 + 1	42	(34 + 0 + 8)	0	0	5
December	2 + 0	33	(33 + 0 + 0)	0	0	3
Total		265	(207 + 0 + 58)	0	2	11
1965						
January	2 + 0	32	(32 + 0 + 0)	0	0	1
February	3 + 1	88	(70 + 0 + 18)	0	3	2
March	3 + 1	75	(64 + 0 + 11)	0	8	1
April	4 + 1	93	(65 + 0 + 28)	1	9	2
May	5 + 0	78	(61 + 17 + 0)	0	4	3
June	5 + 0	87	(66 + 21 + 0)	3	9	2
July	5 + 1	99	(65 + 31 + 3)	0	6	4
August	5 + 1	114	(61 + 31 + 22)	0	13	2
September	5 + 1	87	(56 + 22 + 9)	0	13	5
October	5 + 1	120	(63 + 36 + 21)	1	12	3
November	6 + 1	99	(62 + 26 + 11)	0	13	4
December	5 + 0	98	(67 + 31 + 0)	0	12	6
Total		1070	(732 + 215 + 123)	5	102	35
1966						
January	5 + 1	109	(68 + 25 + 16)	0	6	5
February	5 + 2	92	(59 + 27 + 6)	0	10	1
March	5 + 1	119	(62 + 32 + 25)	0	11	3
April	5 + 1	106	(60 + 30 + 16)	0	21	4
May	5 + 1	96	(66 + 28 + 2)	0	9	4
June	6 + 1	111	(60 + 29 + 22)	3	8	6
July	5 + 1	93	(64 + 26 + 3)	1	13	4
August	5 + 1	113	(90 + 3 + 20)	0	11	7
September	5 + 1	107	(91 + 0 + 16)	0	9	4
October	5 + 1	107	(92 + 0 + 15)	2	14	4
November	4 + 1	96	(77 + 0 + 19)	0	6	5
December	5 + 1	104	(93 + 0 + 11)	2	8	2
Total		1253	(882 + 200 + 171)	8	126	49

	NO OF CARRIERS CVA + CVS	TOTAL	NO OF DAYS ON THE LINE (YANKEE + DIXIE + CVS)	AIR COMBAT VICTORIES	AIRCRAFT LOSSES COMBAT	AIRCRAFT LOSSES OPS
1967						
January	4 + 1	116	(93 + 0 + 23)	0	8	5
February	5 + 1	103	(84 + 0 + 19)	0	3	6
March	5 + 1	103	(93 + 0 + 10)	0	10	5
April	5 + 1	106	(91 + 0 + 15)	2	11	3
May	5 + 1	111	(101 + 0 + 10)	6	24	2
June	5 + 1	116	(90 + 0 + 26)	0	10	3
July	5 + 0	92	(92 + 0 + 0)	3	19	4
August	4 + 1	95	(82 + 0 + 13)	2	15	6
September	4 + 1	92	(69 + 0 + 23)	0	2	4
October	4 + 2	89	(75 + 0 + 14)	2	16	4
November	4 + 1	81	(66 + 0 + 15)	0	8	5
December	4 + 1	93	(73 + 0 + 20)	1	7	1
Total		1197	(1009 + 0 + 188)	16	133	48
1968						
January	5 + 1	104	(91 + 0 + 13)	0	8	9
February	6 + 1	106	(88 + 0 + 18)	0	3	3
March	5 + 1	111	(92 + 0 + 19)	0	5	4
April	5 + 1	99	(91 + 0 + 8)	0	2	6
May	6 + 1	116	(93 + 0 + 23)	0	12	2
June	6 + 2	110	(91 + 0 + 19)	1	7	6
July	5 + 1	111	(93 + 0 + 18)	4	4	5
August	5 + 1	102	(93 + 0 + 9)	1	6	7
September	5 + 1	107	(90 + 0 + 17)	1	7	5
October	5 + 1	107	(93 + 0 + 14)	0	4	2
November	5 + 1	103	(87 + 0 + 16)	0	1	2
December	5 + 1	104	(85 + 0 + 19)	0	2	0
Total		1280	(1087 + 0 + 193)	7	61	51

Left: HC-7 personnel relax on the helicopter pad of a destroyer in the Gulf of Tonkin. The helo is one of the six Seasprites modified by Kaman to the HH-2C Combat SAR configuration with twin turbines and armor around the cockpit, engines, and other critical areas. The minigun has been removed from the nose-mounted General Electric TAT-102 turret. (Kaman Aerospace)

Above: The Naval Air Rework Facility in Alameda, California, was responsible for the TACOS (Tactical and Countermeasures Strike Support Aircraft) program which turned A-3B heavy attack aircraft into dual role EKA-3Bs equipped for operations in the tanking and ECM roles. This EKA-3B of VAQ-132 is seen recovering aboard USS America *(CVA-66) on 13 July 1970. The blisters on the fuselage sides contained antennas for the AN/ALT-92 VHF noise jammer and the ventral canoe housed antennas for the AN/ALT-27 S-band jammer and AN/APA-69 direction finder. The HRU (Hose Refueling Unit) was housed at the aft end of the ventral canoe.* (US Navy)

	NO OF CARRIERS CVA + CVS	TOTAL	NO OF DAYS ON THE LINE (YANKEE + DIXIE + CVS)	AIR COMBAT VICTORIES	AIRCRAFT LOSSES COMBAT	OPS
1969						
January	5 + 1	95	(77 + 0 + 18)	0	1	2
February	4 + 1	88	(69 + 0 + 19)	0	3	7
March	5 + 1	85	(67 + 0 + 18)	0	1	3
April	5 + 1	91	(75 + 0 + 16)	0	1	4
May	5 + 1	77	(65 + 0 + 12)	0	1	6
June	5 + 1	84	(66 + 0 + 18)	0	1	1
July	4 + 1	88	(77 + 0 + 11)	0	1	9
August	4 + 1	79	(65 + 0 + 14)	0	0	7
September	4 + 0	61	(61 + 0 + 0)	0	0	2
October	5 + 0	64	(64 + 0 + 0)	0	1	1
November	4 + 0	62	(62 + 0 + 0)	0	3	3
December	4 + 0	62	(62 + 0 + 0)	0	0	4
Total		936	(810 + 0 + 126)	0	13	49
1970						
January	4 + 0	63	(63 + 0 + 0)	0	2	1
February	4 + 0	56	(56 + 0 + 0)	0	2	6
March	4 + 0	66	(66 + 0 + 0)	1	2	3
April	4 + 0	62	(62 + 0 + 0)	0	3	5
May	5 + 0	90	(90 + 0 + 0)	0	0	8
June	5 + 0	63	(63 + 0 + 0)	0	1	3
July	4 + 0	65	(65 + 0 + 0)	0	0	2
August	4 + 0	65	(65 + 0 + 0)	0	0	2
September	4 + 0	62	(62 + 0 + 0)	0	0	1
October	4 + 0	62	(62 + 0 + 0)	0	0	1
November	5 + 0	50	(50 + 0 + 0)	0	0	2
December	3 + 0	51	(51 + 0 + 0)	0	1	2
Total		755	(755 + 0 + 0)	1	11	36

During the Southeast Asia War, Reconnaissance Heavy Attack Squadron Five (RVAH-5) deployed five times to the Gulf of Tonkin. Its first, third, and fifth deployments were aboard USS Ranger *(CVA-61). This RVAH-5 Vigilante was one of the aircraft which were aboard* Ranger *during the 1972-73 cruise.* (By courtesy of Cloud 9 Photography)

	NO OF CARRIERS CVA + CVS	TOTAL	NO OF DAYS ON THE LINE (YANKEE + DIXIE + CVS)	AIR COMBAT VICTORIES	AIRCRAFT LOSSES COMBAT	AIRCRAFT LOSSES OPS
1971						
January	3 + 0	43	(43 + 0 + 0)	0	0	3
February	3 + 0	57	(57 + 0 + 0)	0	0	4
March	3 + 0	70	(70 + 0 + 0)	0	1	1
April	3 + 0	61	(61 + 0 + 0)	0	1	0
May	4 + 0	49	(49 + 0 + 0)	0	0	0
June	3 + 0	48	(48 + 0 + 0)	0	0	2
July	3 + 0	53	(53 + 0 + 0)	0	0	0
August	3 + 0	39	(39 + 0 + 0)	0	0	1
September	3 + 0	30	(30 + 0 + 0)	0	0	2
October	3 + 0	31	(31 + 0 + 0)	0	0	2
November	3 + 0	48	(48 + 0 + 0)	0	0	1
December	3 + 0	58	(58 + 0 + 0)	0	2	0
Total		587	(587 + 0 + 0)	0	4	16
1972						
January	3 + 0	50	(50 + 0 + 0)	1	0	2
February	3 + 0	62	(62 + 0 + 0)	0	1	2
March	4 + 0	64	(64 + 0 + 0)	1	2	4
April	5 + 0	110	(110 + 0 + 0)	0	6	0
May	6 + 0	147	(147 + 0 + 0)	16	14	4
June	7 + 0	119	(119 + 0 + 0)	3	9	1
July	6 + 0	122	(122 + 0 + 0)	0	9	1
August	6 + 0	120	(120 + 0 + 0)	1	7	1
September	6 + 0	118	(118 + 0 + 0)	1	11	6
October	6 + 0	123	(123 + 0 + 0)	0	2	2
November	6 + 0	121	(121 + 0 + 0)	0	6	4
December	6 + 0	125	(125 + 0 + 0)	1	7	2
Total		1281	(1281 + 0 + 0)	24	74	29
1973						
January	7 + 0	123	(123 + 0 + 0)	1	4	5
February	6 + 0	94	(94 + 0 + 0)	0	0	0
March	5 + 0	85	(85 + 0 + 0)	0	0	0
April	4 + 0	80	(80 + 0 + 0)	0	0	0
May	4 + 0	60	(60 + 0 + 0)	0	0	0
June	3 + 0	50	(50 + 0 + 0)	0	0	0
July	3 + 0	45	(45 + 0 + 0)	0	0	0
August	3 + 0	17	(17 + 0 + 0)	0	0	0
Total		554	(554 + 0 + 0)	1	4	5
GRAND TOTAL 1964–73		9178	(7904 + 415 + 859)	62	530	329

Photographed at NAS Miramar on 16 March 1973, this RF-8G of VFP-63 Det 1 carries the NP tail code of CVW-21. It deployed once more aboard USS Hancock *(CVA-19) between 8 May 1973 and 8 January 1974.* (Peter B Lewis)

***Table 8*: Operational Carriers (Homeports and Assigned Air Wings/Air Groups) 30 September 1973**

COMNAVAIRLANT, Norfolk Virginia		
Multi-purpose Aircraft Carriers		
USS *Independence* (CV-62)	Norfolk, Virginia	CVW-7
USS *John F. Kennedy* (CV-67)	Norfolk, Virginia	CVW-1
USS *Saratoga* (CV-60)	Mayport, Florida	CVW-3
Attack Carriers		
USS *America* (CVA-66)	Norfolk, Virginia	CVW-8
USS *Forrestal* (CVA-59)	Norfolk, Virginia	CVW-17
USS *Franklin D. Roosevelt* (CVA-42)	Mayport, Florida	CVW-6
COMNAVAIRPAC, San Diego, California		
Multi-purpose Aircraft Carriers		
USS *Kitty Hawk* (CV-63)	North Island, California	CVW-11
Attack Carriers		
USS *Constellation* (CVA-64)	North Island, California	CVW-9
USS *Coral Sea* (CVA-43)	Alameda, California	CVW-15
USS *Enterprise* (CVAN-65)	Alameda, California	CVW-14
USS *Hancock* (CVA-19)	North Island, California	CVW-21
USS *Midway* (CVA-41)	Alameda, California	CVW-5
USS *Oriskany* (CVA-34)	Alameda, California	CVW-19
USS *Ranger* (CVA-61)	Alameda, California	CVW-2

Grumman EA-6B Prowlers were deployed only three times to the Gulf of Tonkin as initially few were available following entry into service with VAQ-129 in January 1971. By 30 September 1973, however, the number of EA-6Bs in service with Fleet combat units had risen to forty-nine and Prowlers outnumbered by more than two-to-one the EKA-3Bs they were replacing. (Grumman History Center)

***Table* 9: Fleet Combat Units (Carrier Aircraft Inventory) 30 September 1973**

	COMNAVAIRLANT USN + USMC	COMNAVAIRPAC USN + USMC	TOTAL
Fighters			
F-4B/J/N	140 + 64	156 + 88	448
F-8H/J	0 + 0	43 + 0	43
F-14A	0 + 0	13 + 0	13
Attack aircraft			
A-4E/F/M	8 + 39	53 + 72	172
A-6A/B/C/E	78 + 31	69 + 22	200
A-7A/B/C/E	168 + 0	238 + 0	406
AV-8A	0 + 40	0 + 0	40
Photo-reconnaissance aircraft			
RF-4B*	0 + 9	0 + 18	27
RF-8G	0 + 0	17 + 0	17
RA-5C	35 + 0	0 + 0	35
Tanker aircraft			
KA-6D	17 + 0	16 + 0	33

	COMNAVAIRLANT USN + USMC	COMNAVAIRPAC USN + USMC	TOTAL
ECM aircraft			
EKA-3B	0 + 0	21 + 0	21
EA-3B*	4 + 0	7 + 0	11
EA-6A/B	0 + 9	29 + 11	49
AEW aircraft			
E-1B	4 + 0	11 + 0	15
E-2B/C	19 + 0	17 + 0	36
ASW aircraft			
S-2E/G	45 + 0	44 + 0	89
COD aircraft			
C-1A	10 + 0	11 + 0	21
C-2A	3 + 0	4 + 0	7
Helicopters			
SH-3A/D/G/H	73 + 0	66 + 0	139
TOTAL	604 + 192	815 + 211	1822

* Usually land-based but deployed aboard carriers when required

USS *Coral Sea* at War

With 875 days on the line, USS *Coral Sea* (CVA-43) accounted for nearly one-tenth of the total number of days spent in the war zone by the twenty-one attack and antisubmarine carriers deployed to the Gulf of Tonkin. Hence, *Coral Sea* is a fitting choice for a more detailed look at the men and units of the Tonkin Gulf Yacht Club.

Launching her first strike on 7 February 1965 at the onset of the Flaming Dart air interdiction campaign against the Democratic Republic of Vietnam, *Coral Sea* was last on the line on 8 August 1973, just one week before the Congress of the United States mandated an end to American combat involvement in Southeast Asia. In the intervening years, her aircrew personnel were credited with the destruction of six MiG-17s but her human and matériel losses were heavy. Fifty-five of her Naval Aviators were either killed or reported missing. With sixty-nine aircraft failing to return from combat missions and twenty-six others lost in operational accidents, her total aircraft losses approximately equalled the full complement of a representative air wing.

Ordered from the Newport News Shipbuilding and Drydock Company on 14 June 1943 as the third Aircraft Carrier, Large (CVB) *Coral Sea* had her keel laid on 10 July 1944. Launched on 2 April 1946, she was commissioned as CVB-43 on 1 October 1947. (The CVBs were the first class of US carriers to receive an armored deck—other ships in this class were hull numbers 41 (USS *Midway*) and 42 (USS *Franklin D. Roosevelt*) and the unnamed hull numbers 44, 56, and 57 which were cancelled in March 1945 prior to being launched.)

Following her shakedown cruise in the Caribbean at the

USS Coral Sea *(CVA-43) in the Western Pacific on 4 December 1971, four days before chopping to the Seventh Fleet for her sixth war cruise. In addition to aircraft from her CVW-15, she has on board at least one Douglas EA-3B from VQ-1; the 'Queer Whale' is on the starboard edge of the deck, aft of the island.* (US Navy by courtesy of Captain Joseph J Frick)

This F-4B of VF-151, seen framed beneath the tail of an RA-3B of VAP-61 during a combat sortie in the spring of 1965, returned to Coral Sea *for the 1971-72 war cruise. Then assigned to VF-51 and carrying the modex 113, BuNo 149457 was the aircraft in which Lt Winston W Copeland and Lt Donald R Bouchoux shot down a MiG-17 on 11 June 1972.* (Don J Willis)

beginning of 1948 and a training cruise for midshipmen in the summer of that year, *Coral Sea* made her first operational deployment with the Sixth Fleet from 3 May to 25 September 1949. Remaining homeported in Norfolk, Virginia, until 1957, she deployed seven more times to the Atlantic and Mediterranean prior to being sent to the Puget Sound Naval Shipyard in Bremerton, Washington, to undergo a 33-month conversion and modernization. The so-called SCB 110A modernization included incorporation of an angled deck, fairing of her forward deck and hull to form a hurricane bow, addition of blisters to widen her hull by 8ft (2.44m), installation of three C 11-1 steam catapults and Mk 7 Mod 2 arresting gear, replacement of her two centerline and single deck-edge aircraft elevators with three larger deck-edge elevators, and upgrading of her radar and communications systems.

At the conclusion of the SCB 110A program, *Coral Sea* had the following principal characteristics:

light ship displacement:	45,100 tons (40,914 tonnes)
full load displacement:	62,600 tons (56,790 tonnes)
overall length:	978ft (298.10m)
beam:	231ft (70.41m)
draft (full):	34ft 9in (10.59m)
flight deck dimensions:	978ft × 236ft (298.10m + 71.93m)
length of angled deck:	663ft 6in (202.23m)
elevator dimensions:	56ft × 44ft (17.07m × 13.41m)
elevator capacity:	74,000lb (33,565kg)
aviation ordnance:	1376 tons (1248 tonnes)
aviation fuel:	600,000 gallons (2,271,200 litres) of JP-5
number of aircraft:	80 (typical)
antiaircraft battery:	six (later three) 5in
ship complement:	162 officers and 2521 men
air group complement:	201 officers and 1537 men
full speed:	30.6 knots
sustained speed:	29.5 knots
endurance:	9500 nautical miles (15 600km) at 20 knots

Recommissioned as CVA-43 on 25 January 1960, *Coral Sea* was then assigned to the Pacific Fleet and homeported in Alameda, California. Embarking Carrier Air Group Fifteen (CVG-15), she made her first WestPac deployment between September 1960 and May 1961 prior to becoming the first carrier to be fitted with the Pilot Landing Aid Television (PLAT)[1] system. Prior to the end of 1963, CVA-43 and CVG-15 (redesignated CVW-15/Carrier Air Wing Fifteen in December 1963) made two more peacetime cruises in the Western Pacific and several port calls in Guam, Hawaii, Japan, and the Philippines.

[1] Designed to provide a film recording (later replaced by video tape) of every landing, the PLAT system was useful for instructional purposes and in the analysis of landing accidents. Within two years from its installation aboard *Coral Sea*, all CVAs were equipped with PLAT.

Photographed from the right-hand seat of an A-3B of VAH-2 during an early war sortie, this F-8D from USS Coral Sea *(CVA-43) has its fin adorned with the* Black Knights' *insignia. On 14 October 1965, while strafing flak emplacements during a strike against military buildings at Dong Hoi on the coast of the North Vietnamese panhandle, this VF-154 aircraft was hit on the port side, aft of the nose wheel well, by small arms fire. Progressive loss of oil and hydraulic pressure led to a complete engine seizure and forced Lt (jg) J A 'Jack' Terhune to eject. He was almost immediately picked up off shore by a Seasprite from* Coral Sea's *HC-1 Det 1 unit D.* (Don J Willis)

In the weeks immediately preceding the Gulf of Tonkin Incident, *Coral Sea* was operating off the coast of Southern California as a unit of the First Fleet. Activities were intense as carrier qualification landings (CarQuals) were conducted in preparation for her next scheduled deployment to WestPac. On 24 July 1964, she established a peacetime record of 536 arrested landings (traps) in 18 hours 56 minutes (a phenomenal average of one trap every 2.12 minutes!) to qualify 375 pilots for day landings and 161 pilots for night landings. After setting this record, *Coral Sea* went back for an inport period at Alameda where she was moored when US Naval Aviation went back to war on 2 August 1964. Her aircrews, however, were fortunate to be allowed to enjoy peace for another six months. At last, following additional training and five weeks in drydock at Hunters Point in San Francisco Bay for underwater body repairs, *Coral Sea* was ready to on-load ammunition and embark CVW-15 for her first deployment to the Gulf of Tonkin.

The First War Cruise, 7 December 1964 to 1 November 1965

Leaving her homeport on 7 December 1964 under the command of Capt George L Cassell, *Coral Sea* and her CVW-15[2] proceeded to the waters around the Hawaiian Islands where additional training and ORI took place prior to a rest period at Pearl Harbor during the year-end holidays. Departing from Pearl Harbor on 6 January 1965, *Coral Sea* proceeded to WestPac where on the 23rd she was placed under the operational control of Carrier Task Group 77.5 (CTG 77.5), Task Force 77, Seventh Fleet. On 1 February, *Coral Sea* first went on the line for a period of thirty-three days. Things were relatively quiet at first and only routine operations took place. However, all changed during the early morning hours of Sunday, 7 February 1965; instead of proceeding to the Philippines for a few days of scheduled liberty, *Coral Sea* steamed at top speed to rejoin *Ranger* (CVA-61) and *Hancock* (CVA-19) off South Vietnam. In retaliation for a Viet Cong attack against US forces at the Pleiku Air Base and nearby Camp Holloway, the three carriers were instructed to mount the Flaming Dart One strike against targets in North Vietnam. Aircraft from CVW-

[2] The squadrons assigned to this Air Wing, the types of aircraft operated by these squadrons, and the tail codes and modexes applied to their aircraft are listed in Appendix 1—Combat Cruises.

Having already flown two bombing missions, as evidenced by the bombs painted beneath the Royal Rampants' *insignia, this A-3B of VAH-2 is about to be loaded with bombs in preparation for a third mission over the North in April 1965.* (Don J Willis)

15 (*Coral Sea*) and CVW-19 (*Hancock*) were to attack barracks and port facilities at Dong Hoi, while aircraft from CVW-9 (*Ranger*) were to bomb the Vit Thu Lu barracks.

For its first war mission in the early afternoon of 7 February, CVW-15 launched twenty aircraft: A-1Hs from VA-165 *Boomers* led by Cdr Ray Chamberlin; A-4Cs from VA-153 *Blue Tail Flies* under the command of Cdr Peter Mongilardi, Jr; A-4Es from VA-155 *Silver Foxes* of Cdr Jack Harris; and F-8Ds of Cdr Bill Donnelly's VF-154 *Black Knights*. In addition, VAH-2 *Royal Rampants* sent A-3Bs to act as tankers for the twenty strike aircraft and fighters. Even though weather over the target had deteriorated, with a 700ft (215m) ceiling and local rain squalls, and the North Vietnamese were putting up light to moderate AAA fire, the strike aircraft proceeded with their briefed low-level high-speed delivery. Ten buildings were destroyed, two were heavily damaged, and others left burning by the aircraft of *Coral Sea* and *Hancock*. Unfortunately, Lt Edward A Dickson's A-4E (BuNo 150075 of VA-155) was hit by small arms or light AAA fire during a Snakeye[3] bombing run at 450 knots (835kmh), 200ft (60m) above the ground. As flames engulfed the port wing of his Skyhawk and trailed approximately 50ft (15m) aft, Lt Dickson was instructed by his flight leader to prepare to eject. After reaching the relative safety of the sea, Lt Dickson did eject and the seat and canopy were seen to separate. However, the parachute failed to deploy and Lt Dickson became the first *Coral Sea* pilot and second US Naval Aviator to be killed in action in Vietnam.

Again, on 11 February, during Flaming Dart Two, CVW-15 did not have much luck as three of its aircraft were hit during an attack against the Chanh Hoa barracks: LCdr Robert H Shumaker of VF-154 was reported missing in action (but later was found to have been taken prisoner) when his F-8D was shot down by 37mm or 57mm guns; Lt W T Majors of VA-153 was recovered by a USAF helicopter after bailing out over the sea as the engine of his A-4C seized as a result of AAA damage; and Lt E G Hiebert of VA-155 fortunately walked away from his burning A-4E after making a wheels-up landing at Da Nang Air Base with some hung ordnance. Furthermore, during a tanking sortie on 24 February, an A-3B of VAH-2 developed a malfunction and its four crew members bailed out 8 miles (15km) from *Coral Sea*. Only three crew were recovered by Seasprite and Sea King helicopters of HU-1 and HS-4, the latter squadron operating from the ASW carrier *Yorktown* (CVS-10). Notwithstanding these losses, *Coral Sea* remained on the line for twenty-two more days before finally steaming into Subic Bay after two full months at sea.

On 18 March, three days after returning on the line, CVA-43 launched her third strike when aircraft bombed supply buildings in Phu Van and Vinh Son. No aircraft

[3] Snakeyes are retarded weapons obtained by fitting retarding fins to standard 250lb (113kg) Mk 81 and 500lb (227kg) Mk 82 GP bombs.

were lost during this first Rolling Thunder mission but this happy situation did not last, and *Coral Sea*'s second period on the line, which lasted thirty-three days, was once again marred by losses: six aircraft were shot down and LCdr Kenneth E Hume of VF-154 and Lt William M Roark of VA-153 were killed in action on 29 March and 7 April. Fortunately, the four other pilots were recovered. On the positive side, this period on the line saw the Crusaders and Skyhawks of CVW-15 fly the Navy's first night armed reconnaissance mission of the war on the night of 15 April and its Skywarriors operate in the bombing role for the first time. During the first Flaming Dart and Rolling Thunder missions, A-3Bs had been used as tankers but on 29 March six A-3Bs from the *Royal Rampants* of VAH-2 bombed a radar site, headquarters buildings, and barracks on Bach Long Vi Island. Although successful and followed by other bombing sorties by VAH-2 and Heavy Attack Squadrons operating from other carriers, this use of the A-3 was discontinued by the end of 1965 as Skywarriors were more valuable as tankers.

As the pace of operations quickened, living conditions aboard *Coral Sea* became harsher for Naval Aviators and sailors. Fresh water, always a precious commodity at sea, had to be drastically conserved as distillation equipment could not keep up with the steam catapults' increased water consumption resulting from the large number of launches of heavily-laden aircraft. In spite of the heat and humidity, uniforms and flight suits could not be washed, latrines were not flushed, and showers were prohibited. Finally, when

What the well-dressed combat crew was supposed to wear! 'Aussie' style bush hats were the big thing to buy during quick shopping trips to Saigon. The three Royal Rampants *in this April 1965 photograph are, from left to right: AMH1 M L Sutherland, third crewman, LCdr L P Hettinger, pilot, and Lt (jg) W H Haushalter, bombardier-navigator.* (Don J Willis)

Dark-shirted deck hands prepare to load 20mm ammunition into A-1Hs from VA-152 aboard USS Oriskany *(CVA-34) during operations in the Gulf of Tonkin in 1965. The two sailors in white T-shirts carry 'hernia bars', used to lift bombs from carts to racks.* (Jerry Edwards)

flight operations were curtailed or suspended after days on end of misery and discomfort, the height of luxury for the exhausted and no longer dashing aircrews was to be allowed to take a sailor's shower (10 seconds to get wet and 10 seconds to rinse) and to exchange their soiled flight suits, so dirty and impregnated with sweat that they were almost 'free standing', for freshly laundered suits or uniforms. For sailors confined deep down in the steamy entrails of the ship, life was even less bearable. No wonder R&R, be it in Olongapo, Hong Kong, or Yokosuka, was awaited with near desperation and enjoyed with so much wild enthusiasm.

Enemy fighters were first encountered on 3 April when MiG-17s made an inconclusive hit-and-run pass at aircraft from CVW-15 and CVW-21 (the latter then embarked aboard *Hancock*) before diving away to safety. More foreboding was the evidence brought back two days later by one of *Coral Sea*'s reconnaissance aircraft. Intelligence had expected that North Vietnamese defenses would be beefed up with SAM missiles, and the accuracy of this prediction was confirmed by an RF-8A of VFP-63 Det Delta which, on 5 April, photographed a SAM site being constructed some 15 miles (24km) southeast of Hanoi. Plans were made at once to hit this site but the well-grounded recommendation of local commanders was not endorsed by Washington. Thus, during the next four months, construction of additional SAM sites proceeded without US interference. This new weapon's worth was first proven on 24 July 1965 when an SA-2 brought down a F-4C of the 47th TFS/15th TFW, USAF. By the time American involvement in the Southeast Asia War ended on 15 August 1973, 197 US fixed-wing aircraft (including thirteen from *Coral Sea*) and

Three different types, an F-4B from VF-151, an RF-8G from VFP-63 Det 43, and an A-6A from VA-35, undergo routine maintenance in the tightly-packed confines of the hangar. (Jerry Edwards)

Taking advantage of a break in operations, Coral Sea *crewmen stroll on deck during a quiet April day in the South China Sea. Such peaceful moments were few and far between during the record length war cruise of CVA-43 when she and her crew spent 331 days away from home. The aircraft closest to the bow, NL413 is the F-8D in which Lt David A Kardell was killed on 9 May 1965 when he flew into the ground while strafing a truck in Route Package IV.* (Don J Willis)

Mk 82 bombs and other stores clutter the hangar floor as F-48s and A-6As are being serviced in preparation for a strike mission (Jerry Edwards)

The tail markings on BuNo 142676, NL 406, clearly identify the A-7E in the center of this photograph as belonging to the Sidewinders of VA-86. The F-4B on the right side is an aircraft from the Vigilantes of VF-151. (Jerry Edwards)

seven helicopters had been lost to SA-2s and SA-7s.

R&R was given to the crew of *Coral Sea* during visits to Subic Bay and Hong Kong in the second half of April, but the men were back on the line on 1 May for a period of twenty-seven days. Primary targets for Rolling Thunder strikes continued to be bridges, while armed reconnaissance sorties were flown to interdict North Vietnamese transportation of men and supplies. An F-8D of VF-154 was lost during this period and Lt David A Kardell was killed on 9 May while strafing a truck.

Leaving the line on 27 May, *Coral Sea* was scheduled to return to her homeport and, accordingly, proceeded to Subic Bay to unload ammunition. A few days later, while the carrier was in port at Yokosuka, word was received that she was to return to the Gulf of Tonkin and remain in the war zone for an indefinite period. In fact, *Coral Sea* did not return to Alameda until 1 November, after setting a new duration record for deployment by a USN carrier: 331 days.

On the second day of the fourth line period, which began on 24 June and ended on 23 July, CVW-15 lost its CAG, Cdr Peter Mongilardi, Jr, west of Tanh Hoa.[4] During the same line period, on 15 July, another CVW-15 pilot, Lt A

[4] Leading a three-aircraft armed reconnaissance mission, Cdr Mongilardi was apparently hit by 37mm fire at the start of a run on a small bridge. More than four months earlier, on 7 February, he had led *Coral Sea*'s first war mission. Then, during a Rolling Thunder sortie on 29 March when his A-4C received numerous AAA hits in the tail section, suffered a utility hydraulic failure, and was losing fuel rapidly, he had managed to reach the carrier only by tanking continuously until the final straight-in approach and trap. One month later, Cdr Mongilardi relinquished command of VA-153 to assume that of CVW-15 from Cdr Henry P Glindeman.

Maintenance personnel from VA-35 work on one of the Pratt and Whitney J52-P-8A turbojets from a Grumman A-6A. The tail markings of the Black Panthers from VA-35 are noteworthy. (Jerry Edwards)

Right: With Coral Sea on her way back to Alameda in June 1970, boxes cluttering her hangar deck now contain goods of a less belligerent nature: 'loot' accumulated by her crew during final R&R stays in Cubi Point on 3–4 June and in Sydney on 13–18 June. (Jerry Edwards)

The Skyhawks in this photograph taken in the South China Sea in April 1965 belong to the two light attack squadrons assigned to CVW-15 for the first war cruise aboard Coral Sea. *The aircraft on the left is an A-4C of VA-153, that on the right an A-4E of VA-155. During that cruise the* Blue Tail Flies *of VA-153 lost six A-4Cs, including that flown on 25 June 1965 by CAG Peter Mongilardi, while the* Silver Foxes *of VA-155 lost five A-4Es.* (Don J Willis)

J Bennett of VA-153, was shot down by North Vietnamese AAA on 15 July but was rescued by a USN destroyer.

Notwithstanding her combat losses, *Coral Sea* was awarded the Admiral Flatley Memorial Award for Aviation Safety for Fiscal Year 1965 (1 July 1964 to 30 June 1965). This award was particularly meaningful as CVA-43 had been operating on a war footing for five months during that Fiscal Year and its crew had handled thousands of combat sorties.

From 24 July until 11 August, *Coral Sea* and her crew were given a well-deserved rest, including R&R in Hong Kong. During the next 30-day line period (nine of which were spent on Dixie Station, the only time during combat operations when CVA-43 was not on Yankee Station), *Coral Sea* logged her 100th underway replenishment (Unrep)[5] of the cruise. More importantly, her CVW-15 lost seven aircraft and four pilots: Cdr Harry E Thomas of VA-153 and Lt (jg) Edward B Shaw of VA-165 were killed in action, Lt (jg) Charles B Goodwin of VFP-63 was reported missing after his RF-8A failed to return from a night photo-reconnaissance sortie over North Vietnam, and LCdr Wendell B Rivers was taken prisoner of war.

The sixth and final line period of *Coral Sea*'s first war deployment began on 1 October and lasted only fourteen days. In spite of its short duration, it was quite notable. On 6 October, LCdr Dan MacIntyre and Lt (jg) Alan Johnson, the pilot and RIO of a F-4B from VF-151 *Vigilantes*, shot down a MiG-17 with an AIM-17D Sparrow. Although this air combat victory was confirmed, news about it was not released for several years; apparently, it had been scored over Chinese territory and the victim was likely to have been an aircraft belonging not to the Vietnam People's Air Force but to the Air Force of the People's Liberation Army, the air force of the allegedly neutral People's Republic of China.

During the same period CVW-15 lost two more aircraft to AAA fire and one in an operational accident; fortunately, all pilots were recovered. Last to be hit, Lt Jack Terhune was forced to abandon his crippled VF-154 Crusader before reaching *Coral Sea*. Closely watched by his wingman, Lt James Glinn, and by Lt (jg) Al Zink, an RF-8A pilot of VFP-63, Lt Terhune safely ejected—the whole procedure being spectacularly recorded by the RF-8A's cameras—and

[5] During her first 100 Unreps (50 times from oilers, 35 times from ammunition ships, 11 times from stores ships, and four times from general cargo ships), CVA-43 received 18,940,669 US gallons (71,696,726 litres) of fuel oil, 11,508,442 gallons (43,563,277 litres) of JP-5, 1,052,979 gallons (3,985,875 litres) of avgas, and over 3000 tons (2720 tonnes) of ordnance.

BuNo 147899 is ready for launch on the No 1 catapult. The missile on the fuselage pylon is an AIM-9B Sidewinder. The name of Lt Ronald E McKeown, the pilot who made the 150,000th arrested landing aboard Coral Sea, is painted on the cockpit's sill. However, for the benefit of readers unfamiliar with operational practices, it should be pointed out that this does not necessarily indicate that Ron McKeown was in the cockpit when this photograph was taken as a carrier pilot flies whatever aircraft is available, not just that bearing his name. (Don J Willis)

was recovered by a UH-2 Seasprite of the carrier's HU-1 Det 1 Unit E. On a more positive side, *Coral Sea* set a new record for the numer of arrested landings when on 2 October 1965, Lt Ronald E McKeown[6] made the 150,000th trap aboard CVA-43 in an F-8D of VF-154 while returning from a combat sortie over the North.

After unloading ammunition at Subic Bay on 16 October, *Coral Sea* reached her homeport sixteen days later. During her record 331-day deployment, she had been at sea for 245 days and had steamed 105,000 nautical miles (195,000km). Her CVW-15 had flown over 10,800 combat sorties, participated in 160 major strikes, dropped over 6000 tons (5450 tonnes) of ordnance, and recorded over 16,500 launches. Eight of her aircrew had been killed, one pilot was missing in action, and two had been taken prisoner of war. One of her A-3Bs, two of her A-1Hs, three of her RF-8As, six F-8Ds, and eleven of her A-4Cs and A-4Es had been lost in combat and operational accidents. For their first war cruise, *Coral Sea* and CVW-15 were awarded a Navy Unit Commendation for 'exceptionally meritorious service' and CVW-15 personnel won over 1000 medals, including one Navy Cross, four Silver Stars, seventeen Distinguished Flying Crosses, and five Purple Hearts.

[6] On 23 May 1972, not quite seven years later, by which time he was a LCdr, and was flying F-4Bs with VF-161 aboard *Midway* (CVA-41), Ron McKeown gained greater reknown by shooting down two MiG-17s.

The Second War Cruise, 29 July 1966 to 23 February 1967

Needing much attention after her long combat cruise, *Coral Sea* entered the San Francisco Naval Shipyard at Hunters Point on 22 November 1965 for repairs (including replacement of a turbine) and testing until the end of April 1966. Refresher training, carrier qualifications, and exercises kept CVA-43 busy until 29 July when Capt Frank W Ault, who had relieved Capt Cassell and assumed command on 18 February, and his crew sailed the carrier from Alameda for her second war cruise. This time the air wing was CVW-2 with two fighter squadrons flying Phantom IIs, two light attack squadrons with Skyhawks, an attack squadron with Skyraiders, a tanker detachment equipped with A-3Bs, a reconnaissance detachment with RF-8Gs, an airborne early warning detachment with new Grumman E-2As, and a helicopter detachment with Seasprites. After arriving in the war zone, CVW-2s capabilities were further strengthened

This tanker-configured A-3B, one of the aircraft assigned to VAH-2 Det A during the 1966-67 cruise, was photographed during a stopover at Da Nang Air Base in South Vietnam. The Tracker parked forward of the Skywarrior is an S-2E of VS-35 which normally operated from the deck of USS Yorktown *(CVS-10).* (Robert C Mikesh)

Below: The Fighting Redcocks *of VA-22 first went to war aboard USS* Midway *(CVA-41) and then went aboard* Coral Sea *for their second war cruise. This A-4C, with 'USS CORAL SEA' painted on its rear fuselage, was photographed at NAS Lemoore, the home for all light attack squadrons of the Pacific Fleet.* (Peter B Lewis)

by the addition during line periods of an ECM detachment equipped with EA-1Fs.

After undergoing ORI in Hawaiian waters, making port calls in Pearl Harbor and Yokosuka, and loading ammunition and supplies at Subic Bay, *Coral Sea* departed the Philippines on 26 August to join TF 77 in the Gulf of Tonkin. However, the loss of a blade on the number 3 screw during transit caused a two-week delay while she was dry-docked for repairs in Yokosuka prior to relieving her sistership, *Franklin D. Roosevelt* (CVA-42), and joining *Constellation* (CVA-64) and *Intrepid* (CVS-11) on Yankee Station on 12 September.

Combat operations began the next day, but strikes flown against North Vietnamese LOCs and supply facilities proved uneventful. The following day, however, *Coral Sea* lost her first aircraft to a SAM when an A-1H of VA-25 was brought down as it crossed the coast during an armed reconnaissance over RP III. The pilot, Cdr C W Stoddard, was apparently hit and died in the crash of his aircraft. Thereafter, as *Coral Sea* remained on the line for thirty-eight consecutive days, losses mounted rapidly. Eight aircraft were shot down between 17 September and 12 October; three crew members were taken prisoner of war, three were killed, two were reported missing, and two were recovered. In addition, an A-3B was lost in a catapult launch accident on 2 October but, fortunately, its four crew members were recovered.

Preceded by ten days at Subic Bay, where repairs were made to the machinery and aircraft elevators, the second period on the line began on 30 October and lasted until 4 December. For most of these seven weeks, CVW-2 shared responsibility for combat operations over the North with CVW-1, which was embarked aboard *Franklin D. Roosevelt* (CVA-42), CVW-14 aboard *Ticonderoga* (CVA-14), and CVW-15 aboard *Constellation* (CVA-64). Activities were less hectic than they had been earlier in the fall and, consequently, losses were lighter. Nevertheless, Lt (jg) W T Arnold of VA-22 was killed on 17 November when his A-4C crashed, and the pilot and RIO of a Phantom II from VF-154 were taken prisoner of war on 2 December. The crew of another F-4B lost to enemy action on 3 November and the pilot of a Skyhawk lost in a mid-air collision on 11 November were recovered.

Once more in need of repairs, *Coral Sea* returned to Subic Bay on 6 December and then went to Hong Kong where the crew enjoyed the Christmas holidays. On the way back to Yankee Station, *Coral Sea* lost an A-4C which was being launched for a test hop on 27 December, but the lucky *Fighting Redcock* was quickly recovered from the China Sea waters.

Arriving the next day in the Gulf of Tonkin, *Coral Sea* found *Kitty Hawk* and *Enterprise* on station and all were joined by *Ticonderoga* on 4 January 1967. Following the Christmas and New Year interludes, *Rolling Thunder* operations began with a new fury on 2 January when Air Force fighters shot down seven MiG-21s during Operation Bolo and carrier aircraft renewed their offensive against lines of communications. Although the Air Force success against the MiGs substantially reduced the air threat, strike aircraft still had to contend with formidable defenses. During 1966, the North Vietnamese had increased the number of SAM sites from 87 to 151 and the number of radar installations from 130 to 389. Particularly significant was the fact that seven out of ten new radar installations were AAA fire control radars. The results were soon evident to all: *Coral Sea* alone lost four aircraft (a Phantom and three Skyhawks) to North Vietnamese guns in eleven days during operations against road and rail targets in RP II and RP III. On 4 January, Lt (jg) J M Hays of VA-22 and Lt A M Van Pelt and Ens R A Morris of VF-154, who managed to get feet wet before being forced to eject, were rescued by Navy helicopters. Less fortunate, Lt (jg) M P Cronin of VA-23 was taken prisoner of war on 13 January and two days later Lt (jg) D H Moran, Jr, another VA-23 pilot, ejected over the Gulf but was dead from flak wounds when recovered by a helicopter.

Although heavy operations took place during a break in the monsoon weather between 19 and 23 January, CVW-2 suffered no further losses prior to the carrier's departure from the line on 31 January. Released by TF 77 on 16 February, *Coral Sea* proceeded back home after off loading ammunition and supplies at Subic Bay and stopping for nine days in Yokosuka. The carrier's second combat deployment, for which she received another Navy Unit Commendation, was completed when she moored at Alameda on 23 February 1967.

The usual post deployment refit, CarQuals and refresher training activities then kept *Coral Sea* close to home for five months. During that period, a change of command ceremony held on 18 March while she was in the San Francisco Naval Shipyard at Hunters Point saw Capt William H Shawcross relieve Capt Ault as Commanding Officer.

The Third War Cruise, 26 July 1967 to 6 April 1968

Again teamed with CVW-15, *Coral Sea* departed Alameda on 26 July 1968 for Hawaiian waters where ORI was conducted before joining the Seventh Fleet on 10 August. Nine days later, while CVA-43 was sailing between Yokosuka and Subic Bay prior to going on the line, LCdr F H Gates was killed when his A-1H crashed while attempting to land on board the carrier after having experienced engine troubles.

The first combat related loss incurred during that cruise was recorded on 29 August when an A-4E of VA-153 failed to pull up during a bombing attack against the Nhan Thap cave storage in RP II and its pilot, Lt M J Allard, was killed. The next day, VA-25 lost one of its Skyraiders during a strike against water-borne logistic craft but its pilot, Lt (jg) L E Gardiner, was recovered.

The penultimate day of the month also saw TF 77 carriers (*Coral Sea*, *Constellation*, and *Oriskany*) mount a major effort to isolate Haiphong from the rest of North Vietnam. Although the targeted railroad and highway bridges in and around Haiphong were protected by heavy flak concentration, numerous SAM batteries and MiG-17 protective patrols, Skyhawk pilots from VA-153 and VA-155 succeeded in cutting a highway bridge and damaging two other bridges on 18 September and a couple of days later tore up a fourth rail and highway bridge in Haiphong while Phantom crews from VF-151 and VF-161 kept the MiGs away from the strike aircraft. The only aircraft loss during this offensive was an RF-8G from VFP-63 Det 43 which was hit by AAA near the Kien An highway bridge during a Blue Tree damage-assessment reconnaissance sortie on 21 September. LCdr M H Vescelius, ejected but was taken prisoner of war. Earlier during this line period, CVW-15 crews had inflicted heavy damage to marine installations in Cam Pha, North Vietnam's third largest port.

The second line period lasted only fifteen days but was marked by two operational accidents: *Coral Sea* damaged her two starboard aircraft elevators in a collision with the ammunition ship *Mount Katmai* (AE-16) during underway replenishment on 18 October and one week later almost became the third TF 77 carrier to experience a catastrophic fire when a Zuni rocket ignited accidentally during a routine test on deck. Fortunately, only nine sailors suffered burns and damage was light. For CVW-15, the period was equally traumatic as four of its Naval Aviators were taken prisoner, a fifth died in captivity, and a sixth was killed when the controls of his A-4E locked after being damaged due to ordnance malfunction during a rocket attack against a storage area in RP VIB. In addition, on 23 October only one crew member could be rescued when an SH-3A of HS-6, the ASW helicopter squadron embarked aboard *Kearsarge* (CVS-33), settled into the water after one of its blades struck the ship during cross-deck operation aboard *Coral Sea*. However, this two-week period also provided CVW-15 and *Coral Sea* with a chance to gain the first 'PT boat ace' and attack a worthwhile target, the Phuc Yen Air Base. The first of these events took place on 21 October when LCdr W P Cook, who had previously sunk another PT boat, was credited with the destruction of four of the six P-4 fast attack craft which he and his *Silver Foxes* wingman had surprised at dawn just off Thanh Hoa harbor.

Bearing sixty-three missions marks and the name 'Cdr W H Harris', as well as the words 'COMMANDER ATTACK CARRIER AIRWING TWO' on its mid fuselage, the CAG bird of VA-23 was photographed at NAS China Lake, California, on 16 March 1967 after Coral Sea *had returned from her second war cruise.* (Peter B Lewis)

Long requested by pilots and senior commanders alike, the coordinated Air Force/Navy operation against Phuc Yen Air Base, the main MiG base located 11 miles (18km) north of Hanoi, was finally authorized by Washington and

began on 24 October. During Alpha strikes against that airfield, CVW-15 lost two Phantoms and one Skyhawk (the crews of which were among the prisoners of war mentioned above) to SAMs, while CVW-16, *Oriskany*'s air wing, lost three A-4Es and the Air Force an F-105D. Bombing results were satisfactory but runway, taxiway and revetments were quickly repaired by the North Vietnamese as the Johnson Administration did not authorize follow-on strikes, thus enabling the MiGs to return to Phuc Yen only a few days

Taken on 28 September 1967, toward the end of the first line period of the third war cruise, this photograph shows an A-1H from VA-25 and a pair of F-4Bs from VF-151 ready for a midday launch. Other aircraft on the deck of Coral Sea are four A-4Es from VA-153 and VA-155, three KA-3Bs from VAH-2 Det 43, and an EA-1F from VAW-13. (US Navy)

after they had sought sanctuary in China.

Leaving Yankee Station on 27 October, *Coral Sea* went to Subic Bay where in less than six days her damaged elevators were repaired. However, this Philippine interlude was curtailed as the carrier and her escort were forced out to sea by an approaching typhoon. While *Coral Sea* was on her way to R&R in Hong Kong, two Seasprites from HC-1 Det 43 saved thirty-seven Chinese crew members from the freighter *Loyal Fortunes* which had been grounded on Pratas Reef, some 170 miles (315km) southeast of the Crown Colony.

Coordinated Rolling Thunder missions, Alpha strikes, and armed reconnaissance sorties were flown over the North, mainly in RP VIB, while *Coral Sea* remained on Yankee Station for twenty-six days between 12 November and 7 December. Again North Vietnamese defenses took a heavy toll as CVW-15 lost another four aircraft. The first of these losses occurred on the fifth day on the line when a F-4B of VF-151 ran into a barrage of four SA-2 missiles (the *Vigilantes* ejected and were taken prisoner) as it was providing flak support for a strike against the Hai Duong rail bridge while other aircraft were bombing a newly authorized target, the Haiphong Shipyard. The next day, Cdr W D McGrath and Lt R G Emrich were killed in the crash of their VF-161 Phantom near Hanoi after they either stalled and spun out of control or were caught in a heavy AAA barrage while taking SAM evasive maneuvers below 6000ft (1800m). Two more F-4Bs were lost on 19 November when a VF-151 section providing TarCAP for a strike near Haiphong was jumped by several MiG-17s. The lead aircraft, flown by LCdr C D Clower and Lt (jg) W O Estes II, had its right wing blown off by an AA-2 air-to-air missile and the wingman aircraft, flown by Lt (jg) J E Teague and Lt (jg) T G Stier, was either gunned down by a MiG or flew into debris from the lead aircraft. All four crew members were initially listed as missing in action but, in fact, they had been taken prisoner and were released in 1973. During this line period, CVW-15 also lost one of its squadron commanders; Cdr W H Searfus drowned when he could not get out from his sinking A-4E which had been blown off *Coral Sea*'s deck by the jet blast of another aircraft.

Preceded by six days in Subic Bay and straddling the year end holidays, the fourth line period saw *Coral Sea* on Yankee Station from 17 December until 6 January for intensive operations, with three Alpha strikes being flown each day, when weather permitted, against North Vietnamese LOCs and ammunition and fuel storage complexes. First to be lost during this period was LCdr Cook, the VA-155's 'PT boat ace'. Flying an armed reconnaissance sortie along Route 67 in the North Vietnamese panhandle near Vinh on 22 December, LCdr Cook safely ejected from his A-4E after his aircraft was damaged by the blast of its own Mk 82 bombs following a shallow dive and low pull out during an attack against a pontoon bridge. The crew of the SAR helicopter found him near the wreckage of his Sky-

This dusk recovery scene symbolizes Crusader operations on Yankee Station. During the first war cruise of Coral Sea, *VF-154 flew F-8Ds while VFP-63 Det Delta had RF-8As. For the next six cruises the only Crusaders aboard CVA-43 were RF-8Gs from VFP-63 detachments.* (US Navy by courtesy of Captain Joseph J Frick)

hawk; unfortunately, he was dead from massive head injuries caused by bomb fragments. More fortunate were the pilot and RIO of a VF-61 Phantom who successfully ejected and were recovered at sea after their aircraft was hit by 37mm fire during a weather reconnaissance sortie near Cam Pha on 29 December 1967.

Taking advantage of the 24-hour Christmas truce, the North Vietnamese immediately sent a stream of trucks down the Ho Chi Minh Trail to bring in supplies for their planned Tet Offensive. This move, however, had been anticipated and at the end of the truce Air Force and Navy aircraft struck in force, CVW-15 alone being credited with the destruction of at least 455 trucks.

During the last weeks of 1967 and, following a 36-hour New Year truce, the first weeks of 1968, pre-emptive Alpha strikes were flown against targets in Hanoi, Haiphong and Thanh Hoa by aircraft from *Coral Sea*, *Kitty Hawk*, and *Oriskany* and heavy vehicle losses were inflicted on the North Vietnamese. Nevertheless, the Communists went ahead with their planning for a major offensive south of the DMZ, thus causing a change of venue for most of the next line period.

Off the line for only nine days, during which Subic Bay and Hong Kong were again visited, *Coral Sea* arrived back on Yankee Station on 16 January. Taking advantage of a break in the unusually heavy northeast monsoon, CVW-15 flew Alpha strikes against the Dong Phong Thuong railroad and highway bridge on the 18th and 19th and against the infamous Than Hoa bridge on the 28th. Skyhawks scored hits with 2000lb (907kg) bombs but failed to destroy this stubborn target. An unrelated combat loss was recorded on 25 January when a *Blue Tail Flies* A-4E was shot down by a SAM while attacking coastal batteries at Cuong Gian which had taken HMAS *Perth* under fire. The pilot, Cdr Woolcock, ejected and was recovered at sea by a USN helicopter.

After the first war cruise, the E-1Bs from the Early Eleven *of VAW-11 Det Delta were replaced aboard* Coral Sea *by E-2As. For the second war cruise the Hawkeyes were those from VAW-11 Det Alpha while those taken aboard for the third, fourth, and fifth cruises were operated by the* Sun Kings *of VAW-116. Tracers came back on board for the sixth and seventh war cruises when they were flown and maintained by VAW-111 Det 4 (note Det 4 inscription on the nose gear door of this E-1B.)* (US Navy by courtesy of Captain Joseph J Frick)

As weather to the north continued to worsen, CVW-15 turned its attention to South Vietnam where major Communist infiltrations were reported in I Corps near Lang Vei and Khe Sanh. Notwithstanding air support provided by aircraft from *Coral Sea*, ground fighting south of the DMZ became increasingly heavy. Finally on 29 January, during the first night of the Tet cease-fire, the North Vietnamese launched their powerful offensive with uncoordinated attacks against Da Nang and Pleiku. During the next night, thirty-six of the forty-four South Vietnamese provincial capitals, sixty-four of the 242 district capitals, and twenty-three airfields came under fire as the Tet Offensive gained tempo.

Initially USAF, USMC, and VNAF operations were impaired by Communist attacks against airfields in South Vietnam and the Navy was called to provide air support

A destroyer stands plane guard off the stern of Coral Sea *as an A-1H from VA-25 comes in for recovery aboard the carrier following air operations over North Vietnam during the line period which began on 16 January 1968. All ordnance have been expended and the only external store is a centerline tank.* (US Navy)

Right: The last Navy Skyraider attack sorties were flown by the Fist of the Fleet *of VA-25 on 20 February 1968 during the last day on the line before* Coral Sea *returned to Alameda at the end of her third war cruise. The venerable 'Spad', however, was far from disappearing from the Southeast Asian scene. Navy EA-1Fs, were flown by VAQ-33 Det 11 from Yankee Station until December 1968; the 1st Special Operations Squadron, 56th Special Operations Wing, USAF, flew A-1s until the end of 1972; and, finally, the VNAF flew its last Skyraider sorties as the Republic of Vietnam collapsed in the spring of 1975.* (US Navy)

for the hard pressed ground forces. The timing, however, was bad. On 23 January, *Enterprise* (CVAN-65) and her screen had been detached to a Task Group in the Sea of Japan for possible operations against North Korea following the seizure by that nation of the USS *Pueblo* (AGER-2). Accordingly, instead of being released from the control of TF 77 at the end of January to return to California as scheduled, *Coral Sea* remained on the line until 20 February and her aircraft, alongside those of *Kitty Hawk* and *Ticonderoga*, took part in Operation Niagara in support of the besieged Marine garrison at Khe Sanh. CVW-15 incurred no losses during operations over South Vietnam but Lt (jg) J P Dunn was reported missing in action when, on 14 February, his A-1H was shot down by Chinese MiGs after straying too close to Hainan during a ferry flight from NAS Cubi Point in the Philippines.

Leaving the line on 20 February, *Coral Sea* remained under the operational control of ComSeventhFlt until 29 March and made port calls in Subic Bay and Sasebo, where Capt James Ferris relieved Capt Shawcross. She moored back at Alameda on 6 April 1968. During 132 days on the line, her aircraft had flown 11,328 combat and combat support sorties, nearly 10 per cent more than during the record length cruise in 1964–65.

The Fourth War Cruise, 7 September 1968 to 18 April 1969

After spending two months in the San Francisco Naval Shipyard at Hunters Point, *Coral Sea* remained in Californian waters until September 1968. During that time, she was used on 18 July for the carrier suitability trials of the F-4K, the Phantom II version for the Royal Navy, and on 23 and 24 July for those of the F-111B, the unsuccessful carrier

NL
39680

A Kaman UH-2C Seasprite landing on the forward portion of the angled deck during training operations off the Californian coast. The NL tail code and three-digit modex indicate that it belonged to HC-1 Det 9, the Pacific Fleet Angels' *detachment which was aboard* Coral Sea *for her fifth war cruise in 1969-70.*
(Jerry Edwards)

version of the General Dynamics variable geometry strike fighter.

For the fourth combat cruise of *Coral Sea*, CVW-15 packed a more potent punch following the substitution of the Intruder-equipped VA-52 for the Skyraider-equipped VA-25 and the conversion of VA-153 to the A-4F version of the Skyhawk. Conversely, heavy losses incurred during the previous $2\frac{1}{2}$ years by Navy Skyhawk squadrons forced the replacement of the *Silver Foxes*' A-4Es by the older A-4Cs of VA-216. For that cruise, CVW-15 also embarked two small Skywarrior detachments. One, equipped with EKA-3Bs, started the cruise as VAW-13 Det 43 but was redesignated VAQ-130 Det 43 on 1 October 1968. The other, with KA-3Bs, was furnished by VAH-10, the last operational HATRON.

Having left Alameda on 7 September, *Coral Sea* chopped to the Seventh Fleet on the 23rd and began combat operations on 10 October. By then, things were markedly quieter than when she had last been on the line, as President Johnson, on 31 March 1968, had ordered an end to bombing north of the 20th parallel as a concession opening the way to peace talks with the North Vietnamese. Operating against lines of communication in RP II and RP III alongside CVW-6 (*America*), CVW-10 (*Intrepid*), and CVW-21 (*Hancock*), CVW-15 found few lucrative targets to offset the loss of an A-6A and its crew to unknown causes during a night armed reconnaissance sortie on 13 October.

On the last day of this line period, 1 November, all bombing of North Vietnam was halted by Presidential order and thereafter air operations over the North were limited to photographic reconnaissance flights. Thus, when *Coral Sea* returned on the line after spending nine days in Subic Bay, CVW-15 aircraft divided their attention between South Vietnam and Laos prior to concentrating their efforts almost exclusively on LOCs in southern Laos. The only loss during that period was an A-4C from VA-216 which hit the water after a catapult launch at the start of a strike sortie on 21 November. Unfortunately, Cdr M J Naschek was lost in this crash.

Off the line from 9 to 29 December, the *Coral Sea* crew enjoyed an abbreviated Christmas holiday in Japan prior to returning to the Gulf of Tonkin to resume combat operations on the penultimate day of 1968. As poor weather and the New Year and Tet truce periods resulted in a curtailment of operations over Laos and South Vietnam, CVW-15 ended this line period by losing only one aircraft. A *Black Diamonds* A-4C was hit by light aimed automatic weapons during an armed reconnaissance sortie in Laos on 3 January 1969 and, after nursing his aircraft back to the China Sea, the pilot was forced to eject after the engine failed and was recovered.

Preceded by R&R in Singapore, the next line period, from 10 February to 3 March, was unfortunately costlier for CVW-15. Two A-4Cs from VA-216 were shot down over Laos on 14 February (one pilot was recovered and one reported missing in action), fatigue was suspected as the cause for the loss of a KA-3B and its three *Vikings* crew members during a tanking sortie on the 17th, and all four HC-1 crew members were recovered on the 21st when their UH-2C helicopter went down at sea after suffering a dual engine failure.

Less than six weeks after enjoying a week's stay in Singapore, the *Coral Sea* crew was treated to another period of R&R when CVA-43 spent six days in Hong Kong beginning on 12 March. After this luxury (frequent R&R periods were unknown during the previous three years, when the pace of operations had been frantic), the fifth and final line period of the cruise lasted but eleven days and was relatively uneventful. The only significant event occurred on 25 March when a *Vigilantes* F-4B was lost due to an engine failure and its crew recovered. Five days later, *Coral Sea* left the Gulf of Tonkin and, after stopping in Subic Bay and Yokosuka, reached Alameda on 18 April 1969.

This A-6A from VA-35 was photographed off the coast of California in August 1969 before the Black Panthers *deployed aboard* Coral Sea *as part of CVW-15. During the ensuing deployment, CVA-43's fifth war cruise, VA-35 primarily operated A-6As and KA-6Ds but also had a few of the rare A-6Cs. The only Intruder lost during this cruise was an A-6A which crashed into the sea on 26 December 1969.* (US Navy)

The Fifth War Cruise, 23 September 1969 to 1 July 1970

Upon taking office in January 1969, President Nixon confirmed the three-month old bombing halt imposed by his predecessor and five months later announced a plan progressively to withdraw US ground troops from Vietnam. Nonetheless, the need to maintain carriers on station in the Gulf of Tonkin remained and the grueling pace, keeping Pacific Fleet carriers in home waters for work-up cycles of less than six-month duration, continued unabated. For *Coral Sea*, this fast-paced turnaround schedule led to a brief reduced availability (RAV) period in the Puget Sound Naval Shipyard in Bremerton during the late spring of 1969, CarQuals and refresher training during the summer, and a departure from Alameda on 23 September. Once again, the air wing was CVW-15 with the previously embarked VF-151, VF-161, and VAW-116 and the familiar detachments from VFP-63 and HC-1. However, two Corsair II squadrons, VA-82 and VA-86, were substituted for the usual Skyhawk squadrons and VA-35 replaced VA-52 as the Intruder squadron.

On their way to the China Sea, *Coral Sea* and CVW-15 completed ORI in Hawaiian waters, made a port call in Yokosuka, and loaded ammunition in Subic Bay prior to starting the first of five line periods on 27 October 1969. The final period on the line ended on 1 June 1970, with sailors and aircrews getting a chance to unwind from 125 days spent in the Gulf of Tonkin during R&R in Hong Kong, Sasebo, Subic Bay and Yokosuka.

Throughout this less eventful deployment, air operations consisted mostly of ground support and road interdiction sorties against limited value targets in Laos and South Vietnam while operations over the North were restricted to reconnaissance flights. Consequently, as the enemy had not yet deployed heavy anti-aircraft guns or SAM batteries outside North Vietnam, CVW-15 only lost one aircraft to hostile fire during this combat cruise. Unfortunately, its VA-86 pilot, LCdr M G Hoff, failed to eject when his A-7A was hit during a strafing run against trucks in Laos on 7 January 1970. Operational losses, conversely, were much higher than in previous deployments: four A-7As, three F-4Bs, one A-6B, and one E-2A were lost and only seven of their seventeen aircrews recovered.

On her way back to Alameda, *Coral Sea* made a detour to Sydney, where her crew enjoyed warm Australian hospitality during a five-day visit, prior to sailing back home on 1 July 1970. In spite of the growing sound and fury of antiwar protesters, the always joyous family reunions were made happier for the crew by the knowledge that much needed repairs and overhaul were going to keep CVA-43 at the San Francisco Bay Naval Shipyard for nine months. After that, short at-sea periods for training and CarQuals off the coast of California kept the ship and her crew out of the war for another eight months. Moreover, in the fall of 1971 hopes were high that peace talks in Paris would result in a quick ending of the war. This was not to be the case and the cruise which started when *Coral Sea* departed Alameda on 12 November 1971 proved more demanding and costlier than the previous two.

An F-4B of VF-161 is being readied for launch during operations in February 1970. The Chargers of VF-161 went to war in 1966 aboard USS Constellation *(CVA-64), then made three war cruises aboard USS* Coral Sea *(CVA-43), and ended the war with two cruises aboard USS* Midway *(CVA-41).* (Jerry Edwards)

The Sixth War Cruise, 12 November 1971 to 17 July 1972

Although CVW-15 was on board when *Coral Sea* sailed for the South China Sea, only the EKA-3Bs of VAQ-135 and the RF-8Gs of VFP-63 had been part of the previous deployment. HC-1 was still supplying the helicopter detachment flying plane guard and SAR sorties, but it had traded its UH-2Cs for Sikorsky SH-3Gs. The E-2As of VAW-116 had given place to older and less capable E-1Bs flown by a VAW-111 detachment as Hawkeyes were in short supply. More importantly, all five fighter and attack squadrons were new to the air wing as the F-4Bs of the *Vigilantes* and *Chargers* were replaced by those of VF-51 and VF-111, the A-7As of the *Marauders* and *Sidewinders* by the A-7Es of VA-22 and VA-94, and the A-6As of the *Black Panthers* by the A-6As, A-6Bs and KA-6Ds of a Marine squadron, VMA(AW)-224. Notwithstanding these numerous changes, CVW-15 was combat ready when on 14 December *Coral Sea* arrived once again on Yankee Station.

As had been the case when she had last been on the line more than eighteen months earlier, strike emphasis was still placed on interdiction sorties in Laos. The tactical situation, however, had changed. In October 1971, the North Vietnamese had begun to deploy pairs of MiGs to Bai Thuong, Quan Lang, and Vinh from where they posed a threat to strike aircraft operating over the Laotian panhandle. Additionally, protective reaction strikes were flown more frequently to take out North Vietnamese SAM and AAA batteries firing against US reconnaissance aircraft flying over the North.

Commencing on 15 December, interdiction sorties along the Laotian sections of the Ho Chi Minh Trail and occasional strikes in support of ARVN troops in South Vietnam kept CVW-15 busy, especially so as *Enterprise*

(CVAN-65) and her screen had left the line on the 10th to proceed to the Indian Ocean as a show of force during the Indo-Pakistani war. With *Coral Sea* remaining in the Gulf of Tonkin through the year-end holidays, her A-6As and A-7Es joined those from *Constellation* (CVA-64) in flying 423 Proud Deep sorties between 26 and 30 December as part of the major Air Force/Navy response to increased North Vietnamese opposition to US reconnaissance activities designed to uncover preparations for the anticipated Communist offensive against the South. Two Intruders, one from each carrier, were lost to SAMs on 30 December; the Marine pilot and the BN of the *Coral Sea* aircraft were taken prisoner, the pilot from the *Constellation* aircraft was killed, but his BN was recovered by a Navy SAR helicopter.

Interspersed with infrequent air support sorties over South Vietnam and occasional retaliatory strikes over the beginning of March. Returning on the line on 2 March to take part in stepped-up interdiction efforts, *Coral Sea* spent thirteen eventful days on the line. Her air wing lost an F-4B on 3 March (the aircraft's controls failed during a BarCAP sortie but the two *Screaming Eagles* were recovered) and three days later obtained its second air combat victory during a photo-reconnaissance mission of Quang Lang airfield. Flying one of two VF-111 Phantom IIs assigned ForCAP, Lt Garry Weigand and Lt (jg) Bill Freckelton surprised a MiG-17 making a gun pass at their flight leader as they were flying west of Vinh Son and shot it down with a Sidewinder. This was but a foretaste of things to come as the long awaited Communist offensive was launched on the night of 29–30 March, six days after *Coral Sea* had returned from a brief upkeep period in Subic Bay.

When the offensive was launched, led by six NVA

The Black Ravens *of VAQ-135 went on their first deployment in September 1969 when they embarked aboard* Coral Sea. *They were back aboard CVA-43 for two more war cruises and before the war ended also sent EKA-3B detachments aboard USS* Kitty Hawk *(CVA-63) and USS* Hancock *(CVA-19). This EKA-3B of VAQ-135 Det 3 was photographed at NAS Alameda, California, where the squadron was commissioned in May 1969 and where it was based when ashore.* (Peter B Lewis)

the North, interdiction missions in Laos were the main contribution made by CVW-15 to the diminishing US war effort in Southeast Asia during the 'calm before the storm' period which prevailed in January and February 1972. For *Coral Sea* there were no aircraft combat losses during the first nine weeks of the year but two of her A-7Es were lost in operational accidents on 18 January and 4 February. In the former incident, the *Shrikes* pilot was recovered and, in the latter, the *Fighting Redcocks* pilot was killed.

Although an ominous increase in North Vietnamese infiltration and logistic stockpiling had been detected, an anticipated Communist offensive during the Tet holiday did not materialize and a period of relative calm prevailed until

divisions, TF 77 had only *Coral Sea* and *Hancock* on the line as *Constellation* and *Kitty Hawk* were respectively in Japan and the Philippines. Moreover, the Air Force had by then reduced its tactical inventory in Thailand and South

Vietnam to barely 370 aircraft, all USMC aircraft had been withdrawn from the theater, and the VNAF attack aircraft inventory had reached the 200-aircraft level for the first time. Consequently, CVW-15's sixty-eight fighter and attack aircraft (twenty-six Corsairs, twenty-five Phantoms, and seventeen Intruders) represented a significant portion of the force available to help repulse the NVA and were immediately thrown into the fray, initially concentrating their attacks on enemy troops and vehicles in South Vietnam.

While air operations in direct support of South Vietnamese and US forces were much needed, full containment of the enemy offensive could only be achieved by striking back against the North Vietnamese logistics network. Accordingly, as part of Operation Freedom Train which began on 5 April, US aircraft were again allowed to strike targets in North Vietnam south of the 19th parallel and to attack selected targets further north. Then, respectively on 9 and 10 April, President Nixon authorized Operation Pocket Money, the mining campaign against major North Vietnamese ports, and Operation Linebacker I, the major offensive against North Vietnam. For CVW-15, this meant an all-out effort during which fifty consecutive days were spent on the line, two enemy aircraft destroyed, seven of its aircraft lost in combat and one in an operational accident.

Right: A pair of Grumman A-6As from VMA-(AW)-224 flies over Coral Sea *during operations on the line on 8 March 1972. For this cruise, the Marine squadron had a few A-6Bs and KA-6Ds. Marine All-Weather Attack Squadron 224 took part in Operation Freedom Train, the strikes launched to blunt the North Vietnamese 1972 spring offensive, Operation Pocket Money, the sowing of mines in the approaches to Haiphong Harbor and other North Vietnamese ports, and in Linebacker I, the major air offensive launched against North Vietnam in May 1972.* (US Navy)

Below: With sharkmouth markings under the nose and a red and white sunburst on the tail, the F-4Bs of VF-111 were among the most colorful aircraft flying combat sorties over North Vietnam. This aircraft, BuNo 153019, was the aircraft flown by Lt Garry L Weigand and Lt (jg) William C Freckelton when they shot down a MiG-17 on 6 March 1972. (Peter B Lewis)

As soon as operations over North Vietnam were once again authorized, CVW-15 not only continued flying interdiction sorties over Laos and sorely needed sorties in support of allied forces in Military Regions One and Two but also joined other Navy and Air Force aircraft flying armed reconnaissance and strike missions over the North against increasingly significant targets, including power plants and factories. In addition, at the onset of Operation Pocket Money, CAG Roger Sheets led three A-6As from VMA(AW)-224 and six A-7Es from VA-94 to initiate the mining campaign by sowing thirty-two Mk 52-2s with 72-hour arming delays in the outer channel of Haiphong Harbor. Beginning on 11 May, mine-sowing missions were extended to include additional ports, as well as river mouths and coastal waters.

During this busy line period no *Coral Sea* aircraft were lost over South Vietnam but one of its A-6As was shot down by 37mm fire during a dusk armed reconnaissance sortie in the Steel Tiger area in Laos (the pilot was recovered but the BN was reported missing in action) and six other aircraft failed to return from missions over the North. Five of these losses were caused by SAMs: two A-7Es and an A-6A were downed during armed reconnaissance sorties just north of the DMZ, an A-7E went down while providing flak support for an Iron Hand mission in the same area, and another A-7E was hit during an Alpha strike in the Haiphong area (two of the Naval Aviators crewing these aircraft were recovered, two were killed, one was reported missing in action, and one prisoner of war). The other loss over North Vietnam occurred on 27 April 1972 when Lt Molinare and LCdr Souder were taken prisoner of war after their F-4B was hit by an air-to-air missile while flying CAP near Bai Thuong.

During May, when faced with increased pressure threatening their ability to continue their offensive in South Vietnam, the North Vietnamese committed their air force in a futile attempt to inflict heavy losses to US strike aircraft. The results were quite the opposite as Navy and Air Force fighters respectively shot down sixteen and eleven MiGs. Two of these US victories were obtained by *Screaming Eagles*; flying from *Coral Sea*, Cdr Jerry Houston and Lt

Kevin Moore claimed a MiG-17 on 6 May and Lt Ken Cannon and Lt Roy Morris did so on 10 May.

Even though the urgency of the situation required maximum effort for seven weeks, thus increasing crew fatigue and the risk of accident, the only operational loss during this line period was that of an SH-3G from *Coral Sea*'s HC-1 Det 6 which crashed while attempting a night landing aboard a missile cruiser, USS *Providence* (CLG-6), on 8 May. Five of the eight crew members of this HC-1 Det 6 helicopter were recovered. Three days later *Coral Sea* left the Gulf of Tonkin and proceeded first to Subic Bay for some urgently needed upkeep and then to Hong Kong for a well deserved R&R week.

The fifth line period, which began on 23 May and during which *Coral Sea* extracted a heavy price from the North Vietnamese for their aggression in the South, was also costly for CVW-15. An A-7E from VA-94 was shot down by a SAM after launching a pair of Shrike anti-radiation missiles during an Iron Hand mission near Haiphong on 24 May, an A-6A from VMA(AW)-224 was hit by light AAA during a strike against the Uong Bi railroad yard on 29 May, and another Intruder from the Marine squadron was brought down near Nam Dinh by guns from the AAA battery it was bombing on 11 June. The crews from the first two aircraft were recovered but the pilot of the third, Capt Wilson, was reported missing in action while his BN, Capt Angus, was taken prisoner.

On the last day of that line period—10 June according to the deployment schedule which uses CONUS dates but actually 11 June as the Gulf of Tonkin is on the other side of the International Date Line—two VF-51 crews, Cdr 'Tooter' Teague and Lt Ralph Howell and Lt Winston Copeland and Lt Don Bouchoux, shot down a pair of MiG-17s, bringing *Coral Sea*'s wartime score to six MiGs. Her 2.0:1 kill ratio, however, was disappointing as it trailed that achieved by both the USAF (2.17:1) and the Navy (3.93:1 overall and 6.0:1 in fighter-vs-fighter combat).

The sixth and final line period of the cruise lasted nine days during which CVW-15 aircraft flew mainly against targets in the North as the need for Navy tactical air attack sorties in South Vietnam had decreased markedly after the Air Force had beefed up its strength in Southeast Asia as part of the Constant Guard deployment. For *Coral Sea*, these last days on the line were marred by the loss of an A-7E pilot from VA-22 on 25 June when Lt Shumway apparently flew into the ground while attacking parked trucks in RP III.

A-7Es from VA-94 took part with A-6As from VMA-(AW)-224 in the first Pocket Money mission on 9 May 1972 when they sowed mines in the outer channel of Haiphong Harbor. This A-7E was photographed at NAAS Fallon on 25 July 1971 when the Mighty Shrikes *of VA-94 and other CVW-15 squadrons were training in preparation for their 1971-72 deployment to the Gulf of Tonkin.* (Peter B Lewis)

Below: Also photographed at NAAS Fallon on 25 July 1971, the CAG bird of VA-22 has its rudder adorned with stripes in the colors of each of the squadrons in CVW-15. During the 1971-72 cruise, the Fighting Redcocks *of VA-22 lost three A-7Es in combat and one in an operational accident. Three pilots were killed and one taken prisoner of war.* (Peter B Lewis)

To celebrate the end of a combat cruise, twenty-three CVW-15 aircraft (twelve Corsairs, six Phantoms, and five Intruders) fly a neat formation for the benefit of the crew looking up from the deck of CVA-43. An SH-3G from HC-1 is flying plane guard off the starboard side. (US Navy by courtesy of Captain Joseph J Frick)

Released by the Seventh Fleet on 11 July, *Coral Sea* proceeded directly back to Alameda where the exhausted ship complement and CVW-15 personnel were glad to arrive six days later. Although rumors of 'peace with honor' were beginning to sound believable, *Coral Sea* still had to prepare for yet another war cruise as the Paris peace talks were not proceeding as fast as expected. To that effect, CVA-43 went back to Hunters Point for repairs before starting a new cycle with refresher training (RefTra) and CarQuals in November and December and a holiday standdown at Alameda. Luckily, while *Coral Sea*'s sailors and Naval Aviators were enjoying the comforts of home, Linebacker II finally convinced the North Vietnamese to return to the negotiating table. All air operations against North Vietnam and over South Vietnam ceased on 27 January 1973. Nevertheless, *Coral Sea* was still needed in the Gulf of Tonkin and, with CVW-15 unchanged except for the replacement of VMA(AW)-224 by VA-95, departed Alameda on 9 March.

The Seventh and Final War Cruise, 9 March 1973 to 8 November 1973

When *Coral Sea* took her place on the line on 31 March, she joined *Constellation*, *Enterprise*, and *Ranger* which were already in the Gulf of Tonkin either on the Mine Logistics Carrier Station, supporting Task Force 78 ships taking part in Operation Endsweep, or further south at the relocated Yankee Station off the northern coast of South Vietnam, to fly combat support sorties over Laos and Cambodia.

Still demanding, operations were by then less risky and the tempo of activities much reduced since the previous war deployment. Line periods were shorter, and more frequent and longer inport periods were enjoyed by the *Coral Sea* crew in Subic Bay, Sasebo, and Hong Kong. More importantly, for the first time in eight years, CVA-43 lost no aircraft in combat. Finally, after Operation Endsweep and combat operations in Cambodia ended on 27 July and 15 August respectively, US involvement in an unpopular war was over. *Coral Sea*, however, spent another thirty-eight days on the line after the official ending of the war and showed the flag in the area prior to being released by TF 77 on 30 October 1973. A fast transit brought her back to Alameda on 8 November to enjoy thirteen months in and off California prior to departing for what was expected to be a routine peacetime deployment to WestPac.

NAVY
NL
NL
NL
NL
CORAL SEA

Once More in Anger

As *Coral Sea* lacked the facilities needed to maintain the sophisticated electronic equipment of the Grumman EA-6B and as VAQ-130, the last squadron to be equipped with Douglas EKA-3Bs, had stood down five months earlier, CVW-15 was forced to deploy without a tactical electronic warfare detachment when CVA-43 left Alameda on 5 December 1974. However, for the first peacetime cruise in ten years, CVW-15 was strengthened by the re-equipment of its two fighter squadrons with F-4Ns.

During the first three months of 1975, the military situation in South Vietnam and Cambodia deteriorated rapidly and soon it was obvious that Congress would not again authorize the use of US forces to bolster the Saigon and Phnom Penh governments. Instead, aerial evacuation plans were activated and Naval Aviation was called to provide air cover. During Operation Eagle Pull, the evacuation of American citizens, Cambodian officials and Third Country Nationals from Phnom Penh on 12 April, *Coral Sea* remained on standby status. A week later, however, CVA-43 was back on the line as she joined TF 76 in the waters off South Vietnam to provide air support for Operation Frequent Wind, the evacuation of Saigon, which ended when the South Vietnamese capital was overrun during the early morning of 29 April 1975.

Off the line after witnessing the sad end of the Republic of Vietnam, *Coral Sea* visited Singapore between 6 and 10 May and was on her way to Perth, Australia, when on 12 May the SS *Mayaguez*, a US-registered 10,776-ton container ship of Sea-Land Service, Inc., was seized by Khmer Rouge patrol boats while steaming in international waters some 60 nautical miles (110km) southwest of Democratic Kampuchea (Cambodia). Immediately, CVA-43 and her three destroyer escorts were diverted to take position in the Gulf of Siam while an Air Force/Marine rescue plan was organized in Thailand. On 15 May, as Marines fought the Khmer Rouge on the island of Koh Tang, CVW-15 launched two morning strikes, with A-7Es and A-6As covered by F-4Ns, against installations on the Cambodian mainland. The first resulted in the destruction of several North American T-28Ds of the Air Force of the Kampuchea Liberation Army on the Ream airfield and the other in that of an oil depot near Kompong Som. Later in the day, with the *Mayaguez* and her crew safely back with their Marine rescuers, the Southeast Asia War finally was over for the USS *Coral Sea*, her officers and sailors, and her air wing personnel. They arrived back in Alameda on 8 November 1975, nearly eleven years after CVA-43 first sailed to take her place on the line in the Gulf of Tonkin. The long and costly war was at last over.

This stern view of USS Coral Sea *(CVA-43) was taken on 9 December 1971 as she was approaching Cubi Point. After a two-day stay in the Philippines, the ship departed for Yankee Station where she reported as part of Task Group 77.6 on 14 December.* (US Navy by courtesy of Captain Joseph J Frick)

APPENDIX 1
Combat Cruises

All combat cruises made in the Gulf of Tonkin between 2 August 1964 and 15 August 1973 by fifteen attack carriers, two antisubmarine carriers operating in the attack role, and four antisubmarine carriers operating in the ASW role are summarized respectively in the first section (carriers operating in the attack role) and the second section (carriers operating in the ASW role) of the following listing. Data in each of these synopses include:

- carrier name,
- number of her Air Wing (CVW) or ASW Air Group (CVSG),
- dates of departure and return to her homeport,
- date when she was assigned to the operational control of Task Force 77 (in-chop date) and date when she was relieved from that control (out-chop),
- composition of her Air Wing or ASW Air Group,
- air combat victories obtained by her aircrews,
- aircraft combat losses, and
- aircraft operational losses.

NOTE: In the squadron listing provided for each attack carrier deployment, temporary detachments which cross-decked frequently—such as those by VAP-61 with RA-3Bs, VAQ-33 and VAW-13 with EA-1Fs, VQ-1 with EA-3Bs, HC-3 with CH-46Ds, HC-5 with UH-2Cs, and HC-7 with SH-3As and HH-3As—are not included as they were not permanent components of the assigned CVW.

Units of Task Force 77, as seen on 14 October 1967 from the bridge of USS Constellation *(CVA-64), are from left to right: the destroyer* George K. Mackenzie *(DD-836), the attack carrier USS* Oriskany *(CVA-34), the destroyer USS* Rogers *(DD-876), and the ammunition ship USS* Mount Katmai *(AE-16). In addition to aircraft of CVW-14, aircraft on the deck of* Constellation *includes two EA-1Fs from a VAW-13 detachment.* (US Navy)

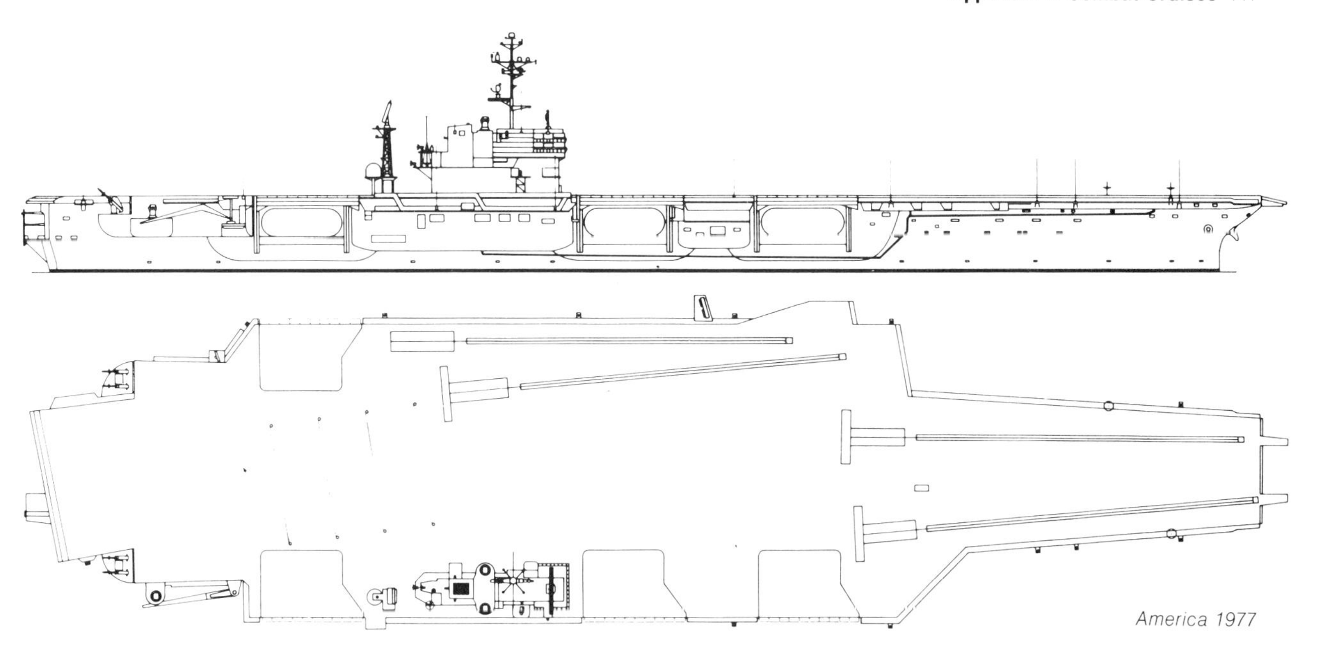

America 1977

Attack Carriers and Antisubmarine Carriers operating as Limited CVAs

USS *America* (CVA-66)

Air Wing: CVW-6

Homeport departure/return: Norfolk, 10 April 1968–16 December 1968

In-chop/out-chop: 12 May 1968–20 November 1968

On Line periods: 31 May 1968–27 June 1968; 7 July 1968–2 August 1968; 18 August 1968–11 September 1968; 28 September 1968–29 October 1968
Total: 112 days on the line

Squadrons:

VF-33	F-4J	AE	2xx
VF-102	F-4J	AE	1xx
VA-82	A-7A	AE	3xx
VA-86	A-7A	AE	4xx
VA-85	A-6A/B	AE	5xx
VAH-10 Det 66	KA-3B	AE	01x
RVAH-13	RA-5C	AE	60x
VAW-13 Det 66	EKA-3B	AE	71x
(became VAQ-130 Det 66 on 1 October 1968)			
VAW-122	E-2A	AE	72x
HC-2 Det 66	UH-2A/B	HU	xx

Air Combat victories (1):

10 July 1968: MiG-21 shot down by F-4J (155553, AE 212, Lt Roy Cash, Jr, and Lt Joseph E Kain, Jr) of VF-33.

Combat losses (10):

31 May 1968: A-7A (153255, AE 304) of VA-82; AAA; Laos; Lt K W Fields, recovered.

4 June 1968: F-4J (155554, AE 204) of VF-33; AAA; North Vietnam; Lt E P Price, KIA, and Lt (jg) W A Simmons, recovered.

10 June 1968: A-7A (153265, AE 404) of VA-86; probably AAA; North Vietnam; LCdr R W Ford, died in captivity.

16 June 1968: F-4J (155548, AE 101) of VF-102; MiG's AAM; North Vietnam; Cdr W E Wilber, POW, and Lt (jg) B F Rupinski, KIA.

18 June 1968: F-4J (155546, AE 210) of VF-33; SAM; North Vietnam; LCdr J W Holtzclaw and LCdr J A Burns, both recovered.

24 July 1968: F-4J (155551, AE 203) of VF-33; AAA; North Vietnam; Cdr O G Elliott and Lt (jg) A Dambekaln, both recovered.

24 July 1968: A-7A (153253, AE 302) of VA-82; cause unknown; North Vietnam; LCdr D S Greiling, died in captivity.

25 July 1968: F-4J (155540, AE 112) of VF-102; AAA; North Vietnam; Lt C C Parish, KIA, Lt R S Fant, POW.

28 August 1968: A-6B (151561, AE 521) of VA-85; SAM; North Vietnam; Lt (jg) R R Duncan and Lt (jg) A F Ashall, both KIA.

6 September 1968: A-6A (154127, AE 506) of VA-85; AAA; North Vietnam; Cdr K L Koskey, POW, and LCdr R G McKee, recovered.

Operational losses (5):

31 May 1968: A-7A (153258) of VA-82; pilot recovered.
21 June 1968: A-7A (153209) of VA-86; pilot recovered.
22 June 1968: A-7A (153257) of VA-82; pilot recovered.
25 June 1968: A-7A (153271) of VA-86; pilot recovered.
2 September 1968: A-7A (153225) of VA-86; pilot recovered.

Assigned to the Atlantic Fleet, USS America *(CVA-66) made three war cruises to the Gulf of Tonkin. She is seen here during an earlier peacetime deployment with aircraft from CVW-6 on deck.* (US Navy via Naval Institute Press)

USS *America* (CVA-66)

Air Wing: CVW-9

Homeport departure/return: Norfolk, 10 April 1970–21 December 1970

In-chop/out-chop: 12 May 1970–23 November 1970

On Line periods: 26 May 1970–15 June 1970; 29 June 1970–13 July 1970; 21 July 1970–3 August 1970; 25 August 1970–17 September 1970; 14 October 1970–8 November 1970
Total: 100 days on the line

Squadrons:

VF-92	F-4J	NG	2xx
VF-96	F-4J	NG	1xx
VA-146	A-7E	NG	3xx
VA-147	A-7E	NG	4xx
VA-165	A-6A/B/C	NG	5xx
RVAH-12	RA-5C	NG	60x
VAQ-132	KA/EKA-3B	NG	61x
VAW-124	E-2A	NG	01x
HC-2 Det 66	UH-2C	HU	0xx

Air Combat victories (0):

Combat losses (0):

Operational losses (3):
20 May 1970: F-4J (155738) of VF-92; crew recovered.
4 July 1970: EKA-3B (142400) of VAQ-132; crew of three recovered.
25 July 1970: F-4J (155789) of VF-92; one crew member recovered and one killed.

USS *America* (CVA-66)

Air Wing: CVW-8

Homeport departure/return: Norfolk, 5 June 1972–24 March 1973

In-chop/out-chop: 1 July 1972–4 March 1973

On Line periods: 14–24 July 1972; 10–27 August 1972; 6 September 1972–7 October 1972; 22 October 1972–30 November 1972; 10–26 December 1972; 9 January 1973–1 February 1973; 13–28 February 1973
Total: 158 days on the line

Squadrons:

VF-74	F-4J	AJ	1xx
VMFA-333	F-4J	AJ	2xx
VA-82	A-7C	AJ	3xx
VA-86	A-7C	AJ	4xx
VA-35	A-6A/C and KA-6D	AJ	5xx
RVAH-6	RA-5C	AJ	60x
VAQ-132	EA-6B	AJ	61x
VAW-124	E-2B	AJ	01x
HC-2 Det 66	SH-3G	AJ	xx

Air Combat victories (1):

11 September 1972: MiG-21 shot down by F-4J (155526, AJ 201, Maj Lee T Lasseter and Capt John D Cummings) of VMFA-333.

Combat losses (11):

17 July 1972: A-7C (156792, AJ 405) of VA-86; own bomb; South Vietnam; Cdr W D Yonke, recovered.

17 July 1972: A-7C (156771, AJ 401) of VA-86; own bomb; South Vietnam; Lt D K Anderson, recovered.

10 September 1972: A-7C (156798, AJ 310) of VA-82; SAM; North Vietnam; Lt (jg) S O Musselman, MIA.

11 September 1972; F-4J (155526, AJ 201) of VMFA-333; SAM; North Vietnam; Maj L T Lasseter and Capt J D Cummings, both recovered.

11 September 1972: F-4J (154784, AJ 206) of VMFA-333; AAA; North Vietnam; Capt A S Dudley and 1st Lt J W Brady, both recovered.

18 September 1972: A-6A (157028, AJ 504) of VA-35; AAA; North Vietnam; Cdr V G Donnelly and LCdr K R Buell, both KIA.

27 October 1972: A-7C (156775, AJ 401) of VA-86; SAM; North Vietnam; LCdr J W Hall, MIA.

29 October 1972: A-7C (156762, AJ 404) of VA-86; AAA; North Vietnam; LCdr J E Sullivan, died in captivity.

19 December 1972: A-7C (156783, AJ 303) of VA-82; SAM; North Vietnam; Lt C T Wieland, POW.

23 December 1972: F-4J (153885, AJ 201) of VMFA-333; AAA; North Vietnam; LtCol J K Cochran and Maj H S Carr, both recovered.

24 January 1973: A-6A (157007, AJ 507) of VA-35; AAA; South Vietnam; Lt C M Graf and Lt S H Hatfield, both recovered.

Operational losses (3):

13 September 1972: F-4J (153854) of VF-74; one crew recovered and one crew killed.

17 September 1972: A-7C (156781) of VA-82; pilot recovered.

9 November 1972: A-7C (156764) of VA-86; pilot recovered.

USS *Bon Homme Richard* (CVA-31)

Air Wing: CVW-19

Homeport departure/return: Alameda, 28 January 1964–21 November 1964

In-chop/out-chop: 24 February 1964–16 November 1964

On Line periods: Was on the line in other areas prior to the end of August 1964; 31 August 1964–8 October 1964
Total: 39 days on the line

Squadrons:

VF-191	F-8E	NM	1xx
VF-194	F-8C	NM	4xx
VA-192	A-4C	NM	2xx
VA-195	A-4C	NM	5xx
VA-196	A-1H/J	NM	6xx
VAH-4 Det E	A-3B	ZB	xx
VFP-63 Det E	RF-8A	PP	9xx
VAW-11 Det E	E-1B	RR	7xx
HU-1 Det 1 Unit E	UH-2A	UP	xx

Air Combat victories (0):

Combat losses (0):

Operational losses (1):

5 August 1964: F-8E (150139) of VF-191; pilot recovered.

USS *Bon Homme Richard* (CVA-31)

Air Wing: CVW-19

Homeport departure/return: Alameda, 21 April 1965–13 January 1966

In-chop/out-chop: 12 May 1965–4 January 1966

On Line periods: 28–31 May 1965; 2 June 1965–2 July 1965; 19 July 1965–10 August 1965; 11–30 September 1965; 4–28 October 1965; 14 November 1965–16 December 1965
Total: 136 days on the line

Squadrons:

VF-191	F-8E	NM	1xx
VF-194	F-8E	NM	4xx
VA-192	A-4C	NM	2xx
VA-195	A-4C	NM	5xx
VA-196	A-1H/J	NM	6xx
VFP-63 Det E	RF-8A	PP	9xx
VAW-11 Det E	E-1B	RR	7xx
HU-1 Det 1 Unit E	UH-2A/B	UP	xx

(became HC-1 Det 1 Unit E on 1 July 1965)

Air Combat victories (0):

Combat losses (14):

1 June 1965: RF-8A (146852, PP 9??) of VFP-63; AAA; North Vietnam; LCdr F P Crosby, KIA.

30 June 1965: F-8E (150657, NM 4??) of VF-194; AAA; South Vietnam; LCdr R E Weedon, recovered.

29 July 1965: F-8E (150337, NM 102) of VF-191; AAA; South Vietnam; Lt (jg) E D Brown, KIA.

14 September 1965: A-1J (142057, NM 6??) of VA-196; own bomb; South Vietnam; LCdr J T Kearns, KIA.

14 September 1965: A-4C (147682, NM 2??) of VA-192; AAA; South Vietnam; Lt (jg) N B Taylor, KIA.

24 September 1965: A-1H (135274, NM 6??) of VA-196; AAA; South Vietnam; Cdr J Gallager, recovered.

28 September 1965: A-1H (134482, NM 6??) of VA-196; AAA; North Vietnam; LCdr C J Woods, KIA.

19 October 1965: A-4C (148584, NM 512) of VA-195; unknown cause; North Vietnam; Lt (jg) J B Worcester, KIA.

27 October 1965: F-8E (150655, NM 105) of VF-191; SAM; North Vietnam; Lt D A Moore, POW.

17 November 1965: F-8E (150308, NM 402) of VF-194; AAA; North Vietnam; Cdr R S Chew, recovered.

18 November 1965: F-8E (150332, NM 108) of VF-191; AAA; North Vietnam; Lt (jg) W D Sharp, recovered.

28 November 1965: F-8E (150854, NM 411) of VF-194; AAA; North Vietnam; Lt F H Harrington, recovered.

28 November 1965: F-8E (150327, NM 104) of VF-191; AAA; North Vietnam; Cdr H E Rutledge, POW.

2 December 1965: A-1H (139755, NM 612) of VA-196; unknown cause, North Vietnam; LCdr G R Roberts, KIA.

Operational losses (3):

12 September 1965: F-8E (150331) of VF-191; pilot killed.

24 September 1965: F-8E (150668) of VF-194; pilot killed.

25 September 1965: F-8E (149168) of VF-194; pilot recovered.

USS *Bon Homme Richard* (CVA-31)

Air Wing: CVW-21

Homeport departure/return: Alameda, 26 January 1967–25 August 1967

In-chop/out-chop: 10 February 1967–17 August 1967

On Line periods: 26 February 1967–21 March 1967; 18 April 1967–7 May 1967; 15 May 1967–18 June 1967; 28 June 1967–30 July 1967
Total: 112 days on the line

Squadrons:

VF-24	F-8C	NP	4xx
VF-211	F-8E	NP	1xx
VA-76	A-4C	NP	6xx
VA-212	A-4E	NP	2xx
VA-215	A-1H/J	NP	5xx
VAH-4 Det L	A-3B	ZB	8xx
VFP-63 Det L	RF-8G	PP	9xx
VAW-11 Det L (became VAW-111 Det 31 on 20 April 1967)	E-1B	RR	7xx
HC-1 Det 1 Unit L	UH-2B	UP	xx

Air Combat victories (9):

1 May 1967: MiG-17 shot down by A-4C (148609, NP 685, LCdr Ted R Swartz) of VA-76.

1 May 1967: MiG-17 shot down by F-8E (150303, NP 104, LCdr Marshall O Wright) of VF-211.

19 May 1967: MiG-17 shot down by F-8E (150348, NP 101, Cdr Paul H Speer) of VF-211.

19 May 1967: MiG-17 shot down by F-8E (150661, NP 1??, Lt (jg) Joseph M Shea) of VF-211.

19 May 1967: MiG-17 shot down by F-8C (146981, NP 4??, LCdr Bobby C Lee) of VF-24.

19 May 1967: MiG-17 shot down by F-8C (147029, NP 405, Lt Phillip R Wood) of VF-24.

21 July 1967: MiG-17 shot down by F-8C (147018, NP 442, LCdr Marion H Isaacks) of VF-24.

21 July 1967: MiG-17 shot down by F-8C (146992, NP 424, LCdr Robert J Kirkwood) of VF-24.

21 July 1967: MiG-17 shot down by F-8E (150859, NP 1??, LCdr Ray G Hubbard) of VF-211.

Combat losses (21):

15 March 1967: F-8C (147027, NP 452) of VF-24; unknown cause; North Vietnam; Lt (jg) D Smith, KIA.

21 March 1967: A-1H (137516, NP 572) of VA-215; unknown cause; North Vietnam; Lt P C Charvet, MIA.

24 April 1967: F-8C (146915, NP 449) of VF-24; AAA; North Vietnam; LCdr E B Tucker, died in captivity.

25 April 1967: A-4C (147799, NP 603) of VA-76; MiG; North Vietnam; Lt C D Stackhouse, POW.

25 April 1967: A-4E (151102, NP 225) of VA-212; SAM; North Vietnam; Lt (jg) A R Crebo, recovered.

18 May 1967: A-4C (147816, NP 683) of VA-76; AAA; North Vietnam; Cdr K R Cameron, died in captivity.

19 May 1967: F-8E (150930, NP 109) of VF-211; SAM; North Vietnam; LCdr K Russell, POW.

19 May 1967: F-8C (147021, NP 445) of VF-24; AAA; North Vietnam; Lt (jg) W J Metzger, POW.

20 May 1967: A-4E (149652, NP 233) of VA-212; AAA; North Vietnam; Cdr H L Smith, died in captivity.

21 May 1967: F-8E (150348, NP 105) of VF-211; AAA; North Vietnam; LCdr R G Hubbard, recovered.

25 May 1967: A-1H (135366, NP 572) of VA-215; AAA; North Vietnam; Ens R C Graves, KIA.

31 May 1967: A-4E (151113, NP 223) of VA-212; AAA; North Vietnam; LCdr A R Chauncy, POW.

31 May 1967: A-4E (151183, NP 229) of VA-212; AAA; North Vietnam; Lt (jg) M T Daniels, recovered.

5 June 1967: RF-8G (145614, PP 902) of VFP-63; AAA; North Vietnam; LCdr C H Haines, POW.

6 June 1967; F-8E (150303, NP 104) of VF-211; AAA; North Vietnam; Lt (jg) T R Hall, recovered.

10 June 1967: F-8E (150352, NP 101) of VF-211; AAA; North Vietnam; Lt (jg) T R Hall, POW.

11 June 1967: F-8C (147002, NP 450) of VF-24; AAA; North Vietnam; Lt (jg) J R Miller, recovered.

12 July 1967: A-4E (151181, NP 228) of VA-212; AAA; North Vietnam; LCdr J H Kirkpatrick, recovered.

14 July 1967: A-4C (147709, NP 688) of VA-76; SAM; North Vietnam; Cdr R B Fuller, POW.

14 July 1967: A-4C (147759, NP 693) of VA-76; AAA; North Vietnam; Lt J W Donis, recovered.

20 July 1967: A-4E (151119, NP 222) of VA-212; AAA; North Vietnam; Cdr F H Whittemore, recovered.

Operational losses (2):

27 February 1967: UH-2B (151317) of HC-1; four crew members killed.

2 June 1967: F-8C (147031) of VF-24; pilot killed.

USS Bon Homme Richard *(CVA-31) in July 1969 before returning on the line for the third period during her fifth war cruise. The aircraft on her deck belong to CVW-5. Launched on 29 April 1944,* Bon Homme Richard *was brought up to SCB 27C standards between 1952 and 1955, and was decommissioned on 2 July 1971.* (US Navy)

USS *Bon Homme Richard* (CVA-31)

Air Wing: CVW-5

Homeport departure/return: Alameda, 27 January 1968–10 October 1968

In-chop/out-chop: 9 February 1968–29 September 1968

On Line periods: 21 February 1968–25 March 1968; 7–21 April 1968; 10–30 May 1968; 15 June 1968–6 July 1968; 23 July 1968–17 August 1968; 28 August 1968–13 September 1968
Total: 135 days on the line

Squadrons:

VF-51	F-8H	NF	1xx
VF-53	F-8E	NF	2xx
VA-93	A-4F	NF	3xx
VA-94	A-4E	NF	4xx
VA-212	A-4F	NF	5xx
VFP-63 Det 31	RF-8G	NF	60x
VAW-13 Det 31	EKA-3B	NF	03x
(became VAQ-130 Det 31 on 1 October 1968)			
VAW-111 Det 31	E-1B	RR	7xx
HC-1 Det 31	UH-2C	UP	xx

Air Combat victories (3):
26 June 1968: MiG-21 shot down by F-8H (148710, NF 116, Cdr Lowell R Meyers) of VF-51.
29 July 1968: MiG-17 shot down by F-8E (150349, NF 203, Cdr Guy Cane) of VF-53.
1 August 1968: MiG-21 shot down by F-8H (147916, NF 102, Lt Norman K McCoy) of VF-51.

Combat losses (7):
14 May 1968: A-4F (154198, NF 304) of VA-93; unknown cause; North Vietnam; Lt (jg) B E Karger, KIA.
21 May 1968: A-4F (154988, NF 313) of VA-93; AAA; North Vietnam; Lt (jg) J A Douglass, recovered.
22 May 1968: RF-8G (146886, NF 602) of VFP-63; AAA; North Vietnam; Lt (jg) E F Miller, POW.
22 May 1968: A-4F (154974, NF 502) of VA-212; AAA; North Vietnam; LCdr R S Thomas, recovered.
30 May 1968: A-4F (154174, NF 513) of VA-212; unknown cause; North Vietnam; Lt J E Killian, recovered.
26 July 1968: A-4F (154182, NF 303) of VA-93; own bomb; North Vietnam; LCdr F E Fullerton, MIA.
30 August 1968: A-4F (154981, NF 316) of VA-93; AAA; North Vietnam; LCdr H A Eikel, recovered.

Operational losses (6):
12 March 1968: F-8E (150306) of VF-53; pilot recovered.
11 April 1968: A-4F (154995) of VA-93; pilot killed.
28 May 1968: A-4F (154982) of VA-212; pilot recovered.
24 June 1968: F-8E (149158) of VF-53; pilot recovered.
6 September 1968: A-4F (154187) of VA-93; pilot recovered.
10 September 1968: F-8H (148680) of VF-51; pilot recovered.

USS *Bon Homme Richard* (CVA-31)

Air Wing: CVW-5

Homeport departure/return: Alameda, 18 March 1969–29 October 1969

In-chop/out-chop: 6 April 1969–19 October 1969

On Line periods: 18 April 1969–17 May 1969; 5–25 June 1969; 31 July 1969–31 August 1969; 25 September 1969–8 October 1969
Total: 97 days on the line

Squadrons:

VF-51	F-8J	NF	1xx
VF-53	F-8J	NF	2xx
VA-22	A-4F	NF	3xx
VA-94	A-4E	NF	4xx
VA-144	A-4E	NF	5xx
VFP-63 Det 31	RF-8G	NF	60x
VAQ-130 Det 31	KA/EKA-3B	NF	61x
VAW-111 Det 31	E-1B	NF	73x
HC-1 Det 31	UH-2C	UP	00x

Air Combat victories (0):

Combat losses (1):
22 June 1969: A-4E (152029, NF 503) of VA-144; unknown cause; Laos; Lt (jg) L C Sage, KIA.

Operational losses (11):
26 April 1969: F-8J (150341) of VF-51; pilot recovered.
28 April 1969: F-8J (150320) of VF-53; pilot recovered.
4 May 1969: F-8J (150877) of VF-53; pilot recovered.
6 May 1969: A-4E (152043) of VA-94; pilot recovered.
8 May 1969: F-8J (149226) of VF-51; pilot recovered.
2 August 1969: F-8J (149214) of VF-53; pilot recovered.
10 August 1969: UH-2C (149767) of HC-1; crew of four recovered.
10 August 1969: A-4E (151131) of VA-144; pilot killed.
12 August 1969: F-8J (150330) of VF-53; pilot recovered.
13 August 1969: A-4E (152003) of VA-144; pilot recovered.
27 September 1969: F-8J (149172) of VF-53; pilot recovered.

USS *Bon Homme Richard* (CVA-31)

Air Wing: CVW-5

Homeport departure/return: Alameda, 2 April 1970–12 November 1970

In-chop/out-chop: 21 April 1970–3 November 1970

On line periods: 2–25 May 1970; 2–13 June 1970; 2–28 July 1970; 18 August 1970–1 September 1970; 28 September 1970–20 October 1970
Total: 101 days on the line

Squadrons:

VF-51	F-8J	NF	1xx
VF-53	F-8J	NF	2xx
VA-22	A-4F	NF	3xx
VA-94	A-4E	NF	4xx
VA-144	A-4F	NF	5xx
VFP-63 Det 31	RF-8G	NF	60x
VAQ-130 Det 31	EKA-3B	NF	61x
VAW-111 Det 14	E-1B	NF	01x
HC-1 Det 3	UH-2C	NF	00x

Air Combat victories (0):

Combat losses (0):

Operational losses (2):
14 May 1970: F-8J (150326) of VF-53; pilot killed.
7 June 1970: A-4F (154215) of VA-144; pilot recovered.

USS *Constellation* (CVA-64) and her CVG-13 during the shakedown cruise in the Caribbean in 1962. During the war Connie was deployed seven times to the Gulf of Tonkin and her fighters claimed the destruction of fifteen MiGs. (US Navy via Naval Institute press)

USS *Constellation* (CVA-64)

Air Wing: CVW-14

Homeport departure/return: Alameda, 5 May 1964–1 February 1965

In-chop/out-chop: 11 June 1964–24 January 1965

On Line periods: Was on the line in non-combat areas prior to 5 August 1964; 5 August 1964–17 September 1964; 29 October 1964–21 November 1964
Total: 68 days on the line

Squadrons:

VF-142	F-4B	NK	2xx
VF-143	F-4B	NK	3xx
VA-144	A-4C	NK	4xx
VA-146	A-4C	NK	6xx
VA-145	A-1H/J	NK	5xx
VAH-10	A-3B	NK	1xx
VFP-63 Det F	RF-8A	PP	93x
VAW-11 Det F	E-1B	RR	78x
HU-1 Det 1 Unit F	UH-2A	UP	xx

Air Combat victories (0):

Combat losses (2):

5 August 1964: A-1H (139760, NK 5??) of VA-145; AAA; North Vietnam; Lt (jg) R C Sather, KIA.

5 August 1964: A-4C (149578, NK 411) of VA-144; AAA; North Vietnam; Lt (jg) E Alvarez, POW.

Operational losses (3):

13 November 1964: F-4B (151412) of VA-142; crew of two recovered.

13 November 1964: A-4C (??????) of VA-146; pilot recovered.

13 November 1964: RF-8A (146879) of VMJO-1; pilot recovered.

USS *Constellation* (CVA-64)

Air Wing: CVW-15

Homeport departure/return: North Island, 12 May 1966–3 December 1966

In-chop/out-chop: 29 May 1966–24 November 1966

On Line periods: 14–21 June 1966; 23 June 1966–13 July 1966; 27 July 1966–31 August 1966; 8 September 1966–1 October 1966; 19 October 1966–9 November 1966
Total: 111 days on the line

Squadrons:

VF-151	F-4B	NL	1xx
VF-161	F-4B	NL	2xx
VA-153	A 4C	NL	3xx
VA-155	A-4E	NL	5xx
VA-65	A-6A	NL	4xx
VAH-8	A-3B	NL	6xx
RVAH-6	RA-5C	NL	70x
VAW-11 Det D	E-2A	RR	75x
HC-1 Det 1 Unit D	UH-2A/B	UP	xx

Air Combat victories (1):

13 July 1966: MiG-17 shot down by F-4B (151500, NL 216, Lt William M McGuigan and Lt (jg) Robert M Fowler) of VF-161.

Combat losses (12):

25 June 1966: A-6A (151816, NL 406) of VA-65; AAA; North Vietnam; Lt R M Weber, recovered, and Lt (jg) C W Marik, KIA.

27 June 1966: A-4E (152073, NL 507) of VA-155; AAA; North Vietnam; LCdr G A Smith, KIA.

1 July 1966: A-4E (150017, NL 511) of VA-155; AAA; North Vietnam; Cdr C H Peters, KIA.

4 July 1966: A-4E (151026, NL 513) of VA-155; gunboat AAA; off North Vietnam; Lt N E Holben, recovered.

10 July 1966: A-4C (147732, NL 304) of VA-153; AAA; North Vietnam; LCdr G H Wilkins, KIA.

29 July 1966: A-4E (152045, NL 513) of VA-155; AAA; North Vietnam; Lt (jg) V K Cameron, KIA.

19 August 1966: RA-5C (149309, NL 703) of RVAH-6; AAA; North Vietnam; LCdr J K Thompson and Lt (jg) G L Parten, both recovered.

27 August 1966: A-6A (151822, NL 402) of VA-65; AAA; North Vietnam; LCdr J H Fellowes and Lt (jg) G T Coker, both POW.

12 September 1966: A-4C (147763, NL 314) of VA-153; unknown cause; North Vietnam; LCdr W F Coakley, KIA.

20 October 1966: A-4C (148592, NL 311) of VA-153; AAA; North Vietnam; Lt (jg) H S Edwards, KIA.

22 October 1966: F-4B (151009, NL 214) of VF-161; AAA; North Vietnam; LCdr E P McBride, KIA, and Lt (jg) E U Turner, recovered.

22 October 1966: RA-5C (150030, NL 705) of RVAH-6; SAM; North Vietnam; LCdr T C Kolstad and Lt (jg) W B Klenert, both KIA.

Operational losses (3):

23 June 1966: F-4B (152324) of VF-151; both crew members killed.

10 August 1966: A-4E (151065) of VA-155; pilot killed.

19 September 1966: F-4B (152315) of VF-151; both crew members killed.

USS *Constellation* (CVA-64)

Air Wing: CVW-14

Homeport departure/return: North Island, 29 April 1967–4 December 1967

In-chop/out-chop: 15 May 1967–26 November 1967

On Line periods: 28 May 1967–11 June 1967; 19 June 1967–24 July 1967; 2 August 1967–3 September 1967; 26 September 1967–13 October 1967; 24 October 1967–11 November 1967
Total: 121 days on the line

Squadrons:

VF-142	F-4B	NK	2xx
VF-143	F-4B	NK	3xx
VA-55	A-4C	NK	5xx
VA-146	A-4C	NK	6xx
VA-196	A-6A	NK	4xx
VAH-8 Det 64	A-3B/KA-3B	NK	1xx
RVAH-12	RA-5C	NK	12x
VAW-113	E-2A	NK	75x
HC-1 Det 64	UH-2A/B	UP	xx

Air Combat victories (4):

10 August 1967: MiG-21 shot down by F-4B (152247, NK 202, Lt Guy H Freeborn and Lt (jg) Robert J Elliot) of VF-142.

10 August 1967: MiG-21 shot down by F-4B (150431, NK 2??, LCdr Robert C Davis and LCdr Gayle O Elie) of VF-142.

26 October 1967: MiG-21 shot down by F-4B (149411, NK 1??, Lt (jg) Robert P Hickey, Jr, and Lt (jg) Jeremy G Morris) of VF-143.

30 October 1967: MiG-17 shot down by F-4B (150629, NK 203, LCdr Eugene P Lund and Lt (jg) James R Borst) of VF-142.

Combat losses (12):

19 June 1967: F-4B (150439, NK 207) of VF-142; AAA; North Vietnam; LCdr F L Raines and Ens C L Lewnes, both recovered.

28 June 1967: F-4B (152242, NK 301) of VF-143; AAA; North Vietnam; Cdr W P Lawrence and Lt (jg) J W Bailey, both POW.

30 June 1967: A-4C (147712, NK 605) of VA-146; AAA; North Vietnam; Lt J W McGrawth, POW.

9 July 1967: A-4C (149542, NK 602) of VA-146; SAM; North Vietnam; Lt C R Lee, KIA.

13 August 1967: RA-5C (151634, NK 125) of RVAH-12; AAA; North Vietnam; LCdr L G Hyatt and Lt (jg) W K Goodermote, both POW.

21 August 1967: F-4B (152247, NK 202) of VF-142; AAA; North Vietnam; Cdr R H McGlohn and Lt (jg) J M McIlrath, both recovered.

21 August 1967: A-6A (152638, NK 410) of VA-196; SAM; North Vietnam; Cdr L T Profilet and LCdr W M Hardman, both POW.

21 August 1967: A-6A (152627, NK 402) of VA-196; MiG; China; Lt (jg) D V Scott and Lt (jg) F G Trembley, both KIA.

21 August 1967: A-6A (152625, NK 400) of VA-196; MiG; China; LCdr J L Bookley, KIA, and Lt R J Flynn, POW.

23 August 1967: F-4B (149498, NK 205) of VF-142; SAM; North Vietnam; LCdr T W Sitek and Ens P L Ness, both KIA.

30 October 1967: F-4B (150629, NK 203) of VF-142; own AIM-7E missile; North Vietnam; LCdr H P Lund and Lt (jg) J R Borst, both recovered.

2 November 1967: A-6A (152629, NK 403) of VA-196; AAA; North Vietnam; LCdr R D Morrow, KIA, and Lt J J Wright, MIA.

Operational losses (4):

2 August 1967: A-4C (149632) of VA-55; pilot recovered.

8 August 1967: A-4C (147719) of VA-146; pilot recovered.

17 August 1967: RA-5C (149302) of RVAH-12; both crew members killed.

3 November 1967: KA-3B (147653) of VAH-8; all three crew members killed.

USS *Constellation* (CVA-64)

Air Wing: CVW-14

Homeport departure/return: North Island, 29 May 1968–31 January 1969

In-chop/out-chop: 14 June 1968–23 January 1969

On Line periods: 28 June 1968–22 July 1968; 3–27 August 1968; 12 September 1968–9 October 1968; 30 October 1968–28 November 1968; 10–21 December 1968; 30 December 1968–7 January 1969

Total: 129 days on the line

Squadrons:

VF-142	F-4B	NK	2xx
VF-143	F-4B	NK	3xx
VA-27	A-7A	NK	6xx
VA-97	A-7A	NK	5xx
VA-196	A-6A/B	NK	4xx
VAH-2 Det 64	KA-3B	NK	11x
(became VAQ-132 Det 64 on 1 November 1968)			
VAW-13 Det 64	EKA-3B	NK	10x
(became VAQ-130 Det 64 on 1 October 1968)			
RVAH-5	RA-5C	NK	12x
VAW-113	E-2A	NK	7xx
HC-1 Det 64	UH-2C	UP	xx

Air Combat victories (0):

Combat losses (9):

17 August 1968: F-4B (151404, NK 206) of VF-142; own AIM-9D; North Vietnam; Lt (jg) M L Gartley and Lt W J Mayhew, both POW.

24 August 1968: A-7A (154359, NK 613) of VA-27; AAA; North Vietnam; Lt J R Lee, recovered.

14 September 1968: A-7A (154344, NK 610) of VA-27; AAA; North Vietnam; Cdr G T Pappas, recovered.

17 September 1968: A-7A (153214, NK 507) of VA-97; AAA; North Vietnam; LCdr B D Woods, POW.

30 September 1968: A-6A (154149, NK 404) of VA-196; SAM; North Vietnam; Lt (jg) L Van Renselaar and Lt D A Spinelli, both MIA.

6 October 1968: A-7A (153273, NK 612) of VA-27; SAM; North Vietnam; Lt (jg) G M Biery, recovered.

25 November 1968: RA-5C (149293, NK 123) of RVAH-5; cause unknown; North Vietnam; Cdr E A Stamm, died in captivity, and Lt (jg) R C Thum, KIA.

18 December 1968: A-6A (147764, NK 405) of VA-196; AAA; Laos; Lt (jg) J R Babcock and Lt G J Meyer, both KIA.

19 December 1968: A-6A (154152, NK 407) of VA-196; AAA; Laos; Lt M L Bouchard, KIA, and Lt R W Colyar, recovered.

Operational losses (7):

16 July 1968: A-7A (153234) of VA-97; pilot recovered.

17 August 1968: UH-2C (155202) of HC-1; all four crew members recovered.

20 August 1968: A-6B (151560) of VA-196; both crew members recovered.

24 August 1968: F-4B (150434) of VF-143; one crew member recovered and one killed.

16 September 1968: F-4B (149443) of VF-143; both crew members recovered.

31 October 1968: A-7A (153175) of VA-27; pilot recovered.

7 January 1969: UH-2A (149764) of HC-7; both crew members recovered.

USS *Constellation* (CVA-64)

Air Wing: CVW-14

Homeport departure/return: North Island, 11 August 1969–8 May 1970

In-chop/out-chop: 1 September 1969–29 April 1970

On Line periods: 12 September 1969–3 October 1969; 1–23 November 1969; 7–22 December 1969; 5–30 January 1970; 12 February 1970–1 March 1970; 26 March 1970–17 April 1970

Total: 128 days on the line

Squadrons:

VF-142	F-4J	NK	2xx
VF-143	F-4J	NK	1xx
VA-27	A-7A	NK	4xx
VA-97	A-7A	NK	3xx
VA-85	A-6A/B	NK	5xx
RVAH-7	RA-5C	NK	60x
VAQ-133	KA/EKA-3B	NK	61x
VAW-113	E-2A	NK	01x
HC-1 Det 5	SH-3A	NK	00x

Air Combat victories (1):

28 March 1970: MiG-21 shot down by F-4J (155875, NK 201, Lt Jerome E Beaulier and Lt Steven J Barkley) of VF-142.

Combat losses (5):

1 October 1969: A-7A (153252, NK 300) of VA-97; AAA; Laos; Lt P E Mullowney, recovered.

22 November 1969: F-4J (155889, NK 110) of VF-143; AAA; Laos; Lt (jg) H C Wheeler, recovered, and Lt (jg) H J Bedinger, POW.

28 February 1970: A-7A (153143, NK 411) of VA-27; AAA; Laos; Lt R E Karp, recovered.

3 April 1970: A-7A (154358, NK 313) of VA-97; AAA; Laos; Lt H P Hoffman, recovered.

7 April 1970: A-7A (153233, NK 302) of VA-97; AAA; Laos; Lt M P Hamilton, recovered.

Operational losses (2):

15 November 1969: A-7A (153156) of VA-27; pilot recovered.

8 April 1970: A-7A (153153) of VA-97; pilot recovered.

USS *Constellation* (CVA-64)

Air Wing: CVW-9

Homeport departure/return: North Island, 1 October 1971–1 July 1972

In-chop/out-chop: 27 October 1971–24 June 1972

On Line periods: 4–21 November 1971; 30 November 1971–30 December 1971; 10 January 1972–1 February 1972; 9 February 1972–1 March 1972; 14–22 March 1972; 9–30 April 1972; 1 May 1972–13 June 1972
Total: 169 days on the line

Squadrons:

VF-92	F-4J	NG	2xx
VF-96	F-4J	NG	1xx
VA-146	A-7E	NG	3xx
VA-147	A-7E	NG	4xx
VA-165	A-6A and KA-6D	NG	5xx
RVAH-11	RA-5C	NG	60x
VAQ-130 Det 1	EKA-3B	NG	61x
VAW-116	E-2B	NG	01x
HC-1 Det 3	SH-3G	NG	0xx

Air Combat victories (9):

19 January 1972: MiG-21 shot down by F-4J (157267, NG 112, Lt Randall H Cunningham and Lt (jg) William P Driscoll) of VF-96.

8 May 1972: MiG-17 shot down by F-4J (157267, NG 112, Lt Randall H Cunningham and Lt (jg) William P Driscoll) of VF-96.

10 May 1972: Two MiG-17s shot down by F-4J (155769, NG 106, Lt Michael J Connelly and Lt Thomas J J Blonski) of VF-96.

10 May 1972: MiG-17 shot down by F-4J (155749, NG 111, Lt Steven C Shoemaker and Lt (jg) Keith V Crenshaw) of VF-96.

10 May 1972: Three MiG-17s shot down by F-4J (155800, NG 100, Lt Randall H Cunningham and Lt (jg) William P Driscoll) of VF-96.

10 May 1972: MiG-21 shot down by F-4J (157269, NG 211, Lt Curt Dose and LCdr James McDevitt) of VF-92.

Combat losses (5):

30 December 1971: A-6A (155677, NG 506) of VA-165; SAM; North Vietnam; LCdr F L Holmes, KIA, and Lt C W Burton, recovered.

18 February 1972: F-4J (157266, NG 207) of VF-92; AAA; Laos; Lt B P Rowe, KIA, and Lt (jg) D E Spence, recovered.

10 May 1972: F-4J (155797, NG 212) of VF-92; AAA; North Vietnam; Cdr H L Blackburn and Lt S A Rudloff, both POW.

10 May 1972: F-4J (155800, NG 100) of VF-96; SAM; North Vietnam; Lt R H Cunningham and Lt (jg) W P Driscoll, both recovered.

17 May 1972: A-7E (158015, NG 404) of VA-147; AAA; North Vietnam; Cdr T R Wilkinson, recovered.

Operational losses (2):

22 January 1972: A-7E (156849) of VA-146; pilot recovered.

10 February 1972: SH-3G (148935) of HC-1; crew recovered.

USS *Constellation* (CVA-64)

Air Wing: CVW-9

Homeport departure/return: North Island, 5 January 1973–11 October 1973

In-chop/out-chop: 16 January 1973–2 October 1973

On Line periods: 31 January 1973; 27 February 1973–13 March 1973; 20 March 1973–2 April 1973; 12–25 April 1973; 5–17 May 1973; 29 May 1973–12 June 1973; 28 June 1973–2 July 1973; 5–15 July 1973; 6–15 August 1973; remained on the line for two more periods after the cut-off date of 15 August 1973
Total: 98 days on the line

Squadrons:

VF-92	F-4J	NG	2xx
VF-96	F-4J	NG	1xx
VA-146	A-7E	NG	3xx
VA-147	A-7E	NG	4xx
VA-165	A-6A and KA-6D	NG	5xx
RVAH-12	RA-5C	NG	60x
VAQ-134	EA-6B	NG	61x
VAW-116	E-2B	NG	01x
HS-6 Det 1	SH-3G	NG	00x

Air Combat victories (0):

Combat losses (0):

Operational losses (1):

29 January 1973: A-7E (156837) of VA-147; pilot missing.

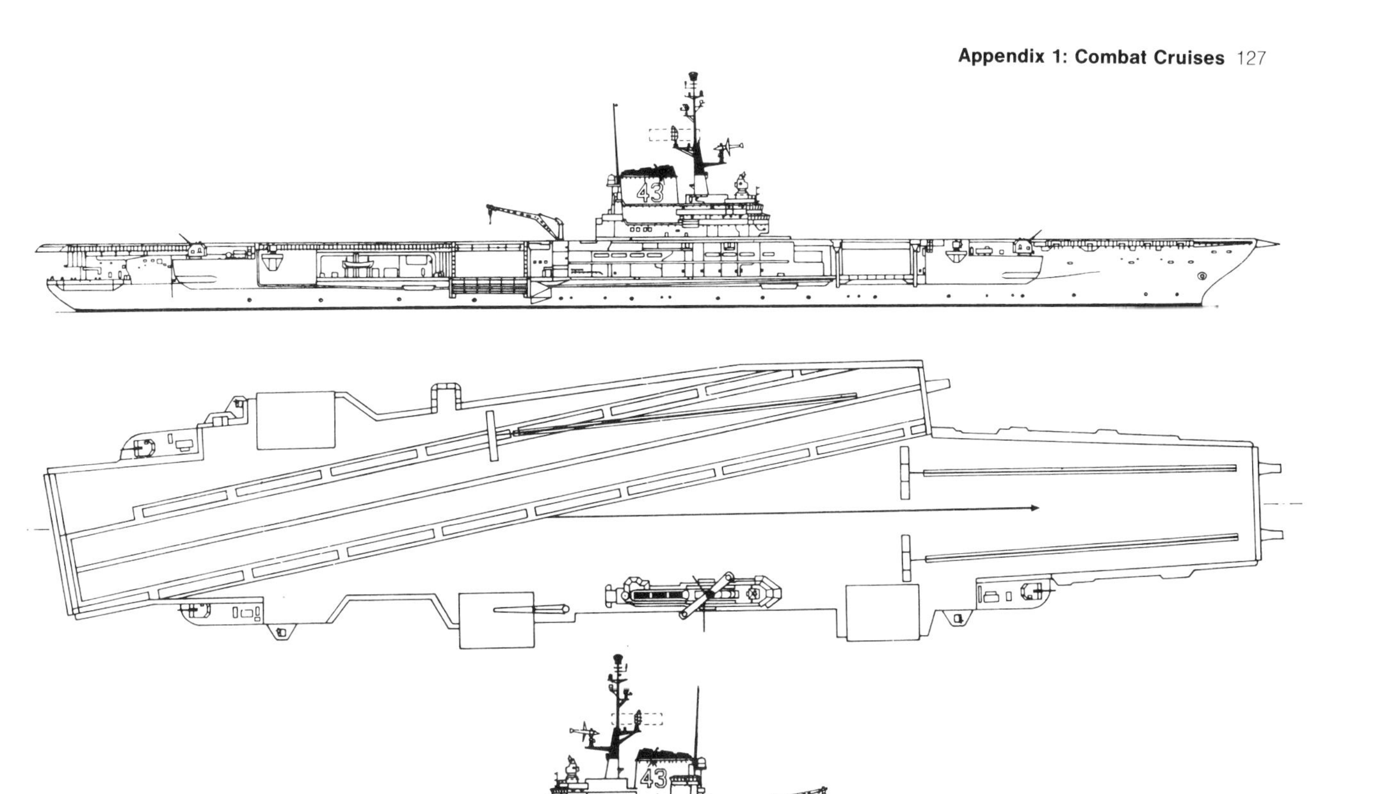

Coral Sea *from 1962*

USS *Coral Sea* (CVA-43)

Air Wing: CVW-15

Homeport departure/return: Alameda, 7 December 1964–1 November 1965

In-chop/out-chop: 23 January 1965–23 October 1965

On Line periods: 1 February 1965–5 March 1965; 15 March 1965–16 April 1965; 1–27 May 1965; 24 June 1965–23 July 1965; 12 August 1965–10 September 1965; 1–14 October 1965
Total: 167 days on the line

Squadrons:

VF-151	F-4B	NL	1xx
VF-154	F-8D	NL	4xx
VA-153	A-4C	NL	3xx
VA-155	A-4E	NL	5xx
VA-165	A-1H/J	NL	2xx
VAH-2	A-3B	NL	6xx
VFP-63 Det D	RF-8A	PP	9xx
VAW-11 Det D	E-1B	RR	7xx
HU-1 Det 1 Unit D	UH-2A/B	UP	x

(became HC-1 Det 1 Unit D on 1 July 1965)

Air Combat victories (1):

6 October 1965: MiG-17 shot down by F-4B (150634, NL 107, LCdr Dan MacIntyre and Lt (jg) Alan Johnson) of VF-151.

Combat losses (21):

7 February 1965: A-4E (150075, NL 503) of VA-155; AAA or small arms fire; North Vietnam; Lt E A Dickson, KIA.

11 February 1965: F-8D (148633, NL 403) of VF-154; AAA; North Vietnam; LCdr R H Shumaker, POW.

11 February 1965: A-4C (149572, NL 3??) of VA-153; AAA; North Vietnam; Lt W T Majors, recovered.

26 March 1965: F-8D (148644, NL 400) of VF-154; AAA; North Vietnam; Lt C E Wangeman, Jr, recovered.

29 March 1965: A-4E (150078, NL 5??) of VA-155; AAA; North Vietnam; Cdr J H Harris, recovered.

29 March 1965: F-8D (148642, NL 407) of VF-154; AAA; North Vietnam; Cdr W N Donnelly, recovered.

29 March 1965: F-8D (148668, NL 408) of VF-154; AAA; North Vietnam; LCdr K E Hume, KIA.

7 April 1965: A-4C (148317, NL 3??) of VA-153; AAA; North Vietnam; Lt W M Roark, KIA.

9 April 1965: A-4C (148841, NL 3??) of VA-153; AAA; North Vietnam; LCdr C H McNeil, recovered.

9 May 1965: F-8D (148673, NL 413) of VF 154; cause unknown; North Vietnam; Lt D A Kardell, KIA.

25 June 1965: A-4C (149574, NL 306) of VA-153; AAA; North Vietnam; Cdr P Mongilardi, KIA.

15 July 1965: A-4C (149576, NL 308) of VA-153; AAA; North Vietnam; Lt A J Bennett, recovered.

12 August 1965: A-4E (150067, NL 5??) of VA-155; AAA; North Vietnam; Lt W T Fidelibus, recovered.

13 August 1965: A-1H (139772, NL 206) of VA-165; AAA; North Vietnam; Lt R Hyland, recovered.
13 August 1965: RF-8A (146849, PP 920) of VFP-63; AAA; North Vietnam; Maj P A Manning, recovered.
13 August 1965: A-4C (148475, NL 312) of VA-153; AAA; North Vietnam; Cdr H E Thomas, KIA.
4 September 1965: A-1H (139693, NL 203) of VA-165; AAA; North Vietnam; Lt (jg) E B Shaw, KIA.
7 September 1965: RF-8A (146826, PP 992) of VFP-63; cause unknown; North Vietnam; Lt (jg) C B Goodwin, MIA.
10 September 1965: A-4E (149991, NL 500) of VA-155; AAA; North Vietnam; LCdr W B Rivers, POW.
11 October 1965: A-4E (152016, NL 5??) of VA-155; AAA; North Vietnam; LCdr P M Moore, recovered.
14 October 1965: F-8D (147899, NL 406) of VF-154; small arms fire; North Vietnam; Lt J A Terhune, recovered.

Operational losses (2):
24 February 1965: A-3B (147664) of VAH-2; three crew members recovered, one killed.
8 October 1965: RF-8A (145617) of VFP-63; pilot recovered.

USS *Coral Sea* (CVA-43)

Air Wing: CVW-2

Homeport departure/return: Alameda, 29 July 1966–23 February 1967

In-chop/out-chop: 11 August 1966–16 February 1967

On Line periods: 12 September 1966–19 October 1966; 30 October 1966–4 December 1966; 28 December 1966–31 January 1967
Total: 109 days on the line

Squadrons:

VF-21	F-4B	NE	1xx
VF-154	F-4B	NE	4xx
VA-22	A-4C	NE	2xx
VA-23	A-4E	NE	3xx
VA-25	A-1H	NE	5xx
VAH-2 Det A	A-3B	ZA	6xx
VFP-63 Det A	RF-8G	PP	89x
VAW-11 Det A	E-2A	RR	74x
HC-1 Det 1 Unit A	UH-2A/B	UP	xx

Air Combat victories (0):

Combat losses (16):
14 September 1966: A-1H (139756, NE 5??) of VA-25; SAM; North Vietnam; Cdr C W Stoddard, KIA.
17 September 1966: A-4C (148488, NE 200) of VA-22; AAA; North Vietnam; Lt (jg) R A Hegstrom, recovered.
19 September 1966: F-4B (152085, NE 451) of VF-154; SAM; North Vietnam; Lt (jg) D B Parsons, Jr, and Lt (jg) T H Pilkington, both KIA.
20 September 1966: F-4B (152073, NE 101) of VF-21; cause unknown; North Vietnam; LCdr J R Bauder and Lt (jg) J B Mills, both MIA.
4 October 1966: A-4C (147737, NE 224) of VA-22; AAA; North Vietnam; LCdr J D Burns, POW.
8 October 1966: RF-8G (146899, PP 896) of VFP-63; AAA; North Vietnam; Lt (jg) F D Litvin, recovered.
9 October 1966: F-4B (152093, NE 452) of VF-154; AAA; North Vietnam; LCdr C N Tanner and Lt R R Terry, both POW.
10 October 1966: A-4E (151150, NE 340) of VA-23; cause unknown; North Vietnam; Lt (jg) M S Confer, KIA.
12 October 1966: A-1H (135323, NE 572) of VA-25; AAA; North Vietnam; Lt R D Woods, POW.
3 November 1966: F-4B (148433, NE 461) of VF-154; AAA; North Vietnam; Lt R W Schaffer and Lt (jg) J P Piccoli, both recovered.
17 November 1966: A-4C (148496, NE 222) of VA-22; cause unknown; North Vietnam; Lt (jg) W T Arnold, MIA.
2 December 1966: F-4B (151014, NE 461) of VF-154; AAA; North Vietnam; Lt (jg) D E McRae, KIA, and Ens D G Rehman, POW.
4 January 1967: A-4C (150584, NE 233) of VA-22; AAA; North Vietnam; Lt (jg) J M Hays, recovered.
4 January 1967: F-4B (152974, NE 451) of VF-154; AAA; North Vietnam; Lt A M Van Pelt and Ens R A Morris, both recovered.
13 January 1967: A-4E (151158, NE 345) of VA-23; AAA; North Vietnam; Lt (jg) M P Cronin, POW.
15 January 1967: A-4E (151168, NE 346) of VA-23; AAA; North Vietnam; Lt (jg) D H Moran, Jr, KIA.

Operational losses (3):
2 October 1966: A-3B (142633) of VAH-2; all four crew members recovered.
11 November 1966: A-4C (147718) of VA-22; pilot recovered.
27 December 1966: A-4C (149641) of VA-22; pilot recovered.

USS *Coral Sea* (CVA-43)

Air Wing: CVW-15

Homeport departure/return: Alameda, 26 July 1967–6 April 1968

In-chop/out-chop: 10 August 1967–29 March 1968

On Line periods: 28 August 1967–30 September 1967; 13–27 October 1967; 12 November 1967–7 December 1967; 17 December 1967–6 January 1968; 16 January 1968–20 February 1968
Total: 132 days on the line

Squadrons:

VF-151	F-4B	NL	1xx
VF-161	F-4B	NL	2xx
VA-153	A-4E	NL	3xx

USS *Coral Sea (CVA-43) during RefTra off the Californian coast in the fall of 1964. Launched on 2 April 1946,* Coral Sea *underwent SCB 110A modernization between 1957 and 1960. Reclassified CV-43 on 30 June 1975, she is expected to remain operational until the early- to mid-1990s and will then replace USS* Lexington *(AVT-16) as a training carrier.* (US Navy by courtesy of Don J Willis)

VA-155	A-4E	NL	5xx
VA-25	A-1H/J	NL	4xx
VAH-2 Det 43	KA-3B	NL	6xx
VFP-63 Det 43	RF-8G	NL	71x
VAW-116	E-2A	NL	70x
HC-1 Det 43	UH-2A	UP	xx

Air Combat victories (0):

Combat losses (15):

29 August 1967: A-4E (151025, NL 313) of VA-153; cause unknown; North Vietnam; Lt M J Allard, KIA.

30 August 1967: A-1H (135390, NL 412) of VA-25; cause unknown; off North Vietnam; Lt (jg) L E Gardiner, recovered.

21 September 1967: RF-8G (144623, NL 710) of VFP-63; AAA; North Vietnam; LCdr M J Vescelius, POW.

17 October 1967: A-4E (152038, NL 512) of VA-155; own 2.75in rockets; North Vietnam; Lt (jg) F J Fortner, KIA.

24 October 1967: F-4B (150421, NL 1??) of VF-151; SAM; North Vietnam; Cdr C R Gillepsie, POW, and Lt (jg) R C Clark, died in captivity.

24 October 1967: F-4B (150995, NL 1??) of VF-151; SAM; North Vietnam; Lt (jg) R F Frishman and Lt (jg) E G Lewis, Jr, both POW.

26 October 1967: A-4E (150059, NL 501) of VA-155; SAM; North Vietnam; Cdr V W Daniels, POW.

16 November 1967: F-4B (152987, NL 104) of VF-151; SAM; North Vietnam; LCdr F H Schultz and Lt (jg) T B Sullivan, both POW.

17 November 1967: F-4B (151488, NL 207) of VF-161; AAA; North Vietnam; Cdr W D McGrath and Lt R G Emrich, both KIA.

19 November 1967: F-4B (150997, NL 110) of VF-151; MiG's AAM; North Vietnam; LCdr C D Clower and Lt (jg) W O Estes II, both POW.

19 November 1967: F-4B (152304, NL 115) of VF-151; MiG; North Vietnam; Lt (jg) J E Teague and Lt (jg) T G Stier, both POW.

22 December 1967: A-4E (152071, NL 506) of VA-155; own Mk-82 bombs; North Vietnam; LCdr W P Cook, KIA.

29 December 1967: F-4B (150449, NL 203) of VF-161; AAA; North Vietnam; Lt J F Dowd and Lt (jg) G K Flint, both recovered.

25 January 1968: A-4E (150057, NL 312) of VA-153; SAM; North Vietnam; Cdr T E Woolcock, recovered.

14 February 1968: A-1H (134499, NL 404) of VA-25; Chinese MiG; off China; Lt (jg) J P Dunn, MIA.

Operational losses (3):

19 August 1967: A-1H (137575) of VA-25; pilot killed.

8 October 1967: F-4B (150474) of VF-161; one crew member recovered, one killed.

25 November 1967: A-4E (150037); taxi accident on deck; pilot killed.

USS *Coral Sea* (CVA-43)

Air Wing: CVW-15

Homeport departure/return: Alameda, 7 September 1968–18 April 1969

In-chop/out-chop: 23 September 1968–11 April 1969

On Line periods: 10 October 1968–1 November 1968; 14 November 1968–8 December 1968; 30 December 1968–27 January 1969; 10 February 1969–3 March 1969; 20–30 March 1969
Total: 110 days on the line

Squadrons:

VF-151	F-4B	NL	1xx
VF-161	F-4B	NL	2xx
VA-153	A-4F	NL	3xx
VA-216	A-4C	NL	6xx
VA-52	A-6A	NL	4xx
VAH-10 Det 43	KA-3B	NL	60x
VFP-63 Det 43	RF-8G	NL	5xx
VAW-13 Det 43	EKA-3B	VR	01x
(became VAQ-130 Det 43 on 1 October 1968)			
VAW-116	E-2A	NL	01x
HC-1 Det 43	UH-2C	UP	xx

Air Combat victories (0):

Combat losses (4):
13 October 1968: A-6A (154141, NL 411) of VA-52; cause unknown; North Vietnam; Cdr O R Orell, MIA, and Lt J D Hunt, KIA.
3 January 1969: A-4C (147764, NL 610) of VA-216; AAA; Laos; Lt (jg) R M Aaron, recovered.
14 February 1969: A-4C (149529, NL 607) of VA-216; AAA; Laos; Lt (jg) L J Stevens, MIA.
14 February 1969: A-4C (148547, NL 601) of VA-216; AAA and/or debris from wingman's aircraft; Laos; LCdr J F Meeham, recovered.

Operational losses (4):
21 November 1968: A-4C (148608) of VA-216; pilot killed.
17 February 1969: KA-3B (138943) of VAH-10; all three crew members killed.
21 February 1969: UH-2C (150144) of HC-1; all four crew members recovered.
25 March 1969: F-4B (150447) of VF-151; both crew members recovered.

USS *Coral Sea* (CVA-43)

Air Wing: CVW-15

Homeport departure/return: Alameda, 23 September 1969–1 July 1970

In-chop/out-chop: 14 October 1969–18 June 1970

On Line periods: 27 October 1969–18 November 1969; 23 December 1969–18 January 1970; 18 February 1970–8 March 1970; 20 March 1970–10 April 1970; 29 April 1970–1 June 1970
Total: 125 days on the line

Squadrons:

VF-151	F-4B	NL	1xx
VF-161	F-4B	NL	2xx
VA-82	A-7A	NL	3xx
VA-86	A-7A	NL	4xx
VA-35	A-6A	NL	5xx
VFP-63 Det 43	RF-8G	NL	60x
VAQ-135	KA/EKA-3B	NL	61x
VAW-116	E-2A	NL	01x
HC-1 Det 9	UH-2C	NL	00x

Air Combat victories (0):

Combat losses (1):
7 January 1970: A-7A (153231, NL 414) of VA-86; AAA; Laos; LCdr M G Hoff, MIA.

Operational losses (10):
15 November 1969: A-7A (152679) of VA-86; pilot recovered.
26 December 1969: A-6A (152891) of VA-35; both crew members killed.
25 February 1970: F-4B (152286) of VF-161; both crew members recovered.
3 March 1970: A-7A (153136) of VA-86; pilot killed.
5 April 1970: F-4B (152325) of VF-151; one crew member recovered, one missing.
8 April 1970: E-2A (151711) of VAW-116; all five crew members killed.
1 May 1970: A-7A (152680) of VA-82; pilot recovered.
16 May 1970: EKA-3B (142657) of VAQ-135; one crew member killed, two missing.
17 May 1970: F-4B (152239) of VF-161; one crew member recovered, one missing.
29 May 1970: A-7A (153146) of VA-82; pilot recovered.

USS *Coral Sea* (CVA-43)

Air Wing: CVW-15

Homeport departure/return: Alameda, 12 November 1971–17 July 1972

In-chop/out-chop: 8 December 1971–11 July 1972

On Line periods: 14 December 1971–16 January 1972; 26 January 1972–17 February 1972; 2–14 March 1972; 23 March 1972–11 May 1972; 23 May 1972–10 June 1972; 22–30 June 1972
Total: 148 days on the line

Squadrons:

VF-51	F-4B	NL	1xx
VF-111	F-4B	NL	2xx
VA-22	A-7E	NL	3xx
VA-94	A-7E	NL	4xx
VMA(AW)-224	A-6A/B and KA-6D	NL	5xx
VFP-63 Det 5	RF-8G	NL	60x
VAQ-135 Det 3	EKA-3B	NL	61x
VAW-111 Det 4	E-1B	NL	01x
HC-1 Det 6	SH-3G	NL	0xx

Air Combat victories (5):

6 March 1972: MiG-17 shot down by F-4B (153019, NL 201, Lt Garry L Weigand and Lt (jg) William C Freckelton) of VF-111.

6 May 1972: MiG-17 shot down by F-4B (150456, NL 100, LCdr Jerry B Houston and Lt Kevin T Moore) of VF-51.

10 May 1972: MiG-17 shot down by F-4B (151398, NL 111, Lt Kenneth L Cannon and Lt Roy A Morris, Jr) of VF-51.

11 June 1972: MiG-17 shot down by F-4B (149473, NL 114, Cdr Foster S Teague and Lt Ralph M Howell) of VF-51.

11 June 1972: MiG-17 shot down by F-4B (149457, NL 113, Lt Winston W Copeland and Lt Donald R Bouchoux) of VF-51.

Combat losses (12):

30 December 1971: F-4B (150418, NL 203) of VF-111; SAM; North Vietnam; LCdr D W Hoffman and Lt (jg) N A Charles, both POW.

6 April 1972: A-7E (157590, NL 300) of VA-22; SAM; North Vietnam; Cdr T E Dunlop, KIA.

9 April 1972: A-6A (155652, NL 505) of VMA(AW)-224; AAA; Laos; Maj C D Smith, recovered, and 1st Lt S D Ketchie, MIA.

16 April 1972: A-7E (156860, NL 4??) of VA-94; SAM or AAA; North Vietnam; Cdr D L Moss, recovered.

27 April 1972: F-4B (153025, NL 102) of VF-51; MiG's AAM; North Vietnam; Lt A R Molinare and LCdr J B Souder, both POW.

1 May 1972: A-7E (156888, NL 401) of VA-94; SAM; North Vietnam; Lt M G Surdyk, recovered.

3 May 1972: A-6A (155709, NL 501) of VMA(AW)-224; cause unknown; North Vietnam; 1st Lt J W McDonald, MIA, and Capt D B Williams, KIA.

6 May 1972: A-7E (156879, NL 313) of VA-22; SAM; North Vietnam; Lt M B Wiles, POW.

24 May 1972: A-7E (156877, NL 410) of VA-94; SAM; North Vietnam; LCdr H A Eikel, recovered.

29 May 1972: A-6A (155650, NL 503) of VMA(AW)-224; AAA; North Vietnam; LCdr P Schuyler and Capt L J Ferracane, both recovered.

11 June 1972: A-6A (154145, NL 522) of VMA(AW)-224; AAA; North Vietnam; Capt R E Wilson, MIA, and Capt W K Angus, POW.

25 June 1972: A-7E (157437, NL 311) of VA-22; cause unknown; North Vietnam; Lt G R Shumway, MIA.

Operational losses (4):

18 January 1972: A-7E (156880) of VA-94; pilot recovered.

4 February 1972: A-7E (156870) of VA-22; pilot killed.

3 March 1972: F-4B (150417) of VF-51; both crew members recovered.

8 May 1972: SH-3G (149699) of HC-1; five crew members recovered and three killed.

USS *Coral Sea* (CVA-43)

Air Wing: CVW-15

Homeport departure/return: Alameda, 9 March 1973–8 November 1973

In-chop/out-chop: 20 March 1973–30 October 1973

On Line periods: 31 March 1973–24 April 1973; 7–20 May 1973; 5–6 June 1973; 12–26 June 1973; 1–27 July 1973; 8 August 1973; remained on the line for five more periods after the cut-off date of 15 August 1973
Total: 84 days on the line

Squadrons:

VF-51	F-4B	NL	1xx
VF-111	F-4B	NL	2xx
VA-22	A-7E	NL	3xx
VA-94	A-7E	NL	4xx
VA-95	A-6A/B and KA-6D	NL	5xx
VFP-63 Det 5	RF-8G	NL	60x
VAQ-135 Det 3	EKA-3B	NL	61x
VAW-111 Det 4	E-1B	NL	01x
HC-1 Det 6	SH-3G	NL	00x

Air Combat victories (0):

Combat losses (0):

Data after 29 January 1973 not available.

Operational losses (0):

Data after 29 January 1973 not available.

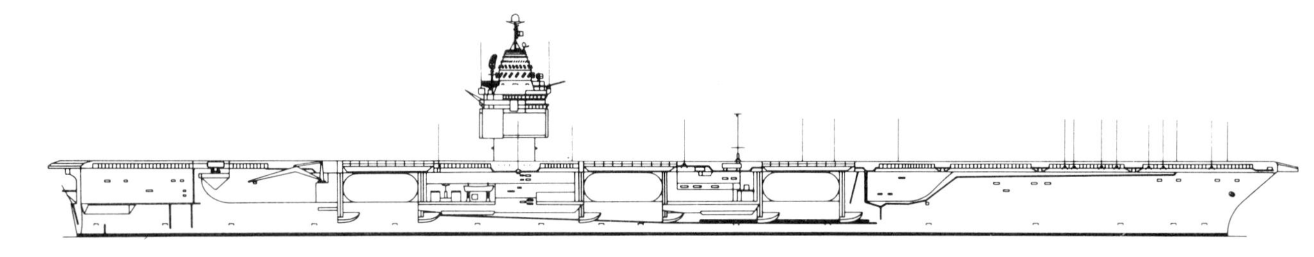

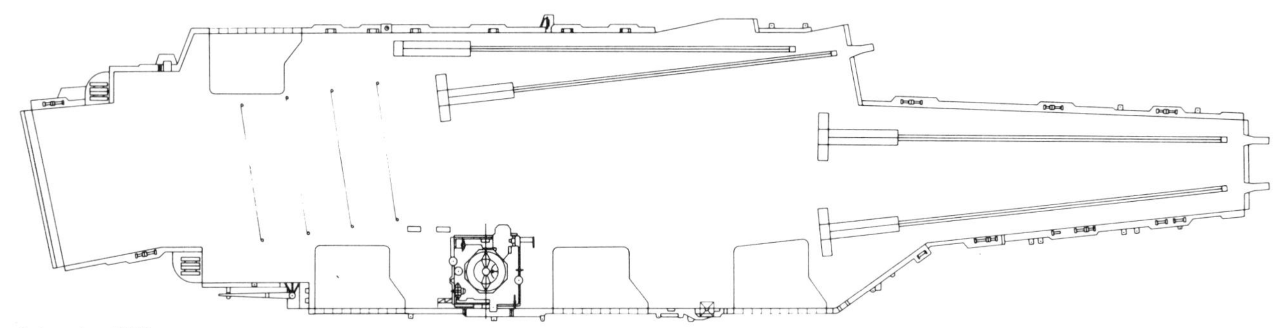

Enterprise *1968*

USS *Enterprise* (CVAN-65)

Air Wing: CVW-9

Homeport departure/return: Norfolk, 26 October 1965–21 June 1966 Alameda

In-chop/out-chop: 21 November 1965–14 June 1966

On Line periods: 2 December 1965–15 January 1966; 4–23 February 1966; 16 March 1966–11 April 1966; 21 April 1966–14 May 1966; 22 May 1966–5 June 1966 *Total*: 131 days on the line

Squadrons:

VF-92	F-4B	NG 2xx
VF-96	F-4B	NG 6xx
VA-36	A-4C	NG 7xx
VA-76	A-4C	NG 5xx
VA-93	A-4C	NG 3xx
VA-94	A-4C	NG 4xx
VAH-4 Det M	A-3B	ZB 11x
RVAH-7	RA-5C	NG 10x
VAW-11 Det M	E-1B	RR 00x
HC-1 Det 1 Unit M	UH-2A/B	UP x

Air Combat victories (0):

Combat losses (16):

2 December 1965: F-4B (151409, NG 206) of VF-92; own Mk-82 bombs; South Vietnam; Lt T J Potter and Lt (jg) D W Schmidt, both recovered.

15 December 1965: RA-5C (151633, NG 1??) of RVAH-7; AAA; South Vietnam; Lt J K Sutor and Lt (jg) G B Dresser, both recovered.

22 December 1965: A-4C (149521, NG 502) of VA-76; AAA; North Vietnam; Lt J D Prudhomme, KIA.

22 December 1965: A-4C (148305, NG 705) of VA-36; AAA; North Vietnam; Lt (jg) W R Alcorn, POW.

23 December 1965: A-4C (149562, NG 414) of VA-94; AAA; North Vietnam; Lt (jg) W L Shankel, POW.

28 December 1965: F-4B (151412, NG 203) of VF-92; cause unknown; Laos; Cdr E A Rawsthorne and Lt A S Hill, Jr, both KIA.

2 January 1966: A-4C (147704, NG 501) of VA-76; AAA; South Vietnam; Lt (jg) D C MacLaughlin, KIA.

14 January 1966: A-4C (147753, NG 713) of VA-36; own Snakeye bomb; Laos; Lt (jg) S B Jordan, recovered.

18 February 1966: F-4B (152297, NG 201) of VF-92; SAM; North Vietnam; Lt (jg) J T Ruffin, KIA, and Lt (jg) L H Spencer, POW.

17 March 1966: A-4C (147740, NG 401) of VA-94; SAM; North Vietnam; Lt (jg) F C Baldock, Jr, POW.

20 March 1966: A-4C (148313, NG 703) of VA-36; AAA; North Vietnam; Cdr J A Mulligan, POW.

20 March 1966: F-4B (151410, NG 202) of VF-92; AAA; North Vietnam; Lt (jg) J S Greenwood, recovered, and Lt (jg) R R Ratzlaff, POW.

21 March 1966: A-4C (149515, NG 406) of VA-94; SAM and/or collision; North Vietnam; Lt F R Compton, KIA.

21 March 1966: A-4C (148499, NG 411) of VA-94; SAM and/or collision; North Vietnam; LCdr J M Tiderman, KIA.

25 March 1966: A-4C (148444, NG 502) of VA-76; AAA; North Vietnam; Lt (jg) B E Smith, POW.

23 May 1966: A-4C (147762, NG 712) of VA-36; AAA; North Vietnam; Ens K W Leuffen, recovered.

Operational losses (4):

2 December 1965: F-4B (149468) of VF-96; both crew members recovered.

28 December 1965: F-4B (151438) of VF-96; both crew members recovered.

23 March 1966: A-4C (147738) of VA-93; pilot killed.

1 April 1966: A-3B (142665) of VAH-4; all three crew members killed.

USS *Enterprise* (CVAN-65)

Air Wing: CVW-9

Homeport departure/return: Alameda, 19 November 1966–6 July 1967

In-chop/out-chop: 3 December 1966–30 June 1967

On Line periods: 18 December 1966–16 January 1967; 1 February 1967–2 March 1967; 22 March 1967–17 April 1967; 29 April 1967–27 May 1967; 5–20 June 1967
Total: 132 days on the line

Squadrons:

VF-92	F-4B	NG 2xx
VF-96	F-4B	NG 6xx
VA-56	A-4C	NG 4xx
VA-113	A-4C	NG 3xx
VA-35	A-6A	NG 5xx
VAH-2 Det M	A-3B	ZA 11x
RVAH-7	RA-5C	NG 10x
VAW-11 Det M (became VAW-112 on 20 April 1967)	E-2A	RR 75x
HC-1 Det 1 Unit M	UH-2A/B	UP xx

Air Combat victories (0):

Combat losses (8):

12 February 1967: RA-5C (151623, NG 105) of RVAH-7; AAA; North Vietnam; Cdr D H Jarvis and Lt (jg) P H Artlip, Jr, both recovered.

20 February 1967: F-4B (150413, NG 614) of VF-96; AAA; North Vietnam; Maj R C Goodman, KIA, and Ens G L Thornton, POW.

8 April 1967: F-4B (152978, NG 610) of VF-96; AAA; North Vietnam; Lt J R Ritchie and Ens F A Schumacher, both recovered.

4 May 1967: A-4C (148514, NG 314) of VA-113; AAA; North Vietnam; Lt (jg) J S Graham, POW.

18 May 1967; A-4C (147842, NG 316) of VA-113; AAA; North Vietnam; Lt R J Haughton, POW.

19 May 1967: A-6A (152594, NG 502) of VA-35; SAM; North Vietnam; LCdr E B McDaniel, POW, and Lt J K Patterson, died in captivity.

19 May 1967: F-4B (152264, NG 604) of VF-96; SAM; North Vietnam; Cdr R Rich, MIA, and LCdr W R Stark, POW.

The nuclear powered USS Enterprise *(CVAN-65) in the South China Sea during her fourth war cruise in 1969. In addition to aircraft of CVW-9, an EA-3B of VQ-1 (with the tail code PR) can be seen on her deck. Launched on 24 September 1960,* Enterprise *was extensively modernized in the 1979-82 period and, homeported at Alameda, was still assigned to PACFLT in 1988.* (US Navy)

10 June 1967: A-4C (145145, NG 406) of VA-56; SAM; North Vietnam; Cdr P W Sherman, KIA.

Operational losses (6):

14 January 1967: A-4C (145087) of VA-56; pilot killed.

14 January 1967: A-4C (147724) of VA-56; pilot recovered.

12 February 1967: F-4B (152219) of VF-96; both crew members killed.

25 February 1967: F-4B (152989) of VF-96; both crew members recovered.

4 April 1967: F-4B (152984) of VF-92; one crew member recovered, one killed.

4 April 1967: F-4B (151493) of VF-92; one crew member recovered, one killed.

USS *Enterprise* (CVAN-65)

Air Wing: CVW-9

Homeport departure/return: Alameda, 3 January 1968–18 July 1968

In-chop/out-chop: 14 January 1968–12 July 1968

On Line periods: 22 February 1968–17 March 1968; 27 March 1968–24 April 1968; 2–20 May 1968; 1–26 June 1968
Total: 100 days on the line

Squadrons:

VF-92	F-4B	NG 2xx
VF-96	F-4B	NG 6xx
VA-56	A-4E	NG 4xx
VA-113	A-4F	NG 3xx
VA-35	A-6A	NG 5xx
VAH-2 Det 65	KA-3B	ZA x
RVAH-1	RA-5C	NG 10x
VAW-13 Det 65	EKA-3B	VR xx
VAW-112	E-2A	NG 70x
HC-1 Det 65	UH-2C	UP xx

Air Combat victories (1):

9 May 1968: MiG-21 shot down by F-4B (153036, NG 6xx, Maj John P Hefferman, USAF, and Lt (jg) Frank A Schumacher) of VF-96.

Combat losses (11):

28 February 1968: A-6A (152938, NG 512) of VA-35; cause unknown; off North Vietnam; LCdr H A Coons and Lt T Stegman, both KIA.

1 March 1968: A-6A (152944, NG 504) of VA-35; cause unknown; North Vietnam; LCdr T E Scheurich, MIA, and Lt (jg) R C Lannon, KIA.

16 March 1968: A-6A (152940, NG 510) of VA-35; AAA; North Vietnam; LCdr E A Shuman III and LCdr D W Doss, both POW.

5 May 1968: RA-5C (149278, NG 102) of RVAH-1; AAA; North Vietnam; Lt G R Worrington and Lt R G Tangeman, both POW.

7 May 1968: F-4B (151485, NG 210) of VF-92; MiG's AAM; North Vietnam; LCdr E S Christensen and Lt (jg) W A Kramer, both recovered.

7 May 1968: A-4F (154214, NG 302) of VA-113; cause unknown; North Vietnam; LCdr P W Paine, KIA.

8 May 1968: A-4E (152005, NG 406) of VA-56; AAA; North Vietnam; Lt D A Lawrence, recovered.

13 May 1968: A-6A (152951, NG 510) of VA-35; AAA; North Vietnam; Lt B B Brehner and Lt J T Fardy, both recovered.

15 June 1968: A-4E (149665, NG 414) of VA-56; small arms fire; North Vietnam; Lt J M Wright, recovered.

23 June 1968: A-4F (154216, NG 301) of VA-113; AAA; North Vietnam; Lt E E Christensen, recovered.

24 June 1968: A-6A (152949, NG 503) of VA-35; AAA; North Vietnam; Lt N M Carpenter, KIA, and Lt (jg) J S Mobley, POW.

Operational losses (4):

12 March 1968: A-6A (152943) of VA-35; both crew members killed.

5 April 1968: F-4B (150463) of VF-96; both crew members recovered.

2 June 1968: F-4B (150453) of VF-92; both crew members recovered.

7 June 1968: F-4B (150994) of VF-92; both crew members recovered.

USS *Enterprise* (CVAN-65)

Air Wing: CVW-9

Homeport departure/return: Alameda, 6 January 1969–2 July 1969

In-chop/out-chop: 17 March 1969–26 June 1969

On Line periods: 31 March 1969–17 April 1969; 31 May 1969–16 June 1969
Total: 35 days on the line

Squadrons:

VF-92	F-4J	NG 2xx
VF-96	F-4J	NG 1xx
VA-146	A-7B	NG 3xx
VA-215	A-7B	NG 4xx
VA-145	A-6A/B	NG 5xx
RVAH-6	RA-5C	NG 60x
VAQ-132	KA/EKA-3B	NG 61x
VAW-112	E-2A	NG 01x
HC-1 Det 65	UH-2C	UP 00x

Air Combat victories (0):

Combat losses (1):

31 March 1969: RA-5C (150842, NG 604) of RVAH-6; AAA; Laos; Cdr D E White and Lt R L Carpenter, both KIA.

Operational losses (1):

8 June 1969: A-7B (154383) of VA-215; pilot recovered.

Remarks:

14 January 1969: Major fire during ORI off Hawaii: 27 men died, 344 were injured, and 15 aircraft were lost.

USS *Enterprise* (CVAN-65)

Air Wing: CVW-14

Homeport departure/return: Alameda, 11 June 1971–12 February 1972

In-chop/out-chop: 27 June 1971–2 February 1972

On Line periods: 16–31 July 1971; 16 August 1971–4 September 1971; 11 October 1971–3 November 1971; 19 November 1971–10 December 1971; 19–24 January 1972
Total: 88 days on the line

Squadrons:

VF-142	F-4J	NK	2xx
VF-143	F-4J	NK	1xx
VA-27	A-7E	NK	4xx
VA-97	A-7E	NK	3xx
VA-196	A-6A/B and KA-6D	NK	5xx
RVAH-5	RA-5C	NK	60x
VAQ-130 Det 4	EKA-3B	NK	61x
VAW-113	E-2B	NK	01x
HC-1 Det 4	SH-3G	NK	00x

Air Combat victories (0):

Combat losses (0):

Operational losses (2):

12 October 1971: A-7E (156866) of VA-97; pilot recovered.

17 October 1971: RA-5C (156634) of RVAH-5; both crew members killed.

USS *Enterprise* (CVAN-65)

Air Wing: CVW-14

Homeport departure/return: Alameda, 12 September 1972–12 June 1973

In-chop/out-chop: 19 September 1972–3 June 1973

On Line periods: 3–22 October 1972; 1 November 1972–9 December 1972; 19 December 1972–12 January 1973; 24 January 1973–25 February 1973; 1 March 1973–6 April 1973; 16 April 1973–6 May 1973; 21–28 May 1973
Total: 183 days on the line

Squadrons:

VF-142	F-4J	NK	2xx
VF-143	F-4J	NK	1xx
VA-27	A-7E	NK	4xx
VA-97	A-7E	NK	3xx
VA-196	A-6A/B and KA-6D	NK	5xx
RVAH-13	RA-5C	NK	60x
VAQ-131	EA-6B	NK	61x
VAW-113	E-2B	NK	01x
HS-2 Det 1	SH-3G	NK	00x

Air Combat victories (1):

28 December 1972: MiG-21 shot down by F-4J (155846, NK 214, Lt (jg) Scott H Davis and Lt (jg) Geoffrey H Ulrich) of VF-142.

Combat losses (3):

20 December 1972: A-6A (155594, NK 511) of VA-196; AAA; North Vietnam; Cdr G R Nakagawa and Lt K H Higon, both POW.

28 December 1972: RA-5C (156633, NK 603) of RVAH-13; MiG's AAM; North Vietnam; LCdr A H Agnew, POW, and Lt M F Haifley, KIA.

27 January 1973: F-4J (155768, NK 113) of VF-143; AAA; South Vietnam; Cdr H H Hall and LCdr P A Kientzler, both POW.

Data after 29 January 1973 not available.

Operational losses (1):

23 November 1972: A-7E (157592) of VA-27; pilot recovered.

Data after 29 January 1973 not available.

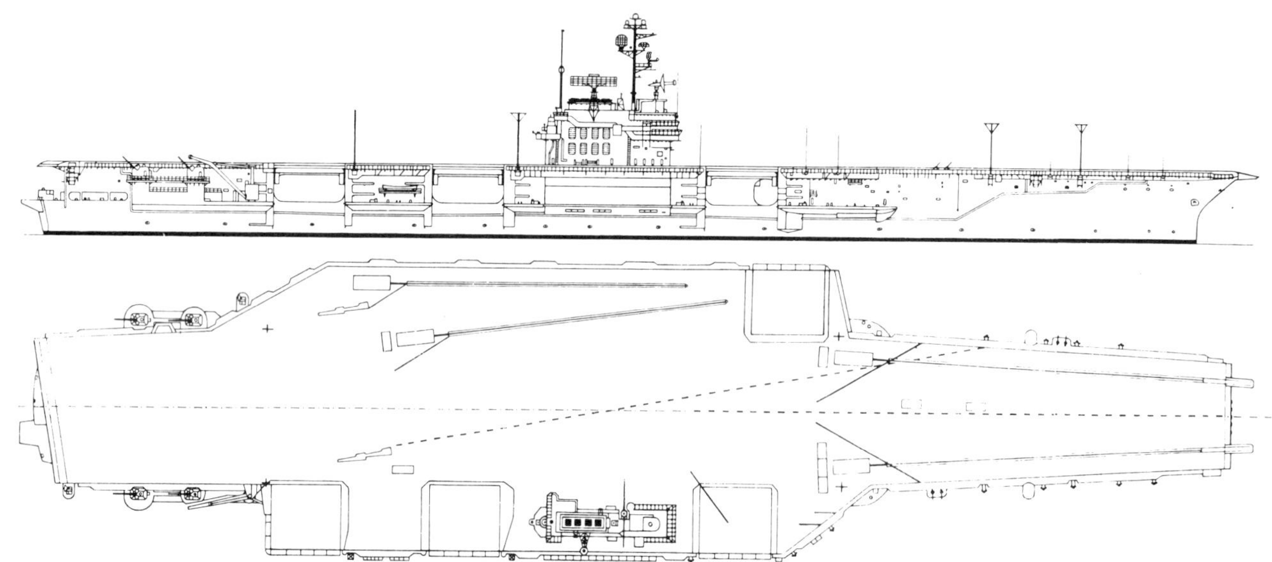

Forrestal *and* Saratoga *in 1965*

USS *Forrestal* (CVA-59)

Air Wing: CVW-17

Homeport departure/return: Norfolk, 6 June 1967–14 September 1967

In-chop/out-chop: 8 July 1967–22 August 1967

On Line periods: 25–29 July 1967
Total: 5 days on the line

Squadrons:

VF-11	F-4B	AA	1xx
VF-74	F-4B	AA	2xx
VA-46	A-4E	AA	4xx
VA-106	A-4E	AA	3xx
VA-65	A-6A	AA	5xx
RVAH-11	RA-5C	AA	60x
VAH-10 Det 59	KA-3B	AA	61x
VAW-123	E-2A	AA	70x
HC-2 Det 59	UH-2A/B	HU	xx

Air Combat victories (0):

Combat losses (0):

Operational losses (0):

Remarks:

29 July 1967: A catastrophic fire while on the line in the Gulf of Tonkin resulted in 134 officers and enlisted men being killed or lost and sixty-two injured. The following twenty-one aircraft were lost as a result of this fire: seven F-4B's (BuNos 153046, 153054, 153060, 153061, 153066, 153069, and 153912), eleven A-4E's (BuNos 149996, 150064, 150068, 150084, 150115, 150118, 150129, 152018, 152024, 152036, and 152040), and three RA-5C's (BuNos 148932, 149282, and 149305).

The unlucky USS Forrestal *(CVA-59) spent only five days on the line as she suffered serious damage and heavy casualties during a fire on 29 July 1967.* (US Navy via Naval Institute Press)

USS *Hancock* (CVA-19)

Air Wing: CVW-21

Homeport departure/return: North Island, 21 October 1964–29 May 1965

In-chop/out-chop: 16 November 1964–11 May 1965

On Line periods: 28 December 1964–16 January 1965; 1–11 February 1965; 15–17 February 1965; 5 March 1965–5 April 1965; 17 April 1965–2 May 1965
Total: 82 days on the line

Squadrons:

VF-211	F-8E	NP	1xx
VF-24	F-8C	NP	4xx
VA-212	A-4E	NP	2xx
VA-216	A-4C	NP	6xx
VA-215	A-1H/J	NP	5xx
VAH-4 Det L	A-3B	ZB	x
VFP-63 Det L	RF-8A	PP	9xx
VAW-11 Det L	E-1B	RR	x
HU-1 Det 1 Unit L	UH-2A	UP	xx

Air Combat victories (0):

Combat losses (7):

26 March 1965: A-1H (139790, NP 5??) of VA-215; AAA; North Vietnam; Lt (jg) C E Gudmunson, recovered.

26 March 1965; A-4E (150130, NP 2??) of VA-212; AAA; North Vietnam; Cdr K L Shugart, recovered.

31 March 1965: A-1H (137584, NP 5??) of VA-215; AAA; North Vietnam; Lt (jg) G W McKinley, KIA

2 April 1965: A-1H (139721, NP 5??) of VA-215; AAA; Laos; LCdr J J Evans, KIA.

3 April 1965: A-4C (148557, NP 6??) of VA-216; small arms fire; North Vietnam; LCdr R A Vohden, POW.

19 April 1965: A-1H (139818, NP 5??) of VA-215; cause unknown; North Vietnam; Lt (jg) J P Shea, KIA.

27 April 1965: A-1H (137545, NP 5??) of VA-215; AAA; Laos; Lt (jg) S B Wilkes, recovered.

Operational losses (5):

22 December 1964: A-3B (142250) of VAH-4; three crew members recovered, one killed.

30 December 1964: A-4C (149625) of VA-216; pilot killed.

13 January 1965: F-8C (147011) of VF-24; pilot recovered.

21 February 1965: F-8E (150897) of VF-211; pilot recovered.

3 March 1965: A-4C (149612) of VA-216; pilot killed

USS *Hancock* (CVA-19)

Air Wing: CVW-21

Homeport departure/return: North Island, 10 November 1965–1 August 1966

In-chop/out-chop: 6 December 1965–21 July 1966

On Line periods: 17 December 1965–23 January 1966; 12 February 1966–5 March 1966; 22 March 1966–9 April 1966; 28 April 1966–13 May 1966; 15–28 May 1966; 6–21 June 1966; 23 June 1966–10 July 1966
Total: 143 days on the line

Squadrons:

VF-24	F-8C	NP	4xx
VF-211	F-8E	NP	1xx
VA-212	A-4E	NP	2xx
VA-216	A-4C	NP	6xx
VA-215	A-1H/J	NP	5xx
VFP-63 Det L	RF-8A	PP	90x
VAW-11 Det L	E-1B	RR	72x
HC-1 Det 1 Unit L	UH-2A/B	UP	xx

Air Combat victories (3):

12 June 1966: MiG-17 shot down by F-8E (150924, NP 1??, Cdr Harold L Marr) of VF-211.

21 June 1966: MiG-17 shot down by F-8E (150924, NP 1??, Lt (jg) Phillip V Vampatella) of VF-211.

21 June 1966: MiG-17 shot down by F-8E (150867, NP 1?? Lt Eugene J Chancy) of VF-211.

Combat losses (16):

5 March 1966: A-1H (137589, NP 5??) of VA-215; AAA; North Vietnam; Cdr R C Hesson, KIA.

3 April 1966: F-8E (146919, NP 450) of VF-24; AAA; North Vietnam; Lt R L Laws, KIA.

9 April 1966: RF-8A (144611, PP 908) of VFP-63; AAA; North Vietnam; Lt (jg) T G Walster, KIA.

29 April 1966: F-8E (150867, NP 111) of VF-211; cause unknown; North Vietnam; Lt (jg) T E Brown, KIA.

29 April 1966: A-1H (137576, NP 567) of VA-215; small arms fire; Laos; LCdr W P Egan, KIA.

1 May 1966: A-4E (151179, NP 228) of VA-212; own rocket; North Vietnam; Lt R H Mansfield, recovered.

2 May 1966: F-8E (149169, NP 100) of VF-211; AAA; North Vietnam; Lt E J Chancy, recovered.

5 May 1966: RF-8A (146831, PP 908) of VFP-63; AAA; North Vietnam; Lt J Heilig, POW.

9 May 1966: A-1H (139616, NP 570) of VA-215; cause unknown; South Vietnam; LCdr C W Sommers, recovered.

21 May 1966: A-4C (148473, NP 690) of VA-216; small arms fire; North Vietnam; LCdr O F Baldwin, recovered.

23 May 1966: F-8E (150901, NP 102) of VF-211; AAA; North Vietnam; Lt L S Miller, recovered.

17 June 1966: A-4C (149528, NP 693) of VA-216; AAA; North Vietnam; Lt (jg) P E Galanti, POW.

21 June 1966: RF-8A (146830, PP 909) of VFP-63; AAA; North Vietnam; Lt L C Eastman, POW.

21 June 1966: F 8E (149152, NP 100) of VF 211; AAA; North Vietnam; Lt C Black, POW.

4 July 1966: A-4C (149616, NP 688) of VA-216; AAA; North Vietnam; LCdr O F Baldwin, recovered.

7 July 1966: A-4C (148456, NP 685) of VA-216; AAA; North Vietnam; LCdr W J Isenhour, recovered.

Operational losses (9):

24 December 1965: F-8E (150891) of VF-211; pilot recovered.
10 January 1966: UH-2A (149751) of HC-1; four crew members recovered.
16 January 1966: F-8C (147012) of VF-24; pilot killed.
27 March 1966: A-4E (150128) of VA-212; pilot recovered.
6 April 1966: A-4E (152052) of VA-212; pilot killed.
14 May 1966: A-1J (142050) of VA-215; pilot recovered.
20 June 1966: EA-1F (135010) of VAW-13; two crew members recovered, one killed.
27 June 1966: A-4E (150000) of VA-212; pilot recovered.
8 July 1966: A-4C (149494) of VA-216; pilot recovered.

USS *Hancock* (CVA-19)

Air Wing: CVW-5

Homeport departure/return: North Island, 5 January 1967–22 July 1967

In-chop/out-chop: 20 January 1967–14 July 1967

On Line periods: 5–25 February 1967; 16 March 1967–11 April 1967; 28 April 1967–4 June 1967; 12–27 June 1967
Total: 102 days on the line

Squadrons:

VF-51	F-8E	NF	1xx
VF-53	F-8E	NF	2xx
VA-93	A-4E	NF	3xx
VA-94	A-4C	NF	4xx
VA-115	A-1H/J	NF	5xx
VAH-4 Det B	A-3B	ZB	x
VFP-63 Det B	RF-8G	PP	91x
VAW-11 Det B	E-1B	RR	72x
(became VAW-111 Det 19 on 20 April 1967)			
HC-1 Det 19	UH-2A/B	UP	x

Air Combat victories (0):

Combat losses (9):

17 March 1967: A-1H (135297, NF 514) of VA-115; small arms fire, North Vietnam; LCdr A H Henderson, recovered.
17 March 1967: A-1H (139768, NF 504) of VA-115; small arms fire; North Vietnam; Lt R B Moore, recovered.
6 May 1967: A-4E (151002, NF 310) of VA-93; AAA; North Vietnam; Lt (jg) R E Wideman, POW.
10 May 1967: A-4C (149509, NF 404) of VA-94; SAM; North Vietnam; Cdr R M Netherland, KIA.
17 May 1967: F-8E (149138, NF 101) of VF-51; AAA; North Vietnam; Lt R W Dodge, POW.
24 May 1967: A-4E (151076, NF 311) of VA-93; AAA; North Vietnam; Lt (jg) M Alsop, recovered.
26 May 1967: A-4E (152022, NF 300) of VA-93; AAA; North Vietnam; Lt (jg) R B McCleary, POW.
30 May 1967: A-4E (151049, NF 301) of VA-93; SAM; North Vietnam; Cdr J P Mehl, POW.
22 June 1967: A-4E (151106, NF 302) of VA-93; AAA; North Vietnam; LCdr J G Pirie, POW.

Operational losses (7):

11 February 1967: F-8E (149192) of VF-51; pilot recovered.
14 February 1967: A-1H (139805) of VA-115; pilot killed.
17 March 1967: A-1H (135225) of VA-115; pilot killed.
17 March 1967: A-1H (134625) of VA-115; pilot recovered.
25 March 1967: F-8E (149147) of VF-53; pilot killed.
30 March 1967: A-4C (147844) of VA-94; pilot recovered.
1 May 1967: F-8E (150301) of VF-51; pilot recovered.

USS *Hancock* (CVA-19)

Air Wing: CVW-21

Homeport departure/return: North Island, 18 July 1968–3 March 1969

In-chop/out-chop: 6 August 1968–23 February 1969

On Line periods: 23 August 1968–4 September 1968; 14 September 1968–14 October 1968; 3–28 November 1968; 20 December 1968–14 January 1969; 30 January 1969–9 February 1969
Total: 107 days on the line

Squadrons:

VF-24	F-8H	NP	2xx
VF-211	F-8H	NP	1xx
VA-55	A-4F	NP	5xx
VA-163	A-4E	NP	3xx
VA-164	A-4E	NP	4xx
VFP-63 Det 19	RF-8G	NP	6xx
VAW-13 Det 19	EKA-3B	NP	84x
(became VAQ-130 Det 19 on 1 October 1968)			
VAW-111 Det 19	E-1B	NP	72x
HC-1 Det 19	UH-2C	UP	x

Air Combat victories (0):

Combat losses (4):

17 September 1968: F-8H (148648, NP 204) of VF-24; AAA; North Vietnam; Lt (jg) P E Swigart, recovered.
23 September 1968: A-4F (155015, NP 507) of VA-55; AAA; North Vietnam; LCdr D H Osborne, POW.
28 September 1968: A-4F (155011, NP 511) of VA-55; AAA; North Vietnam; Lt D J Wright, recovered.
2 October 1968: A-4E (151126, NP 411) of VA-164; AAA; North Vietnam; Cdr D E Erwin, KIA.

Operational losses (7):

19 August 1968: F-8H (147924) of VF-24; pilot recovered.
24 August 1968: F-8H (148694) of VF-211; pilot recovered.
30 August 1968: F-8H (147897) of VF-24; pilot killed.
3 October 1968: RF-8G (144620) of VFP-63; pilot killed.
15 November 1968: F-8H (147923) of VF-211; pilot recovered.
4 February 1969: F-8H (147919) of VF-24; pilot killed.
8 February 1969: A-4E (151103) of VA-164; pilot killed.

With a total of eight, USS Hancock *(CVA-19) set the record for the number of combat cruises. On all but one of these cruises, her Air Wing was CVW-21, the exception being the January–July 1967 cruise when CVW-5 was embarked.* (US Navy via Naval Institute Press)

USS *Hancock* (CVA-19)

Air Wing: CVW-21

Homeport departure/return: North Island, 2 August 1969–15 April 1970

In-chop/out-chop: 21 August 1969–6 April 1970

On Line periods: 1–24 September 1969; 4–27 October 1969; 24 November 1969–17 December 1969; 19 January 1970–11 February 1970; 8–26 March 1970
Total: 115 days on the line

Squadrons:

VF-24	F-8H	NP	2xx
VF 211	F 8J	NP	1xx
VA-55	A-4F	NP	5xx
VA-164	A-4F	NP	4xx
VA-212	A-4F	NP	3xx
VAH-10 Det 19	KA-3B	NP	61x
VFP-63 Det 19	RF-8G	NP	60x
VAW-111 Det 19	E-1B	NP	01x
HC-1 Det 19	SH-3A	NP	00x

Air Combat victories (0):

Combat losses (2):
14 March 1970: A-4F (155010, NP 501) of VA-55; AAA; Laos; Lt (jg) P A Schranz, recovered.
15 March 1970: A-4F (155044, NP 307) of VA-212; AAA; Laos; LCdr R W Hunter, recovered.

Operational losses (6).
28 November 1969: F-8J (150349) of VF-211; pilot recovered.
16 December 1969: RF-8G (145611) of VFP-63; pilot killed.
8 February 1970: SH-3A (149707) of HC-1; all seven crew members recovered.
9 February 1970: A-4F (155005) of VA-212; pilot killed.
10 February 1970: A-4F (155023) of VF-164; pilot recovered.
8 March 1970: A-4F (154994) of VA-212; pilot recovered.

USS *Hancock* (CVA-19)

Air Wing: CVW-21

Homeport departure/return: North Island, 22 October 1970–2 June 1971

In-chop/out-chop: 7 November 1970–19 May 1971

On Line periods: 20 November 1970–7 December 1970; 30 December 1970–4 January 1971; 24 January 1971–20 February 1971; 9 March 1971–9 April 1971; 18 April 1971–3 May 1971
Total: 100 days on the line

Squadrons:

VF-24	F-8J	NP	2xx
VF-211	F-8J	NP	1xx
VA-55	A-4F	NP	5xx
VA-164	A-4F	NP	4xx
VA-212	A-4F	NP	3xx
VFP-63 Det 1	RF-8G	NP	60x
VAQ-129 Det 19	EKA-3B	NP	61x
VAW-111 Det 3	E-1B	NP	01x
HC-1 Det 7	UH-2C	NP	00x

Air Combat victories (0):

Combat losses (0):

Operational losses (3):

26 January 1971: A-4F (154930) of VA-164; pilot recovered.

5 February 1971: F-8J (149197) of VF-211; pilot recovered.

16 March 1971: F-8J (150294) of VF-211; pilot recovered.

USS *Hancock* (CVA-19)

Air Wing: CVW-21

Homeport departure/return: North Island, 7 January 1972–3 October 1972

In-chop/out-chop: 28 January 1972–25 September 1972

On Line periods: 7 February 1972–8 March 1972; 26 March 1972–29 April 1972; 12 May 1972–4 June 1972; 14 June 1972–14 July 1972; 23 July 1972–16 August 1972; 27 August 1972–14 September 1972
Total: 165 days on the line

Squadrons:

VF-24	F-8J	NP	2xx
VF-211	F-8J	NP	1xx
VA-55	A-4F	NP	5xx
VA-164	A-4F	NP	4xx
VA-212	A-4F	NP	3xx
VFP-63 Det 1	RF-8G	NP	60x
VAQ-135 Det 5	EKA-3B	NP	61x
VAW-111 Det 2	E-1B	NP	01x
HC-1 Det 7	SH-3G	NP	00x

Air Combat victories (0):

Combat losses (8):

8 March 1972: A-4F (154205, NP 502) of VA-55; AAA; Laos; Cdr G J Fenzl, recovered.

24 May 1972: F-8J (150311, NP 201) of VF-24; SAM or MiG; North Vietnam; Lt C R Beeler, POW.

25 May 1972: A-4F (155045, NP 301) of VA-212; AAA; North Vietnam; Cdr H H Strong, MIA.

27 May 1972: A-4F (155048, NP 512) of VA-55; AAA; North Vietnam; Lt T B Latendresse, POW.

20 June 1972: F-8J (150923, NP 102) of VF-211; AAA; South Vietnam; Cdr J W Davis, recovered.

9 July 1972: A-4F (154972, NP 312) of VA-212; probably AAA; North Vietnam; Cdr F C Greene, MIA.

11 July 1972: A-4F (155046, NP 501) of VA-55; SAM; North Vietnam; LCdr H D Lesesne, POW.

6 September 1972: A-4F (155021, NP 304) of VA-212; AAA; North Vietnam; Lt W F Pear, recovered.

Operational losses (4):

27 May 1972: A-4F (154197) of VA-55; pilot recovered.

12 August 1972: F-8J (150336) of VF-24; pilot killed.

5 September 1972: RF-8G (146861) of VFP-63; pilot recovered.

5 September 1972: F-8J (150229) of VF-24; pilot recovered.

USS *Hancock* (CVA-19)

Air Wing: CVW-21

Homeport departure/return: North Island, 8 May 1973–8 January 1974

In-chop/out-chop: 19 May 1973–24 December 1973

On Line periods: 1 June 1973; 3–9 June 1973; 21–30 June 1973; 27 July 1973–6 August 1973; remained on the line for four more periods after the cut-off date of 15 August 1973
Total: 29 days on the line

Squadrons:

VF-24	F-8J	NP	2xx
VF-211	F-8J	NP	1xx
VA-55	A-4F	NP	5xx
VA-164	A-4F/TA-4F	NP	4xx
VA-212	A-4F	NP	3xx
VFP-63 Det 1	RF-8G	NP	6xx
VAQ-135 Det 5	EKA-3B	NP	61x
VAW-111 Det 2	E-1B	NP	01x
HC-1 Det 3	SH-3G	NP	0xx

Air Combat victories (0):

Combat losses (0):

Data after 29 January 1973 not available.

Operational losses (0):

Data after 29 January 1973 not available.

Seen here prior to the Southeast Asia War, when her fighter squadrons were still flying Demons and Crusaders, USS Independence (CVA 62) was deployed only once to the Gulf of Tonkin. She spent 100 days on the line between June and November 1965. (US Navy via Naval Institute Press)

USS *Independence* (CVA-62)

Air Wing: CVW-7

Homeport departure/return: Norfolk, 10 May 1965–13 December 1965

In-chop/out-chop: 5 June 1965–21 November 1965

On Line periods: 27 June 1965–8 August 1965; 25 August 1965–21 September 1965; 14 October 1965–11 November 1965

Total: 100 days on the line

Squadrons:

VF-41	F-4B	AG	1xx
VF-84	F-4B	AG	2xx
VA-72	A-4E	AG	3xx
VA-86	A-4E	AG	4xx
VA-75	A-6A	AG	5xx
VAH-4 Det 62	A-3B	ZB	x, then AG 8xx
RVAH-1	RA-5C	AG	60x
VAW-12 Det 62	E-1B	AG	7xx
HU-2 Det 62	UH-2A	HU	xx

(became HC-2 Det 62 on 1 July 1965)

Air Combat victories (0):

Combat losses (13):

14 July 1965: A-6A (151584, AG 507) of VA-75; own Mk-82 bombs; Laos; Lt D Boecker and Lt D R Eaton, both recovered.

18 July 1965: A-6A (151577, AG 500) of VA-75; own Mk-82 bombs; Laos; Cdr J A Denton and Lt (jg) W M Tschudy, both POW.

24 July 1965: A-6A (151585, AG 508) of VA-75; own Mk-82 bombs; Laos; LCdr R P Bordone and Lt (jg) P F Moffett, both recovered.

13 September 1965: A-4E (149999, AG 304) of VA-72; AAA; North Vietnam; Lt (jg) J R Mossman, KIA.

17 September 1965: A-6A (151588, AG 511) of VA-75; AAA; North Vietnam; Cdr L F Vogt, Jr, and Lt R F Barber, both KIA.

20 September 1965: A-4E (151115, AG 313) of VA-72; AAA; North Vietnam; Lt (jg) J R Harris, recovered.

16 October 1965: RA-5C (151615, AG 601) of RVAH-1; AAA; North Vietnam; LCdr J F Bell and LCdr J L Hutton, both POW.

17 October 1965: F-4B (151515, AG 205) of VF-84; AAA; North Vietnam; LCdr S E Olmstead, KIA, and Lt (jg) P A Halyburton, POW.

17 October 1965: F-4B (151494, AG 210) of VF-84; AAA; North Vietnam; Ens R E Gaither and Lt (jg) R A Knutson, both POW.

17 October 1965: F-4B (150631, AG 105) of VF-41; small arms fire; North Vietnam; Lt R L Mayer and Lt (jg) D R Wheat, both POW.

25 October 1965: F-4B (151505, AG 208) of VF-84; AAA; North Vietnam; Lt G G Ericksen and Lt (jg) J L Perry, both recovered.

28 October 1965: F-4B (150626, AG 104) of VF-41; small arms fire; Laos; LCdr A M Lindsey and Lt (jg) R W Cooper, both recovered.

1 November 1965: A-4E (151142, AG 409) of VA-86; AAA; North Vietnam; LCdr B V Wheat, recovered.

Operational losses (4):

20 July 1965: RA-5C (151619) of RVAH-1; both crew members killed.

30 August 1965: C-1A (146047); all seven crew members and passengers recovered.

12 September 1965: C-1A (136784) of VR-21; nine crew members and passengers recovered, one killed.

22 September 1965: E-1B (148918) of VAW-12; all four crew members recovered.

USS *Intrepid* (CVS-11)

Air Wing: CVW-10

Homeport departure/return: Norfolk, 4 April 1966–21 November 1966

In-chop/out-chop: 1 May 1966–30 October 1966

On Line periods: 15 May 1966–14 June 1966; 9 July 1966–9 August 1966; 1–23 September 1966; 1–17 October 1966
Total: 103 days on the line

Squadrons:

VA-15	A-4B	AK	3xx
VA-95	A-4B	AK	5xx
VA-165	A-1H	AK	2xx
VA-176	A-1H	AK	4xx
HC-2 Det 11	UH-2A/B	HU	x

Air Combat victories (1):
9 October 1966: MiG-17 shot down by A-1H (137543, AK 409, Lt (jg) William T Patton) of VA-176.

Combat losses (3):
2 September 1966: A-1H (137534, AK 206) of VA-165; AAA; North Vietnam; Cdr W S Jett, III, recovered.
13 September 1966: A-1H (134534, AK 208) of VA-165; AAA; North Vietnam; Lt (jg) T J Dwyer, recovered.
22 September 1966: A-1H (135239, AK 401) of VA-176; AAA; North Vietnam; Lt C A Knochel, KIA.

Operational losses (2):
19 June 1966: UH-2A (149757) of HC-2; one crew member recovered, three killed.
7 August 1966: A-4B (145040) of VA-15; pilot killed.

USS *Intrepid* (CVS-11)

Air Wing: CVW-10

Homeport departure/return: Norfolk, 11 May 1967–30 December 1967

In-chop/out-chop: 9 June 1967–9 December 1967

On Line periods: 21 June 1967–13 July 1967; 30 July 1967–27 August 1967; 15 September 1967–12 October 1967; 1–23 November 1967
Total: 103 days on the line

Squadrons:

VF-111 Det 11	F-8C	AH	1x
VSF-3	A-4B	AK	1xx
VA-15	A-4C	AK	2xx
VA-34	A-4C	AK	3xx
VA-145	A-1H/J	AK	5xx
VFP-63 Det 11	RF-8G	AK	4xx
VAW-121 Det 11	E-1B	AK	7xx
HC-2 Det 11	UH-2A/B	HU	xx

Air Combat victories (0):

Combat losses (12):
30 June 1967: A-4C (148466, AK 205) of VA-15; AAA; North Vietnam; Lt L O Cole, Jr, MIA.
2 July 1967: A-4B (145002, AK 112) of VSF-3; AAA; North Vietnam; Lt (jg) F M Kasch, KIA.
4 July 1967: A-4C (148544, AK 208) of VA-15; AAA; North Vietnam; Lt P C Craig, MIA.
9 July 1967: A-4C (149603, AK 312) of VA-34; SAM; North Vietnam; LCdr E H Martin, POW.
2 August 1967: A-4C (147670, AK 212) of VA-15; AAA; North Vietnam; Lt D W Thornhill, recovered.
12 August 1967: F-8C (146993, AH 12) of VF-111; AAA; North Vietnam; LCdr F S Teague, recovered.
25 August 1967: A-4C (148440, AK 211) of VA-15; AAA; North Vietnam; Lt (jg) R W Gerard, recovered.
18 September 1967: A-4C (149590, AK 301) of VA-34; SAM; North Vietnam; LCdr S H Hawkins, recovered.
3 October 1967: A-4B (142114, AK 102) of VSF-3; AAA; North Vietnam; Lt (jg) A D Perkins, recovered.
4 October 1967: A-4C (149619, AK 200) of VA-15; AAA; North Vietnam; LCdr P V Schoeffel, POW.
7 November 1967: A-4C (148566, AK 314) of VA-34; AAA; North Vietnam; Lt (jg) M A Krebs, recovered.
17 November 1967: A-4C (149546, AK 306) of VA-34; SAM; North Vietnam; Lt W D Key, POW.

Operational losses (2):
14 June 1967: UH-2A (147983) of HC-2; four crew members recovered.
26 November 1967: A-4B (142742) of VSF-3; pilot recovered.

USS *Intrepid* (CVS-11)

Air Wing: CVW-10

Homeport departure/return: Norfolk, 4 June 1968–8 February 1969

In-chop/out-chop: 6 July 1968–16 January 1969

On Line periods: 24 July 1968–22 August 1968; 5–27 September 1968; 15 October 1968–13 November 1968; 5–27 December 1968
Total: 106 days on the line

Squadrons:

VF-111 Det 11	F-8C	AK	1xx

VA-36	A-4C	AK	5xx
VA-66	A-4C	AK	3xx
VA-106	A-4E	AK	2xx
VFP-63 Det 11	RF-8G	AK	4xx
VAW-121 Det 11	E-1B	AK	7xx
HC-2 Det 11	UH-2A/B	HU	xx

Although USS Intrepid *had been reclassified as an Antisubmarine Warfare Support Carrier in March 1962, she made three deployments to the Gulf of Tonkin as a limited capability Attack Carrier. In that role she embarked CVW-10 with Skyhawks and Skyraiders replacing the usual complement of Trackers and Sea Kings.* (US Navy via Naval Institute Press)

Air Combat victories (1):

19 September 1968: MiG-21 shot down by F-8C (146961, AK 103, Lt Anthony J Nargi) of VF-111.

Combat losses (2):

1 August 1968: A-4C (148599, AK 301) of VA-66; AAA; North Vietnam; Lt (jg) E J Broms, Jr, KIA.

21 October 1968: A-4E (151160, AK 217) of VA-106; AAA; North Vietnam; Lt K K Knabb, MIA.

Operational losses (3):

21 July 1968: RF-8G (145642) of VFP-63; pilot recovered.

20 August 1968: A-4C (148470) of VA-36; pilot recovered.

23 September 1968: A-4E (152091) of VA-106; pilot killed.

USS *Kitty Hawk* (CVA-63)

Air Wing: CVW-11

Homeport departure/return: North Island, 19 October 1965–13 June 1966

In-chop/out-chop: 15 November 1965–6 June 1966

On Line periods: 26 November 1965–24 December 1965; 14 January 1966–4 February 1966; 17 February 1966–15 March 1966; 31 March 1966–27 April 1966; 7–22 May 1966
Total: 122 days on the line

Squadrons:

VF-114	F-4B	NH 4xx
VF-213	F-4G/B	NH 1xx
VA-113	A-4C	NH 3xx
VA-115	A-1H/J	NH 5xx
VA-85	A-6A	NH 8xx
VAH-4 Det C	A-3B	ZB x
RVAH-13	RA-5C	NH 60x
VAW-11 Det C	E-2A	RR 70x
HC-1 Det 1 Unit C	UH-2A/B	UP xx

Air Combat victories (0):

Combat losses (20):

2 December 1965: F-4B (152220, NH 412) of VF-114; cause unknown; North Vietnam; Cdr C B Austin and Lt (jg) J B Logan, both KIA.

20 December 1965: RA-5C (151624, NH 604) of RVAH-13; cause unknown; North Vietnam; LCdr G D Johnson, MIA, and Lt (jg) L E Nordhal, KIA.

21 December 1965: A-6A (151781, NH 801) of VA-85; SAM; North Vietnam; Cdr B J Cartwright, KIA, and Lt E F Gold, MIA.

22 December 1965: RA-5C (151632, NH 603) of RVAH-13; AAA; North Vietnam; LCdr M D Sukenbach, KIA, and Lt (jg) G H Daigle, POW.

31 January 1966: F-4B (152233, NH 402) of VF-114; AAA; Laos; Lt W F Klumpp, II, and Lt (jg) J N Stineman, both recovered.

1 February 1966: A-1J (142038, NH 513) of VA-115; AAA; Laos; Lt (jg) B S Eakin, recovered.

3 February 1966: RA-5C (151625, NH 605) of RVAH-13; AAA; North Vietnam; Lt G L Coffee, POW, and Lt (jg) R T Hanson, Jr, died in captivity.

18 February 1966: A-6A (151797, NH 812) of VA-85; cause unknown; North Vietnam; Lt (jg) J V Murray and Lt (jg) T A Schroeffel, both KIA.

5 March 1966: F-4B (152224, NH 413) of VF-114; hit by target debris; South Vietnam; LCdr M N Guess and Lt R E Pile, both recovered.

12 April 1966: A-3B (142653, ZB 3) of VAH-4; MiG; South China Sea; LCdr W A Glasson, Lt (jg) L M Jordan, and unidentified third crew member, all KIA.

17 April 1966: A-6A (151794, NH 814) of VA-85; AAA; North Vietnam; LCdr S L Sayers and LCdr C D Hawkins, Jr, both recovered.

17 April 1966: A-1H (135398, NH 511) of VA-115; cause unknown; North Vietnam; Lt (jg) W L Tromp, died in captivity.

20 April 1966: A-4C (148512, NH 314) of VA-113; AAA; North Vietnam; Cdr J Abbott, died in captivity.

20 April 1966: A-4C (149495, NH 303) of VA-113; AAA; North Vietnam; Lt (jg) H G Welch, recovered.

21 April 1966: A-6A (151798, NH 805) of VA-85; AAA; North Vietnam; Cdr J E Keller and LCdr E E Austin, both KIA.

22 April 1966: A-6A (151785, NH 805) of VA-85; AAA; North Vietnam; LCdr R F Weimorts and Lt (jg) W B Nickerson, both KIA.

26 April 1966: F-4B (152255, NH 414) of VF-114; hit by target debris; North Vietnam; Lt (jg) W W Smith and Lt (jg) R Blake, both recovered.

27 April 1966: A-6A (151788, NH 811) of VA-85; AAA; North Vietnam; Lt W R Westerman and Lt (jg) B E Weston, both recovered.

28 April 1966: F-4G (150645, NH 111) of VF-213; AAA; North Vietnam; Lt R A Schiltz and Lt (jg) D C Lewis, both recovered.

18 May 1966: F-4B (152257, NH 113) of VF-213; AAA; Laos; LCdr C N Sommers II and LCdr W K Sullivan, both recovered.

Operational losses (5):

17 December 1965: A-4C (148510) of VA-113; pilot killed.

11 March 1966: A-1J (142071) of VA-115; pilot recovered.

17 April 1966: A-4C (148583) of VA-113; pilot recovered.

15 May 1966: A-6A (151800) of VA-85; both crew members recovered.

19 May 1966: A-1J (142051) of VA-115; pilot recovered.

USS *Kitty Hawk* (CVA-63)

Air Wing: CVW-11

Homeport departure/return: North Island, 5 November 1966–20 June 1967

In-chop/out-chop: 17 November 1966–12 June 1967

On Line periods: 4 December 1966–3 January 1967; 17 January 1967–14 February 1967; 3–28 March 1967; 12–28 April 1967; 8–22 May 1967
Total: 118 days on the line

Squadrons:

VF-114	F-4B	NH 2xx
VF-213	F-4B	NH 1xx
VA-112	A-4C	NH 4xx
VA-144	A-4C	NH 3xx
VA-85	A-6A	NH 5xx
VAH-4 Det C	A-3B	ZB x
RVAH-13	RA-5C	NH 60x

VAW-11 Det C	E-2A	RR	70x
(became VAW-114 on 20 April 1967)			
HC-1 Det 1 Unit C	UH-2A/B	UP	xx

Air Combat victories (4):

20 December 1966: An-2 shot down by F-4B (153022, NH 215, Lt H Dennis Wisely and Lt (jg) David L Jordan) of VF-114.

20 December 1966: An-2 shot down by F-4B (153019, NH 110, Lt David McCrea and Ens David Nichols) of VF-213.

24 April 1967: MiG-17 shot down by F-4B (153037, NH ?10, Lt Charles E Southwick and Ens James W Laing) of VF-114.

24 April 1967: MiG-17 shot down by F-4B (153037, NH ?00, Lt Dennis Wisely and Lt (jg) Gareth L Anderson) of VF-114.

Combat losses (14):

21 December 1966: A-4C (148507, NH 303) of VA-144; AAA; North Vietnam; Lt (jg) D E Glenn, POW.

19 January 1967: A-6A (151590, NH 510) of VA-85; AAA; North Vietnam; Cdr A C Brady, POW, and LCdr W P Yardbrough, KIA.

20 January 1967: A-4C (145144, NH 415) of VA-112; cause unknown; North Vietnam; Lt (jg) J F Hogan, MIA.

4 February 1967: F-4B (153007, NH 102) of VF-213; AAA; North Vietnam; Lt D E Thompson, MIA, and Lt A P Collamore, KIA.

8 March 1967: A-3B (144627, ZB 5) of VAH-4; cause unknown; North Vietnam; LCdr C O Crain, Lt (jg) G F Pawlish, and unidentified third crew member, all KIA.

9 March 1967; RA-5C (151627, NH 605) of RVAH-13; AAA; North Vietnam; Cdr C L Putnam, POW, and Lt (jg) F S Prendergast, recovered.

24 March 1967: A-6A (151587, NH 511) of VA-85; AAA; North Vietnam: LCdr J C Ellison and Lt (jg) J E Plowman, both KIA.

27 March 1967: A-4C (148519, NH 415) of VA-112; cause unknown; North Vietnam; Lt A J Palenscar, KIA.

24 April 1967: F-4B (153000, NH 210) of VF-114; AAA; North Vietnam; LCdr C E Southwick and Ens J W Laing, both recovered.

24 April 1967: A-6A (152589, NH 512) of VA-85; AAA; North Vietnam Lt (jg) L I Williams, Jr, and Lt (jg) M D Christian, both recovered.

14 May 1967: F-4B (153001, NH 201) of VF-114; own Zuni rockets; North Vietnam; LCdr C E Southwick and Lt D J Rollins, both POW.

19 May 1967: F-4B (153004, NH 204) of VF-114; SAM; North Vietnam; Lt (jg) J C Plumb and Lt (jg) G L Anderson, both POW.

19 May 1967: RA-5C (150826, NH 602) of RVAH-13; AAA; North Vietnam; LCdr J L Griffin and Lt J Walters, both died in captivity.

21 May 1967: F-4B (153040, NH 213) of VF-114; AAA; North Vietnam; Lt H D Wisely and Ens J W Laing, both recovered.

Operational losses (3):

19 January 1967: F-4B (153029) of VF-114; both crew members killed.

6 April 1967: F-4B (152990) of VF-114; both crew members recovered.

8 May 1967: F-4B (152997) of VF-114; one crew member recovered, one killed.

Commissioned on 29 April 1961, USS Kitty Hawk *(CVA-63) joined the Pacific Fleet after completing her shakedown cruise in the Caribbean. CVA-63 and CVW-11 left North Island on 19 October 1965 at the start of the first of their six war cruises.* (US Navy via Naval Institute Press)

USS *Kitty Hawk* (CVA-63)

Air Wing: CVW-11

Homeport departure/return: North Island, 18 November 1967–28 June 1968

In-chop/out-chop: 6 December 1967–20 June 1968

On Line periods: 23 December 1967–21 February 1968; 4–27 March 1968; 12 April 1968–1 May 1968; 13 May 1968–1 June 1968
Total: 125 days on the line

Squadrons:

VF-114	F-4B	NH 2xx
VF-213	F-4B	NH 1xx
VA-112	A-4C	NH 4xx
VA-144	A-4E	NH 3xx
VA-75	A-6A/B	NH 5xx
VAH-4 Det 63	KA-3B	ZB x
RVAH-11	RA-5C	NH 6xx
VAW-13 Det 63	EA-1F	VR 01x
VAW-114	E-2A	NH 74x
HC-1 Det 63	UH-2C	UP xx

Air Combat victories (0):

Combat losses (8):

27 December 1967: F-4B (153005, NH 205) of VF-114; cause unknown; North Vietnam; LCdr L M Lee and Lt (jg) R B Innes, both MIA.

31 December 1967: A-6A (152917, NH 501) of VA-75; SAM; North Vietnam; LCdr J D Peace and Lt G S Perisho, both KIA.

3 January 1968: A-4C (148486, NH 405) of VA-112; SAM; North Vietnam; LCdr E D Estes, POW.

5 January 1968: A-4E (152074, NH 304) of VA-144; AAA; North Vietnam; Cdr R J Schweitzer, POW.

6 March 1968: A-6A (152922, NH 511) of VA-75; cause unknown; North Vietnam; Lt R C Nelson, MIA, and Lt G L Mitchell, KIA.

13 March 1968: A-4E (152088, NH 300) of VA-144; AAA; Laos; Lt R E Curtis, recovered.

27 April 1968: A-4E (151070, NH 303) of VA-144; AAA; North Vietnam; LCdr R Saavedra, KIA.

18 May 1968: RA-5C (149283, NH 606) of RVAH-11; AAA; North Vietnam; Cdr C N James and LCdr V D Monroe, both POW.

Operational losses (7):

10 January 1968: F-4B (153063) of VF-114; both crew members recovered.

16 January 1968: C-1A (146054); seven crew members and passengers recovered, three killed.

18 January 1968: F-4B (153055) of VF-114; both crew members killed.

29 January 1968: A-4E (151055) of VA-144; pilot recovered.

15 April 1968: F-4B (153002) of VF-114; both crew members recovered.

15 April 1968: F-4B (153043) of VF-114; both crew members recovered.

20 April 1968: F-4B (153003) of VF-114; both crew members recovered.

USS *Kitty Hawk* (CVA-63)

Air Wing: CVW-11

Homeport departure/return: North Island, 30 December 1968–4 September 1969

In-chop/out-chop: 15 January 1969–27 August 1969

On Line periods: 28 January 1969–28 February 1969; 13 March 1969–4 April 1969; 18 April 1969–9 May 1969; 29 June 1969–14 July 1969; 30 July 1969–16 August 1969
Total: 111 days on the line

Squadrons:

VF-114	F-4B	NH 2xx
VF-213	F-4B	NH 1xx
VA-37	A-7A	NH 3xx
VA-105	A-7A	NH 4xx
VA-65	A-6A/B	NH 5xx
RVAH-11	RA-5C	NH 60x
VAQ-131	KA/EKA-3B	NH 61x
VAW-114	E-2A	NH 01x
HC-1 Det 63	UH-2C	UP 0x

Air Combat victories (0):

Combat losses (3):

14 February 1969: A-7A (153181, NH 412) of VA-105; unknown gunfire; Laos; Lt (jg) W C Wiedecken, KIA.

3 April 1969: A-6A (155587, NH 507) of VA-65; AAA; Laos; LCdr E G Redden and Lt J F Ricci, both recovered.

2 May 1969: A-7A (153180, NH 413) of VA-105; AAA; Laos; LCdr W J O'Connor, recovered.

Operational losses (4):

13 March 1969: F-4B (153018) of VF-114; both crew members recovered.

28 April 1969: A-7A (153164) of VA-37; pilot recovered.

3 July 1969: F-4B (153015) of VF-213; both crew members recovered.

1 August 1969: A-7A (153185) of VA-37; pilot killed

USS *Kitty Hawk* (CVA-63)

Air Wing: CVW-11

Homeport departure/return: North Island, 6 November 1970–17 July 1971

In-chop/out-chop: 27 November 1970–6 July 1971

On Line periods: 8–28 December 1970; 13 January 1971–3 February 1971; 21 February 1971–2 April 1971; 10–25 April 1971; 4–16 May 1971; 30 May 1971–23 June 1971

Total: 138 days on the line

Squadrons:

VF-114	F-4J	NH 2xx
VF-213	F-4J	NH 1xx
VA-192	A-7E	NH 3xx
VA-195	A-7E	NH 4xx
VA-52	A-6A/B	NH 5xx
RVAH-6	RA-5C	NH 60x
VAQ-133	KA/EKA-3B	NH 61x
VAW-114	E-2B	NH 01x
HC-1 Det 2	UH-2C	NH 00x

Air Combat victories (0):

Combat losses (0):

Operational losses (1):

27 February 1971: A-7E (157458) of VA-195; pilot recovered.

USS *Kitty Hawk* (CVA-63)

Air Wing: CVW-11

Homeport departure/return: North Island, 17 February 1972–28 November 1972

In-chop/out-chop: 1 March 1972–17 November 1972

On Line periods: 8–25 March 1972; 3 April 1972–25 June 1972; 8 July 1972–3 August 1972; 14 August 1972–4 September 1972; 15 September 1972–2 October 1972; 13 October 1972–4 November 1972

Total: 192 days on the line

Squadrons:

VF-114	F-4J	NH 2xx
VF-213	F-4J	NH 1xx
VA-192	A-7E	NH 3xx
VA-195	A-7E	NH 4xx
VA-52	A-6A/B and KA-6D	NH 5xx
RVAH-7	RA-5C	NH 60x
VAQ-135 Det 1	EKA-3B	NH 61x
VAW-114	E-2B	NH 01x
HC-1 Det 1	SH-3G	NH 00x

Air Combat victories (2):

6 May 1972: MiG-21 shot down by F-4J (157249, NH 206, Lt Robert G Hughes and Lt (jg) Adolph J Cruz) of VF-114.

6 May 1972: MiG-21 shot down by F-4J (157245, NH 201, LCdr Kenneth W Pettigrew and Lt (jg) Michael J McCabe) of VF-114.

Combat losses (10):

23 March 1972: A-7E (157520, NH 307) of VA-192; cause unknown; Laos; Lt D S Pike, MIA.

6 April 1972: A-7E (158006, NH 415) of VA-195; SAM; North Vietnam; Cdr M C Gilfry, recovered.

14 April 1972: F-4J (157252, NH 203) of VF-114; AAA; South Vietnam; Lt J G Greenleaf and Lt C McKinney, both KIA.

7 May 1972: RA-5C (151618, NH 604) of RVAH-7; AAA; North Vietnam; Cdr C R Polfer and Lt (jg) J E Kerman, both POW.

17 June 1972: A-7E (157531, NH 304) of VA-192; SAM; North Vietnam; Cdr D D Owens, recovered.

18 June 1972: F-4J (157273, NH 107) of VF-213; AAA; North Vietnam; LCdr R Cash, Jr, and Lt R J Laib, both recovered.

16 August 1972: F-4J (157262, NH 211) of VF-114; SAM; North Vietnam; Cdr J R Pitzen and Lt O J Pender, Jr, both MIA.

19 August 1972: A-6A (157018, NH 502) of VA-52; cause unknown; North Vietnam; Lt R B Lester, MIA, and Lt H S Mossman, KIA.

19 September 1972: A-7E (158653, NH 304) of VA-192; AAA; North Vietnam; Lt W A Robb, recovered.

2 November 1972: A-7E (157530, NH 300) of VA-192; AAA; North Vietnam; Lt R G Deremer, recovered.

Operational losses (3):

6 March 1972: A-7E (158655) of VA-195; pilot killed.

19 March 1972: A-7E (157529) of VA-192; pilot recovered.

23 March 1972: A-7E (157520) of VA-192; pilot killed.

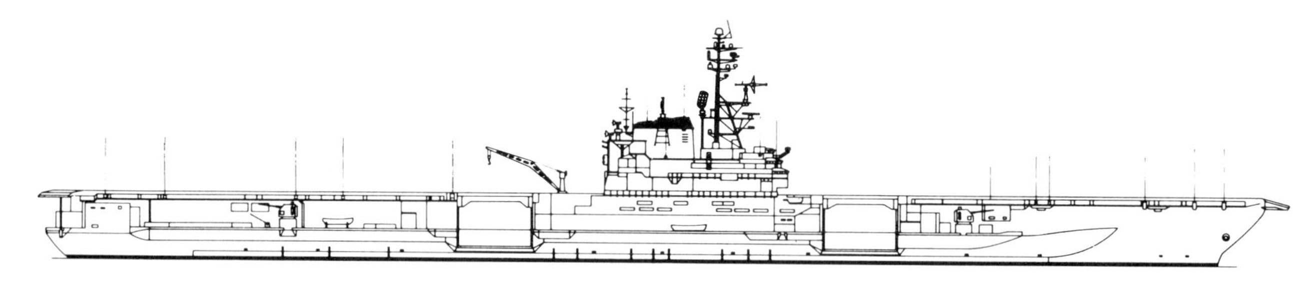

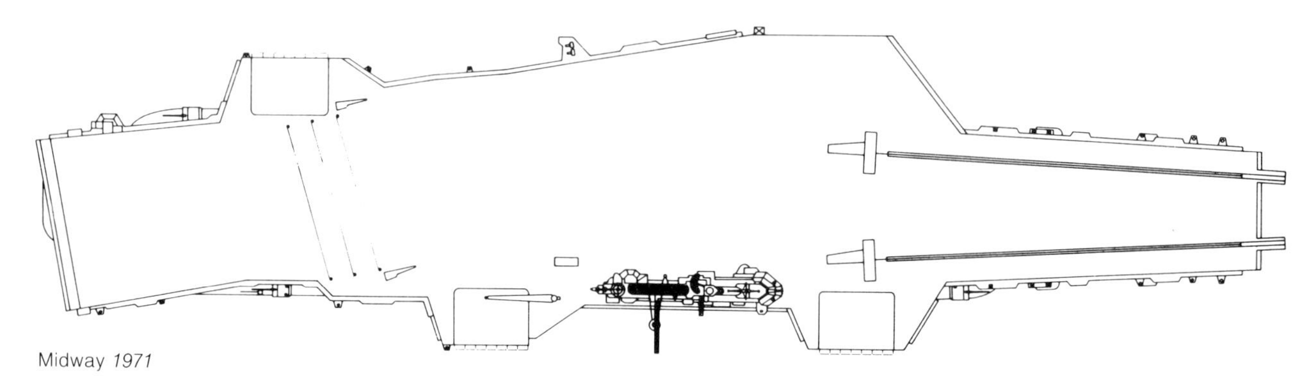

Midway *1971*

USS *Midway* (CVA-41)

Air Wing: CVW-2

Homeport departure/return: Alameda, 6 March 1965–23 November 1965

In-chop/out-chop: 22 March 1965–14 November 1965

On Line periods: 10 April 1965–9 May 1965; 20 May 1965–27 June 1965; 23 July 1965–25 August 1965; 15 September 1965–8 October 1965; 19 October 1965–4 November 1965
Total: 144 days on the line

Squadrons:

VF-21	F-4B	NE	1xx
VF-111	F-8D	NE	4xx
VA-22	A-4C	NE	2xx
VA-23	A-4E	NE	3xx
VA-25	A-1H/J	NE	5xx
VAH-8	A-3B	NE	6xx
VFP-63 Det A	RF-8A	PP	9xx
VAW-11 Det A	E-1B	RR	7xx
HU-1 Det 1 Unit A	UH-2A	UP	xx

(became HC-1 Det 1 Unit A on 1 July 1965)

Air Combat victories (3):

17 June 1965: MiG-17 shot down by F-4B (151488, NE 101, Cdr Louis Page and Lt John C Smith, Jr) of VF-21.

17 June 1965: MiG-17 shot down by F-4B (152219, NE 102, Lt Jack E D Batson, Jr, and LCdr Robert B Doremus) of VF-21.

20 June 1965: MiG-17 shot down by A-1H (137523, NE 573, Lt Charlie Hartman, and 139768, NE 577, Lt Clinton B Johnson) of VA-25.

Combat losses (17):

20 April 1965: A-4C (149507, NE 204) of VA-22; own Mk-81 bombs; North Vietnam; Lt P N Butler, POW.

8 May 1965: F-8D (148637, NE 4??) of VF-111; AAA; North Vietnam; Cdr L D La Haye, KIA.

8 May 1965: RF-8A (145628, PP 9??) of VFP-63; AAA; North Vietnam; Lt (jg) W B Wilson, recovered.

27 May 1965: F-8D (148706, NE 4??) of VF-111; AAA; North Vietnam; Cdr D W Lynn, KIA.

1 June 1965: RF-8A (146881, PP 9??) of VFP-63; AAA; North Vietnam; Lt (jg) M R Fields, recovered.

2 June 1965: A-4E (151144, NE 3??) of VA-23; small arms fire; North Vietnam; Lt (jg) D M Christian, KIA.

2 June 1965: EA-1F (132540, VR 70?) of VAW-13; AAA; North Vietnam; Lt (jg) M D McMikan, Lt (jg) G M Romano and two unidentified crew members, KIA.

2 June 1965: A-4E (151161, NE 3??) of VA-23; small arms fire; North Vietnam; Lt J B McKamey, POW.

3 June 1965: A-4C (148577, NE 2??) of VA-22; AAA; Laos; Lt R P Ilg, recovered.

10 June 1965: A-1H (137521, NE 5??) of VA-25; AAA; North Vietnam; Lt (jg) C L Doughtie, KIA.

28 July 1965: A-4E (149962, NE 3??) of VA-23; own Mk-82 bombs; North Vietnam; Lt (jg) G R Townsend, Jr, recovered.

7 August 1965: A-1H (135329, NE 5??) of VA-25; AAA; North Vietnam; LCdr H E Gray, Jr, KIA.

11 August 1965: A-4E (151185, NE 345) of VA-23; SAM; North Vietnam; Lt (jg) D H Brown, Jr, KIA.

12 August 1965: F-8D (147911, NE 4??) of VF-111; AAA; North Vietnam; Lt (jg) G R Gollahon, KIA.

13 August 1965: A-4C (148564, NE 2??) of VA-22; AAA; North Vietnam; Lt W E Newman, recovered.

24 August 1965: F-4B (152215, NE 112) of VF-21; SAM; North Vietnam; Cdr F A Franke and LCdr R B Doremus, both POW.

24 August 1965: A-4C (149490, NE 2??) of VA-22; cause unknown; North Vietnam; Lt (jg) R M Brunhaver, POW.

Operational losses (5):

11 May 1965: A-4C (148489) of VA-22; pilot recovered.

24 June 1965: A-1H (137523) of VA-25; pilot recovered.

28 July 1965: F-4B (150646) of VF-21; both crew members recovered.

28 October 1965: A-4C (146596) of VA-22; pilot killed.

3 November 1965: F-8D (148635) of VF-111; pilot recovered.

USS *Midway* (CVA-41)

Air Wing: CVW-5

Homeport departure/return: Alameda, 16 April 1971–6 November 1971

In-chop/out-chop: 7 May 1971–24 October 1971

On Line periods: 18 May 1971–9 June 1971; 30 June 1971–20 July 1971; 1–16 August 1971; 27 September 1971–10 October 1971
Total: 74 days on the line

Squadrons:

VF-151	F-4B	NF 2xx
VF-161	F-4B	NF 1xx
VA-56	A-7B	NF 4xx
VA-93	A-7B	NF 3xx
VA-115	A-6A and KA-6D	NF 5xx
VFP-63 Det 3	RF-8G	NF 60x
VAQ-130 Det 2	EKA-3B	NF 61x
VAW-115	E-2B	NF 01x
HC-1 Det 8	SH-3G	NF 00x

Air Combat victories (0):

Combat losses (0):

Operational losses (2):

11 June 1971: E-2B (151719) of VAW-115; all five crew members missing.

12 August 1971: KA-6D (152598) of VA-115; both crew members recovered.

USS Midway *(CVA-41), with CVW-2 aircraft on deck, was photographed on 21 July 1965 as she was steaming toward the Gulf of Tonkin to take her place on the line for the third time. Launched on 20 March 1945,* Midway *underwent SCB 110 modernization between 1955 and 1957 and was again modernized under SCB 101 between 1966 and 1970. Reclassified CV-41 on 30 June 1975, she is expected to remain operational with PACFLT until the mid-1990s.* (US Navy)

USS *Midway* (CVA-41)

Air Wing: CVW-5

Homeport departure/return: Alameda, 10 April 1972–3 March 1973

In-chop/out-chop: 21 April 1972–23 February 1973

On Line periods: 30 April 1972–31 May 1972; 11 June 1972–7 July 1972; 17 July 1972–13 August 1972; 24 August 1972–9 September 1972; 20 September 1972–12 October 1972; 23 October 1972–23 November 1972; 2–19 December 1972; 4–24 January 1973; 3–12 February 1973
Total: 208 days on the line

Squadrons:

VF-151	F-4B	NF	2xx
VF-161	F-4B	NF	1xx
VA-56	A-7B	NF	4xx
VA-93	A-7B	NF	3xx
VA-115	A-6A and KA-6D	NF	5xx
VFP-63 Det 3	RF-8G	NF	60x
VAQ-130 Det 2	EKA-3B	NF	61x
VAW-115	E-2B	NF	01x
HC-1 Det 2	SH-3G	NF	00x

Air Combat victories (5):

18 May 1972: MiG-19 shot down by F-4B (153068, NF 110, Lt Henry A Bartholomay and Lt Oran R Brown) of VF-161.
18 May 1972: MiG-19 shot down by F-4B (153915, NF 105, Lt Patrick E Arwood and Lt James M Bell) of VF-161.
23 May 1972: Two MiG-17s shot down by F-4B (153020, NF 100, LCdr Ronald E McKeown and Lt John C Ensch) of VF-161.
12 January 1973: MiG-17 shot down by F-4B (153045, NF 102, Lt Victor T Kovaleski and Lt (jg) James A. Wise) of VF-161.

Combat losses (15):

19 May 1972: A-7B (154541, NF 411) of VA-56; AAA; North Vietnam; Lt A A Nichols, POW.
23 May 1972: A-7B (154405, NF 302) of VA-93; probably SAM; North Vietnam; Cdr C E Barnett, KIA.
16 June 1972: RF-8G (145613, NF 601) of VFP-63; AAA; North Vietnam; Lt P Ringwood, recovered.
22 July 1972: RF-8G (146873, NF 601) of VFP-63; AAA; North Vietnam; LCdr G C Paige, POW.
23 July 1972: A-7B (154531, NF 414) of VA-56; AAA; North Vietnam; Lt (jg) G L Shank KIA.
23 July 1972: A-7B (154532, NF 400) of VA-56; AAA; North Vietnam; LCdr C O Tolbert, recovered.
6 August 1972: A-7B (154508, NF 403) of VA-56; SAM; North Vietnam; Lt (jg) M G Penn, POW.
25 August 1972: F-4B (153020, NF 100) of VF-161; SAM; North Vietnam; LCdr M W Doyle and Lt J C Ensch, both POW.
27 August 1972: F-4B (151013, NF 210) of VF-151; SAM; North Vietnam; Lt T W Triebel and Lt (jg) D A Everett, both POW.
7 September 1972: A-7B (154393, NF 307) of VA-93; cause unknown; North Vietnam; LCdr D A Gerstel, MIA.
5 November 1972: A-7B (154540, NF 403) of VA-56; AAA; North Vietnam; LCdr C O Tolbert, MIA.
10 November 1972: A-7B (154506, NF 314) of VA-93; AAA; North Vietnam; Lt M J Cobb, recovered.
10 November 1972: A-7B (154399, NF 401) of VA-56; AAA; North Vietnam: Lt W P Lotsberg, recovered.
9 January 1973: A-6A (155693, NF 511); SAM; North Vietnam; Lt M T McCormick, KIA, and Lt (jg) R A Clark, MIA.
14 January 1973: F-4B (153068, NF 110) of VF-161; AAA; North Vietnam; Lt V T Kovaleski and Ens D H Plautz, both recovered.
Data after 29 January 1973 not available.

Operational losses (5):

2 May 1972: KA-6D (152597) of VA-115; both crew members recovered.
21 May 1972: F-4B (153032) of VF-151; both crew members recovered.
29 October 1972: F-4B (153031); no fatalities.
29 October 1972: A-6A (155705) of VA-115; one crew member recovered, one killed.
6 January 1973: A-7B (154543) of VA-56; pilot killed.
Data after 29 January 1973 not available.

USS *Oriskany* (CVA-34)

Air Wing: CVW-16

Homeport departure/return: Alameda, 5 April 1965–16 December 1965

In-chop/out-chop: 27 April 1965–6 December 1965

On Line periods: 8–31 May 1965; 11 June 1965–18 July 1965; 10 August 1965–10 September 1965; 30 September 1965–18 October 1965; 29 October 1965–25 November 1965
Total: 141 days on the line

Squadrons:

VF-162	F-8E	AH	2xx
VMF(AW)-212	F-8E	WD	1xx
VA-163	A-4E	AH	3xx
VA-164	A-4E	AH	4xx

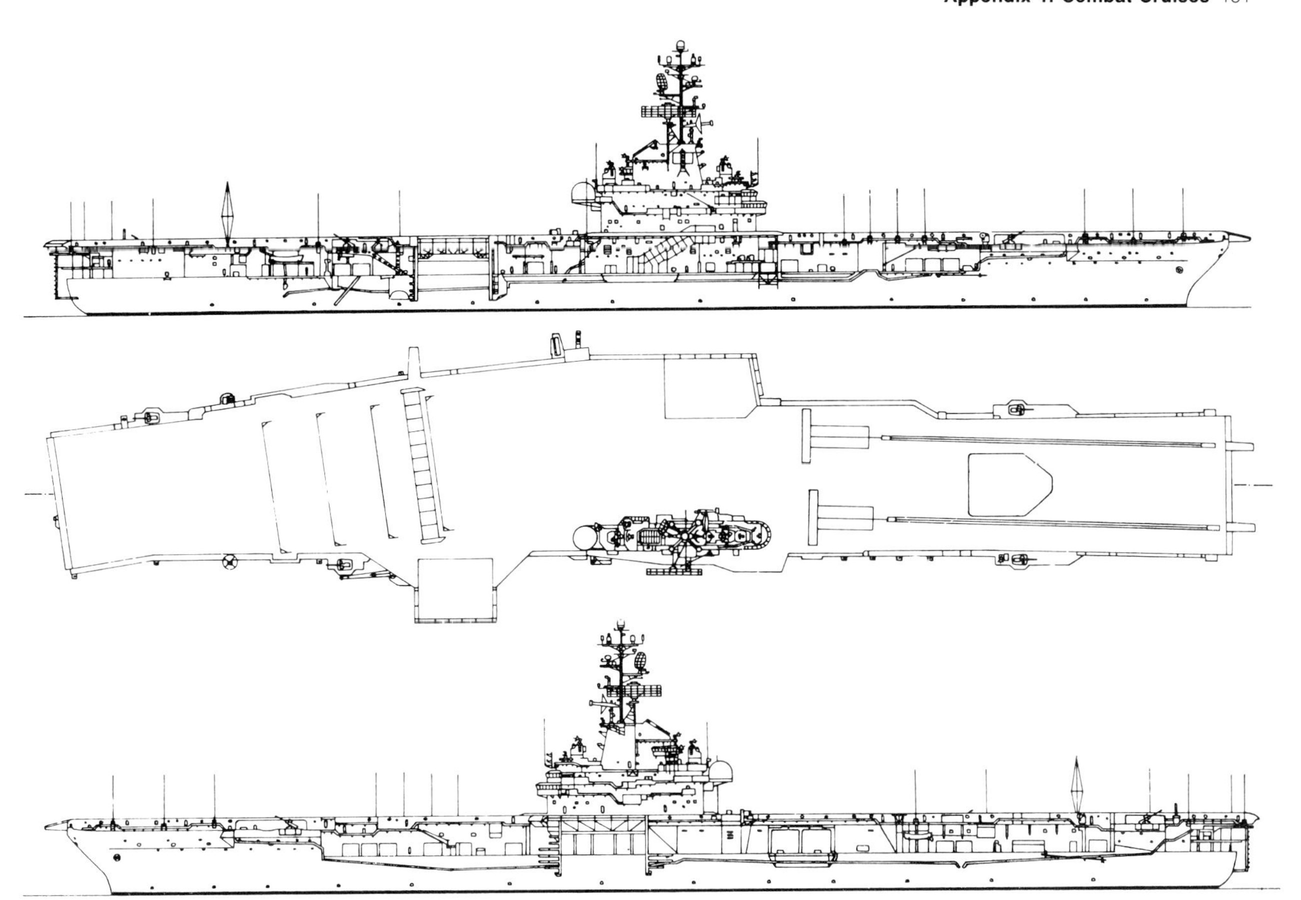

Oriskany *1973*

VA-152	A-1H/J	AH	5xx
VAH-4 Det G	A-3B	ZB	xx
VFP-63 Det G	RF-8A	PP	9xx
VAW-11 Det G	E-1B	RR	75x
HU-1 Det 1 Unit G	UH-2A	UP	xx

(became HC-1 Det 1 Unit G on 1 July 1965)

Air Combat victories (0):

Combat losses (15):

26 August 1965: A-1H (139720, AH 592) of VA-152; AAA; North Vietnam; Lt (jg) E A Davis, POW.

29 August 1965: A-1H (134619, AH 586) of VA-152; AAA; North Vietnam; Lt E D Taylor, KIA.

29 August 1965; RF-8A (146828, PP 919) of VFP-63; AAA; North Vietnam; Lt H S McWhorter, KIA.

6 September 1965: A-4E (152042, AH 475) of VA-164; AAA; North Vietnam; Lt J L Burton, recovered.

8 September 1965: RF-8A (146825, PP 918) of VFP-63; AAA; North Vietnam; Lt (jg) R D Rudolph, KIA.

9 September 1965: A-4E (151134, AH352) of VA-163; AAA; North Vietnam; Cdr J B Stockdale, POW.

5 October 1965: F-8E (150848, AH 227) of VF-162; SAM; North Vietnam; Lt (jg) R F Adams, recovered.

31 October 1965: A-4E (151173, AH 466) of VA-164; AAA; North Vietnam; LCdr T R Powers, died in captivity.

5 November 1965: F-8E (150665, WD 106) of VMF (AW)212; AAA; North Vietnam; Capt H P Chapman, POW.

7 November 1965: A-4E (150071, AH 343) of VA-163; AAA; North Vietnam; LCdr C G Wack, recovered.

9 November 1965: A-1H (137566, AH 590) of VA-152; AAA; North Vietnam; LCdr P G Merchant, recovered.

13 November 1965: A-4E (151067, AH 340) of VA-163; AAA; North Vietnam; Cdr H T Jenkins, POW.

17 November 1965: F-8E (150675, WD 103) of VMF(AW)-212; AAA; North Vietnam; Capt R C Chaimson, recovered.

17 November 1965: A-4E (151083, AH 350) of VA-163; AAA; North Vietnam; LCdr R H Bowling, POW.

17 November 1965: A-1H (135244, AH 588) of VA-152; AAA; North Vietnam; LCdr J J Taylor, KIA.

Operational losses (7):

25 May 1965: A-3B (138947) of VAH-4; all four crew members recovered.

30 June 1965: A-1H (139708) of VA-152; pilot recovered.

18 July 1965: A-4E (151089) of VA-163; pilot killed.

21 July 1965: A-1H (139636) of VA-152; pilot recovered.

10 August 1965: A-1J (142012) of VA-152; pilot killed.

17 October 1965: F-8E (149198) of VMF(AW)-212; pilot recovered.

17 November 1965: F-8E (150875) of VMF(AW)-212; pilot recovered.

USS *Oriskany* (CVA-34)

Air Wing: CVW-16

Homeport departure/return: Alameda, 26 May 1966–16 November 1966

In-chop/out-chop: 11 June 1966–8 November 1966

On Line periods: 30 June 66; 8–27 July 1966; 6 August 1966–7 September 1966; 24 September 1966–26 October 1966
Total: 87 days on the line

Squadrons:

VF-111	F-8E	AH	1xx
VF-162	F-8E	AH	2xx
VA-163	A-4E	AH	3xx
VA-164	A-4E	AH	4xx
VA-152	A-1H	AH	5xx
VAH-4 Det G	A-3B	ZB	61x
VFP-63 Det G	RF-8G	AH	6xx
VAW-11 Det G	E-1B	RR	70x
HC-1 Det 1 Unit G	UH-2A/B	UP	xx

Air Combat victories (1):

9 October 1966: MiG-17 shot down by F-8E (149159, AH 210, Cdr Richard M Bellinger) of VF-162.

Combat losses (16):

12 July 1966: F-8E (150902, AH 203) of VF-162; AAA; North Vietnam; Lt (jg) R F Adams, recovered.

14 July 1966: F-8E (150908, AH 202) of VF-162; MiG; North Vietnam; Cdr R M Bellinger; recovered.

19 July 1966: F-8E (150919, AH 210) of VF-162; SAM; North Vietnam; Lt T A Dennison, died in captivity.

23 July 1966: A-4E (152100, AH 301) of VA-163; AAA; North Vietnam; Cdr W F Foster, recovered.

28 July 1966: A-4E (152077, AH 407) of VA-164; SAM; North Vietnam; Ens G P McSwain, POW.

7 August 1966: A-1H (139701, AH 501) of VA-152; AAA; North Vietnam; Lt C L Fryer, KIA.

11 August 1966: F-8E (150880, AH 112) of VF-111; AAA; North Vietnam; Lt (jg) C A Balisteri, recovered.

13 August 1966: F-8E (150866, AH 113) of VF-111; AAA; North Vietnam; LCdr N S Levy, recovered.

18 August 1966: F-8E (150300, AH 211) of VF-162; AAA; North Vietnam; LCdr D A Verich, recovered

28 August 1966: A-1H (135231, AH 506) of VA-152; AAA; North Vietnam; Cdr G H Smith, recovered.

31 August 1966: RF-8G (146874, AH 602) of VFP-63; AAA; North Vietnam; LCdr T A Tucker, recovered.

5 September 1966: F-8E (150896, AH 106) of VF-111; MiG; North Vietnam; Capt W K Abbott, POW.

6 October 1966: F-8E (150924, AH 201) of VF-162; cause unknown; North Vietnam; Lt R D Leach, recovered.

8 October 1966: A-1H (137629, AH 510) of VA-152; AAA; North Vietnam; Lt J A Feldhaus, MIA.

12 October 1966: A-4E (152075, AH 411) of VA-164; SAM; North Vietnam; Lt F C Elkins, MIA.

14 October 1966: A-1H (139731, AH 511) of VA-152; cause unknown; North Vietnam; Ens D J Thomas, KIA.

Operational losses (9):

29 July 1966: A-4E (152095) of VA-164; pilot killed.
23 August 1966: F-8E (150907) of VF-111; pilot recovered.
25 August 1966: A-4E (152084) of VA-164; pilot killed.
25 August 1966: A-1H (135236) of VA-152; pilot recovered.
26 August 1966: A-4E (152093) of VA-164; pilot recovered.
27 August 1966: A-4E (150079) of VA-163; pilot recovered.
16 September 1966: UH-2B (152196) of HC-1; three crew members recovered.
5 October 1966: A-1H (137610) of VA-152; pilot killed.
23 October 1966: A-4E (150072) of VA-163; pilot recovered.

Remarks:

26 October 1966: As a result of a fire which started in a flare locker, forty-four officers and enlisted men died and thirty-eight were injured. Three A-4s were damaged, and one A-4E (151075) and two UH-2A/Bs (149774 and 150183) were destroyed.

USS *Oriskany* (CVA-34)

Air Wing: CVW-16

Homeport departure/return: Alameda, 16 June 1967–31 January 1968

In-chop/out-chop: 26 June 1967–23 January 1968

On Line periods: 14 July 1967–7 August 1967; 18 August 1967–15 September 1967; 5 October 1967–2 November 1967; 20 November 1967–16 December 1967; 31 December 1967–11 January 1968
Total: 122 days on the line

Squadrons:

VF-111	F-8C	AH	1xx
VF-162	F-8E	AH	2xx
VA-163	A-4E	AH	3xx
VA-164	A-4E	AH	4xx
VA-152	A-1H/J	AH	5xx
VAH-4 Det G	KA-3B	AH	61x
VFP-63 Det G	RF-8G	AH	6xx
VAW-111 Det 34	E-1B	RR	70x
HC-1 Det G	UH-2A/B	UP	xx

During these deployments to the Gulf of Tonkin between April 1965 and January 1968, CVW-16 suffered very heavy losses while operating from USS Oriskany *(CVA-34). The worst losses were taken during the June 1967–January 1968 deployments when, during 122 days on the line, twenty aircrewmen were killed or missing in action, seven taken prisoner of war and thirty-nine aircraft lost.* (US Navy via Naval Institute Press)

Air Combat victories (1):

14 December 1967: MiG-17 shot down by F-8E (150879, AH 204, Lt Richard E Wyman) of VF-162.

Combat losses (29):

14 July 1967: A-4E (152049, AH 407) of VA-164; AAA; North Vietnam; Lt (jg) L J Cunningham, recovered.

15 July 1967: A-1H (135288, AH 504) of VA-152; AAA; North Vietnam; Lt (jg) R B Cassell, KIA.

16 July 1967: F-8E (150925, AH 201) of VF-162; SAM; North Vietnam; LCdr D A Verich, recovered.

18 July 1967: A-4E (151986, AH 404) of VA-164; AAA; North Vietnam; LCdr R D Hartman, died in captivity.

18 July 1967: A-4E (151175, AH 415) of VA-164; AAA; North Vietnam; Lt (jg) L J Duthie, recovered.

18 July 1967: A-4E (152034, AH 401) of VA-164; AAA; North Vietnam; Lt (jg) B T Wood, recovered.

19 July 1967: F-8E (150899, AH 206) of VF-162; AAA; North Vietnam; Cdr H P Hunter, Jr, KIA.

20 July 1967: A-4E (150097, AH 312) of VA-163; AAA; North Vietnam; Lt R. W. Kuhl, recovered.

25 July 1967: A-4E (149961, AH 304) of VA-163, small arms fire; North Vietnam; LCdr D V Davis, KIA.

31 July 1967: F-8C (146984, AH 110) of VF-111; SAM; North Vietnam; Lt (jg) C P Zuhoski, POW.

4 August 1967: A-4E (150052, AH 313) of VA-163; SAM; North Vietnam; Lt (jg) R C Bisz, POW.

31 August 1967: A-4E (152028, AH 315) of VA-163; SAM; North Vietnam; Lt (jg) D J Carey, POW.

31 August 1967: A-4E (149975, AH 310) of VA-163; SAM; North Vietnam; LCdr H A Stafford, POW.

31 August 1967: A-4E (151991, AH 402) of VA-164; SAM; North Vietnam; LCdr R C Perry, KIA.

5 October 1967: F-8C (146938, AH 114) of VF-111; AAA; North Vietnam; Ens D P Matheny, POW.

7 October 1967: A-4E (152086, AH 413) of VA-164; SAM; North Vietnam; Lt D L Hodges, KIA.

9 October 1967: A-4E (152085, AH 416) of VA-164; unknown gunfire; North Vietnam; Lt (jg) L J Cunningham, recovered.

18 October 1967: A-4E (152048, AH 402) of VA-164; AAA; North Vietnam; LCdr J F Barr, KIA.

22 October 1967: A-4E (150116, AH 306) of VA-163; SAM; North Vietnam; Lt (jg) J E Dooley, KIA

24 October 1967: A-4E (149963, AH 311) of VA-163; AAA; North Vietnam; Lt (jg) R A Foulks, recovered.

25 October 1967: A-4E (150086, AH 315) of VA-163; AAA; North Vietnam; Lt J M Krommenhoek, MIA.

26 October 1967: F-8E (150310, AH 206) of VF-162; SAM; North Vietnam; Lt (jg) C D Rice, POW.

26 October 1967: A-4E (149959, AH 300) of VA-163; SAM; North Vietnam; LCdr J S McCain III, POW.

2 November 1967: A-4E (151985, AH 414) of VA-164; AAA; North Vietnam; Lt (jg) F W Knapp, KIA.

5 December 1967: F-8C (146907, AH 102) of VF-111; AAA; North Vietnam; Lt H J Meadows, recovered.

2 January 1968: F-8C (146989, AH 106) of VF-111; AAA; North Vietnam; Lt (jg) C M Taylor, recovered.

4 January 1968: F-8E (150865, AH 206) of VF-162; SAM; North Vietnam; Lt (jg) R W Minnich, MIA.

5 January 1968: A-4E (150131, AH 303) of VA-163; AAA; North Vietnam; Lt (jg) R E Foulks, Jr, KIA.

11 January 1968: A-4E (151152, AH 404) of VA-164; small arms fire; Laos; LCdr D R Weichman, recovered.

Operational losses (10):

12 July 1967: A-4E (150102) of VA-163; pilot recovered.

20 July 1967: F-8E (150916) of VF-162; pilot recovered.

28 July 1967: KA-3B (142658) of VAH-4; one crew member recovered, two killed.

8 September 1967: F-8C (146929) of VF-111; pilot recovered.

10 September 1967: A-4E (150047) of VA-163; pilot recovered.

11 September 1967: F-8E (150910) of VF-162; pilot recovered.

8 October 1967: E-1B (148132) of VAW-111; all five crew members killed.

21 October 1967: KA-3B (142655) of VAH-4; all four crew members recovered.

19 November 1967: F-8C (147004) of VF-111; pilot killed.

1 January 1968: A-4E (151133) of VA-164; pilot recovered.

USS *Oriskany* (CVA-34)

Air Wing: CVW-19

Homeport departure/return: Alameda, 16 April 1969–17 November 1969

In-chop/out-chop: 5 May 1969–10 November 1969

On Line periods: 16 May 1969–3 June 1969; 16 June 1969–29 July 1969; 15 August 1969–12 September 1969; 8–31 October 1969

Total: 116 days on the line

Squadrons:

VF-191	F-8J	NM 1xx
VF-194	F-8J	NM 2xx
VA-23	A-4F	NM 3xx
VA-192	A-4F	NM 4xx
VA-195	A-4E	NM 5xx
VFP-63 Det 34	RF-8G	NM 6xx
VAQ-130 Det 34	EKA-3B	NM 61x
VAW-111 Det 34	E-1B	NM 01x
HC-1 Det 34	UH-2C	NM 00x

Air Combat victories (0):

Combat losses (1):

20 July 1969: A-4F (154993, NM 306) of VA-23; small arms fire; Laos; Lt S K Smiley, KIA.

Operational losses (8):

21 May 1969: F-8J (150926) of VF-194; pilot recovered.

24 May 1969: RF-8G (146844) of VFP-63; pilot recovered.

21 July 1969: A-4F (155003) of VA-192; pilot recovered.
21 July 1969: A-4F (154199) of VA-192; pilot recovered.
29 July 1969: A-4F (154184) of VA-23; pilot recovered.
15 August 1969: A-4F (154206) of VA-195; pilot recovered.
11 September 1969: F-8J (150861) of VF-194; pilot recovered.
26 October 1969: F-8J (150284) of VF-191, pilot recovered.

USS *Oriskany* (CVA-34)

Air Wing: CVW-19

Homeport departure/return: Alameda, 14 May 1970–10 December 1970

In-chop/out-chop: 1 June 1970–29 November 1970

On Line periods: 14–29 June 1970; 13–21 July 1970; 3–25 August 1970; 18 September 1970–13 October 1970; 7–22 November 1970.
Total: 90 days on the line

Squadrons:

VF-191	F-8J	NM 1xx
VF-194	F-8J	NM 2xx
VA-153	A-7A	NM 3xx
VA-155	A-7B	NM 5xx
VAQ-130 Det 1	EKA-3B	NM 61x
VFP-63 Det 34	RF-8G	NM 6xx
VAW-111 Det 34	E-1B	NM 01x
HC-1 Det 6	UH-2C	NM 00x

Air Combat victories (0):

Combat losses (1):
28 June 1970: A-7A (153176, NM 303) of VA-153; cause unknown; Laos; Cdr D D Aldern, MIA.

Operational losses (3):
25 June 1970: A-7B (154525) of VA-155; pilot recovered.
6 November 1970: F-8J (150289) of VF-191; pilot killed.
14 November 1970: RF-8G (145624) of VFP-63; pilot killed.

USS *Oriskany* (CVA-34)

Air Wing: CVW-19

Homeport departure/return: Alameda, 14 May 1971–18 December 1971

In-chop/out-chop: 4 June 1971–8 December 1971

On Line periods: 16 June 1971–10 July 1971; 25 July 1971–7 August 1971; 5–26 September 1971; 4–5 November 1971; 8–19 November 1971
Total: 75 days on the line

Squadrons:

VF-191	F-8J	NM 1xx
VF-194	F-8J	NM 2xx
VA-153	A-7A	NM 3xx
VA-155	A-7B	NM 5xx
VA-215	A-7B	NM 4xx
VFP-63 Det 4	RF-8G	NM 60x
VAQ-130 Det 3	EKA-3B	NM 61x
VAW-111 Det 2	E-1B	NM 01x
HC-1 Det 5	UH-2C	NM 00x

Air Combat victories (0):

Combat losses (0):

Operational losses (4):
21 June 1971: F-8J (150868) of VF-194; pilot killed.
8 September 1971: A-7A (153223) of VA-153, pilot recovered.
22 September 1971: A-7B (154430) of VA-215; pilot recovered.
1 November 1971: A-7A (153189) of VA-153; pilot killed.

USS *Oriskany* (CVA-34)

Air Wing: CVW-19

Homeport departure/return: Alameda, 5 June 1972–30 March 1973

In-chop/out-chop: 21 June 1972–20 March 1973

On Line periods: 29 June 1972; 1–22 July 1972; 15 August 1972–1 September 1972; 11–27 September 1972; 8–31 October 1972; 23 November 1972–18 December 1972; 27 December 1972–30 January 1973; 8 February 1973–5 March 1973
Total: 169 days on the line

Squadrons:

VF-191	F-8J	NM 1xx
VF-194	F-8J	NM 2xx
VA-153	A-7A	NM 3xx
VA-155	A-7B	NM 5xx
VA-215	A-7B	NM 4xx
VAQ-130 Det 3	EKA-3B	NM 61x
VFP-63 Det 4	RF-8G	NM 60x
VAW-111 Det 6	E-1B	NM 01x
HC-1 Det 5	SH-3G	NM 00x

Air Combat victories (0):

Combat losses (2):
17 July 1972: A-7B (154521, NM 510) of VA-155; cause unknown; North Vietnam; Lt L F Haas, KIA.
24 September 1972: A-7B (154486, NM 500) of VA-155; AAA; South Vietnam; Lt D V Borah, POW.
Data after 29 January 1973 not available.

Operational losses (4):
20 September 1972: A-7B (154363) of VA-155; pilot recovered.
27 September 1972: F-8J (150325) of VF-194; pilot killed.
26 November 1972: F-8J (150887) of VF-191; pilot recovered.
13 December 1972: RF-8G (144608) of VFP-63; pilot recovered.
Data after 29 January 1973 not available.

With a UH-2A from HC-1 Det Fox flying plane guard, USS Ranger (CVA-61) is shown sailing off the South Vietnam coast on 13 April 1966 during her second war cruise. Launched on 29 September 1956 and reclassified CV-61 on 30 June 1975. Ranger remained assigned to PACFLT in 1988 and is due to undergo SLEP (Ship Life Extension Program) in mid-1991. (US Navy)

USS *Ranger* (CVA-61)

Air Wing: CVW-9

Homeport departure/return: Alameda, 5 August 1964–6 May 1965

In-chop/out-chop: 17 August 1964–25 April 1965

On Line periods: 18–20 September 1964; 28 November 1964–29 December 1964; 16 January 1965–15 March 1965; 4–12 April 1965
Total: 103 days on the line

Squadrons:

VF-92	F-4B	NG	2xx
VF-96	F-4B	NG	6xx
VA-93	A-4C	NG	3xx
VA-94	A-4C	NG	4xx
VA-95	A-1H/J	NG	5xx
VAH-2 Det M	A-3B	NL	81x
VFP-63 Det M	RF-8A	PP	9xx
RVAH-5	RA-5C	NG	10x
VAW-11 Det M	E-1B	RR	77x
HU-1 Det 1 Unit M	UH-2A	UP	x

Air Combat victories (1):

9 April 1965: MiG-17 shot down by F-4B (151403, NG 602, Lt (jg) Terence M Murphy and Ens Ronald J Fegan) of VF-96.

Combat losses (3):

15 March 1965: A-1H (135375, NG 512) of VA-95; AAA; North Vietnam; Lt (jg) C F Clydesdale, KIA.

9 April 1965: F-4B (151403, NG 602) of VF-96; either MiG or friendly aircraft; over China Sea; Lt (jg) T M Murphy and Ens R J Fegan, both KIA.

11 April 1965: A-1H (135226, NG 5??) of VA-95; AAA; Laos; Lt (jg) W E Swanson, KIA.

Operational losses (2):

9 December 1964: RA-5C (149306) of RVAH-5; both crew members killed.

9 April 1965: F-4B (151425) of VF-96; both crew members recovered.

USS *Ranger* (CVA-61)

Air Wing: CVW-14

Homeport departure/return: Alameda, 10 December 1965–25 August 1966

In-chop/out-chop: 3 January 1966–18 August 1966

On Line periods: 15 January 1966–11 February 1966; 23 February 1966–21 March 1966; 12 April 1966–8 May 1966; 30 May 1966–29 June 1966; 13 July 1966–5 August 1966
Total: 137 days on the line

Squadrons:

VF-142	F-4B	NK	2xx
VF-143	F-4B	NK	3xx
VA-55	A-4E	NK	4xx
VA-146	A-4C	NK	6xx
VA-145	A-1H/J	NK	5xx
VAH-2 Det F	A-3B	ZA	81x
RVAH-9	RA-5C	AC	9xx
VAW-11 Det F	E-2A	RR	70x
HC-1 Det F	UH-2A/B	UP	x

Air Combat victories (0):

Combat losses (15):

31 January 1966: A-4E (152066, NK 407) of VA-55; AAA; North Vietnam; LCdr S G Chumley, recovered.

1 February 1966: A-1J (142031, NK 504) of VA-145; cause unknown; Laos; Lt (jg) D Dengler, escaped.

1 February 1966: A-4C (149527, NK 600) of VA-146; AAA; North Vietnam; Cdr H B Loheed, KIA.

10 February 1966: A-1H (137627, NK 506) of VA-145; AAA; North Vietnam; Lt G D Hopps, KIA.

1 March 1966: F-4B (150443, NK 310) of VF-143; cause unknown; North Vietnam; Lt W D Frawley and Lt (jg) W M Christensen, both KIA.

1 March 1966: A-4E (152057, NK 401) of VA-55; cause unknown; North Vietnam; Lt (jg) D J Wolszyk, MIA.

23 April 1966: A-4E (152025, NK 404) of VA-55; AAA; South Vietnam; LCdr O A Gray, recovered.

30 April 1966: A-4E (151145, NK 406) of VA-55; cause unknown; Laos; Lt J S Buzby, recovered.

2 May 1966: A-4E (151034, NK 412) of VA-55; small arms fire; North Vietnam; LCdr W S Wood, KIA.

15 June 1966: F-4B (152251, NK 310) of VF-143; AAA; North Vietnam; Lt C W Bennett and Ens D W Vermilyea, both recovered.

15 June 1966: A-4E (152063, NK 403) of VA-55; AAA; North Vietnam; LCdr T F Kopfman, POW.

25 June 1966: A-4C (149567, NK 604) of VA-146; AAA; North Vietnam; Lt F H Magee, recovered.

15 July 1966: A-4E (151024, NK 410) of VA-55; AAA; North Vietnam; Lt J Connell, died in captivity.

24 July 1966: A-4E (150040, NK 415) of VA-55; AAA; North Vietnam; Lt E L Foss, recovered.

3 August 1966: A-1H (134586, NK 515) of VA-145; small arms fire; North Vietnam; Lt D Frantz, recovered.

Operational losses (6):

16 January 1966: RA-5C (149312) of RVAH-9; both crew members killed.

25 January 1966: A-4E (152021) of VA-55; pilot recovered.

5 May 1966: A-4C (149571) of VA-146; pilot recovered.

1 June 1966: A-4E (151057) of VA-55; pilot recovered.

20 June 1966: A-1H (139806) of VA-145; pilot killed.

11 July 1966: F-4B (152262) of VF-143; both crew members recovered.

USS *Ranger* (CVA-61)

Air Wing: CVW-2

Homeport departure/return: Alameda, 4 November 1967–25 May 1968

In-chop/out-chop: 20 November 1967–18 May 1968

On Line periods: 3–27 December 1967; 7–27 January 1968; 19 March 1968–11 April 1968; 22 April 1968–9 May 1968
Total: 88 days on the line

Squadrons:

VF-21	F-4B	NE	1xx
VF-154	F-4B	NE	4xx
VA-22	A-4C	NE	2xx
VA-147	A-7A	NE	3xx
VA-165	A-6A	NE	5xx
VAH-2 Det 61	KA-3B	ZA	6xx
RVAH-6	RA-5C	NE	70x
VAW-13 Det 61	EKA-3B	VR	72x
VAW-115	E-2A	NE	75x
HC-1 Det 61	UH-2A/C	UP	xx

Air Combat victories (0):

Combat losses (4):

16 December 1967: F-4B (151492, NE 101) of VF-21; AAA; North Vietnam; LCdr D E Hernandez and Lt (jg) S L Vanhorn, both recovered.

22 December 1967: A-7A (153239, NE 313) of VA-147; SAM; North Vietnam; LCdr J M Hickerson, POW.

26 January 1968: A-6A (152901, NE 501) of VA-165; cause unknown; North Vietnam; LCdr N E Eidsmoe, MIA, and Lt M E Dunn, KIA.

28 April 1968: F-4B (153014, NE 103) of VF-21; AAA; North Vietnam; LCdr D E Hernandez and Lt (jg) D J Lortscher, both recovered.

Operational losses (6):

4 December 1967: UH-2C (149741) of HC-1; four crew members recovered.

10 January 1968: F-4B (151506) of VF-154; both crew members recovered.

10 January 1968: F-4B (151499) of VF-154; both crew members recovered.

23 January 1968: A-6A (152932) of VA-165; one crew member recovered, one killed.

23 January 1968: UH-2B (151315) of HC-7; four crew members recovered.

14 April 1968: F-4B (150644) of VF-154; both crew members recovered.

USS *Ranger* (CVA-61)

Air Wing: CVW-2

Homeport departure/return: Alameda, 26 October 1968–17 May 1969

In-chop/out-chop: 12 November 1968–10 May 1969

On Line periods: 29 November 1968–10 December 1968; 14–29 December 1968; 8–30 January 1969; 16 February 1969–15 March 1969; 5–16 April 1969
Total: 91 days on the line

Squadrons:

VF-21	F-4J	NE	1xx
VF-154	F-4J	NE	2xx
VA-147	A-7A	NE	3xx
VA-155	A-4F	NE	4xx
VA-165	A-6A	NE	5xx
RVAH-9	RA-5C	NE	60x
VAH-10 Det 61	KA-3B	NE	61x
VAQ-130 Det 61	EKA-3B	NE	61x
VAW-115	E-2A	NE	01x
HC-1 Det 61	UH-2C	UP	00x

Air Combat victories (0):

Combat losses (0):

Operational losses (4):

16 January 1969: A-4F (155059) of VA-155; pilot killed.

17 February 1969: F-4J (155760) of VF-21; both crew members recovered.

20 February 1969: F-4J (155763) of VF-21; one crew member recovered, one killed.

12 April 1967: A-7A (1532?2) of VA-147; pilot recovered.

USS *Ranger* (CVA-61)

Air Wing: CVW-2

Homeport departure/return: Alameda, 14 October 1969–1 June 1970

In-chop/out-chop: 4 November 1969–23 May 1970

On Line periods: 17 November 1969–6 December 1969; 18 December 1969–4 January 1970; 30 January 1970–17 February 1970; 1–20 March 1970; 17 April 1970–12 May 1970
Total: 103 days on the line with TF 77 and 8 days (6–13 April 1970) on the line with TF 71 off Korea

Squadrons:

VF-21	F-4J	NE	1xx
VF-154	F-4J	NE	2xx
VA-56	A-7B	NE	4xx
VA-93	A-7B	NE	3xx
VA-196	A-6A	NE	5xx
RVAH-5	RA-5C	NE	60x
VAQ-134	KA-3B/EKA-3B	NE	61x
VAW-115	E-2A	NE	01x
HC-1 Det 8	SH-3A	NE	00x

Air Combat victories (0):

Combat losses (4):

22 November 1969: A-6A (155613, NE 513) of VA-196; cause unknown; Laos; Cdr L W Richards, recovered, and Lt (jg) R C Deuter, MIA.

22 November 1969: A-6A (155607, NE 507) of VA-196; cause unknown; Laos; LCdr R F Collins and Lt M E Quinn, both MIA.

2 January 1970: A-6A (152937, NE 507) of VA-196; AAA; Laos; Lt B C Fryar, KIA, and Lt N G Brooks, MIA.

6 February 1970: A-6A (155618, NE 516) of VA-196; AAA; Laos; LCdr E P Reese and Lt (jg) E R Frazer, both recovered.

Operational losses (7):

17 December 1969: A-7B (154542) of VA-56; pilot recovered.

26 December 1969: A-7B (154517) of VA-56; pilot recovered.

11 January 1970: F-4J (155750) of VF-154; both crew members killed.

5 February 1970: A-7B (154391) of VA-93; pilot killed.

28 February 1970: A-6A (155605) of VA-196; both crew members recovered.

9 March 1970: F-4J (155775) of VF-21; both crew members missing.

9 May 1970: A-7B (154555) of VA-93; pilot recovered.

USS *Ranger* (CVA-61)

Air Wing: CVW-2

Homeport departure/return: Alameda, 27 October 1970–17 June 1971

In-chop/out-chop: 11 November 1970–9 June 1971

On Line periods: 21 November 1970–17 December 1970; 28 December 1970–12 January 1971; 3 February 1971–16 March 1971; 1–16 April 1971; 26 April 1971–17 May 1971
Total: 123 days on the line

Squadrons:

VF-21	F-4J	NE	1xx
VF-154	F-4J	NE	2xx
VA-25	A-7E	NE	4xx
VA-113	A-7E	NE	3xx
VA-145	A-6A/C	NE	5xx
RVAH-1	RA-5C	NE	60x
VAQ-134	KA/EKA-3B	NE	61x
VAW-111 Det 6	E-1B	NE	01x
HC-1 Det 1	SH-3G	NE	00x

Air Combat victories (0):

Combat losses (3):
28 December 1970: A-7E (157509, NE 406) of VA-25; cause unknown; Laos; LCdr R W Castle, Jr, recovered.
13 March 1971: A-7E (157589, NE 315) of VA-113; AAA; Laos; Lt B S Creed, MIA.
17 April 1971: A-7E (157511, NE 305) of VA-113; AAA; Laos; Lt R E Forman, Jr, recovered.

Operational losses (6):
3 December 1970: A-7E (157483) of VA-25; pilot recovered.
15 December 1970: C-2A (155120) of VRC-50; nine crew members and passengers killed.
5 January 1971: F-4J (155577) of VF-21; one crew member recovered, one killed.
8 January 1971: A-6C (155647) of VA-145; one crew member recovered, one killed.
24 February 1971: A-6A (156994) of VA-145; both crew members recovered.
27 February 1971: F-4J (155884) of VF-21; one crew member recovered, one missing.

USS *Ranger* (CVA-61)

Air Wing: CVW-2

Homeport departure/return: Alameda, 16 November 1972–22 June 1973

In-chop/out-chop: 28 November 1972–14 June 1973

On Line periods: 9 December 1972–2 January 1973; 14 January 1973–7 February 1973; 17 February 1973–12 March 1973; 21 March 1973–12 April 1973; 24–30 April 1973; 16–31 May 1973
Total: 120 days on the line

Squadrons:

VF-21	F-4J	NE	2xx
VF-154	F-4J	NE	1xx
VA-25	A-7E	NE	4xx
VA-113	A-7E	NE	3xx
VA-145	A-6A/B and KA-6D	NE	5xx
RVAH-5	RA-5C	NE	60x
VAQ-130 Det 4	EKA-3B	NE	61x
VAW-111 Det 1	E-1B	NE	01x
HC-1 Det 4	SH-3G	NE	00x

Air Combat victories (0):

Combat losses (1):
24 December 1972: A-7E (157503, NE 314) of VA-113; cause unknown; North Vietnam; Lt P S Clark, Jr, MIA.

Data after 29 January 1973 not available.

Operational losses (3):
21 January 1973: EKA-3B (142634) of VAQ-130; all three crew members killed.
29 January 1973: F-4J (158361) of VF-21; both crew members killed.
29 January 1973: F-4J (158366) of VF-21; both crew members recovered.

Data after 29 January 1973 not available.

USS Franklin D. Roosevelt *(CVA-42), the least successful of the three* Midway *class carriers, was deployed only once during the war. With CVW-1 on board,* FDR *spent ninety-five days on the line between July 1966 and January 1967.* (US Navy via Naval Institute Press)

USS *Franklin D. Roosevelt* (CVA-42)

Air Wing: CVW-1

Homeport departure/return: Mayport, 21 June 1966–21 February 1967

In-chop/out-chop: 25 July 1966–29 January 1967

On Line periods: 10 August 1966–12 September 1966; 1–2 October 1966; 20 October 1966–12 November 1966; 23 November 1966–27 December 1966
Total: 95 days on the line

Squadrons:

VF-14	F-4B	AB	1xx
VF-32	F-4B	AB	2xx
VA-12	A-4E	AB	4xx
VA-72	A-4E	AB	5xx
VA-172	A-4C	AB	3xx
VAH-10 Det 42	A-3B	AB	6xx
VFP-62 Det 42	RF-8G	AB	9xx
VAW-12 Det 42	E-1B	AB	71x
HC-2 Det 42	UH-2A/B	HU	xx

Air Combat victories (0):

Combat losses (7):

21 August 1966: A-4E (151109, AB 505) of VA-72; AAA; North Vietnam; Lt A R Carpenter, recovered.

22 August 1966: A-4E (149992, AB 510) of VA-72; own rockets; North Vietnam; Lt K G Craig, recovered.

20 October 1966: A-4C (147775, AB 302) of VA-172; AAA; North Vietnam; Lt (jg) F R Purrington, POW.

1 November 1966: A-4E (151138, AB 508) of VA-72; AAA; North Vietnam; Lt A R Carpenter, POW.

2 December 1966: A-4C (145116, AB 304) of VA-172; SAM; North Vietnam; Ens P L Worrell, MIA.

2 December 1966: A-4C (145143, AB 300) of VA-172; SAM; North Vietnam; Cdr B A Nystrom, MIA.

14 December 1966: A-4E (151068, AB 513) of VA-172; SAM; North Vietnam; Lt C D Wilson, KIA.

Operational losses (8):

31 July 1966: A-4C (147677) of VA-172; pilot recovered.

6 September 1966: RF-8G (144624) of VFP-62; pilot killed.

10 September 1966: EA-1F (132543) of VAW-13; all four crew members recovered.

5 October 1966: F-4B (152328) of VF-32; both crew members recovered.

3 November 1966: F-4B (151018) of VF-14; both crew members recovered.

12 November 1966: A-4E (150048) of VA-12; pilot killed.

12 November 1966: A-4E (155051) of VA-12; pilot killed.

14 December 1966: E-1B (147218) of VAW-12; two crew members recovered, three killed.

USS Saratoga *(CV-60) made only one war cruise to Southeast Asia. She is seen here in the Atlantic Ocean in April 1972 shortly after departing Mayport, Florida, at the start of that deployment. Aircraft on her deck bear the AC tail code of CVW-3. Launched on 6 June 1958 and reclassified CV-60 on 30 June 1972,* Saratoga *remained assigned to LANTFLT in 1988 after undergoing SLEP between October 1980 and February 1983.* (US Navy)

USS *Saratoga* (CV-60)

Air Wing: CVW-3

Homeport departure/return: Mayport, 11 April 1972–13 February 1973

In-chop/out-chop: 8 May 1972–16 January 1973

On Line periods: 18 May 1972–20 June 1972; 1–16 July 1972; 28 July 1972–22 August 1972; 2–20 September 1972; 29 September 1972–20 October 1972; 5 November 1972–8 December 1972; 18 December 1972–8 January 1973
Total: 173 days on the line

Squadrons:

VF-31	F-4J	AC	1xx
VF-103	F-4J	AC	2xx
VA-37	A-7A	AC	3xx
VA-105	A-7A	AC	4xx
VA-75	A-6A/B and KA-6D	AC	5xx
RVAH-1	RA-5C	AC	6xx
VAW-123	E-2B	AC	01x
HS-7	SH-3A/D	AC	00x

Air Combat victories (2):

21 June 1972: MiG-21 shot down by F-4J (157293, AC 101, Cdr Samuel C Flynn, Jr, and Lt William H John) of VF-31.

10 August 1972: MiG-21 shot down by F-4J (157299, AC 296, LCdr Robert E Tucker, Jr, and Lt (jg) Stanley B Edens) of VF-103.

Combat losses (13):

7 June 1972: RA-5C (156616, AC 601) of RVAH-1; SAM; North Vietnam; LCdr C H Smith and Lt L G Kunz, both recovered.

13 June 1972: A-7A (153206, AC 305) of VA-37; SAM; North Vietnam; LCdr F J Davis, KIA.

17 June 1972: A-7A (153230, AC 406) of VA-105; AAA; North Vietnam; Lt L R Kilpatrick, MIA.

10 July 1972: F-4J (155803, AC 212) of VF-103; MiG; North Vietnam; Lt R I Randall and Lt F J Masterson, both POW.

6 August 1972: A-7A (153147, AC 407) of VA-105; AAA; North Vietnam; Lt J R Lloyd, recovered.

17 August 1972: A-7A (153207, AC 306) of VA-37; SAM; North Vietnam; LCdr D V Raebel, POW.

6 September 1972: A-6A (155626, AC 505) of VA-75; SAM; North Vietnam; LCdr D F Lindland and Lt R G Lerseth, both POW.

8 September 1972: F-4J (157302, AC 202) of VF-103; AAA; North Vietnam; Cdr P P Bordone and Lt J H Findley, both recovered.

12 September 1972: A-7A (153213, AC 312) of VA-37; AAA; North Vietnam; Lt G H Averett, recovered.

10 November 1972: A-7A (153161, AC 300) of VA-37; AAA; North Vietnam; LCdr F W Wright III, KIA.

20 November 1972: F-4J (157288, AC 210) of VF-103; SAM; North Vietnam; LCdr V E Lesh and Lt (jg) D L Cordes, both recovered.

21 December 1972: A-6A (152946, AC 500) of VA-75; AAA; North Vietnam; LCdr R S Graustein, KIA, and LCdr B S Wade, MIA.

23 December 1972: SH-3A (151552, AC00?) of HS-7; small arms fire; North Vietnam; all crew members recovered.

Operational losses (4):

15 June 1972: A-7A (153197) of VA-105; pilot killed.

31 July 1972: A-7A (153193) of VA-105; pilot recovered.

28 November 1972: A-6A (155622) of VA-75; one crew member recovered, one killed.

31 December 1972: SH-3D (156494) of HS-7; four crew members recovered.

USS Shangri-La *(CVS-38) and her CVW-8 working up off Roosevelt Roads, Puerto Rico, on 11 February 1970, three weeks prior to departing for the Gulf of Tonkin.* (US Navy)

USS *Shangri-La* (CVS-38)

Air Wing: CVW-8

Homeport departure/return: Mayport, 5 March 1970–17 December 1970

In-chop/out-chop: 30 March 1970–24 November 1970

On Line periods: 12 April 1970–1 May 1970; 13–28 May 1970; 14 June 1970–2 July 1970; 29 July 1970–17 August 1970; 31 August 1970–28 September 1970; 21 October 1970–5 November 1970

Total: 120 days on the line

Squadrons:

VF-111	F-8H	AJ	1xx
VF-162	F-8H	AJ	2xx
VA-12	A-4C	AJ	4xx
VA-152	A-4E	AJ	5xx
VA-172	A-4C	AJ	3xx
VFP-63 Det 38	RF-8G	AJ	6xx
VAH-10 Det 38	KA-3B	AJ	61x
(became VAQ-129 Det 38 on 1 September 1970)			
VAW-121 Det 38	E-1B	AJ	01x
HC-2 Det 38	UH-2C	HU	xx

Air Combat victories (0):

Combat losses (1):

21 April 1970: A-4C (148184, AJ 305) of VA-172; AAA; Laos; Lt (jg) J B Golz, KIA.

Operational losses (8):

28 April 1970: A-4C (147803) of VA-12; pilot recovered.

29 April 1970: F-8H (148650) of VF-162; pilot recovered.

26 May 1970: A-4E (149993) of VA-152; pilot recovered.

22 June 1970: A-4C (148495) of VA-172; pilot killed.

6 August 1970: A-4C (149553) of VA-12; pilot recovered.

12 August 1970: F-8H (148660) of VF-162; pilot recovered.

22 September 1970: A-4C (149525) of VA-172; pilot recovered.

20 October 1970: F-8H (148643) of VF-162; pilot recovered.

USS *Ticonderoga* (CVA-14)

Air Wing: CVW-5

Homeport departure/return: Alameda, 14 April 1964–15 December 1964

In-chop/out-chop: 11 May 1964–10 December 1964

On Line periods: Was on the line in non-combat areas prior to 5 August 1964; 5–30 August 1964; 5–29 October 1964; 2–5 November 1964; 22–27 November 1964
Total: 61 days on the line

Squadrons:

VF-51	F-8E	NF	1xx
VF-53	F-8E	NF	2xx
VA-55	A-4E	NF	5xx
VA-56	A-4E	NF	4xx
VA-52	A-1H/J	NF	3xx
VAH-4 Det B	A-3B	ZB	x
VFP-63 Det B	RF-8A	PP	93x
VAW-11 Det B	E-1B	RR	76x
HU-1 Det 1 Unit B	UH-2A	UP	xx

Air Combat victories (0)

Combat losses (0):

Operational losses (5):
13 August 1964: A-4E (150018) of VA-56; pilot recovered.
19 August 1964: A-4E (150033) of VA-55; pilot recovered.
6 September 1964: A-4E (150024) of VA-56; pilot killed.
1 November 1964: F-8E (149141) of VF-53; pilot killed.
23 November 1964: A-4E (151037) of VA-55; pilot recovered.

USS *Ticonderoga* (CVA-14)

Air Wing: CVW-5

Homeport departure/return: Alameda, 28 September 1965–13 May 1966

In-chop/out-chop: 25 October 1965–7 May 1966

On Line periods: 5 November 1965–2 December 1965; 21–31 December 1965; 4–14 January 1966; 23 January 1966–16 February 1966; 6–31 March 1966, 10–20 April 1966
Total: 112 days on the line

Squadrons:

VF-51	F-8E	NF	1xx
VF-53	F-8E	NF	2xx
VA-56	A-4E	NF	4xx
VA-144	A-4C	NF	5xx
VA-52	A-1H/J	NF	3xx
VAH-4 Det B	A-3B	ZB	8xx
VFP-63 Det B	RF-8A	PP	93x
VAW-11 Det B	E-1B	RR	70x
HC-1 Det 1 Unit B	UH-2A/B	UP	xx

Air Combat victories (0):

Combat losses (11):
1 December 1965: A-4C (149560, NF 547) of VA-144; AAA; North Vietnam; Lt (jg) J V McCormick, KIA.
3 January 1966: A-1J (142081, NF 387) of VA-52; AAA; South Vietnam; Lt J W Donahue, recovered.
7 February 1966: A-4E (152027, NF 462) of VA-56; AAA; North Vietnam; LCdr R Crayton, POW.
9 February 1966: A-4C (149557, NF 546) of VA-144; SAM; North Vietnam; LCdr J L Snyder, recovered.
14 February 1966: A-4C (149552, NF 543) of VA-144; cause unknown; Laos; Lt (jg) J C Durham, recovered.
20 March 1966: A-4C (145081, NF 553) of VA-144; AAA; South Vietnam; Lt (jg) J L Pinneker, KIA.
14 April 1966: A-1H (139692, NF 381) of VA-52; SAM; North Vietnam; Cdr J C Mape, KIA.
17 April 1966: A-4E (151058, NF 463) of VA-56; AAA; North Vietnam; LCdr V O Hough, recovered.
18 April 1966: A-1J (142032, NF 391) of VA-52; AAA; North Vietnam; Lt A D Wilson, recovered.
19 April 1966: RF-8A (146843, PP 937) of VFP-63; AAA; North Vietnam; Lt R F Ball, recovered.
19 April 1966: F-8E (150853, NF 2??) of VF-53; AAA; North Vietnam; Cdr R F Mohrhardt, recovered.

Operational losses (5):
16 November 1965: A-1H (137590) of VA-52; pilot recovered.
30 November 1965: F-8E (149176) of VF-53; pilot killed.
1 December 1965: A-1H (137621) of VA-52; pilot recovered.
26 December 1965: F-8E (150843) of VF-53; pilot recovered.
14 April 1966: F-8E (149179) of VF-51; pilot recovered.

USS *Ticonderoga* (CVA-14)

Air Wing: CVW-19

Homeport departure/return: Alameda, 15 October 1966–29 May 1967

In-chop/out-chop: 27 October 1966–22 May 1967

On Line periods: 13 November 1966–16 December 1966; 4 January 1967–4 February 1967; 15 February 1967–15 March 1967; 29 March 1967–28 April 1967
Total: 126 days on the line

Squadrons:

VF-191	F-8E	NM	1xx
VF-194	F-8E	NM	4xx
VA-192	A-4E	NM	2xx
VA-195	A-4C	NM	5xx
VA-52	A-1H	NM	3xx

For her fifth and last war cruises, USS Ticonderoga (CVA-14) embarked CVW-16 and spent ninety-seven days on the line between February and September 1969. (USN via Naval Institute Press)

VAH-4 Det E	A-3B	ZB	xx
VFP-63 Det E	RF-8G	PP	91x
VAW-11 Det E	E-1B	RR	72x
(became VAW-111 Det 14 on 20 April 1967)			
HC-1 Det 1 Unit E	UH-2A/B	UP	xx

Air Combat victories (0):

Combat losses (14):

23 November 1966: A-4E (151172, NM 204) of VA-192; AAA; North Vietnam; Cdr A E Hill, recovered.

27 November 1966: A-1H (135341, NM 309) of VA-52; AAA; North Vietnam; Lt (jg) W H Natter, recovered.

13 December 1966: A-4C (147776, NM 502) of VA-195; AAA; North Vietnam; Lt (jg) D O Taylor, recovered.

13 December 1966: A-4C (147819, NM 500) of VA-195; SAM; North Vietnam; LCdr C E Barnett, recovered.

14 December 1966: F-8E (149148, NM 408) of VF-194; SAM; North Vietnam; Lt M T Newell, KIA.

5 January 1967: A-4E (151136, NM 200) of VA-192; own rockets; North Vietnam; LCdr R A Stratton, POW.

6 January 1967: F-8E (149184, NM 110) of VF-191; AAA; North Vietnam; LCdr R D Mullen, POW.

7 March 1967: A-4E (152087, NM 200) of VA-192; small arms fire; Laos; Lt S N Young, recovered.

11 March 1967: A-4E (151108, NM 209) of VA-192; SAM; North Vietnam; Cdr E M Moore, Jr, POW.

7 April 1967: A-4C (149639, NM 506) of VA-195; AAA; North Vietnam; Cdr C E Hathaway, recovered.

10 April 1967: A-4E (151200, NM 212) of VA-192; AAA; North Vietnam; LCdr G W Shattuck, recovered.

25 April 1967: A-4E (151116, NM 204) of VA-192; SAM; North Vietnam; LCdr F J Almberg, recovered.

26 April 1967: A-4E (152076, NM 200) of VA-192; AAA; North Vietnam; Lt (jg) J W Cain, recovered.

26 April 1967: A-4E (151073, NM 208) of VA-192; SAM; North Vietnam; LCdr M J Estocin, KIA.

Operational losses (3):

18 January 1967: A-1H (139748) of VA-52; pilot killed.

27 February 1967: A-4C (148607) of VA-195; pilot recovered.

7 March 1967: F-8E (150350) of VF-191; pilot killed.

USS *Ticonderoga* (CVA-14)

Air Wing: CVW-19

Homeport departure/return: Alameda 27 December 1967–17 August 1968

In-chop/out-chop: 13 January 1968–9 August 1968

On Line periods: 26 January 1968–3 March 1968; 26 March 1968–6 April 1968; 25 April 1968–12 May 1968; 21 May 1968–14 June 1968; 27 June 1968–23 July 1968
Total: 120 days on the line

Squadrons:

VF-191	F-8E	NM	1xx
VF-194	F-8E	NM	4xx
VA-23	A-4F	NM	3xx
VA-192	A-4F	NM	2xx
VA-195	A-4C	NM	5xx
VAH-4 Det 14	KA-3B	ZB	xx
VFP-63 Det 14	RF-8G	NM	6xx
VAW-111 Det 14	E-1B	RR	72x
HC-1 Det 14	UH-2B	UP	xx

Air Combat victories (1):

9 July 1968: MiG-17 shot down by F-8E (150926, NM 107, LCdr John B Nichols, III) of VF-191.

Combat losses (2):

14 February 1968: F-8E (150909, NM 402) of VF-194; SAM; North Vietnam; Lt (jg) R C McMahan, MIA.

28 March 1968: RF-8G (144616, NM 601) of VFP-63; small arms fire; Laos; LCdr M W Wallace, KIA.

Operational losses (6):

2 February 1968: F-8E (150667) of VF-191; pilot killed.

15 February 1968: UH-2A (152197) of HC-1; four recovered.

24 February 1968: F-8E (150335) of VF-191; pilot recovered.

4 July 1968: A-4F (155002) of VA-192; pilot recovered.

4 July 1968: F-8E (149165) of VF-194; pilot recovered.

23 July 1968: A-4F (154189) of VA-23; pilot killed.

USS *Ticonderoga* (CVA-14)

Air Wing: CVW-16

Homeport departure/return: Alameda, 1 February 1969–18 September 1969

In-chop/out-chop: 18 February 1969–10 September 1969

On Line periods: 4–19 March 1969; 30 March 1969–16 April 1969; 10 May 1969–4 June 1969; 26 June 1969–1 August 1969
Total: 97 days on the line

Squadrons:

VF-111	F-8H	AH	1xx
VF-162	F-8J	AH	2xx
VA-25	A-7B	AH	5xx
VA-87	A-7B	AH	3xx
VA-112	A-4C	AH	4xx
VFP-63 Det 14	RF-8G	AH	60x
VAQ-130 Det 14	EKA-3B	AH	61x
VAW-111 Det 14	E-1B	AH	01x
HC-1 Det 14	UH-2C	UP	xx

Air Combat victories (0):

Combat losses (0):

Operational losses (7):

9 March 1969: A-7B (154473) of VA-25; pilot recovered.

12 May 1969: A-7B (154441) of VA-25; pilot recovered.

3 July 1969: F-8J (150656) of VF-162; pilot recovered.

6 July 1969: F-8H (148636) of VF-111; pilot recovered.

19 July 1969: A-7B (154423) of VA-87; pilot recovered.

22 July 1969: A-4C (148310) of VA-112; pilot recovered.

26 July 1969: A-4C (147833) of VA-112; pilot killed.

Antisubmarine Carriers

USS *Bennington* (CVS-20)

Air Wing: CVSG-59

Homeport departure/return: North Island, 22 March 1965–7 October 1965

In-chop/out-chop: ? ? 1965–? ? 1965

On Line periods: 29 July 1965–17 August 1965; 27 August 1965–9 September 1965
Total: 34 days on the line

Squadrons:

VS-33	S-2E	NT	1x/2x
VS-38	S-2E	NT	3x/4x
HS-8	SH-3A	NT	5x/6x
VAW-11 Det Q	E-1B	RR	7xx
VA-113 Det Q	A-4B		

Air Combat victories (0):

Combat losses (0):

Operational losses (1):

21 May 1965: A-4B (144938) of VA-113; pilot recovered.

USS *Bennington* (CVS-20)

Air Wing: CVSG-59

Homeport departure/return: North Island, 4 November 1966–23 May 1967

In-chop/out-chop: ? ? 1966–? ? 1967

On Line periods: 21 December 1966–23 January 1967; 10 February 1967–8 March 1967; 30 March 1967–15 April 1967
Total: 78 days on the line

Squadrons:

VS-33	S-2E	NT	1x/2x
VS-38	S-2E	NT	3x/4x
HS-8	SH-3A	NT	5x/6x
VAW-11 Det Q	E-1B	RR	7xx

(became VAW-111 Det 20 on 20 April 1967)

Air Combat victories (0):

Combat losses (0):

Operational losses (1):

12 January 1967: SH-3A (149909) of HS-8; four crew members recovered and two killed.

USS Bennington *(CVS-20) steaming into San Diego Bay to tie up at North Island on 25 November 1967. She was then between her second and third deployments to the Gulf of Tonkin. Sixteen days earlier, on 9 November,* Bennington *had recovered the unmanned Apollo 4 spacecraft about 600 miles northwest of Hawaii. Launched on 26 February 1944,* Bennington *was brought up to SCB 27A standards between 1950 and 1952 and to SCB 125 standards in 1954-55, was reclassified as an antisubmarine warfare support carrier on 30 June 1959, and was decommissioned on 15 January 1970.* (US Navy)

USS *Bennington* (CVS-20)

Air Wing: CVSG-59

Homeport departure/return: North Island, 1 May 1968–9 November 1968

In-chop/out-chop: ? ? 1968–? ? 1968

On Line periods: 25 June 1968–18 July 1968; 23 August 1968–2 September 1968; 4 September 1968; 6–19 September 1968; 7–20 October 1968
Total: 64 days on the line

Squadrons:

VS-33	S-2E	NT	1x/2x
VS-38	S-2E	NT	3x/4x
HS-8	SH-3A	NT	5x/6x
VAW-111 Det 20	E-1B	RR	76x

Air Combat victories (0):

Combat losses (1):

29 August 1968: SH-3A (149729) of HC-7; all crew members recovered.

Operational losses (1):

26 March 1968: SH-3A (149901) of HS-8; one crew member recovered, three killed.

USS *Hornet* (CVS-12)

Air Wing: CVSG-57

Homeport departure/return: Bremerton, 12 August 1965–23 March 1966

In-chop/out-chop: ? ? 1965–8 February 1966

On Line periods: 11 October 1965–1 November 1965; 16–25 November 1965; 16 January 1966–2 February 1966
Total: 50 days on the line

Squadrons:

VS-35	S-2D/S-2E	NV	1x/2x
VS-37	S-2E	NV	3x/4x
HS-2	SH-3A	NV	5x/6x
VAW-11 Det N	E-1B	RR	76x
H&MS-15 Det N	A-4C	YV	8x

Air Combat victories (0):

Combat losses (2):

7 November 1965: SH-3A (148993) of HS-2; small arms fire; North Vietnam; four crew members recovered.

21 January 1966: S-2D (149252, NV-12) of VS-35; cause unknown; North Vietnam; Lt W S Forman, Lt (jg) E B Templin, Jr, AMHC E H Frenyea, and R R Sennett, all MIA.

Operational losses (0):

USS *Hornet* (CVS-12)

Air Wing: CVSG-57

Homeport departure/return: Bremerton, 27 March 1967–28 October 1967

In-chop/out-chop: 25 April 1967–18 October 1967

On Line periods: 22 May 1967–26 June 1967; 2–14 August 1967; 8 September 1967–5 October 1967
Total: 77 days on the line

Squadrons:

VS-35	S-2E	NV	1x/2x
VS-37	S-2E	NV	3x/4x
HS-2	SH-3A	NV	5x/6x
VAW-11 Det N	E-1B	RR	76x

(became VAW-111 Det 12 on 20 April 1967)

Air Combat victories (0):

Combat losses (3):

21 May 1967: SH-3A (151530) of HS-2; AAA; North Vietnam; four crew members recovered.

23 May 1967: SH-3A (148985) of HS-2; unknown; North Vietnam; four crew members killed.

19 July 1967: SH-3A (151538) of HS-2; AAA; North Vietnam; four crew members killed

Operational losses (5):

20 June 1967: SH-3A (149685) of HS-2; five crew members recovered.

6 July 1967: SH-3A (149924) of HS-2; three crew members recovered.

8 August 1967: C-1A (146016); five crew members recovered and one killed.

26 August 1967: SH-3A (148982) of HS-2; six crew members recovered.

27 September 1967: US-2C (133371) of VC-5; all four crew members recovered.

Between her first and second war cruises, USS Hornet *(CVS-12) was also used to recover an unmanned Apollo spacecraft, doing so about 500 miles southeast of Wake Island on 25 August 1966. She is seen here underway in the Central Pacific on 9 August 1966. Launched on 29 August 1943,* Hornet *was brought up to SCB 27A standards between 1951 and 1953 and to SCB 125 standards in 1955-56, was reclassified as an antisubmarine warfare support carrier on 27 June 1958, and was decommissioned on 26 May 1970.* (US Navy)

USS *Hornet* (CVS-12)

Air Wing: CVSG-57

Homeport departure/return: Bremerton, 30 September 1968–12 May 1969

In-chop/out-chop: ? ? 1968–? ? 1969

On Line periods: 3–15 November 1968; 28 November 1968–19 December 1968; 5–22 January 1969; 5–23 February 1969; 5–22 March 1969; 2–17 April 1969
Total: 106 days on the line

Squadrons:

VS-35	S-2E	NV	1x/2x
VS-37	S-2E	NV	3x/4x
HS-2	SH-3A	NV	5x/6x
VAW-111 Det 12	E-1B	RR	7xx

Air Combat victories (0):

Combat losses (0):

Operational losses (1):
8 February 1969: SH-3A (151534) of HS-2; four crew members recovered.

USS *Kearsarge* (CVS-33)

Air Wing: CVSG-53

Homeport departure/return: Long Beach, 19 June 1964–16 December 1964

In-chop/out-chop: ? ? 1964–? ? 1964

On Line periods: 11 August 1964–24 September 1964; 4–8 October 1964; 1–8 November 1964
Total: 58 days on the line

Squadrons:

VS-21	S-2F	NS	1x/2x
VS-29	S-2F	NS	3x/4x
HS-6	SH-3A	NS	5x/6x
VAW-11 Det R	EA-1E	RR	7xx
VA-153 Det R	A-4B		
HU-1 Det 1 Unit R	UH-2A	UP	xx

Air Combat victories (0):

Combat losses (0):

Operational losses (0):

USS *Kearsarge* (CVS-33)

Air Wing: CVSG-53

Homeport departure/return: Long Beach, 9 June 1966–20 December 1966

In-chop/out-chop: 11 July 1966–11 December 1966

On Line periods: 12 August 1966–3 September 1966; 12–22 September 1966; 29 September 1966–7 October 1966; 18–25 October 1966; 6–24 November 1966
Total: 70 days on the line

Squadrons:

VS-21	S-2E	NS	1x/2x
VS-29	S-2E	NS	3x/4x
HS-6	SH-3A	NS	5x/6x
VAW-11 Det R	E-1B	RR	72x

Air Combat victories (0):

Combat losses (2):
16 October 1966: SH-3A (150618, NS ? ?) of HS-6; small arms fire; North Vietnam; four crew members recovered.
7 November 1966: SH-3A (??????, NS ? ?) of HS-6; small arms fire; North Vietnam; four crew members recovered.

Operational losses (1):
10 November 1966: S-2E (152351) of VS-21; all four crew members killed.

USS *Kearsarge* (CVS-33)

Air Wing: CVSG-53

Homeport departure/return: Long Beach, 17 August 1967–6 April 1968

In-chop/out-chop: 12 October 1967–28 March 1968

On Line periods: 23 October 1967–13 November 1967; 29 November 1967–20 December 1967; 7–19 January 1968; 2–19 February 1968
Total: 75 days on the line

Squadrons:

VS-21	S-2E	NS	1x/2x
VS-29	S-2E	NS	3x/4x
HS-6	SH-3A	NS	5x/6x
VAW-111 Det 33	E-1B	RR	76x

Air Combat victories (0):

Combat losses (0):

Photographed in Hawaiian waters on 5 July 1966, USS Kearsarge *(CVS-33) and her CVSG-53 had just completed ORE at the start of their second war cruise.* Kearsarge *chopped to Seventh Fleet six days later and took her place on the line on 12 August. Launched on 5 May 1945,* Kearsarge *was brought up to SCB 27A standards between 1950 and 1952 and to SCB 125 standards in 1955-57, was reclassified as an antisubmarine warfare support carrier on 1 October 1958, and was decommissioned on 15 January 1970.* (US Navy)

Operational losses (2):

23 October 1967: SH-3A (151522) of HS-6; one crew member recovered.

20 November 1967: S-2E (150602) of VS-21; two crew members killed.

USS *Kearsarge* (CVS-33)

Air Wing: CVSG-53

Homeport departure/return: Long Beach, 29 March 1969–4 September 1969

In-chop/out-chop: ? ? 1969–? ? 1969

On Line periods: 4–15 May 1969; 1–5 June 1969; 18 June 1969–5 July 1969; 26 July 1969–14 August 1969
Total: 55 days on the line

Squadrons:

VS-21	S-2E	NS	1x/2x
VS-29	S-2E	NS	3x/4x
HS-6	SH-3A	NS	5x/6x
VAW-111 Det 33	E-1B	RR	01x

Air Combat victories (0):

Combat losses (0):

Operational losses (0):

With her crew manning the rails, a Marine honor guard standing over the bow, and CVSG-55 aircraft neatly aligned, USS Yorktown *(CVS-10) is ready for inspection. Two weeks after this photograph was taken,* Yorktown *departed Bremerton for her first wartime deployment to the Gulf of Tonkin. Launched on 21 January 1943,* Yorktown *was brought up to SCB 27A standards between 1951 and 1953 and to SCB 125 standards in 1954-55, was reclassified as an antisubmarine warfare support carrier on 1 September 1957, and was stricken on 1 June 1973.* (US Navy)

USS *Yorktown* (CVS-10)

Air Wing: CVSG-55

Homeport departure/return: Bremerton, 23 October 1964–16 May 1965

In-chop/out-chop: ? ? 1965–? ? 1965

On Line periods: 9–26 February 1965; 21 March 1965–28 April 1965
Total: 57 days on the line

Squadrons:

VS-23	S-2E	NU	1x/2x
VS-25	S-2E	NU	3x/4x
HS-4	SH-3A	NU	5x/6x
VAW-11 Det T	EA-1E	RR	7xx
VMA-223 Det T	A-4C	WP	xx

Air Combat victories (0):

Combat losses (0):

Operational losses (1):

15 April 1965: EA-1E (139603) of VAW-11; all three crew members recovered.

USS *Yorktown* (CVS-10)

Air Wing: CVSG-55

Homeport departure/return: Bremerton, 5 January 1966–27 July 1966

In-chop/out-chop: ? ? 1966–? ? 1966

On Line periods: 25 February 1966–25 March 1966; 13–28 April 1966; 30 May 1966–15 June 1966; 24 June 1966–3 July 1966
Total: 72 days on the line

Squadrons:

VS-23	S-2E	NU	1x/2x
VS-25	S-2E	NU	3x/4x
HS-4	SH-3A	NU	5x/6x
VAW-11 Det T	E-1B	RR	71x

Air Combat victories (0):

Combat losses (0):

Operational losses (2):
15 January 1966: SH-3A (150619) of HS-4; five crew members recovered.
5 February 1966: SH-3A (149926) of HS-4; fifteen crew members and passengers recovered.

USS *Yorktown* (CVS-10)

Air Wing: CVSG-55

Homeport departure/return: Bremerton, 28 December 1967–5 July 1968

In-chop/out-chop: ?? ??? 1968–?? ??? 1968

On Line periods: 13 March 1968–8 April 1968; 5–27 May 1968; 4–16 June 1968
Total: 63 days on the line

Squadrons:

VS-23	S-2E	NU	1x/2x
VS-25	S-2E	NU	3x/4x
HS-4	SH-3A	NU	5x/6x
VAW-111 Det 10	E-1B	RR	71x

Air Combat victories (0):

Combat losses (0):

Operational losses (1):
17 March 1968: S-2E (149274) of VS-23; all four crew members killed.

APPENDIX 2

Aircraft of Task Force 77

Carriers operating in the Gulf of Tonkin between 1964 and 1973 embarked fourteen different types of fixed-wing and rotary-wing aircraft. In the following pages, the development and combat history of each type is briefly summarized and its combat deployments are listed by squadrons. The principal characteristics and performance of these aircraft appear in Tables 10 and 11 at the end of this appendix.

Shore-based at NAS Cubi Point, the Philippines, VAW-13 Detachment One sent temporary detachments to operate from carriers in the Gulf of Tonkin. This EA-1F from the Zappers *of VAW-13 was photographed at Cubi Point in 1965.* (Jerry Edwards)

Douglas A1-J and EA-1E

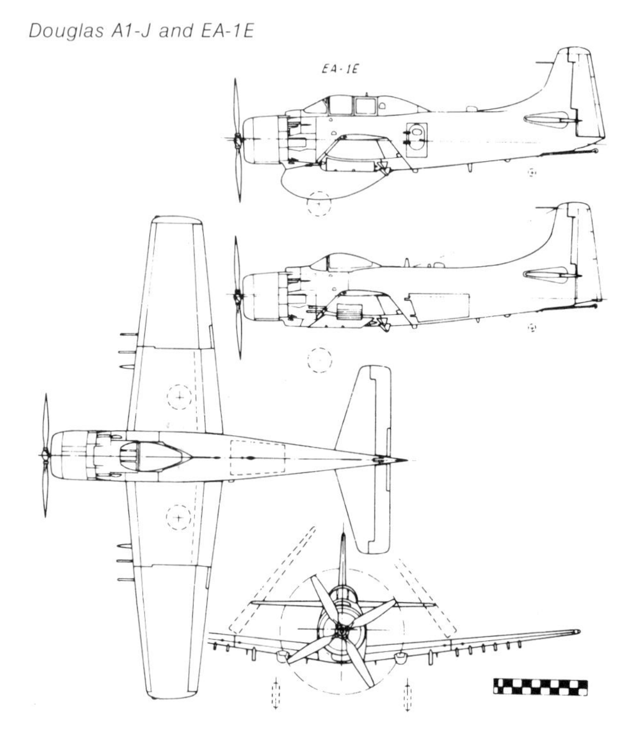

Douglas A-1 and EA-1 Skyraider

Designed during the last year of World War II as a single-seat bomber intended to replace two-seat scout bombers and three-seat torpedo bombers aboard carriers, the XBT2D-1 prototype of the piston-engined Skyraider series first flew on 18 March 1945. The first production variant, the AD-1, entered service with VA-19A in December 1946. Production totalled 3180 aircraft in eight major models and thirty-seven versions, with the last AD-7 (redesignated A-1J in September 1962) coming off the lines in February 1957. On 31 July 1964, the Navy combat aircraft inventory still included 198 A-1H and A-1J single-seat attack aircraft, thirty EA-1F four-seat ECM support aircraft, and thirty-one EA-1E four-seat AEW aircraft.

Although they were already considered obsolete when they took part in retaliatory strikes at the time of the Tonkin Gulf Incident in August 1964, carrier-based A-1Hs and A-1Js fought on for another forty-four months during which they flew attack sorties, proved most valuable during ResCAPs on account of their long endurance and heavy offensive load, and were credited with the destruction of two MiG-17s. Moreover, EA-1E detachments provided AEW support during a war cruise aboard USS *Kearsarge* (CVS-33) and one aboard USS *Yorktown* (CVS-10) in 1964–65, and EA-1F detachments flew ECM support for the ships and aircraft of TF 77. The last Skyraider bombing sorties were flown by aircraft from VA-25 operating from USS *Coral Sea* (CVA-43) during operations in support of ground troops in South Vietnam on 20 February 1968, and the last combat support sorties were flown in December 1968 by EA-1Fs from VAQ-33 Det 11 aboard USS *Intrepid* (CVS-11).

While equipped with Skyraiders, the Wild Aces *of VA-152 made three deployments aboard USS* Oriskany *(CVA-34) during the Southeast Asia War. These A-1Hs were photographed at NAS Alameda, California, on 10 February 1968, ten days after VA-152 had returned from the third of these cruises.* (Peter B Lewis)

A-1 and EA-1 Skyraider Deployments

Squadron/Air Wing	Aircraft	Carrier	Tail Code & Modex	Deployment Dates
VA-25 *Fist of the Fleet*				
VA-25/CVW-2	A-1H/J	USS *Midway* (CVA-41)	NE 5xx	6 March 65–23 November 65
VA-25/CVW-2	A-1H	USS *Coral Sea* (CVA-43)	NE 5xx	29 July 66–23 February 67
VA-25/CVW-15	A-1H/J	USS *Coral Sea* (CVA-43)	NL 4xx	26 July 67–6 April 68
VA-52 *Knightriders*				
VA-52/CVW-5	A-1H/J	USS *Ticonderoga* (CVA-14)	NF 3xx	14 April 64–15 December 64
VA-52/CVW-5	A-1H/J	USS *Ticonderoga* (CVA-14)	NF 3xx	28 September 65–13 May 66
VA-52/CVW-19	A-1H	USS *Ticonderoga* (CVA-14)	NM 3xx	15 October 66–29 May 67
VA-95 *Skyknights*				
VA-95/CVW-9	A-1H/J	USS *Ranger* (CVA-61)	NG 5xx	5 August 64–6 May 65
VA-115 *Arabs*				
VA-115/CVW-1	A-1H/J	USS *Kitty Hawk* (CVA-63)	NH 5xx	19 October 65–13 June 66
VA-115/CVW-5	A-1H/J	USS *Hancock* (CVA-19)	NF 5xx	5 January 67–22 July 67
VA-145 *Swordsmen*				
VA-145/CVW-14	A-1H/J	USS *Constellation* (CVA-64)	NK 5xx	5 May 64–1 February 65
VA-145/CVW-14	A-1H/J	USS *Ranger* (CVA-61)	NK 5xx	10 December 65–25 August 66
VA-145/CVW-10	A-1H/J	USS *Intrepid* (CVS-11)	AK 5xx	11 May 67–30 December 67
VA-152 *Wild Aces*				
VA-152/CVW-16	A-1H/J	USS *Oriskany* (CVA-34)	AH 5xx	5 April 65–16 December 65
VA-152/CVW-16	A-1H/J	USS *Oriskany* (CVA-34)	AH 5xx	26 May 66–16 November 66
VA-152/CVW-16	A-1H/J	USS *Oriskany* (CVA-34)	AH 5xx	16 June 67–31 January 68
VA-165 *Boomers*				
VA-165/CVW-15	A-1H/J	USS *Coral Sea* (CVA-43)	NL 2xx	7 December 64–1 November 65
VA-165/CVW-10	A-1H	USS *Intrepid* (CVS-11)	AK 2xx	4 April 66–21 November 66
VA-176 *Thunderbolts*				
VA-176/CVW-10	A-1H	USS *Intrepid* (CVS-11)	AK 4xx	4 April 66–21 November 66
VA-196 *Main Battery*				
VA-196/CVW-19	A-1H/J	USS *Bon Homme Richard* (CVA-31)	NM 6xx	28 January 64–21 November 64
VA-196/CVW-19	A-1H/J	USS *Bon Homme Richard* (CVA-31)	NM 6xx	21 April 65–13 January 66
VA-215 *Barn Owls*				
VA-215/CVW-21	A-1H/J	USS *Hancock* (CVA-19)	NP 5xx	21 October 64–29 May 65
VA-215/CVW-21	A-1H/J	USS *Hancock* (CVA-19)	NP 5xx	10 November 65–1 August 66
VA-215/CVW-21	A-1H/J	USS *Bon Homme Richard* (CVA-31)	NP 5xx	26 January 67–25 August 67
VAQ-33 *Knight Hawks*				
VAQ-33 Det 14/CVW-19	EA-1F	USS *Ticonderoga* (CVA-14)	NM 70x	27 December 67–17 August 68
VAQ-33 Det 11/CVW-10	EA-1F	USS *Intrepid* (CVS-11)	AK 8xx	4 June 68–8 February 69
VAW-11 *Early Eleven*				
VAW-11 Det R/CVSG-53	EA-1E	USS *Kearsarge* (CVS-33)	RR 7xx	19 June 64–16 December 64
VAW-11 Det T/CVSG-55	EA-1E	USS *Yorktown* (CVS-10)	RR 7xx	23 October 64–16 May 65
VAW-13 *Zappers*				
VAW-13 Det A/CVW-2	EA-1F	USS *Midway* (CVA-41)	VR 70x	6 March 65–23 November 65
VAW-13 Det E/CVW-19	EA-1F	USS *Bon Homme Richard* (CVA-31)	VR 70x	21 April 65–13 January 66
VAW-13 Det 1/CVW-7	EA-1F	USS *Independence* (CVA-62)	VR 70x	10 May 65–13 December 65
VAW-13 Det A/CVW-19	EA-1F	USS *Coral Sea* (CVA-43)	VR 72x	29 July 66–23 February 67
VAW-13 Det M/CVW-9	EA-1F	USS *Enterprise* (CVAN-65)	VR 77x	19 November 66–6 July 77
VAW-13 Det 31/CVW-21	EA-1F	USS *Bon Homme Richard* (CVA-31)	VR 77x	26 January 67–25 August 67
VAW-13 Det 64/CVW-14	EA-1F	USS *Constellation* (CVA-64)	VR 77x	29 April 67–4 December 67
VAW-13 Det 43/CVW-15	EA-1F	USS *Coral Sea* (CVA-43)	VR 77x	26 July 67–6 April 68
VAW-13 Det 63/CVW-11	EA-1F	USS *Kitty Hawk* (CVA-63)	VR 01x	18 November 67–28 June 68

(*Note*: These VAW-13 detachments moved from one carrier to another to remain on the line when a carrier went off the line. Hence, these detachments did not serve aboard the indicated carriers for the entire duration of the deployments.)

Squadron/Air Wing	Aircraft	Carrier	Tail Code & Modex	Deployment Dates
VAW-33 *Knighthawks*				
VAW-33 Det 11/CVW-10	EA-1F	USS *Intrepid* (CVS-11)	AK 6xx	11 May 67–30 December 67

Although operating primarily from land bases, RA-3Bs from VAP-61 were occasionally detached to carriers operating in the Gulf of Tonkin. To reduce their visual detectability during night operations over the Ho Chi Minh Trail, several VAP-61 Skywarriors were camouflaged in three tones of gray. (Toshiuki Todo by courtesy of Cloud 9 Photography)

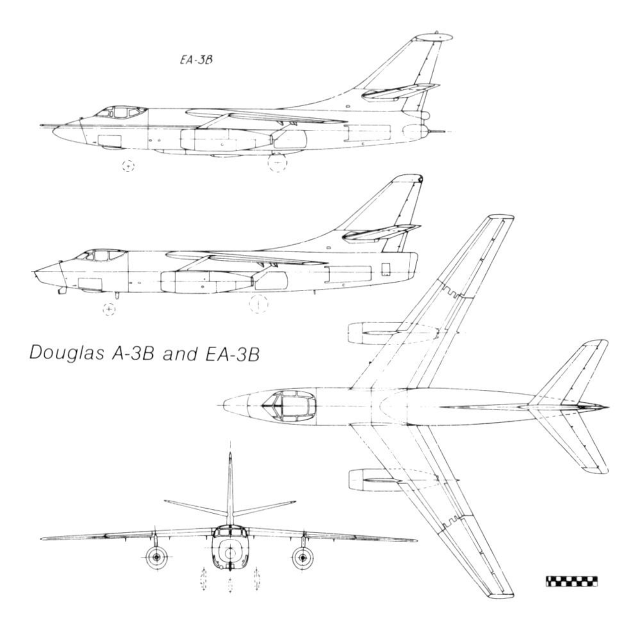

Douglas A-3B and EA-3B

Douglas A-3, EA-3, EKA-3, KA-3, and RA-3 Skywarrior

Developed as a carrier-based heavy attack aircraft primarily intended to carry special weapons (nuclear bombs), the Skywarrior first flew on 28 October 1952 and entered service with VAH-1 in the spring of 1956. Although the main production version of this twin-jet aircraft, the three-seat A3D-2 (redesignated A-3B in September 1982), lost its primary nuclear deterrence role shortly after the entry into service of ballistic missile submarines, it gained a new lease on life as the primary naval tanker aircraft. On 31 July 1964, the Navy had 105 A-3Bs in service, most of which were configured as tankers with an A-12B-7 hose reel unit occupying the rear half of the bomb bay. In addition, the Fleet inventory included twenty-two seven-seat EA-3B electronic reconnaissance aircraft, twenty-three three-seat RA-3B photo-reconnaissance aircraft, and eleven eight-seat TA-3B bombardier-navigator trainers.

A-3Bs did fly some bombing missions over both North and South Vietnam beginning in March 1965 but these aircraft soon proved more valuable as tankers. Accordingly, the Naval Air Rework Facility at NAS Alameda developed two specialized variants using A-3B airframes: the KA-3B which was a dedicated tanker and the EKA-3B, a dual-role tanker/tactical jammer aircraft. Both saw much service in support of war operations. During the Southeast Asian War, RA-3Bs and EA-3Bs from land-based squadrons (VAP-61, VAP-62, and VQ-1) made frequent but short duration deployments aboard carriers operating in the Gulf of Tonkin. The RA-3Bs proved especially useful in detecting camouflaged targets during night and infrared photography missions, and the EA-3Bs gathered data on North Vietnamese radar and communications networks during ELINT and SIGINT operations

With hose extended, this tanker configured A-3B from the Fourrunners *of VAH-4 Det Charlie is ready to refuel a pair of A-4Cs from the* Bombing Broncos *of VA-112. Both squadrons were assigned to CVW-11 aboard USS* Kitty Hawk *during the November 1966-June 1967 deployment.* (US Navy)

When operating from their shore base at NAS Alameda, California, the EKA-3Bs from the Zappers of VAQ-130 carried the tail code VR. Between October 1968 and June 1973, VAQ-130 detachments made eighteen deployments aboard ten different carriers. (L S Smalley)

A-3, EKA-3, and KA-3 Skywarrior Deployments

Squadron/Air Wing	*Aircraft*	*Carrier*	*Tail Code & Modex*	*Deployment Dates*
VAH-2 *Royal Rampants*				
VAH-2 Det M/CVW-9	A-3B	USS *Ranger* (CVA-61)	ZA 81x	5 August 64–6 May 65
VAH-2/CVW-15	A-3B	USS *Coral Sea* (CVA-43)	NL 6xx	7 December 64–1 November 65
VAH-2 Det F/CVW-14	A-3B	USS *Ranger* (CVA-61)	ZA 81x	10 December 65–25 August 66
VAH-2 Det A/CVW-2	A-3B	USS *Coral Sea* (CVA-43)	ZA 6xx	29 July 66–23 February 67
VAH-2 Det M/CVW-9	A-3B	USS *Enterprise* (CVAN-65)	ZA 11x	19 November 66–6 July 67
VAH-2 Det 43/CVW-15	KA-3B	USS *Coral Sea* (CVA-43)	NL 6xx	26 July 67–6 April 68
VAH-2 Det 61/CVW-2	KA-3B	USS *Ranger* (CVA-61)	ZA 6xx	4 November 67–25 May 68
VAH-2 Det 65/CVW-9	KA-3B	USS *Enterprise* (CVAN-65)	ZA x	3 January 68–18 July 68
VAH-2 Det 64/CVW-14	KA-3B	USS *Constellation* (CVA-64)	NK 11x	29 May 68–31 October 68
VAH-4 *Fourrunners*				
VAH-4 Det E/CVW-19	A-3B	USS *Bon Homme Richard* (CVA-31)	ZB xx	28 January 64–21 November 64
VAH-4 Det B/CVW-5	A-3B	USS *Ticonderoga* (CVA-14)	ZB x	14 April 64–15 December 64
VAH-4 Det L/CVW-21	A-3B	USS *Hancock* (CVA-19)	ZB x	21 October 64–29 May 65
VAH-4 Det G/CVW-16	A-3B	USS *Oriskany* (CVA-34)	ZB xx	5 April 65–16 December 65
VAH-4 Det 62/CVW-7	A-3B	USS *Independence* (CVA-62)	ZB x/AG 8xx	10 May 65–13 December 65
VAH-4 Det B/CVW-5	A-3B	USS *Ticonderoga* (CVA-14)	ZB 8xx	28 September 65–13 May 66
VAH-4 Det C/CVW-11	A-3B	USS *Kitty Hawk* (CVA-63)	ZB x	19 October 65–13 June 66
VAH-4 Det M/CVW-9	A-3B	USS *Enterprise* (CVAN-65)	ZB 61x	26 October 65–21 June 66
VAH-4 Det G/CVW-16	A-3B	USS *Oriskany* (CVA-34)	ZB 61x	26 May 66–16 November 66
VAH-4 Det E/CVW-19	A-3B	USS *Ticonderoga* (CVA-14)	ZB 1x	15 October 66–29 May 67
VAH-4 Det C/CVW-11	A-3B	USS *Kitty Hawk* (CVA-63)	ZB x	5 November 66–20 June 67
VAH-4 Det B/CVW-5	A-3B	USS *Hancock* (CVA-19)	ZB x	5 January 67–22 July 67
VAH-4 Det L/CVW-21	A-3B	USS *Bon Homme Richard* (CVA-31)	ZB 8xx	26 January 67–25 August 67
VAH-4 Det 34/CVW-16	KA-3B	USS *Oriskany* (CVA-34)	AH 61x	26 June 67–31 January 68
VAH-4 Det 63/CVW-11	KA-3B	USS *Kitty Hawk* (CVA-63)	ZB x	18 November 67–28 June 68
VAH-4 Det 14/CVW-19	KA-3B	USS *Ticonderoga* (CVA-14)	ZB 1x	28 December 67–17 August 68
VAH-8 *Fireballers*				
VAH-8/CVW-2	A-3B	USS *Midway* (CVA-41)	NE 6xx	6 March 65–23 November 65
VAH-8/CVW-15	A-3B	USS *Constellation* (CVA-64)	NL 6xx	12 May 66–3 December 66
VAH-8/CVW-14	A-3B/KA-3B	USS *Constellation* (CVA-64)	NK 1xx	29 April 67–4 December 67
VAH-10 *Vikings*				
VAH-10/CVW-14	A-3B	USS *Constellation* (CVA-64)	NK 1xx	5 May 64–1 February 65
VAH-10 Det 42/CVW-1	A-3B	USS *Franklin D. Roosevelt* (CVA-42)	AB 6xx	21 June 66–21 February 67
VAH-10 Det 59/CVW-17	KA-3B	USS *Forrestal* (CVA-59)	AA 61x	6 June 67–14 September 67
VAH-10 Det 66/CVW-6	KA-3B	USS *America* (CVA-66)	AE 01x	10 April 68–16 December 68
VAH-10 Det 43/CVW-15	KA-3B	USS *Coral Sea* (CVA-43)	NL 60x	7 September 68–18 April 69
VAH-10 Det 61/CVW-2	KA-3B	USS *Ranger* (CVA-61)	NE 61x	26 October 68–17 May 69
VAH-10 Det 19/CVW-21	KA-3B	USS *Hancock* (CVA-19)	NP 61x	2 August 69–15 April 70
VAH-10 Det 38/CVW-8	KA-3B	USS *Shangri-La* (CVS-38)	AJ 61x	5 March 70–31 August 70
VAQ-129 *Vikings*				
VAQ-129 Det 38/CVW-8	KA-3B	USS *Shangri-La* (CVS-38)	AJ 61x	1 September 70–17 December 70
VAQ-129 Det 19/CVW-21	EKA-3B	USS *Hancock* (CVA-19)	NP 61x	22 October 70–2 June 71

Squadron/Air Wing	*Aircraft*	*Carrier*	*Tail Code & Modex*	*Deployment Dates*
VAQ-130 *Zappers*				
VAQ-130 Det 31/CVW-5	EKA-3B	USS *Bon Homme Richard* (CVA-31)	NF 03x	1 October 68–10 October 68
VAQ-130 Det 66/CVW-6	EKA-3B	USS *America* (CVA-66)	AE 71x	1 October 68–16 December 68
VAQ-130 Det 64/CVW-14	EKA-3B	USS *Constellation* (CVA-64)	NK 10x	1 October 68–31 January 69
VAQ-130 Det 19/CVW-21	EKA-3B	USS *Hancock* (CVA-19)	NP 84x	1 October 68–3 March 69
VAQ-130 Det 43/CVW-15	EKA-3B	USS *Coral Sea* (CVA-43)	VR 01x	1 October 68–18 April 69
VAQ-130 Det 61/CVW-2	EKA-3B	USS *Ranger* (CVA-61)	NE 61x	26 October 68–17 May 69
VAQ-130 Det 14/CVW-16	EKA-3B	USS *Ticonderoga* (CVA-14)	AH 61x	1 February 69–18 September 69
VAQ-130 Det 31/CVW-5	KA/EKA-3B	USS *Bon Homme Richard* (CVA-31)	NF 61x	18 March 69–29 October 69
VAQ-130 Det 34/CVW-19	EKA-3B	USS *Oriskany* (CVA-34)	NM 61x	16 April 69–17 November 69
VAQ-130 Det 31/CVW-5	EKA-3B	USS *Bon Homme Richard* (CVA-31)	NF 61x	2 April 70–12 November 70
VAQ-130 Det 1/CVW-19	EKA-3B	USS *Oriskany* (CVA-34)	NM 61x	16 May 70–10 December 70
VAQ-130 Det 2/CVW-5	EKA-3B	USS *Midway* (CVA-41)	NF 61x	16 April 71–6 November 71
VAQ-130 Det 3/CVW-19	EKA-3B	USS *Oriskany* (CVA-34)	NM 61x	14 May 71–18 December 71
VAQ-130 Det 4/CVW-14	EKA-3B	USS *Enterprise* (CVAN-65)	NK 61x	11 June 71–12 February 72
VAQ-130 Det 1/CVW-9	EKA-3B	USS *Constellation* (CVA-64)	NG 61x	1 October 71–1 July 72
VAQ-130 Det 2/CVW-5	EKA-3B	USS *Midway* (CVA-41)	NF 61x	10 April 72–3 March 73
VAQ-130 Det 3/CVW-19	EKA-3B	USS *Oriskany* (CVA-34)	NM 61x	5 June 72–30 March 73
VAQ-130 Det 4/CVW-2	EKA-3B	USS *Ranger* (CVA-61)	NE 61x	16 November 72–22 June 73
VAQ-131 *Lancers*				
VAQ-131/CVW-11	KA/EKA-3B	USS *Kitty Hawk* (CVA-63)	NH 61x	30 December 68–4 September 69
VAQ-132 *Scorpions*				
VAQ-132 Det 64/CVW-14	KA-3B	USS *Constellation* (CVA-64)	NK 11x	1 November 68–31 January 69
VAQ-132/CVW-9	KA/EKA-3B	USS *Enterprise* (CVAN-65)	NG 61x	6 January 69–2 July 69
VAQ-132/CVW-9	KA/EKA-3B	USS *America* (CVA-66)	NG 61x	10 April 70–21 December 70
VAQ-133 *Wizards*				
VAQ-133/CVW-14	KA/EKA-3B	USS *Constellation* (CVA-64)	NK 61x	11 August 69–8 May 70
VAQ-133/CVW-11	KA/EKA-3B	USS *Kitty Hawk* (CVA-63)	NH 61x	6 November 70–17 July 71
VAQ-134 *Garudas*				
VAQ-134/CVW-2	KA-EKA-3B	USS *Ranger* (CVA-61)	NE 61x	14 October 69–1 June 70
VAQ-134/CVW-2	KA-EKA-3B	USS *Ranger* (CVA-61)	NE 61x	27 October 70–17 July 71
VAQ-135 *Black Ravens*				
VAQ-135/CVW-15	KA/EKA-3B	USS *Coral Sea* (CVA-43)	NL 61x	23 September 69–1 July 70
VAQ-135 Det 3/CVW-15	EKA-3B	USS *Coral Sea* (CVA-43)	NL 61x	12 November 71–17 July 72
VAQ-135 Det 5/CVW-21	EKA-3B	USS *Hancock* (CVA-19)	NP 61x	7 January 72–3 October 72
VAQ-135/CVW-11	EKA-3B	USS *Kitty Hawk* (CVA-63)	NH 61x	17 February 72–28 November 72
VAQ-135 Det 3/CVW-15	EKA-3B	USS *Coral Sea* (CVA-43)	NL 61x	9 March 73–8 November 73
VAQ-135 Det 5/CVW-21	EKA-3B	USS *Hancock* (CVA-19)	NP 61x	8 May 73–8 January 74
VAW-13 *Zappers*				
VAW-13 Det 61/CVW-2	EKA-3B	USS *Ranger* (CVA-61)	VR 72x	4 November 67–25 May 68
VAW-13 Det 65/CVW-9	EKA-3B	USS *Enterprise* (CVAN-65)	ZA x	3 January 68–18 July 68
VAW-13 Det 31/CVW-5	EKA-3B	USS *Bon Homme Richard* (CVA-31)	NF 03x	27 January 68–30 September 68
VAW-13 Det 66/CVW-6	EKA-3B	USS *America* (CVA-66)	AE 71x	10 April 68–30 September 68
VAW-13 Det 64/CVW-14	EKA-3B	USS *Constellation* (CVA-64)	NK 10x	29 May 68–30 September 68
VAW-13 Det 19/CVW-21	EKA-3B	USS *Hancock* (CVA-19)	NP 84x	18 July 68–30 September 68
VAW-13 Det 43/CVW-15	EKA-3B	USS *Coral Sea* (CVA-43)	VR 01x	7 September 68–30 September 68

Douglas A-4 and TA-4 Skyhawk

Going into combat on 5 August 1964, Skyhawk attack bombers went on to fly more bombing sorties than any other carrier aircraft during the entire Rolling Thunder period, and at war's end, still equipped three squadrons of CVW-21 aboard USS *Hancock* (CVA-19). The Skyhawk's intensive war participation, however, was not without its price; 195 Navy A-4s were lost in combat and 77 more in operational accidents, the total representing more than 31 per cent of all aircraft and helicopters lost by the US Navy.

Although the prototype of this outstanding naval aircraft had first flown on 22 June 1954, the type remained in production until February 1979, when the 2960th Skyhawk was completed. In US Naval service, the A-4 entered service with VA-72 in September 1956, and on 30 July 1964, 867 A-4Bs, A-4Cs, and A-4Es were assigned to first line Navy and Marine squadrons. In addition, obsolescent A-4As remained in service with training and reserve units.

With the exception of A-4B deployments by VA-15, VA-95, and VSF-3 aboard USS *Intrepid* (CVS-11) and of A-4B detachments aboard USS *Bennington* (CVS-20) and USS *Kearsarge* (CVS-33) by VA-113 and VA-153, all Skyhawk deployments to the Gulf of Tonkin were made with A-4Cs, A-4Es, and A-4Fs. The latter were fitted on the assembly lines with a humped avionic compartment (which was also retrofitted to many A-4Es and to the A-4Cs modified as A-4Ls for service with reserve units) to house some of the ECM gear (ALQ-51A or ALQ-100 receiver-transmitter and the APR-27 receiver) which had been found necessary to penetrate North Vietnamese defenses. A number of A-4Es and A-4Fs were also fitted with APS-107 RHAW equipment to improve accuracy when operating in the SAM suppression role with Shrike anti-radiation misiles; at that time, to avoid interference with the APS-107, these aircraft received a canted refueling probe. All Skyhawk variants could carry a buddy refueling store beneath the fuselage.

To cope with the increased demand for pilots, the two-seat TA-4F and TA-4J advanced trainer versions were developed during the war. Most served in the United States but a couple of TA-4Fs deployed with VA-164 in May 1973 and others were operated by the Marine Corps in the Tactical Air Control (Airborne) role from Chu Lai Air Base in South Vietnam.

Douglas A-4E Skyhawk and TA-4F

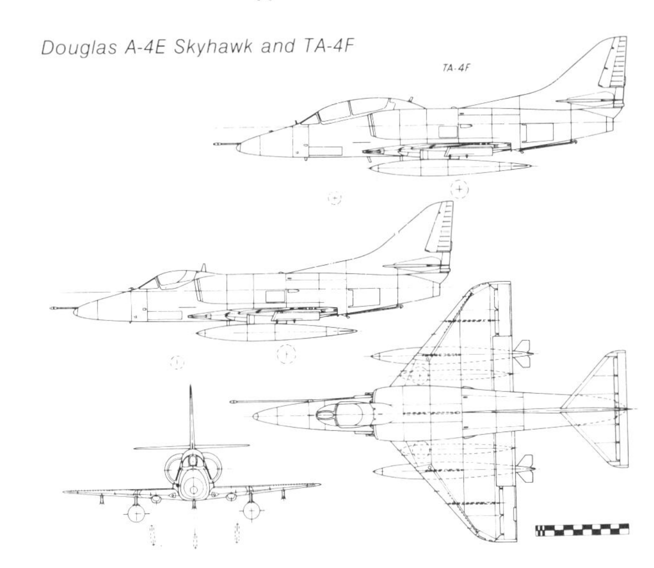

This A-4F from the Fighting Redcocks *of VA-22 was photographed over the Western Pacific in August 1969 while VA-22 was assigned to CVW-5 aboard USS* Bon Homme Richard *(CVA-31). Skyhawk losses during the war were heavy.* (US Navy)

A-4 and TA-4 Skyhawk Deployments

Squadron/Air Wing	Aircraft	Carrier	Tail Code & Modex	Deployment Dates
VA-12 *Flying Ubangis*				
VA-12/CVW-1	A-4E	USS *Franklin D. Roosevelt* (CVA-42)	AB 4xx	21 June 66–21 February 67
VA-12/CVW-8	A-4C	USS *Shangri-La* (CVS-38)	AJ 4xx	5 March 70–17 December 70
VA-15 *Valions*				
VA-15/CVW-10	A-4B	USS *Intrepid* (CVS-11)	AK 3xx	4 April 66–21 November 66
VA-15/CVW-10	A-4C	USS *Intrepid* (CVS-11)	AK 2xx	11 May 67–30 December 67

Squadron/Air Wing	*Aircraft*	*Carrier*	*Tail Code & Modex*	*Deployment Dates*
VA-22 *Fighting Redcocks*				
VA-22/CVW-2	A-4C	USS *Midway* (CVA-41)	NE 2xx	6 March 65–23 November 65
VA-22/CVW-2	A-4C	USS *Coral Sea* (CVA-43)	NE 2xx	29 July 66–23 February 67
VA-22/CVW-2	A-4C	USS *Ranger* (CVA-61)	NE 2xx	4 November 67–25 May 68
VA-22/CVW-5	A-4F	USS *Bon Homme Richard* (CVA-31)	NF 3xx	18 March 69–29 October 69
VA-22/CVW-5	A-4F	USS *Bon Homme Richard* (CVA-31)	NF 3xx	2 April 70–12 November 70
VA-23 *Black Knights*				
VA-23/CVW-2	A-4E	USS *Midway* (CVA-41)	NE 3xx	6 March 65–23 November 65
VA-23/CVW-2	A-4E	USS *Coral Sea* (CVA-43)	NE 3xx	29 July 66–23 February 67
VA-23/CVW-19	A-4F	USS *Ticonderoga* (CVA-14)	NM 3xx	27 December 67–17 August 68
VA-23/CVW-19	A-4F	USS *Oriskany* (CVA-34)	NM 3xx	16 April 69–17 November 69
VA-34 *Blue Blasters*				
VA-34/CVW-10	A-4C	USS *Intrepid* (CVS-11)	AK 3xx	11 May 67–30 December 67
VA-36 *Roadrunners*				
VA-36/CVW-9	A-4C	USS *Enterprise* (CVAN-65)	NG 7xx	26 October 65–21 June 66
VA-36/CVW-10	A-4C	USS *Intrepid* (CVS-11)	AK 5xx	4 June 68–8 February 69
VA-46 *Clansmen*				
VA-46/CVW-17	A-4E	USS *Forrestal* (CVA-59)	AA 4xx	6 June 67–14 September 67
VA-55 *Warhorses*				
VA-55/CVW-5	A-4E	USS *Ticonderoga* (CVA-14)	NF 5xx	14 April 64–15 December 64
VA-55/CVW-14	A-4E	USS *Ranger* (CVA-61)	NK 4xx	10 December 65–25 August 66
VA-55/CVW-14	A-4C	USS *Constellation* (CVA-64)	NK 5xx	29 April 67–4 December 67
VA-55/CVW-21	A-4F	USS *Hancock* (CVA-19)	NP 5xx	18 July 68–3 March 69
VA-55/CVW-21	A-4F	USS *Hancock* (CVA-19)	NP 5xx	2 August 69–15 April 70
VA-55/CVW-21	A-4F	USS *Hancock* (CVA-19)	NP 5xx	22 October 70–2 June 71
VA-55/CVW-21	A-4F	USS *Hancock* (CVA-19)	NP 5xx	7 January 72–3 October 72
VA-55/CVW-21	A-4F	USS *Hancock* (CVA-19)	NP 5xx	8 May 73–8 January 74
VA-56 *Champions*				
VA-56/CVW-5	A-4E	USS *Ticonderoga* (CVA-14)	NF 4xx	14 April 64–15 December 64
VA-56/CVW-5	A-4E	USS *Ticonderoga* (CVA-14)	NF 4xx	28 September 65–13 May 66
VA-56/CVW-9	A-4C	USS *Enterprise* (CVAN-65)	NG 4xx	19 November 66–6 July 67
VA-56/CVW-9	A-4E	USS *Enterprise* (CVAN-65)	NG 4xx	3 January 68–18 July 68
VA-66 *Waldomen*				
VA-66/CVW-10	A-4C	USS *Intrepid* (CVS-11)	AK 3xx	4 June 68–8 February 69
VA-72 *Blue Hawks*				
VA-72/CVW-7	A-4E	USS *Independence* (CVA-62)	AG 3xx	10 May 65–13 December 65
VA-72/CVW-1	A-4E	USS *Franklin D. Roosevelt* (CVA-42)	AB 5xx	21 June 66–21 February 67

Photographed from the island of USS Bon Homme Richard *(CVA-31), this A-4C from VA-76 had to 'bolt' after its hook failed to engage a cross-deck pendant after returning from a combat sortie on 24 May 1967. The* Spirits *had been part of CVW-9 aboard USS* Enterprise *(CVAN-65) when the nuclear carrier had made her first deployment to the Gulf of Tonkin in 1965-66, transferred to CVW-21 for a war cruise aboard CVA-31 in 1967, and then went to CVW-7 prior to being decommisioned in 1969.* (US Navy)

Squadron/Air Wing	*Aircraft*	*Carrier*	*Tail Code & Modex*	*Deployment Dates*
VA-76 *Spirits*				
VA-76/CVW-9	A-4C	USS *Enterprise* (CVAN-65)	NG 5xx	26 October 65–21 June 66
VA-76/CVW-21	A-4C	USS *Bon Homme Richard* (CVA-31)	NP 6xx	26 January 67–25 August 67
VA-86 *Sidewinders*				
VA-86/CVW-7	A-4E	USS *Independence* (CVA-62)	AG 4xx	10 May 65–13 December 65
VA-93 *Blue Blazers*				
VA-93/CVW-9	A-4C	USS *Ranger* (CVA-61)	NG 3xx	5 August 64–6 May 65
VA-93/CVW-9	A-4C	USS *Enterprise* (CVAN-65)	NG 3xx	26 October 65–21 June 66
VA-93/CVW-5	A-4E	USS *Hancock* (CVA-19)	NF 3xx	5 January 67–22 July 67
VA-93/CVW-5	A-4F	USS *Bon Homme Richard* (CVA-31)	NF 3xx	27 January 68–10 October 68
VA-94 *Mighty Shrikes*				
VA-94/CVW-9	A-4C	USS *Ranger* (CVA-61)	NG 4xx	5 August 64–6 May 65
VA-94/CVW-9	A-4C	USS *Enterprise* (CVAN-65)	NG 4xx	26 October 65–21 June 66
VA-94/CVW-5	A-4C	USS *Hancock* (CVA-19)	NF 4xx	5 January 67–22 July 67
VA-94/CVW-5	A-4E	USS *Bon Homme Richard* (CVA-31)	NF 4xx	27 January 68–10 October 68
VA-94/CVW-5	A-4E	USS *Bon Homme Richard* (CVA-31)	NF 4xx	18 March 69–29 October 69
VA-94/CVW-5	A-4E	USS *Bon Homme Richard* (CVA-31)	NF 4xx	2 April 70–12 November 70
VA-95 *Skyknights*				
VA-95/CVW-10	A-4B	USS *Intrepid* (CVS-11)	AK 5xx	4 April 66–21 November 66
VA-106 *Gladiators*				
VA-106/CVW-17	A-4E	USS *Forrestal* (CVA-59)	AA 3xx	6 June 67–14 September 67
VA-106/CVW-10	A-4E	USS *Intrepid* (CVS-11)	AK 2xx	4 June 68–8 February 69
VA-112 *Bombing Broncos*				
VA-112/CVW-11	A-4C	USS *Kitty Hawk* (CVA-63)	NH 4xx	5 November 66–20 June 67
VA-112/CVW-11	A-4C	USS *Kitty Hawk* (CVA-63)	NH 4xx	18 November 67–28 June 68
VA-112/CVW-16	A-4C	USS *Ticonderoga* (CVA-14)	AH 4xx	1 February 69–18 September 69
VA-113 *Stingers*				
VA-113 Det Q/CVSG-59	A-4B	USS *Bennington* (CVS-20)	???	22 March 65–7 October 65
VA-113/CVW-11	A-4C	USS *Kitty Hawk* (CVA-63)	NH 3xx	19 October 65–13 June 66
VA-113/CVW-9	A-4C	USS *Enterprise* (CVAN-65)	NG 3xx	19 November 66–6 July 67
VA-113/CVW-9	A-4F	USS *Enterprise* (CVAN-65)	NG 3xx	3 January 68–18 July 68
VA-144 *Roadrunners*				
VA-144/CVW-14	A-4C	USS *Constellation* (CVA-64)	NK 4xx	5 May 64–1 February 65
VA-144/CVW-5	A-4C	USS *Ticonderoga* (CVA-14)	NF 5xx	28 September 65–13 May 66
VA-144/CVW-11	A-4C	USS *Kitty Hawk* (CVA-63)	NH 3xx	5 November 66–20 June 67
VA-144/CVW-11	A-4E	USS *Kitty Hawk* (CVA-63)	NH 3xx	18 November 67–28 June 68
VA-144/CVW-5	A-4E	USS *Bon Homme Richard* (CVA-31)	NF 5xx	18 March 69–29 October 69
VA-144/CVW-5	A-4F	USS *Bon Homme Richard* (CVA-31)	NF 5xx	2 April 70–12 November 70

After the Skyraiders were phased out, the smaller carriers which could not accommodate Intruders were forced to replace their A-1 squadron with a third A-4 squadron. In the case of CVA-31, the A-1s of VA-215 were replaced in 1968 by the A-4Fs of VA-212 and in 1969 by the A-4Es of VA-144. This Roadrunners *A-4E, retrofitted with the humped avionic compartment, is seen in flight over the Pacific Ocean on 24 July 1969.* (US Navy)

Squadron/Air Wing	Aircraft	Carrier	Tail Code & Modex	Deployment Dates
VA-146 *Blue Diamonds*				
VA-146/CVW-14	A-4C	USS *Constellation* (CVA-64)	NK 6xx	5 May 64–1 February 65
VA-146/CVW-14	A-4C	USS *Ranger* (CVA-61)	NK 6xx	10 December 65–25 August 66
VA-146/CVW-14	A-4C	USS *Constellation* (CVA-64)	NK 6xx	29 April 67–4 December 67
VA-152 *Wild Aces*				
VA-152/CVW-8	A-4E	USS *Shangri-La* (CVS-38)	AJ 5xx	5 March 70–17 December 70
VA-153 *Blue Tail Flies*				
VA-153 Det R/CVSG-53	A-4B	USS *Kearsarge* (CVS-33)	???	19 June 64–16 December 64
VA-153/CVW-15	A-4C	USS *Coral Sea* (CVS-43)	NL 3xx	7 December 64–1 November 65
VA-153/CVW-15	A-4C	USS *Constellation* (CVA-64)	NL 3xx	12 May 66–3 December 66
VA-153/CVW-15	A-4E	USS *Coral Sea* (CVA-43)	NL 3xx	26 July 67–6 April 68
VA-153/CVW-15	A-4F	USS *Coral Sea* (CVA-43)	NL 3xx	7 September 68–18 April 69
VA-155 *Silver Foxes*				
VA-155/CVW-15	A-4E	USS *Coral Sea* (CVA-43)	NL 5xx	7 December 64–1 November 65
VA-155/CVW-15	A-4E	USS *Constellation* (CVA-64)	NL 5xx	12 May 66–3 December 66
VA-155/CVW-15	A-4E	USS *Coral Sea* (CVA-43)	NL 5xx	26 July 67–6 April 68
VA-155/CVW-2	A-4F	USS *Ranger* (CVA-61)	NE 4xx	26 October 68–17 May 69
VA-163 *Saints*				
VA-163/CVW-16	A-4E	USS *Oriskany* (CVA-34)	AH 3xx	5 April 65–16 December 65
VA-163/CVW-16	A-4E	USS *Oriskany* (CVA-34)	AH 3xx	26 May 66–16 November 66
VA-163/CVW-16	A-4E	USS *Oriskany* (CVA-34)	AH 3xx	16 June 67–31 January 68
VA-163/CVW-21	A-4E	USS *Hancock* (CVA-19)	NP 3xx	18 July 68–3 March 69
VA-164 *Ghost Riders*				
VA-164/CVW-16	A-4E	USS *Oriskany* (CVA-34)	AH 4xx	5 April 65–16 December 65
VA-164/CVW-16	A-4E	USS *Oriskany* (CVA-34)	AH 4xx	26 May 66–16 November 66
VA-164/CVW-16	A-4E	USS *Oriskany* (CVA-34)	AH 4xx	16 June 67–31 January 68
VA-164/CVW-21	A-4E	USS *Hancock* (CVA-19)	NP 4xx	18 July 68–3 March 69
VA-164/CVW-21	A-4F	USS *Hancock* (CVA-19)	NP 4xx	2 August 69–15 April 70
VA-164/CVW-21	A-4F	USS *Hancock* (CVA-19)	NP 4xx	22 October 70–2 June 71
VA-164/CVW-21	A-4F	USS *Hancock* (CVA-19)	NP 4xx	7 January 72–3 October 72
VA-164/CVW-21	A-4F/TA-4F	USS *Hancock* (CVA-19)	NP 4xx	8 May 73–8 January 74
VA-172 *Blue Bolts*				
VA-172/CVW-1	A-4C	USS *Franklin D. Roosevelt* (CVA-42)	AB 3xx	21 June 66–21 February 67
VA-172/CVW-8	A-4C	USS *Shangri-La* (CVS-38)	AJ 3xx	5 March 70–17 December 70
VA-192 *Golden Dragons*				
VA-192/CVW-19	A-4C	USS *Bon Homme Richard* (CVA-31)	NM 2xx	28 January 64–21 November 64
VA-192/CVW-19	A-4C	USS *Bon Homme Richard* (CVA-31)	NM 2xx	21 April 65–13 January 66
VA-192/CVW-19	A-4E	USS *Ticonderoga* (CVA-14)	NM 2xx	15 October 66–29 May 67
VA-192/CVW-19	A-4F	USS *Ticonderoga* (CVA-14)	NM 2xx	27 December 67–17 August 68
VA-192/CVW-19	A-4F	USS *Oriskany* (CVA-34)	NM 4xx	16 April 69–17 November 69
VA-195 *Dambusters*				
VA-195/CVW-19	A-4C	USS *Bon Homme Richard* (CVA-31)	NM 5xx	28 January 64–21 November 64
VA-195/CVW-19	A-4C	USS *Bon Homme Richard* (CVA-31)	NM 5xx	21 April 65–13 January 66
VA-195/CVW-19	A-4C	USS *Ticonderoga* (CVA-14)	NM 5xx	15 October 66–29 May 67
VA-195/CVW-19	A-4C	USS *Ticonderoga* (CVA-14)	NM 5xx	27 December 67–17 August 68
VA-195/CVW-19	A-4E	USS *Oriskany* (CVA-34)	NM 5xx	16 April 69–17 November 69
VA-212 *Rampant Raiders*				
VA-212/CVW-21	A-4E	USS *Hancock* (CVA-19)	NP 2xx	21 October 64–29 May 65
VA-212/CVW-21	A-4E	USS *Hancock* (CVA-19)	NP 2xx	10 November 65–1 August 66
VA-212/CVW-21	A-4E	USS *Bon Homme Richard* (CVA-31)	NP 2xx	26 January 67–25 August 67
VA-212/CVW-5	A-4F	USS *Bon Homme Richard* (CVA-31)	NF 5xx	27 January 68–10 October 68
VA-212/CVW-21	A-4F	USS *Hancock* (CVA-19)	NP 3xx	2 August 69–15 April 70
VA-212/CVW-21	A-4F	USS *Hancock* (CVA-19)	NP 3xx	22 October 70–2 June 71
VA-212/CVW-21	A-4F	USS *Hancock* (CVA-19)	NP 3xx	7 January 72–3 October 72
VA-212/CVW-21	A-4F	USS *Hancock* (CVA-19)	NP 3xx	8 May 73–8 January 74

Squadron/Air Wing	Aircraft	Carrier	Tail Code & Modex	Deployment Dates
VA-216 *Black Diamonds*				
VA-216/CVW-21	A-4C	USS *Hancock* (CVA-19)	NP 6xx	21 October 64–29 May 65
VA-216/CVW-21	A-4C	USS *Hancock* (CVA-19)	NP 6xx	10 November 65–1 August 66
VA-216/CVW-15	A-4C	USS *Coral Sea* (CVA-43)	NL 6xx	7 September 68–18 April 69
VMA-223 *Bulldogs*				
VMA-223 Det T/CVSG-55	A-4C	USS *Yorktown* (CVS-10)	WP xx	23 October 64–16 May 65
VSF-3 *Chessmen*				
VSF-3/CVW-10	A-4B	USS *Intrepid* (CVS-11)	AK 1xx	11 May 67–30 December 67
H&MS-15				
H&MS-15 Det N/CVSG-57	A-4C	USS *Hornet* (CVS-12)	YV 8x	12 August 65–23 March 66

Grumman A-6 and KA-6 Intruder

Carrying a heavier bomb load than any other type of carrier-based aircraft and capable of precision low-level strike under all-weather conditions, the Intruder proved to be an outstanding aircraft after overcoming problems due to premature detonation of its bombs during early operations in July 1965 when it had first deployed with VA-75 aboard USS *Independence* (CVA-62).

Following the prototype's maiden flight on 16 April 1960, the Intruder entered service in February 1963. At the start of the war, A-6As equipped, at least partially, three LANTFLT squadrons and one Marine squadron (with only thirty-five aircraft in service on 31 July 1964). However, production soon gained tempo and A-6As quickly replaced A-1H/Js aboard the large carriers, with one Marine and ten Navy squadrons making one or more deployments to the Gulf of Tonkin.

Specialized Intruder versions taking part in operations during the war were the KA-6D tanker, first deployed by VA-196 aboard USS *Enterprise* (CVAN-65) in June 1971, the A-6B defense suppression aircraft armed with Standard ARMs (anti-radiation missiles), first deployed by VA-75 aboard USS *Kitty Hawk* (CVA-63) in November 1967, and the A-6C, which was fitted with sensors for detecting truck convoys and first deployed by VA-165 aboard USS *America* (CVA-66) in April 1970.

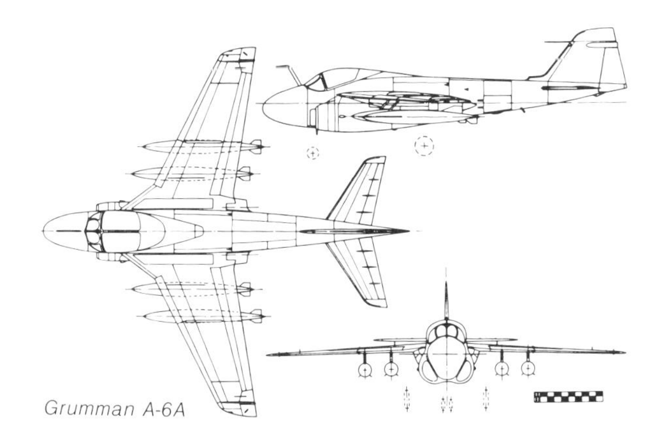

Grumman A-6A

After three war cruises with Skyraiders aboard USS Ticonderoga *(CVA-14), the* Knightriders *of VA-52 converted to Intruders prior to deploying to the Gulf of Tonkin with CVW-15 aboard USS* Coral Sea *(CVA-43) in 1968-69. They then transferred to CVW-11 for two war cruises aboard USS* Kitty Hawk *(CVA-63). BuNo 157022 was photographed at NAS Lemoore, California, on 10 October 1971 between VA-52's first and second cruises aboard CVA-63.* (Peter B Lewis)

A-6 and KA-6 Intruder Deployments

Squadron/Air Wing	Aircraft	Carrier	Tail Code & Modex	Deployment Dates
VA-35 *Black Panthers*				
VA-35/CVW-9	A-6A	USS *Enterprise* (CVAN-65)	NG 5xx	19 November 66–6 July 67
VA-35/CVW-9	A-6A	USS *Enterprise* (CVAN-65)	NG 5xx	3 January 68–18 July 68
VA-35/CVW-15	A-6A	USS *Coral Sea* (CVA-43)	NL 5xx	23 September 69–1 July 70
VA-35/CVW-8	A-6A/C & KA-6D	USS *America* (CVA-66)	AJ 5xx	5 June 72–24 March 73
VA-52 *Knightriders*				
VA-52/CVW-15	A-6A	USS *Coral Sea* (CVA-43)	NL 4xx	7 September 68–18 April 69
VA-52/CVW-11	A-6A/B	USS *Kitty Hawk* (CVA-63)	NH 5xx	6 November 70–17 July 71
VA-52/CVW-11	A-6A/B & KA-6D	USS *Kitty Hawk* (CVA-63)	NH 5xx	17 February 72–28 November 72
VA-65 *Tigers*				
VA-65/CVW-15	A-6A	USS *Constellation* (CVA-64)	NL 4xx	12 May 66–3 December 66
VA-65/CVW-17	A-6A	USS *Forrestal* (CVA-59)	AA 5xx	6 June 67–14 September 67
VA-65/CVW-11	A-6A/B	USS *Kitty Hawk* (CVA-63)	NH 5xx	30 December 68–4 September 69
VA-75 *Sunday Punchers*				
VA-75/CVW-7	A-6A	USS *Independence* (CVA-62)	AG 5xx	10 May 65–13 December 65
VA-75/CVW-11	A-6A/B	USS *Kitty Hawk* (CVA-63)	NH 5xx	18 November 67–28 June 68
VA-75/CVW-3	A-6A/B & KA-6D	USS *Saratoga* (CV-60)	AC 5xx	11 April 72–13 February 73
VA-85 *Black Falcons*				
VA-85/CVW-11	A-6A	USS *Kitty Hawk* (CVA-63)	NH 8xx	19 October 65–13 June 66
VA-85/CVW-11	A-6A	USS *Kitty Hawk* (CVA-63)	NH 5xx	5 November 66–20 June 67
VA-85/CVW-6	A-6A/B	USS *America* (CVA-66)	AE 5xx	10 April 68–16 December 68
VA-85/CVW-14	A-6A/B	USS *Constellation* (CVA-64)	NK 5xx	11 August 69–8 May 70
VA-95 *Green Lizards*				
VA-95/CVW-15	A-6A/B & KA-6D	USS *Coral Sea* (CVA-43)	NL 5xx	9 March 73–8 November 73
VA-115 *Arabs*				
VA-115/CVW-5	A-6A & KA-6D	USS *Midway* (CVA-41)	NF 5xx	16 April 71–6 November 71
VA-115/CVW-5	A-6A & KA-6D	USS *Midway* (CVA-41)	NF 5xx	10 April 72–3 March 73
VA-145 *Swordsmen*				
VA-145/CVW-9	A-6A/B	USS *Enterprise* (CVAN-65)	NG 5xx	6 January 69–2 July 69
VA-145/CVW-2	A-6A/C	USS *Ranger* (CVA-61)	NE 5xx	27 October 70–17 June 71
VA-145/CVW-2	A-6A/B & KA-6D	USS *Ranger* (CVA-61)	NE 5xx	16 November 72–22 June 73
VA-165 *Boomers*				
VA-165/CVW-2	A-6A	USS *Ranger* (CVA-61)	NE 5xx	4 November 67–25 May 68
VA-165/CVW-2	A-6A	USS *Ranger* (CVA-61)	NE 5xx	26 October 68–17 May 69
VA-165/CVW-9	A-6/A/B/C	USS *America* (CVA-66)	NG 5xx	10 April 70–21 December 70
VA-165/CVW-9	A-6A & KA-6D	USS *Constellation* (CVA-64)	NG 5xx	1 October 71–1 July 72
VA-165/CVW-9	A-6A & KA-6D	USS *Constellation* (CVA-64)	NG 5xx	5 January 73–11 October 73
VA-196 *Main Battery*				
VA-196/CVW-14	A-6A	USS *Constellation* (CVA-64)	NK 4xx	29 April 67–4 December 67
VA-196/CVW-14	A-6A/B	USS *Constellation* (CVA-64)	NK 4xx	29 May 68–31 January 69
VA-196/CVW-2	A-6A	USS *Ranger* (CVA-61)	NE 5xx	14 October 69–1 June 70
VA-196/CVW-14	A-6A/B & KA-6D	USS *Enterprise* (CVAN-65)	NK 5xx	11 June 71–12 February 72
VA-196/CVW-14	A-6A/B & KA-6D	USS *Enterprise* (CVAN-65)	NK 5xx	12 September 72–12 June 73
VMA(AW)-224 *Bengals*				
VMA(AW)-224/CVW-15	A-6A/B & KA-6D	USS *Coral Sea* (CVA-43)	NL 5xx	12 November 71–17 July 72

Flight deck crewmen ready an A-6A of Attack Squadron 165 for launching from the flight deck of USS Constellation *(CVA-64) on 25 April 1972. During the war the* Boomers *of VA-165 deployed twice aboard USS* Ranger *(CVA-61), once aboard USS* America *(CVA-66), and again twice aboard USS* Constellation. (US Navy)

Grumman EA-6 Prowler

The Prowler was the first carrier-based aircraft specially developed to suppress enemy electronic activity in support of strike aircraft and ground troops and to obtain tactical electronic intelligence from within combat areas. Its aerodynamic prototype first flew on 25 May 1968. The four-seat EA-6B, which was fitted with five external store stations for TJS (Tactical Jamming System) pods and drop tanks, was received by the Fleet in January 1971.

The first EA-6B deployment to the Gulf of Tonkin was made by VAQ-132 aboard USS *America* (CVA-66) beginning in June 1972. Even though they were restricted to stand-off jamming in support of both Naval and Air Force missions as the Navy was not prepared to risk having a damaged aircraft fall into Communist hands, the Prowlers from that squadron and those from VAQ-131 and VAQ-134 proved most effective during Linebacker II operations.

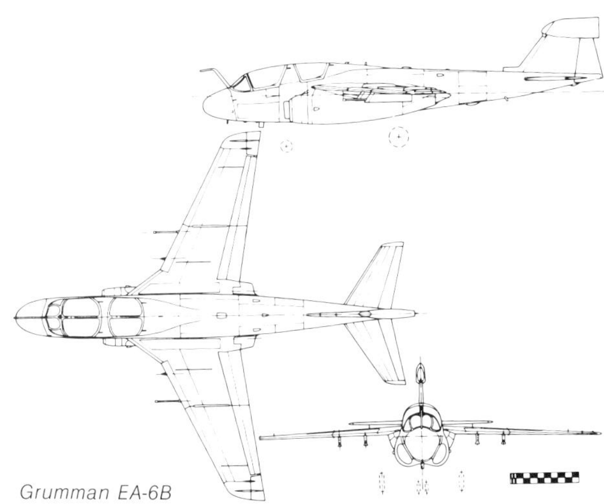

Grumman EA-6B

Left: Grumman EA-6B Prowlers first deployed with VAQ-131 aboard USS America *(CVA-66) in June 1972. The next squadron to take Prowlers to the Gulf of Tonkin was VAQ-131 which departed Alameda aboard USS* Enterprise *(CVA-65) on 12 September 1972* (Peter B Lewis)

EA-6 Prowler Deployments

Squadron/Air Wing	*Aircraft*	*Carrier*	*Tail Code & Modex*	*Deployment Dates*
VAQ-131 *Lancers*				
VAQ-131/CVW-14	EA-6B	USS *Enterprise* (CVAN-65)	NK 61x	12 September 72–12 June 73
VAQ-132 *Scorpions*				
VAQ-132/CVW-8	EA-6B	USS *America* (CVA-66)	AJ 61x	5 June 72–24 March 73
VAQ-134 *Garudas*				
VAQ-134/CVW-9	EA-6B	USS *Constellation* (CVA-64)	NG 61x	5 January 73–11 October 73

Main type of COD transport operated during the war years (and in fact soldiering on until 1986), the Grumman C-1A Trader proved reliable but slow and noisy. This aircraft served as a station hack at NAS Lemoore, the California home of PACFLT's light attack squadrons. (Peter B Lewis)

Grumman E-1 Tracer and C-1 Trader

Both the Tracer AEW aircraft and the Trader transport were derived from the twin-engined Grumman S-2 Tracker ASW aircraft and used the same wing and power plant installation. In the case of the Trader, the fuselage was modified to adapt the aircraft for COD duty carrying either nine passengers in rear-facing seats or 3500lb (1588kg) of cargo in a 1165cu ft (33m^3) fuselage compartment. The Tracer fuselage provided accommodation for the pilot, co-pilot/tactical director, and two radar operators and housed most of the specialized electronic equipment. The antenna for the AN/APS-82 radar was housed in a dish-type radome above the fuselage. On the E-1B, the conventional tail surfaces of the S-2 and C-1 were replaced by a central fin and twin rudder and fin at the end of the horizontal tail surfaces. The Tracer and Trader prototypes had respectively been flown for the first time in December 1956 and January 1955. On 31 July 1964, the Fleet had 80 E-1Bs and 72 C-1As for service aboard carriers.

Although the Tracer's intended successor, the E-2A Hawkeye, had just entered service when carrier-based aircraft flew their first strike against North Vietnam and progressively replaced it aboard most carriers operating in the Gulf of Tonkin, the Tracer made more deployments than the Hawkeye and was still serving with TF 77 carriers when the war ended. Even more enduring were the C-1A Trader COD aircraft which served with all the carriers operating in Southeast Asia as well as with land-based VR and VRC squadrons operating in support of TF 77, notably the VR-21 detachment at NAS Atsugi, Japan, and VRC-50 at NAS Cubi Point, the Philippines.

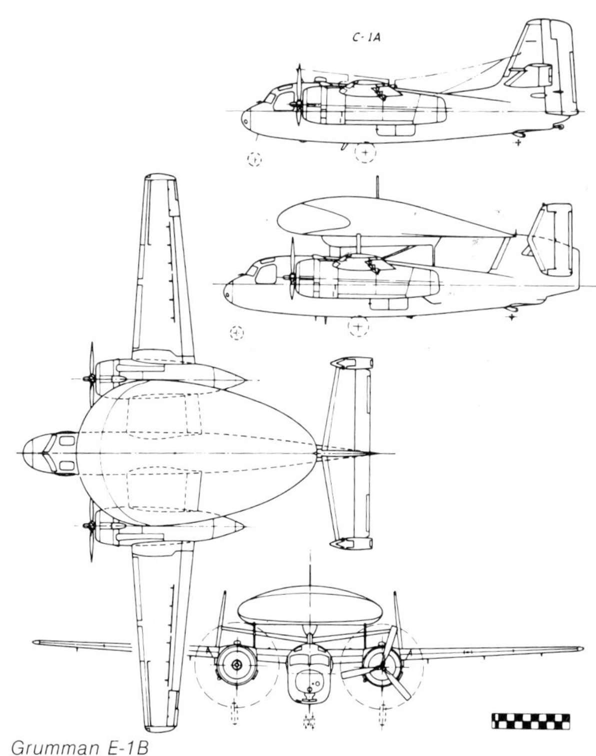

Grumman E-1B

E-1 Tracer Deployments

Squadron/Air Wing	*Aircraft*	*Carrier*	*Tail Code & Modex*	*Deployment Dates*
VAW-11 *Early Eleven*				
VAW-11 Det E/CVW-19	E-1B	USS *Bon Homme Richard* (CVA-31)	RR 7xx	28 January 64–21 November 64
VAW-11 Det B/CVW-5	E-1B	USS *Ticonderoga* (CVA-14)	RR 76x	14 April 64–15 December 64
VAW-11 Det F/CVW-14	E-1B	USS *Constellation* (CVA-64)	RR 78x	5 May 64–1 February 65
VAW-11 Det M/CVW-9	E-1B	USS *Ranger* (CVA-61)	RR 77x	5 August 64–6 May 65
VAW-11 Det L/CVW-21	E-1B	USS *Hancock* (CVA-19)	RR x	21 October 64–29 May 65
VAW-11 Det D/CVW-15	E-1B	USS *Coral Sea* (CVA-43)	RR 7xx	7 December 64–1 November 65
VAW-11 Det A/CVW-2	E-1B	USS *Midway* (CVA-41)	RR 7xx	6 March 65–23 November 65
VAW-11 Det Q/CVSG-59	E-1B	USS *Bennington* (CVS-20)	RR 7xx	22 March 65–7 October 65
VAW-11 Det G/CVW-16	E-1B	USS *Oriskany* (CVA-34)	RR 75x	5 April 65–16 December 65
VAW-11 Det E/CVW-19	E-1B	USS *Bon Homme Richard* (CVA-31)	RR 7xx	21 April 65–13 January 66
VAW-11 Det N/CVSG-57	E-1B	USS *Hornet* (CVS-12)	RR 76x	12 August 65–23 March 66
VAW-11 Det B/CVW-5	E-1B	USS *Ticonderoga* (CVA-14)	RR 70x	28 September 65–13 May 66
VAW-11 Det M/CVW-9	E-1B	USS *Enterprise* (CVAN-65)	RR 00x	26 October 65–21 June 66
VAW-11 Det L/CVW-21	E-1B	USS *Hancock* (CVA-19)	RR 72x	10 November 65–1 August 66

A Grumman E-1B Tracer of VAW-11 Det Echo taxies onto the port catapult aboard USS Bon Homme Richard *(CVA-31) in June 1965. This angle clearly illustrates the odd shape of the radome within which the AN/APS-82 antenna was rotating at 6rpm.* (Jerry Edwards)

VAW-11 Det T/CVSG-55	E-1B	USS *Yorktown* (CVS-10)	RR 71x	5 January 66–27 July 66
VAW-11 Det G/CVW-16	E-1B	USS *Oriskany* (CVA-34)	RR 70x	26 May 66–16 November 66
VAW-11 Det R/CVSG-53	E-1B	USS *Kearsarge* (CVS-33)	RR 72x	9 June 66–20 December 66
VAW-11 Det E/CVW-19	E-1B	USS *Ticonderoga* (CVA-14)	RR 72x	15 October 66–19 April 67
VAW-11 Det Q/CVSG-59	E-1B	USS *Bennington* (CVS-20)	RR 7xx	4 November 66–19 April 67
VAW-11 Det B/CVW-5	E-1B	USS *Hancock* (CVA-19)	RR 72x	5 January 67–19 April 67
VAW-11 Det L/CVW-21	E-1B	USS *Bon Homme Richard* (CVA-31)	RR 7xx	26 January 67–19 April 67
VAW-11 Det N/CVSG-57	E-1B	USS *Hornet* (CVS-12)	RR 76x	27 March 67–19 April 67

VAW-12 ***Bats***

VAW-12 Det 62/CVW-7	E-1B	USS *Independence* (CVA-62)	AG 7xx	10 May 65–13 December 65
VAW-12 Det 42/CVW-1	E-1B	USS *Franklin D. Roosevelt* (CVA-42)	AB 71x	21 June 66–21 February 67

VAW-111 ***Hunters***

VAW-111 Det 20/CVSG-59	E-1B	USS *Bennington* (CVS-20)	RR 7xx	20 April 67–23 May 67
VAW-111 Det 14/CVW-19	E-1B	USS *Ticonderoga* (CVA-14)	RR 72x	20 April 66–29 May 67
VAW-111 Det 19/CVW-5	E-1B	USS *Hancock* (CVA-19)	RR 72x	20 April 67–22 July 67
VAW-111 Det 12/CVSG-57	E-1B	USS *Hornet* (CVS-12)	RR 76x	20 April 67–28 October 67
VAW-111 Det 31/CVW-21	E-1B	USS *Bon Homme Richard* (CVA-31)	RR 7xx	20 April 67–25 August 67
VAW-111 Det 34/CVW-16	E-1B	USS *Oriskany* (CVA-34)	RR 70x	16 June 67–31 January 68
VAW-111 Det 33/CVSG-53	E-1B	USS *Kearsarge* (CVS-33)	RR 76x	17 August 67–6 April 68
VAW-111 Det 14/CVW-19	E-1B	USS *Ticonderoga* (CVA-14)	RR 72x	27 December 67–17 August 68
VAW-111 Det 10/CVSG-53	E-1B	USS *Yorktown* (CVS-10)	RR 71x	28 December 67–5 July 68
VAW-111 Det 31/CVW-5	E-1B	USS *Bon Homme Richard* (CVA-31)	RR 7xx	27 January 68–10 October 68
VAW-111 Det 20/CVSG-59	E-1B	USS *Bennington* (CVS-20)	RR 7xx	1 May 68–9 November 68
VAW-111 Det 19/CVW-21	E-1B	USS *Hancock* (CVA-19)	NP 72x	18 July 68–3 March 69
VAW-111 Det 12/CVSG-57	E-1B	USS *Hornet* (CVS-12)	RR 7xx	30 September 68–12 May 69
VAW-111 Det 14/CVW-16	E-1B	USS *Ticonderoga* (CVA-14)	AH 01x	1 February 69–18 September 69
VAW-111 Det 31/CVW-5	E-1B	USS *Bon Homme Richard* (CVA-31)	NF 73x	18 March 69–29 October 69
VAW-111 Det 33/CVSG-53	E-1B	USS *Kearsarge* (CVS-33)	RR 01x	29 March 69–4 September 69
VAW-111 Det 34/CVW-19	E-1B	USS *Oriskany* (CVA-34)	NM 01x	16 April 69–17 Nov 69
VAW-111 Det 19/CVW-21	E-1B	USS *Hancock* (CVA-19)	NP 01x	2 August 69–15 April 70
VAW-111 Det 14/CVW-5	E-1B	USS *Bon Homme Richard* (CVA-31)	NF 01x	2 April 70–12 Nov 70
VAW-111 Det 34/CVW-19	E-1B	USS *Oriskany* (CVA-34)	NM 01x	14 May 70–10 December 70
VAW-111 Det 3/CVW-21	E-1B	USS *Hancock* (CVA-19)	NP 01x	20 October 70–2 June 71
VAW-111 Det 6/CVW-2	E-1B	USS *Ranger* (CVA-61)	NE 01x	27 October 70–17 June 71
VAW-111 Det 2/CVW-19	E-1B	USS *Oriskany* (CVA-34)	NM 01x	14 May 71–18 December 71
VAW-111 Det 4/CVW-15	E-1B	USS *Coral Sea* (CVA-43)	NL 01x	12 November 71–17 July 72
VAW-111 Det 2/CVW-21	E-1B	USS *Hancock* (CVA-19)	NP 01x	7 January 72–3 October 72
VAW-111 Det 6/CVW-19	E-1B	USS *Oriskany* (CVA-34)	NM 01x	5 June 72–30 March 73
VAW-111 Det 1/CVW-2	E-1B	USS *Ranger* (CVA-61)	NE 01x	16 November 72–22 June 73
VAW-111 Det 4/CVW-15	E-1B	USS *Coral Sea* (CVA-43)	NL 01x	9 March 73–8 November 73
VAW-111 Det 2/CVW-21	E-1B	USS *Hancock* (CVA-19)	NP 01x	8 May 73–8 January 74

VAW-121 ***Griffons***

VAW-121 Det 11/CVW-10	E-1B	USS *Intrepid* (CVS-11)	AK 7xx	11 May 67–30 December 67
VAW-121 Det 11/CVW-10	E-1B	USS *Intrepid* (CVS-11)	AK 7xx	4 June 68–8 February 69
VAW-121 Det 38/CVW-8	E-1B	USS *Shangri-La* (CVS-38)	AJ 01x	5 March 70–17 December 70

Except on occasional training flights, AEW aircraft do not fly in formation. This unusual gathering of two E-2As from VAW-112 was photographed off the coast of Oahu, Hawaii, on 28 February 1969 while their carrier, USS Enterprise *(CVAN-65), was being repaired following the catastrophic fire which had occurred six weeks earlier.* (US Navy)

Grumman E-2 Hawkeye and C-2 Greyhound

The turbine engined successor of the piston-engined E-1B Tracer AEW aircraft first flew on 21 October 1970 and had just entered service with VAW-11, with twelve E-2As being on strength on 31 July 1964, when combat operations began against North Vietnam. The first E-2A combat deployment was made by VAW-11 Det C aboard USS *Kitty Hawk* (CVA-63) beginning in October 1965. The same carrier saw the much improved E-2B version make its operational début when VAW-114 embarked for the war cruise which began in November 1970.

The C-2 Greyhound COD aircraft used the same wings, power plant, and tail unit as the E-2, but had a new fuselage with a rear loading ramp. It could carry up to thirty-nine passengers or 10,000lb (4540kg) of cargo. The C-2A first

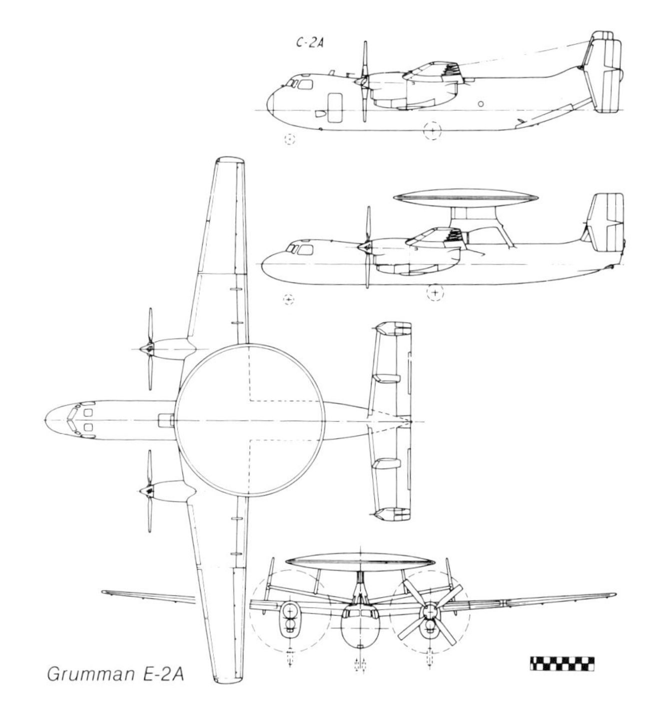

Grumman E-2A

flew in November 1964 and entered service with VRC-50 in December 1966 to provide support for TF 77 from NAS Cubi Point, the Philippines.

E-2 Hawkeye Deployments

Squadron/Air Wing	Aircraft	Carrier	Tail Code & Modex	Deployment Dates
VAW-11 *Early Eleven*				
VAW-11 Det C/CVW-11	E-2A	USS *Kitty Hawk* (CVA-63)	RR 70x	19 October 65–13 June 66
VAW-11 Det F/CVW-14	E-2A	USS *Ranger* (CVA-61)	RR 70x	10 December 65–25 August 66
VAW-11 Det D/CVW-15	E-2A	USS *Constellation* (CVA-64)	RR 75x	12 May 66–3 December 66
VAW-11 Det A/CVW-2	E-2A	USS *Coral Sea* (CVA-43)	RR 74x	29 July 66–23 February 67
VAW-11 Det C/CVW-11	E-2A	USS *Kitty Hawk* (CVA-63)	RR 70x	5 November 66–19 April 67
VAW-11 Det M/CVW-9	E-2A	USS *Enterprise* (CVAN-65)	RR 75x	19 November 66–19 April 67
VAW-112 *Golden Hawks*				
VAW-112/CVW-9	E-2A	USS *Enterprise* (CVAN-65)	RR 75x	20 April 67–6 July 67
VAW-112/CVW-9	E-2A	USS *Enterprise* (CVAN-65)	NG 70x	3 January 68–18 July 68
VAW-112/CVW-9	E-2A	USS *Enterprise* (CVAN-65)	NG 01x	6 January 69–2 July 69
VAW-113 *Black Eagles*				
VAW-113/CVW-14	E-2A	USS *Constellation* (CVA-64)	NK 75x	29 April 67–4 December 67
VAW-113/CVW-14	E-2A	USS *Constellation* (CVA-64)	NK 7xx	29 May 68–31 January 69
VAW-113/CVW-14	E-2B	USS *Enterprise* (CVAN-65)	NK 01x	11 June 71–12 February 72
VAW-113/CVW-14	E-2B	USS *Enterprise* (CVAN-65)	NK 01x	12 September 72–12 June 73
VAW-114 *Hormel Hawgs*				
VAW-114/CVW-11	E-2A	USS *Kitty Hawk* (CVA-63)	RR 70x	20 April 67–20 June 67
VAW-114/CVW-11	E-2A	USS *Kitty Hawk* (CVA-63)	NH 74x	18 November 67–28 June 68
VAW-114/CVW-11	E-2A	USS *Kitty Hawk* (CVA-63)	NH 01x	30 December 68–4 September 69
VAW-114/CVW-11	E-2B	USS *Kitty Hawk* (CVA-63)	NH 01x	6 November 70–17 July 71
VAW-114/CVW-11	E-2B	USS *Kitty Hawk* (CVA-63)	NH 01x	17 February 72–28 November 72
VAW-115 *Liberty Bells*				
VAW-115/CVW-2	E-2A	USS *Ranger* (CVA-61)	NE 75x	4 November 67–25 May 68
VAW-115/CVW-2	E-2A	USS *Ranger* (CVA-61)	NE 01x	26 October 68–17 May 69
VAW-115/CVW-2	E-2A	USS *Ranger* (CVA-61)	NE 01x	14 October 69–1 June 70
VAW-115/CVW-5	E-2B	USS *Midway* (CVA-41)	NF 01x	16 April 71–6 November 71
VAW-115/CVW-5	E-2B	USS *Midway* (CVA-41)	NF 01x	10 April 72–3 March 73
VAW-116 *Sun Kings*				
VAW-116/CVW-15	E-2A	USS *Coral Sea* (CVA-43)	NL 70x	26 July 67–6 April 68
VAW-116/CVW-15	E-2A	USS *Coral Sea* (CVA-43)	NL 01x	7 September 68–18 April 69
VAW-116/CVW-15	E-2A	USS *Coral Sea* (CVA-43)	NL 01x	23 September 69–1 July 70
VAW-116/CVW-9	E-2B	USS *Constellation* (CVA-64)	NG 01x	1 October 71–1 July 72
VAW-116/CVW-9	E-2B	USS *Constellation* (CVA-64)	NG 01x	5 January 73–11 October 73
VAW-122 *Hummer Gators*				
VAW-122/CVW-6	E-2A	USS *America* (CVA-66)	AE 72x	10 April 68–16 December 68
VAW-123 *Screwtops*				
VAW-123/CVW-17	E-2A	USS *Forrestal* (CVA-59)	AA 70x	6 June 67–14 September 67
VAW-123/CVW-3	E-2B	USS *Saratoga* (CV-60)	AC 01x	11 April 72–13 May 73
VAW-124 *Bullseyes*				
VAW-124/CVW-9	E-2A	USS *America* (CVA-66)	NG 01x	10 April 68–16 December 68
VAW-124/CVW-8	E-2B	USS *America* (CVA-66)	AJ 01x	5 June 72–24 March 73

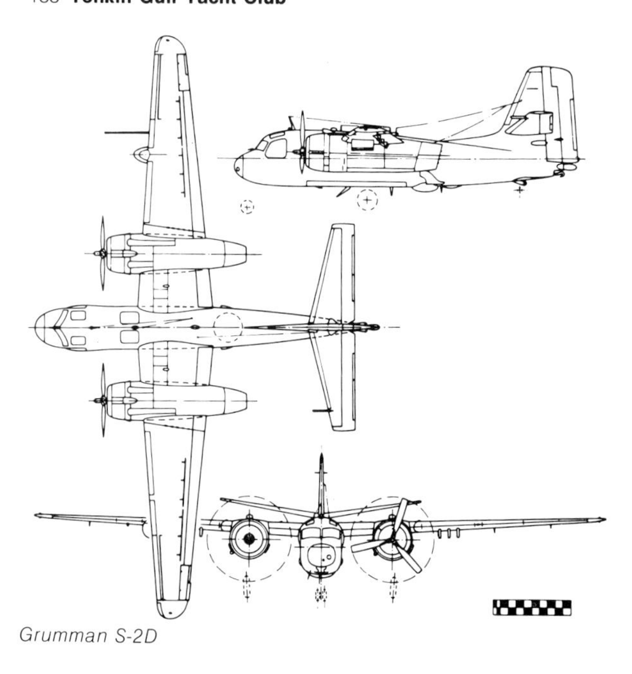

Grumman S-2D

Eight squadrons of S-2 Trackers deployed aboard antisubmarine warfare support carriers during the war. Air Antisubmarine Squadron Thirty-Seven (VS-37) was one of the two squadrons which deployed three times aboard USS Hornet *(CVS-12) between August 1965 and May 1969.* (Peter B Lewis)

Grumman S-2 Tracker

The XS2F-1 prototype of the piston-engined Tracker ASW aircraft had first flown on 4 December 1952, and the type had entered service in February 1954. Aircraft in this series were redesignated S-2s in September 1962. At the time of the Tonkin Gulf Incident, 258 of the S-2D, S-2E and S-2F variants were still serving with carrier units.

During the first five years of the war, eight squadrons of S-2s deployed aboard CVS carriers operating in the Gulf of Tonkin to provide antisubmarine and ocean surveillance support for TF 77. The last of these wartime cruises ended in September 1969 when USS *Kearsarge* (CVS-33) returned to Long Beach.

S-2 Tracker Deployments

Squadron/Air Wing	*Aircraft*	*Carrier*	*Tail Code & Modex*	*Deployment Dates*
VS-21 *Fighting Redtails*				
VS-21/CVSG-53	S-2F	USS *Kearsarge* (CVS-33)	NS 1x/2x	19 June 64–16 December 64
VS-21/CVSG-53	S-2E	USS *Kearsarge* (CVS-33)	NS 1x/2x	9 June 66–20 December 66
VS-21/CVSG-53	S-2E	USS *Kearsarge* (CVS-33)	NS 1x/2x	17 August 67–6 April 68
VS-21/CVSG-53	S-2E	USS *Kearsarge* (CVS-33)	NS 1x/2x	29 March 69–4 September 69
VS-23 *Black Cats*				
VS-23/CVSG-55	S-2E	USS *Yorktown* (CVS-10)	NU 1x/2x	23 October 64–16 May 65
VS-23/CVSG-55	S-2E	USS *Yorktown* (CVS-10)	NU 1x/2x	5 January 66–27 July 66
VS-23/CVSG-55	S-2E	USS *Yorktown* (CVS-10)	NU 1x/2x	28 December 67–5 July 68
VS-25 *Golden Eagles*				
VS-25/CVSG-55	S-2E	USS *Yorktown* (CVS-10)	NU 3x/4x	23 October 64–16 May 65
VS-25/CVSG-55	S-2E	USS *Yorktown* (CVS-10)	NU 3x/4x	5 January 66–27 July 66
VS-25/CVSG-55	S-2E	USS *Yorktown* (CVS-10)	NU 3x/4x	28 December 67–5 July 68
VS-29 *Tromboners* (became ***Yellowtails*** before 1967 deployment)				
VS-29/CVSG-53	S-2F	USS *Kearsarge* (CVS-33)	NS 3x/4x	19 June 64–16 December 64
VS-29/CVSG-53	S-2E	USS *Kearsarge* (CVS-33)	NS 3x/4x	9 June 66–20 December 66
VS-29/CVSG-53	S-2E	USS *Kearsarge* (CVS-33)	NS 3x/4x	17 August 67–6 April 68
VS-29/CVSG-53	S-2E	USS *Kearsarge* (CVS-33)	NS 3x/4x	29 March 69–4 September 69

Squadron/Air Wing	Aircraft	Carrier	Tail Code & Modex	Deployment Dates
VS-33 *Screwbirds*				
VS-33/CVSG-59	S-2E	USS *Bennington* (CVS-20)	NT 1x/2x	22 March 65–7 October 65
VS-33/CVSG-59	S-2E	USS *Bennington* (CVS-20)	NT 1x/2x	4 November 66–23 May 67
VS-33/CVSG-59	S-2E	USS *Bennington* (CVS-20)	NT 1x/2x	1 May 68–9 November 68
VS-35 *Boomerangs*				
VS-35/CVSG-57	S-2D/E	USS *Hornet* (CVS-12)	NV 1x/2x	12 August 65–23 March 66
VS-35/CVSG-57	S-2E	USS *Hornet* (CVS-12)	NV 1x/2x	27 March 67–28 October 67
VS-35/CVSG-57	S-2E	USS *Hornet* (CVS-12)	NV 1x/2x	30 September 68–12 May 69
VS-37 *Sawbucks*				
VS-37/CVSG-57	S-2E	USS *Hornet* (CVS-12)	NV 3x/4x	12 August 65–23 March 66
VS-37/CVSG-57	S-2E	USS *Hornet* (CVS-12)	NV 3x/4x	27 March 67–28 October 67
VS-37/CVSG-57	S-2E	USS *Hornet* (CVS-12)	NV 3x/4x	30 September 68–12 May 69
VS-38 *Red Griffins* (unofficial nickname ***Claw Clan***)				
VS-38/CVSG-59	S-2E	USS *Bennington* (CVS-20)	NT 3x/4x	22 March 65–7 October 65
VS-38/CVSG-59	S-2E	USS *Bennington* (CVS-20)	NT 3x/4x	4 November 66–23 May 67
VS-38/CVSG-59	S-2E	USS *Bennington* (CVS-20)	NT 3x/4x	1 May 68–9 November 68

Kaman UH-2 Seasprite

Designed to meet a 1956 Navy requirement for a long-range, all-weather utility and rescue helicopter, the Seasprite had flown in prototype form on 2 July 1959 and was first delivered in December 1962. Within nineteen months of that date, the type had become the Navy's standard plane guard rescue helicopter, with UH-2 detachments being provided to PACFLT carriers by HU-1 and to LANTFLT carriers by HU-2. On 31 July 1964, these two squadrons operated a total of eighty-six UH-2As and UH-2Bs, the latter differing from the initial production version in being fitted with simplified equipment for VFR operations.

During the war, the single-engined UH-2As and UH-2Bs were progressively supplemented in the utility-rescue role aboard carriers by twin-engined UH-2Cs and then supplanted in that role by Sikorsky SH-3s. Until 1971, UH-2A/B/Cs were also flown from SAR ships on combat rescue missions by detachments from HC-1 and from a specialized squadron, HC-7 *Sea Devils*. The last mentioned unit also briefly operated the HH-2C armed rescue version of the Seasprite.

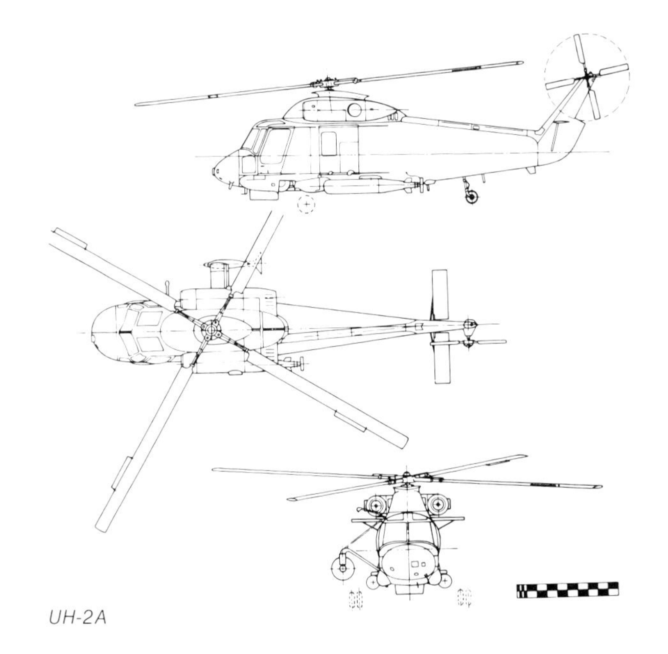

UH-2A

Whereas other Seasprite versions proved most satisfactory (and were still quite valuable in the LAMPS role in the late 1980s), HH-2Cs were quickly replaced in service with HC-7 by SH-3As and HH-3As. This HH-2C from the Sea Devils *of HC-7 was photographed at NAS Imperial Beach, California, on 12 May 1971.* (Peter B Lewis)

One of the four Medals of Honor awarded to Naval Aviators during the Southeast Asian War went to Lt (jg) Clyde E Lassen of HC-7 for his daring rescue of a VF-33 crew near Vinh during the night of 18-19 June 1968. In spite of intense enemy fire, Lt (jg) Lassen and his crew succeeded on their third attempt to pick up the two Tarsiers *and brought them back to the guided missile frigate USS* Jouett *(DLG-29), the duty SAR ship from which HC-7 Det 104 was then operating. Clyde Lassen is seated in the cockpit of an UH-2A after this famous rescue but before being awarded the Medal of Honor.* (Kaman Aerospace)

UH-2 Seasprite Deployments

Squadron/Air Wing	*Aircraft*	*Carrier*	*Tail Code & Modex*	*Deployment Dates*
HC-1 *Pacific Fleet Angels*				
HC-1 Det 1 D/CVW-15	UH-2A/B	USS *Coral Sea* (CVA-43)	UP x	1 July 65–1 November 65
HC-1 Det 1 A/CVW-2	UH-2A	USS *Midway* (CVA-41)	UP xx	1 July 65–23 November 65
HC-1 Det 1 G/CVW-16	UH-2A/B	USS *Oriskany* (CVA-34)	UP xx	1 July 65–16 December 65
HC-1 Det 1 E/CVW-19	UH-2A/B	USS *Bon Homme Richard* (CVA-31)	UP xx	1 July 65–13 January 66
HC-1 Det 1 B/CVW-5	UH-2A/B	USS *Ticonderoga* (CVA-14)	UP xx	28 September 65–13 May 66
HC-1 Det 1 C/CVW-11	UH-2A/B	USS *Kitty Hawk* (CVA-63)	UP xx	19 October 65–13 June 66
HC-1 Det 1 M/CVW-9	UH-2A/B	USS *Enterprise* (CVAN-65)	UP x	26 October 65–21 June 66
HC-1 Det 1 L/CVW-21	UH-2A/B	USS *Hancock* (CVA-19)	UP xx	10 November 65–1 August 66
HC-1 Det 1 F/CVW-14	UH-2A/B	USS *Ranger* (CVA-61)	UP x	10 December 65–25 August 66
HC-1 Det 1 D/CVW-15	UH-2A/B	USS *Constellation* (CVA-64)	UP xx	12 May 66–3 December 66
HC-1 Det 1 G/CVW-16	UH-2A/B	USS *Oriskany* (CVA-34)	UP xx	26 May 66–16 November 66
HC-1 Det 1 A/CVW-2	UH-2A/B	USS *Coral Sea* (CVA-43)	UP xx	29 July 66–23 February 67
HC-1 Det 1 E/CVW-19	UH-2A/B	USS *Ticonderoga* (CVA-14)	UP xx	15 October 66–29 May 67
HC-1 Det 1 C/CVW-11	UH-2A/B	USS *Kitty Hawk* (CVA-63)	UP xx	5 November 66–20 June 67
HC-1 Det 1 M/CVW-9	UH-2A/B	USS *Enterprise* (CVAN-65)	UP xx	19 November 66–6 July 67
HC-1 Det 19/CVW-5	UH-2A/B	USS *Hancock* (CVA-19)	UP x	5 January 67–22 July 67
HC-1 Det 1 L/CVW-21	UH-2B	USS *Bon Homme Richard* (CVA-31)	UP xx	26 January 67–25 August 67
HC-1 Det 64/CVW-14	UH-2A/B	USS *Constellation* (CVA-64)	UP xx	29 April 67–4 December 67
HC-1 Det 34/CVW-16	UH-2A/B	USS *Oriskany* (CVA-34)	UP xx	16 June 67–31 January 68

Squadron/Air Wing	Aircraft	Carrier	Tail Code & Modex	Deployment Dates
HC-1 Det 43/CVW-15	UH-2A	USS *Coral Sea* (CVA-43)	UP xx	26 July 67–6 April 68
HC-1 Det 61/CVW-2	UH-2A/C	USS *Ranger* (CVA-61)	UP xx	4 November 67–25 May 68
HC-1 Det 63/CVW-11	UH-2C	USS *Kitty Hawk* (CVA-63)	UP xx	18 November 67–28 June 68
HC-1 Det 14/CVW-19	UH-2B	USS *Ticonderoga* (CVA-14)	UP xx	27 December 67–17 August 68
HC-1 Det 65/CVW-9	UH-2C	USS *Enterprise* (CVAN-65)	UP xx	3 January 68–18 July 68
HC-1 Det 31/CVW-5	UH-2C	USS *Bon Homme Richard* (CVA-31)	UP xx	27 January 68–10 October 68
HC-1 Det 64/CVW-14	UH-2C	USS *Constellation* (CVA-64)	UP xx	29 May 68–31 January 69
HC-1 Det 19/CVW-21	UH-2C	USS *Hancock* (CVA-19)	UP x	18 July 68–3 March 69
HC-1 Det 43/CVW-15	UH-2C	USS *Coral Sea* (CVA-43)	UP xx	7 September 68–18 April 69
HC-1 Det 61/CVW-2	UH-2C	USS *Ranger* (CVA-61)	UP 00x	26 October 68–17 May 69
HC-1 Det 63/CVW-11	UH-2C	USS *Kitty Hawk* (CVA-63)	UP 0x	30 December 68–4 September 69
HC-1 Det 65/CVW-9	UH-2C	USS *Enterprise* (CVAN-65)	UP 00x	6 January 69–2 July 69
HC-1 Det 14/CVW-16	UH-2C	USS *Ticonderoga* (CVA-14)	UP xx	1 February 69–18 September 69
HC-1 Det 31/CVW-5	UH-2C	USS *Bon Homme Richard* (CVA-31)	UP 00x	18 March 69–29 October 69
HC-1 Det 34/CVW-19	UH-2C	USS *Oriskany* (CVA-34)	NM 00x	16 April 69–17 November 69
HC-1 Det 9/CVW-15	UH-2A	USS *Coral Sea* (CVA-43)	NL 00x	23 September 69–1 July 70
HC-1 Det 3/CVW-5	UH-2C	USS *Bon Homme Richard* (CVA-31)	NF 00x	2 April 70–12 November 70
HC-1 Det 6/CVW-19	UH-2C	USS *Oriskany* (CVA-34)	NM 00x	14 May 70–10 December 70
HC-1 Det 7/CVW-21	UH-2C	USS *Hancock* (CVA-19)	NP 00x	22 October 70–2 June 71
HC-1 Det 2/CVW-11	UH-2C	USS *Kitty Hawk* (CVA-63)	NH 00x	6 November 70–17 July 71
HC-1 Det 5/CVW-19	UH-2C	USS *Oriskany* (CVA-34)	NM 00x	14 May 71–18 December 71
HC-2 *Fleet Angels*				
HC-2 Det 62/CVW-7	UH-2A	USS *Independence* (CVA-62)	HU xx	1 July 65–13 December 65
HC-2 Det 11/CVW-10	UH-2A/B	USS *Intrepid* (CVS-11)	HU x	4 April 66–21 November 66
HC-2 Det 42/CVW-1	UH-2A/B	USS *Franklin D. Roosevelt* (CVA-42)	HU xx	21 June 66–21 February 67
HC-2 Det 11/CVW-10	UH-2A/B	USS *Intrepid* (CVS-11)	HU xx	11 May 67–30 December 67
HC-2 Det 59/CVW-17	UH-2A/B	USS *Forrestal* (CVA-59)	HU xx	6 June 67–14 September 67
HC-2 Det 66/CVW-6	UH-2A/B	USS *America* (CVA-66)	HU xx	10 April 68–16 December 68
HC-2 Det 11/CVW-10	UH-2A/B	USS *Intrepid* (CVS-11)	HU xx	4 June 68–8 February 69
HC-2 Det 38/CVW-8	UH-2C	USS *Shangri-La* (CVS-38)	HU xx	5 March 70–17 December 70
HC-2 Det 66/CVW-6	UH-2C	USS *America* (CVA-66)	HU 0xx	10 April 70–21 December 70
HU-1 *Pacific Fleet Angels*				
HU-1 Det 1 E/CVW-19	UH-2A	USS *Bon Homme Richard* (CVA-31)	UP xx	28 January 64–21 November 64
HU-1 Det 1 B/CVW-5	UH-2A	USS *Ticonderoga* (CVA-14)	UP xx	14 April 64–15 December 64
HU-1 Det 1 F/CVW-14	UH-2A	USS *Constellation* (CVA-64)	UP xx	5 May 64–1 February 65
HU-1 Det 1 R/CVSG-53	UH-2A	USS *Kearsarge* (CVS-33)	UP xx	19 June 64–16 December 64
HU-1 Det 1 M/CVW-9	UH-2A	USS *Ranger* (CVA-61)	UP x	5 August 64–6 May 65
HU-1 Det 1 L/CVW-21	UH-2A	USS *Hancock* (CVA-19)	UP xx	21 October 64–29 May 65
HU-1 Det 1 D/CVW-15	UH-2A/B	USS *Coral Sea* (CVA-43)	UP x	7 December 64–30 June 65
HU-1 Det 1 A/CVW-2	UH-2A	USS *Midway* (CVA-41)	UP xx	6 March 65–30 June 65
HU-1 Det 1 G/CVW-16	UH-2A/B	USS *Oriskany* (CVA-34)	UP xx	5 April 65–30 June 65
HU-1 Det 1 E/CVW-19	UH-2A/B	USS *Bon Homme Richard* (CVA-31)	UP xx	21 April 65–30 June 65
HU-2 *Fleet Angels*				
HU-2 Det 62/CVW-7	UH-2A	USS *Independence* (CVA-62)	HU xx	10 May 65–30 June 65

LTV A-7 Corsair II

Combining increased radius of action and heavier load of conventional ordnance with the nuclear strike capability of its naval predecessor, the Douglas A-4, the A-7 Corsair II retained the general configuration of the F-8 supersonic fighter but had a simpler and stronger airframe optimized for operations at subsonic speeds with a heavy warload. It was first flown on 27 September 1965, entered service one year later, and first deployed to the Gulf of Tonkin in November 1967 with VA-147 aboard USS *Ranger* (CVA-61).

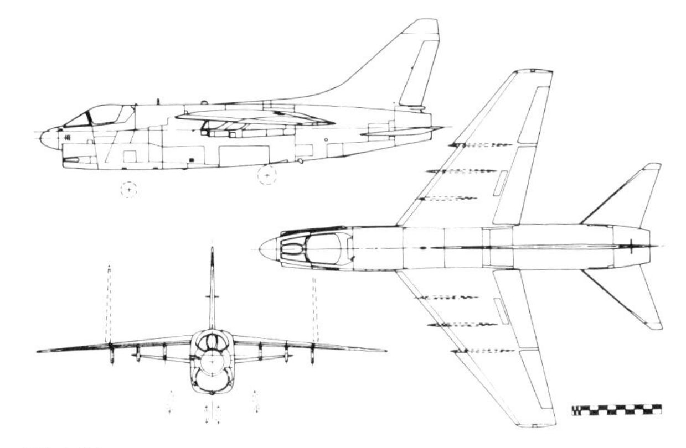

LT A-7A

For their second deployment aboard USS Constellation (CVA-64) as part of CVW-11, the A-7As from the Warhawks of VA-97 had their modex changed from the 500 series to the 300 series as painted on the nose of this Corsair II. (Peter B Lewis)

The first three versions, the A-7A, A-7B and A-7C, were powered by a Pratt and Whitney TF30 engine but the main Navy version, the A-7E, used the Allison TF41 engine first specified by the Air Force for its A-7D variant. With twenty squadrons operating from TF 77 carriers, Corsair IIs flew conventional strikes, Iron Hand defense suppression missions with Shrike anti-radiation missiles, and buddy refueling sorties.

A-7 Corsair II Deployments

Squadron/Air Wing	*Aircraft*	*Carrier*	*Tail Code & Modex*	*Deployment Dates*
VA-22 *Fighting Redcocks*				
VA-22/CVW-15	A-7E	USS *Coral Sea* (CVA-43)	NL 3xx	12 November 71–17 July 72
VA-22/CVW-15	A-7E	USS *Coral Sea* (CVA-43)	NL 3xx	9 March 73–8 November 73
VA-25 *Fist of the Fleet*				
VA-25/CVW-16	A-7B	USS *Ticonderoga* (CVA-14)	AH 5xx	1 February 69–18 September 69
VA-25/CVW-2	A-7E	USS *Ranger* (CVA-61)	NE 4xx	27 October 70–17 June 71
VA-25/CVW-2	A-7E	USS *Ranger* (CVA-61)	NE 4xx	16 November 72–22 June 73
VA-27 *Royal Maces*				
VA-27/CVW-14	A-7A	USS *Constellation* (CVA-64)	NK 6xx	29 May 68–31 January 69
VA-27/CVW-14	A-7A	USS *Constellation* (CVA-64)	NK 4xx	11 August 69–8 May 70
VA-27/CVW-14	A-7E	USS *Enterprise* (CVAN-65)	NK 4xx	11 June 71–12 February 72
VA-27/CVW-14	A-7E	USS *Enterprise* (CVAN-65)	NK 4xx	12 September 72–12 June 73
VA-37 *Bulls*				
VA-37/CVW-11	A-7A	USS *Kitty Hawk* (CVA-63)	NH 3xx	30 December 68–4 September 69
VA-37/CVW-3	A-7A	USS *Saratoga* (CV-60)	AC 3xx	11 April 72–13 February 73
VA-56 *Champions*				
VA-56/CVW-2	A-7B	USS *Ranger* (CVA-61)	NE 4xx	14 October 69–1 June 70
VA-56/CVW-5	A-7B	USS *Midway* (CVA-41)	NF 4xx	16 April 71–6 November 71
VA-56/CVW-5	A-7B	USS *Midway* (CVA-41)	NF 4xx	10 April 72–3 March 73
VA-82 *Marauders*				
VA-82/CVW-6	A-7A	USS *America* (CVA-66)	AE 3xx	10 April 68–16 December 68
VA-82/CVW-15	A-7A	USS *Coral Sea* (CVA-43)	NL 3xx	23 September 69–1 July 70
VA-82/CVW-8	A-7C	USS *America* (CVA-66)	AJ 3xx	5 June 72–24 March 73

Squadron/Air Wing	*Aircraft*	*Carrier*	*Tail Code & Modex*	*Deployment Dates*
VA-86 *Sidewinders*				
VA-86/CVW-6	A-7A	USS *America* (CVA-66)	AE 4xx	10 April 68–16 December 68
VA-86/CVW-15	A-7A	USS *Coral Sea* (CVA-43)	NL 4xx	23 September 69–1 July 70
VA-86/CVW-8	A-7C	USS *America* (CVA-66)	AJ 4xx	5 June 72–24 March 73
VA-87 *Golden Warriors*				
VA-87/CVW-16	A-7B	USS *Ticonderoga* (CVA-14)	AH 3xx	1 February 69–18 September 69
VA-93 *Blue Blazers*				
VA-93/CVW-2	A-7B	USS *Ranger* (CVA-61)	NE 3xx	14 October 69–1 June 70
VA-93/CVW-5	A-7B	USS *Midway* (CVA-41)	NF 3xx	16 April 71–6 November 71
VA-93/CVW-5	A-7B	USS *Midway* (CVA-41)	NF 3xx	10 April 72–3 March 73
VA-94 *Mighty Shrikes*				
VA-94/CVW-15	A-7E	USS *Coral Sea* (CVA-43)	NL 4xx	12 November 71–17 July 72
VA-94/CVW-15	A-7E	USS *Coral Sea* (CVA-43)	NL 4xx	9 March 73–8 November 73
VA-97 *Warhawks*				
VA-97/CVW-14	A-7A	USS *Constellation* (CVA-64)	NK 5xx	29 May 68–31 January 69
VA-97/CVW-14	A-7A	USS *Constellation* (CVA-64)	NK 3xx	11 August 69–8 May 70
VA-97/CVW-14	A-7E	USS *Enterprise* (CVAN-65)	NK 3xx	11 June 71–12 February 72
VA-97/CVW-14	A-7E	USS *Enterprise* (CVAN-65)	NK 3xx	12 September 72–12 June 73
VA-105 *Gunslingers*				
VA-105/CVW-11	A-7A	USS *Kitty Hawk* (CVA-63)	NH 4xx	30 December 68–4 September 69
VA-105/CVW-3	A-7A	USS *Saratoga* (CV-60)	AC 4xx	11 April 72–13 February 73
VA-113 *Stingers*				
VA-113/CVW-2	A-7E	USS *Ranger* (CVA-61)	NE 3xx	27 October 70–17 June 71
VA-113/CVW-2	A-7E	USS *Ranger* (CVA-61)	NE 3xx	16 November 72–22 June 73
VA-146 *Blue Diamonds*				
VA-146/CVW-9	A-7B	USS *Enterprise* (CVAN-65)	NG 3xx	6 January 69–2 July 69
VA-146/CVW-9	A-7E	USS *America* (CVA-66)	NG 3xx	10 April 70–21 December 70
VA-146/CVW-9	A-7E	USS *Constellation* (CVA-64)	NG 3xx	1 October 71–1 July 72
VA-146/CVW-9	A-7E	USS *Constellation* (CVA-64)	NG 3xx	5 January 73–11 October 73
VA-147 *Argonauts*				
VA-147/CVW-2	A-7A	USS *Ranger* (CVA-61)	NE 3xx	4 November 67–25 May 68
VA-147/CVW-2	A-7A	USS *Ranger* (CVA-61)	NE 3xx	26 October 68–17 May 69
VA-147/CVW-9	A-7E	USS *America* (CVA-66)	NG 4xx	10 April 70–21 December 70
VA-147/CVW-9	A-7E	USS *Constellation* (CVA-64)	NG 4xx	1 October 71–1 July 72
VA-147/CVW-9	A-7E	USS *Constellation* (CVA-64)	NG 4xx	5 January 73–11 October 73
VA-153 *Blue Tail Flies*				
VA-153/CVW-19	A-7A	USS *Oriskany* (CVA-34)	NM 3xx	14 May 70–10 December 70
VA-153/CVW-19	A-7A	USS *Oriskany* (CVA-34)	NM 3xx	14 May 71–18 December 71
VA-153/CVW-19	A-7A	USS *Oriskany* (CVA-34)	NM 3xx	5 June 72–30 March 73

After returning from their second deployment aboard USS Ranger (CVA-61), the Argonauts of VA-147 converted from the A-7A to the more capable A-7E and were transferred from CVW-2 to CVW-9 for deployment aboard USS America (CVA-66) between April and December 1970. BuNo 156608 was photographed at NAAS Fallon on 6 December 1969 after returning from a training sortie over the northern Nevada desert. (Peter B Lewis)

Squadron/Air Wing	Aircraft	Carrier	Tail Code & Modex	Deployment Dates
VA-155 *Silver Foxes*				
VA-155/CVW-19	A-7B	USS *Oriskany* (CVA-34)	NM 5xx	14 May 70–10 December 70
VA-155/CVW-19	A-7B	USS *Oriskany* (CVA-34)	NM 5xx	14 May 71–18 December 71
VA-155/CVW-19	A-7B	USS *Oriskany* (CVA-34)	NM 5xx	5 June 72–30 March 73
VA-192 *Golden Dragons*				
VA-192/CVW-11	A-7E	USS *Kitty Hawk* (CVA-63)	NH 3xx	6 November 70–17 July 71
VA-192/CVW-11	A-7E	USS *Kitty Hawk* (CVA-63)	NH 3xx	17 February 72–28 November 72
VA-195 *Dambusters*				
VA-195/CVW-11	A-7E	USS *Kitty Hawk* (CVA-63)	NH 4xx	6 November 70–17 July 71
VA-195/CVW-11	A-7E	USS *Kitty Hawk* (CVA-63)	NH 4xx	17 February 72–28 November 72
VA-215 *Barn Owls*				
VA-215/CVW-9	A-7B	USS *Enterprise* (CVAN-65)	NG 4xx	6 January 69–2 July 69
VA-215/CVW-19	A-7B	USS *Oriskany* (CVA-34)	NM 4xx	14 May 71–18 December 71
VA-215/CVW-19	A-7B	USS *Oriskany* (CVA-34)	NM 4xx	5 June 72–30 March 73

After outscoring the F-4 until 5 June 1972, when Phantom II crews claimed their 18th, 19th and 20th kills and steadily pulled ahead, the F-8 in the end trailed well behind the F-4. The 18th and last confirmed victory obtained by F-8 pilots was a MiG-21 shot down by Lt Anthony J Nargi on 19 September 1968. Seven of the eighteen MiGs shot down by Crusader pilots were credited to the Checkmates *of VF-211. This F-8J was photographed over the Gulf of Tonkin on 18 March 1971 when VF-211 was making its fifth deployment aboard USS* Hancock *(CVA-19).* (US Navy)

LTV F-8 and RF-8 Crusader

Proudly nicknamed 'the last of the gunfighters' by its pilots, the gun-and-missile Crusader was officially credited with the destruction of eighteen MiG fighters during the Southeast Asian War. Its prototype had first flown on 25 March 1955 and squadron deliveries began two years later. With 482 F-8C/D/Es equipping seventeen first-line squadrons and two replacement squadrons on 31 July 1964, Crusaders still outnumbered Phantom IIs by three to two. By the end of the war, however, Crusaders were on their way out with only forty-three F-8H/Js remaining in service with Navy front-line squadrons.

During the war years the original production versions, the F-8A through F-8E, were supplemented by remanufactured variants, the F-8H through F-8L, with strengthened airframes, improved avionics, external stores capability, Shoehorn ECM fit, and more powerful engines. These latter variants served exclusively aboard *Hancock* class carriers and with reserve units.

The RF-8A photo-reconnaisance version differed from the initial fighter variant in having the gun-and-missile armament and AN/APG-30A radar replaced with a five-

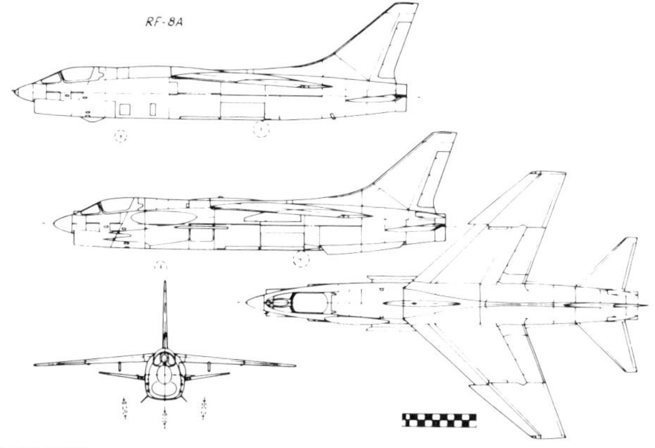

LTV F-8E

camera installation. It had entered service in September 1957, and eighty-seven were operated by Navy and Marine squardons on 31 July 1964.

Seventy-three RF-8As were brought up to the RF-8G standard with strengthened airframes, ventral fins, a new navigation system, improved camera installations, and substitution of an 18,000lb (8165kg) thrust J57-P-20A engine for the originally-fitted 16,000lb (7257kg) thrust J57-P-4.

F-8 and RF-8 Crusader Deployments

Squadron/Air Wing	*Aircraft*	*Carrier*	*Tail Code & Modex*	*Deployment Dates*
VF-24 *Checkertails*				
VF-24/CVW-21	F-8C	USS *Hancock* (CVA-19)	NP 4xx	21 October 64–29 May 65
VF-24/CVW-21	F-8C	USS *Hancock* (CVA-19)	NP 4xx	10 November 65–1 August 66
VF-24/CVW-21	F-8C	USS *Bon Homme Richard* (CVA-31)	NP 4xx	26 January 67–25 August 67
VF-24/CVW-21	F-8H	USS *Hancock* (CVA-19)	NP 2xx	18 July 68–3 March 69
VF-24/CVW-21	F-8H	USS *Hancock* (CVA-19)	NP 2xx	2 August 69–15 April 70
VF-24/CVW-21	F-8J	USS *Hancock* (CVA-19)	NP 2xx	22 October 70–2 June 71
VF-24/CVW-21	F-8J	USS *Hancock* (CVA-19)	NP 2xx	7 January 72–3 October 72
VF-24/CVW-21	F-8J	USS *Hancock* (CVA-19)	NP 2xx	8 May 73–8 January 74
VF-51 *Screaming Eagles*				
VF-51/CVW-5	F-8E	USS *Ticonderoga* (CVA-14)	NF 1xx	14 April 64–15 December 64
VF-51/CVW-5	F-8E	USS *Ticonderoga* (CVA-14)	NF 1xx	28 September 65–13 May 66
VF-51/CVW-5	F-8E	USS *Hancock* (CVA-19)	NF 1xx	5 January 67–22 July 67
VF-51/CVW-5	F-8H	USS *Bon Homme Richard* (CVA-31)	NF 1xx	27 January 68–10 October 68
VF-51/CVW-5	F-8J	USS *Bon Homme Richard* (CVA-31)	NF 1xx	18 March 69–29 October 69
VF-51/CVW-5	F-8J	USS *Bon Homme Richard* (CVA-31)	NF 1xx	2 April 70–12 November 70
VF-53 *Iron Angels*				
VF-53/CVW-5	F-8E	USS *Ticonderoga* (CVA-14)	NF 2xx	14 April 64–15 December 64
VF-53/CVW-5	F-8E	USS *Ticonderoga* (CVA-14)	NF 2xx	28 September 65–13 May 66
VF-53/CVW-5	F-8E	USS *Hancock* (CVA-19)	NF 2xx	5 January 67–22 July 67
VF-53/CVW-5	F-8E	USS *Bon Homme Richard* (CVA-31)	NF 2xx	27 January 68–10 October 68
VF-53/CVW-5	F-8J	USS *Bon Homme Richard* (CVA-31)	NF 2xx	18 March 69–29 October 69
VF-53/CVW-5	F-8J	USS *Bon Homme Richard* (CVA-31)	NF 2xx	2 April 70–12 November 70
VF-111 *Sundowners*				
VF-111/CVW-2	F-8D	USS *Midway* (CVA-41)	NE 4xx	6 March 65–23 November 65
VF-111/CVW-16	F-8E	USS *Oriskany* (CVA-34)	AH 1xx	26 May 66–16 November 66
VF-111 Det 11/CVW-10	F-8C	USS *Intrepid* (CVS-11)	AH 1x	11 May 67–30 December 67
VF-111/CVW-16	F-8C	USS *Oriskany* (CVA-34)	AH 1xx	16 June 67–31 January 68
VF-111 Det 11/CVW-10	F-8C	USS *Intrepid* (CVS-11)	AK 1xx	4 June 68–8 February 69
VF-111/CVW-16	F-8H	USS *Ticonderoga* (CVA-14)	AH 1xx	1 February 69–18 September 69
VF-111/CVW-8	F-8H	USS *Shangri-La* (CVS-38)	AJ 1xx	5 March 70–17 December 70
VF-154 *Black Knights*				
VF-154/CVW-15	F-8D	USS *Coral Sea* (CVA-43)	NL 4xx	7 December 64–1 November 65
VF-162 *Hunters*				
VF-162/CVW-16	F-8E	USS *Oriskany* (CVA-34)	AH 2xx	5 April 65–16 December 65
VF-162/CVW-16	F-8E	USS *Oriskany* (CVA-34)	AH 2xx	26 May 66–16 November 66
VF-162/CVW-16	F-8E	USS *Oriskany* (CVA-34)	AH 2xx	16 June 67–31 January 68
VF-162/CVW-16	F-8J	USS *Ticonderoga* (CVA-14)	AH 2xx	1 February 69–18 September 69
VF-162/CVW-8	F-8H	USS *Shangri-La* (CVS-38)	AJ 2xx	5 March 70–17 December 70

The Sundowners *of VF-111 made their last deployment with Crusaders between March and December 1970 when they took F-8Hs aboard USS* Shangri-La *(CVS-38) as part of CVW-8. After returning to NAS Miramar, California, they converted to F-4Bs for deployment aboard USS* Coral Sea *(CVA-43).* (By courtesy of Cloud 9 Photography)

Squadron/Air Wing	*Aircraft*	*Carrier*	*Tail Code & Modex*	*Deployment Dates*
VF-191 *Satan's Kittens*				
VF-191/CVW-19	F-8E	USS *Bon Homme Richard* (CVA-31)	NM 1xx	28 January 64–21 November 64
VF-191/CVW-19	F-8E	USS *Bon Homme Richard* (CVA-31)	NM 1xx	21 April 65–13 January 66
VF-191/CVW-19	F-8E	USS *Ticonderoga* (CVA-14)	NM 1xx	15 October 66–29 May 67
VF-191/CVW-19	F-8E	USS *Ticonderoga* (CVA-14)	NM 1xx	27 December 67–17 August 68
VF-191/CVW-19	F-8J	USS *Oriskany* (CVA-34)	NM 1xx	16 April 69–17 November 69
VF-191/CVW-19	F-8J	USS *Oriskany* (CVA-34)	NM 1xx	14 May 70–10 December 70
VF-191/CVW-19	F-8J	USS *Oriskany* (CVA-34)	NM 1xx	14 May 71–18 December 71
VF-191/CVW-19	F-8J	USS *Oriskany* (CVA-34)	NM 1xx	5 June 72–30 March 73
VF-194 *Red Lightnings*				
VF-194/CVW-19	F-8C	USS *Bon Homme Richard* (CVA-31)	NM 4xx	28 January 64–21 November 64
VF-194/CVW-19	F-8E	USS *Bon Homme Richard* (CVA-31)	NM 4xx	21 April 65–13 January 66
VF-194/CVW-19	F-8E	USS *Ticonderoga* (CVA-14)	NM 4xx	15 October 66–29 May 67
VF-194/CVW-19	F-8E	USS *Ticonderoga* (CVA-14)	NM 4xx	27 December 67–17 August 68
VF-194/CVW-19	F-8J	USS *Oriskany* (CVA-34)	NM 2xx	16 April 69–17 November 69
VF-194/CVW-19	F-8J	USS *Oriskany* (CVA-34)	NM 2xx	14 May 70–10 December 70
VF-194/CVW-19	F-8J	USS *Oriskany* (CVA-34)	NM 2xx	14 May 71–18 December 71
VF-194/CVW-19	F-8J	USS *Oriskany* (CVA-34)	NM 2xx	5 June 72–30 March 73
VF-211 *Checkmates*				
VF-211/CVW-21	F-8E	USS *Hancock* (CVA-19)	NP 1xx	21 October 64–29 May 65
VF-211/CVW-21	F-8E	USS *Hancock* (CVA-19)	NP 1xx	10 November 65–1 August 66
VF-211/CVW-21	F-8E	USS *Bon Homme Richard* (CVA-31)	NP 1xx	26 January 67–25 August 67
VF-211/CVW-21	F-8H	USS *Hancock* (CVA-19)	NP 1xx	18 July 68–3 March 69
VF-211/CVW-21	F-8J	USS *Hancock* (CVA-19)	NP 1xx	2 August 69–15 April 70
VF-211/CVW-21	F-8J	USS *Hancock* (CVA-19)	NP 1xx	22 October 70–2 June 71
VF-211/CVW-21	F-8J	USS *Hancock* (CVA-19)	NP 1xx	7 January 72–3 October 72
VF-211/CVW-21	F-8H	USS *Hancock* (CVA-19)	NP 1xx	8 May 73–8 January 74
VMF(AW)-212 *Lancers*				
VMF(AW)-212/CVW-16	F-8E	USS *Oriskany* (CVA-34)	WD 1xx	5 April 65–16 December 65
VFP-62 *Fighting Photos*				
VFP-62 Det 42/CVW-1	RF-8G	USS *Franklin D. Roosevelt* (CVA-42)	AB 9xx	21 June 66–21 February 67
VFP-63 *Eyes of the Fleet*				
VFP-63 Det E/CVW-19	RF-8A	USS *Bon Homme Richard* (CVA-31)	PP 9xx	28 January 64–21 November 64
VFP-63 Det B/CVW-5	RF-8A	USS *Ticonderoga* (CVA-14)	PP 93x	14 April 64–15 December 64
VFP-63 Det F/CVW-14	RF-8A	USS *Constellation* (CVA-64)	PP 93x	5 May 64–1 February 65
VFP-63 Det M/CVW-9	RF-8A	USS *Ranger* (CVA-61)	PP 9xx	5 August 64–6 May 65
VFP-63 Det L/CVW-21	RF-8A	USS *Hancock* (CVA-19)	PP 9xx	21 October 64–29 May 65
VFP-63 Det D/CVW-15	RF-8A	USS *Coral Sea* (CVA-43)	PP 9xx	7 December 64–1 November 65
VFP-63 Det A/CVW-2	RF-8A	USS *Midway* (CVA-41)	PP 9xx	6 March 65–23 November 65
VFP-63 Det G/CVW-16	RF-8A	USS *Oriskany* (CVA-34)	PP 9xx	5 April 65–16 December 65
VFP-63 Det E/CVW-19	RF-8A	USS *Bon Homme Richard* (CVA-31)	PP 9xx	21 April 65–13 January 66
VFP-63 Det B/CVW-5	RF-8A	USS *Ticonderoga* (CVA-14)	PP 93x	28 September 65–13 May 66
VFP-63 Det L/CVW-21	RF-8A	USS *Hancock* (CVA-19)	PP 90x	10 November 65–1 August 66
VFP-63 Det G/CVW-16	RF-8A	USS *Oriskany* (CVA-34)	AH 6xx	26 May 66–16 November 66
VFP-63 Det A/CVW-2	RF-8G	USS *Coral Sea* (CVA-43)	PP 89x	29 July 66–23 February 67
VFP-63 Det E/CVW-19	RF-8G	USS *Ticonderoga* (CVA-14)	PP 91x	15 October 66–29 May 67
VFP-63 Det B/CVW-5	RF-8G	USS *Hancock* (CVA-19)	PP 91x	5 January 67–22 July 67

VFP-63 detachments and a detachment from VFP-62 made a total of forty-two war cruises to the Gulf of Tonkin during which nineteen RF-8As and RF-8Gs were lost in combat. This RF-8G of VFP-63 Det 3 was photographed at NAS Miramar, California, shortly after USS Midway *(CVA-41) had returned home at the end of her April 1972-March 1973 cruise.* (Peter B Lewis)

Squadron/Air Wing	Aircraft	Carrier	Tail Code & Modex	Deployment Dates
VFP-63 Det L/CVW-21	RF-8G	USS *Bon Homme Richard* (CVA-31)	PP 9xx	26 January 67–25 August 67
VFP-63 Det 11/CVW-10	RF-8G	USS *Intrepid* (CVS-11)	AK 4xx	11 May 67–30 December 67
VFP-63 Det 34/CVW-16	RF-8G	USS *Oriskany* (CVA-34)	AH 6xx	16 June 67–31 January 68
VFP-63 Det 43/CVW-15	RF-8G	USS *Coral Sea* (CVA-43)	NL 71x	26 July 67–6 April 68
VFP-63 Det 14/CVW-19	RF-8G	USS *Ticonderoga* (CVA-14)	NM 6xx	27 December 67–17 August 68
VFP-63 Det 31/CVW-5	RF-8G	USS *Bon Homme Richard* (CVA-31)	NF 60x	27 January 68–10 October 68
VFP-63 Det 11/CVW-10	RF-8G	USS *Intrepid* (CVS-11)	AK 4xx	4 June 68–8 February 69
VFP-63 Det 19/CVW-21	RF-8G	USS *Hancock* (CVA-19)	NP 6xx	18 July 68–3 March 69
VFP-63 Det 43/CVW-15	RF-8G	USS *Coral Sea* (CVA-43)	NL 5xx	7 September 68–18 April 69
VFP-63 Det 14/CVW-16	RF-8G	USS *Ticonderoga* (CVA-14)	AH 60x	1 February 69–18 September 69
VFP-63 Det 31/CVW-5	RF-8G	USS *Bon Homme Richard* (CVA-31)	NF 60x	18 March 69–29 October 69
VFP-63 Det 34/CVW-19	RF-8G	USS *Oriskany* (CVA-34)	NM 6xx	16 April 69–17 November 69
VFP-63 Det 19/CVW-21	RF-8G	USS *Hancock* (CVA-19)	NP 60x	2 August 69–15 April 70
VFP-63 Det 43/CVW-15	RF-8G	USS *Coral Sea* (CVA-43)	NL 60x	23 September 69–1 July 70
VFP-63 Det 38/CVW-8	RF-8G	USS *Shangri-La* (CVS-38)	AJ 6xx	5 March 70–17 December 70
VFP-63 Det 31/CVW-5	RF-8G	USS *Bon Homme Richard* (CVA-31)	NF 60x	2 April 70–12 November 70
VFP-63 Det 34/CVW-19	RF-8G	USS *Oriskany* (CVA-34)	NM 6xx	14 May 70–10 December 70
VFP-63 Det 1/CVW-21	RF-8G	USS *Hancock* (CVA-19)	NP 60x	22 October 70–2 June 71
VFP-63 Det 3/CVW-5	RF-8G	USS *Midway* (CVA-41)	NF 60x	16 April 71–6 November 71
VFP-63 Det 4/CVW-19	RF-8G	USS *Oriskany* (CVA-34)	NM 60x	14 May 71–18 December 71
VFP-63 Det 5/CVW-15	RF-8G	USS *Coral Sea* (CVA-43)	NL 60x	12 November 71–17 July 72
VFP-63 Det 1/CVW-21	RF-8G	USS *Hancock* (CVA-19)	NP 60x	7 January 72–3 October 72
VFP-63 Det 3/CVW-5	RF-8G	USS *Midway* (CVA-41)	NF 60x	10 April 72–3 March 73
VFP-63 Det 4/CVW-19	RF-8G	USS *Oriskany* (CVA-34)	NM 60x	5 June 72–30 March 73
VFP-63 Det 5/CVW-15	RF-8G	USS *Coral Sea* (CVA-43)	NL 60x	9 March 73–8 November 73
VFP-63 Det 1/CVW-21	RF-8G	USS *Hancock* (CVA-19)	NP 6xx	8 May 73–8 January 74

BuNo 150636, one of the rare F-4Gs flown by the Black Lions *of VF-213, 'bolters' during operations aboard USS* Kitty Hawk *(CVA-63) in 1965-66. During the Southeast Asian War, VF-213 made five more deployments aboard CVA-63.* (US Navy by courtesy of Cloud 9 Photography)

McDonnell F-4 Phantom II

The XF4H-1 prototype of the twinjet, two-seat Phantom II made its maiden flight on 27 May 1958, and the type entered service with VF-121 in December 1960. On 31 July 1964, 320 F-4A/B/Gs equipped fifteen Navy squadrons and six Marine squadrons. First going into action on 5 August 1964 during strikes against North Vietnamese PT boat bases, F-4Bs played a major role throughout the war and were credited with the destruction of forty-one enemy aircraft. During that period, five Navy F-4s were lost to MiGs, thirteen were brought down by SAMs, fifty-three were shot down by AAA and small arms fire, and fifty-four were lost in operational accidents.

With the exception of the F-4Gs which partially equipped VF-213 during a 1965–66 deployment aboard USS *Kitty Hawk* (CVA-63), the only two versions which were flown from carriers during the war were the F-4B and F-4J. The latter, which was first operated in the Gulf of Tonkin by VF-33 and VF-102 aboard USS *America* (CVA-66) in May 1968, had more powerful J79 engines and an AN/AWG-10 fire-control radar in place of the original AN/APQ-72 unit. In all instances, primary air-to-air armament consisted of Sparrow radar-guided missiles and Sidewinder infrared-homing missiles.

With empty multiple ejection racks and bearing 'triple nut' modex, the CAG bird from the Black Aces *of VF-41 has just returned from a strike sortie in August 1965 during the only war cruise of USS* Independence *(CVA-62). The tail of an EA-1F from VAW-13 and the forward fuselage of an UH-2A from HU-2 Det 62 can be seen in the foreground.* (Jerry Edwards)

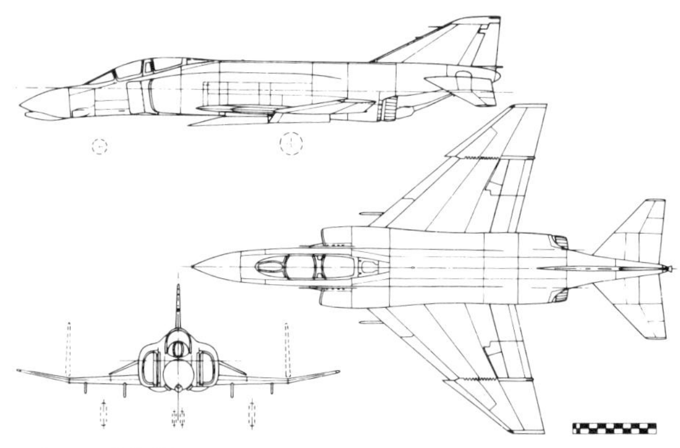

McDonnell F-4B

Right: Carrying a 600-gallon (2271-liter) centerline tank and armed with AIM-9G Sidewinders on underwing pylons and AIM-7E Sparrows recessed into the underside of the fuselage, this F-4J from the Ghostriders *of VF-142 is in the typical configuration adopted for CAP sorties. While equipped with F-4Js, the* Ghostriders *made one war cruise aboard USS* Constellation *(CVA-64) and two aboard USS* Enterprise *(CVAN-65).* (US Navy by courtesy of Rick Morgan)

F-4 and Phantom II Deployments

Squadron/Air Wing	*Aircraft*	*Carrier*	*Tail Code & Modex*	*Deployment Dates*
VF-11 *Red Rippers*				
VF-11/CVW-17	F-4B	USS *Forrestal* (CVA-59)	AA 1xx	6 June 67–14 September 67
VF-14 *Tophatters*				
VF-14/CVW-1	F-4B	USS *Franklin D. Roosevelt* (CVA-42)	AB 1xx	21 June 66–21 February 67
VF-21 *Freelancers*				
VF-21/CVW-2	F-4B	USS *Midway* (CVA-41)	NE 1xx	6 March 65–23 November 65
VF-21/CVW-2	F-4B	USS *Coral Sea* (CVA-43)	NE 1xx	29 July 66–23 February 67
VF-21/CVW-2	F-4B	USS *Ranger* (CVA-61)	NE 1xx	4 November 67–25 May 68
VF-21/CVW-2	F-4J	USS *Ranger* (CVA-61)	NE 1xx	26 October 68–17 May 69
VF-21/CVW-2	F-4J	USS *Ranger* (CVA-61)	NE 1xx	14 October 69–1 June 70
VF-21/CVW-2	F-4J	USS *Ranger* (CVA-61)	NE 1xx	27 October 70–17 June 71
VF-21/CVW-2	F-4J	USS *Ranger* (CVA-61)	NE 2xx	16 November 72–22 June 73
VF-31 *Tomcatters*				
VF-31/CVW-3	F-4J	USS *Saratoga* (CV-60)	AC 1xx	11 April 72–13 February 73
VF-32 *Swordsmen*				
VF-32/CVW-1	F-4B	USS *Franklin D. Roosevelt* (CVA-42)	AB 2xx	21 June 66–21 February 67
VF-33 *Tarsiers*				
VF-33/CVW-6	F-4J	USS *America* (CVA-66)	AE 2xx	10 April 68–16 December 68
VF-41 *Black Aces*				
VF-41/CVW-7	F-4B	USS *Independence* (CVA-62)	AG 1xx	10 May 65–13 December 65
VF-51 *Screaming Eagles*				
VF-51/CVW-15	F-4B	USS *Coral Sea* (CVA-43)	NL 1xx	12 November 71–17 July 72
VF-51/CVW-15	F-4B	USS *Coral Sea* (CVA-43)	NL 1xx	9 March 73–8 November 73

Squadron/Air Wing	Aircraft	Carrier	Tail Code & Modex	Deployment Dates
VF-74 *Be-devilers*				
VF-74/CVW-17	F-4B	USS *Forrestal* (CVA-59)	AA 2xx	6 June 67–14 September 67
VF-74/CVW-8	F-4J	USS *America* (CVA-66)	AJ 1xx	5 June 72–24 March 73
VF-84 *Jolly Rogers*				
VF-84/CVW-7	F-4B	USS *Independence* (CVA-62)	AG 2xx	10 May 65–13 December 65
VF-92 *Silver Kings*				
VF-92/CVW-9	F-4B	USS *Ranger* (CVA-61)	NG 2xx	5 August 64–6 May 65
VF-92/CVW-9	F-4B	USS *Enterprise* (CVAN-65)	NG 2xx	26 October 65–21 June 66
VF-92/CVW-9	F-4B	USS *Enterprise* (CVAN-65)	NG 2xx	19 November 66–6 July 67
VF-92/CVW-9	F-4B	USS *Enterprise* (CVAN-65)	NG 2xx	3 January 68–18 July 68
VF-92/CVW-9	F-4J	USS *Enterprise* (CVAN-65)	NG 2xx	6 January 69–2 July 69
VF-92/CVW-9	F-4J	USS *America* (CVA-66)	NG 2xx	10 April 70–21 December 70
VF-92/CVW-9	F-4J	USS *Constellation* (CVA-64)	NG 2xx	1 October 71–1 July 72
VF-92/CVW-9	F-4J	USS *Constellation* (CVA-64)	NG 2xx	5 January 73–11 October 73

Squadron/Air Wing	Aircraft	Carrier	Tail Code & Modex	Deployment Dates
VF-96 *Fighting Falcons*				
VF-96/CVW-9	F-4B	USS *Ranger* (CVA-61)	NG 6xx	5 August 64–6 May 65
VF-96/CVW-9	F-4B	USS *Enterprise* (CVAN-65)	NG 6xx	26 October 65–21 June 66
VF-96/CVW-9	F-4B	USS *Enterprise* (CVAN-65)	NG 6xx	19 November 66–6 July 67
VF-96/CVW-9	F-4B	USS *Enterprise* (CVAN-65)	NG 6xx	3 January 68–18 July 68
VF-96/CVW-9	F-4J	USS *Enterprise* (CVAN-65)	NG 1xx	6 January 69–2 July 69
VF-96/CVW-9	F-4J	USS *America* (CVA-66)	NG 1xx	10 April 70–21 December 70
VF-96/CVW-9	F-4J	USS *Constellation* (CVA-64)	NG 1xx	1 October 71–1 July 72
VF-96/CVW-9	F-4J	USS *Constellation* (CVA-64)	NG 1xx	5 January 73–11 October 73
VF-102 *Diamondbacks*				
VF-102/CVW-6	F-4J	USS *America* (CVA-66)	AE 1xx	10 April 68–16 December 68
VF-103 *Sluggers*				
VF-103/CVW-3	F-4J	USS *Saratoga* (CV-60)	AC 2xx	11 April 72–13 February 73

Squadron/Air Wing	Aircraft	Carrier	Tail Code & Modex	Deployment Dates
VF-111 *Sundowners*				
VF-111/CVW-15	F-4B	USS *Coral Sea* (CVA-43)	NL 2xx	12 November 71–17 July 72
VF-111/CVW-15	F-4B	USS *Coral Sea* (CVA-43)	NL 2xx	9 March 73–8 November 73
VF-114 *Aardvarks*				
VF-114/CVW-11	F-4B	USS *Kitty Hawk* (CVA-63)	NH 4xx	19 October 65–13 June 66
VF-114/CVW-11	F-4B	USS *Kitty Hawk* (CVA-63)	NH 2xx	5 November 66–20 June 67
VF-114/CVW-11	F-4B	USS *Kitty Hawk* (CVA-63)	NH 2xx	18 November 67–28 June 68
VF-114/CVW-11	F-4B	USS *Kitty Hawk* (CVA-63)	NH 2xx	30 December 68–4 September 69
VF-114/CVW-11	F-4J	USS *Kitty Hawk* (CVA-63)	NH 2xx	6 November 70–17 July 71
VF-114/CVW-11	F-4J	USS *Kitty Hawk* (CVA-63)	NH 2xx	17 February 72–28 November 72
VF-142 *Ghostriders*				
VF-142/CVW-14	F-4B	USS *Constellation* (CVA-64)	NK 2xx	5 May 64–1 February 65
VF-142/CVW-14	F-4B	USS *Ranger* (CVA-61)	NK 2xx	10 December 65–25 August 66
VF-142/CVW-14	F-4B	USS *Constellation* (CVA-64)	NK 2xx	29 April 67–4 December 67
VF-142/CVW-14	F-4B	USS *Constellation* (CVA-64)	NK 2xx	29 May 68–31 January 69
VF-142/CVW-14	F-4J	USS *Constellation* (CVA-64)	NK 2xx	11 August 69–8 May 70
VF-142/CVW-14	F-4J	USS *Enterprise* (CVAN-65)	NK 2xx	11 June 71–12 February 72
VF-142/CVW-14	F-4J	USS *Enterprise* (CVAN-65)	NK 2xx	12 September 72–12 June 73
VF-143 *Pukin Dogs*				
VF-143/CVW-14	F-4B	USS *Constellation* (CVA-64)	NK 3xx	5 May 64–1 February 65
VF-143/CVW-14	F-4B	USS *Ranger* (CVA-61)	NK 3xx	10 December 65–25 August 66
VF-143/CVW-14	F-4B	USS *Constellation* (CVA-64)	NK 3xx	29 April 67–4 December 67
VF-143/CVW-14	F-4B	USS *Constellation* (CVA-64)	NK 3xx	29 May 68–31 January 69
VF-143/CVW-14	F-4J	USS *Constellation* (CVA-64)	NK 3xx	11 August 69–8 May 70
VF-143/CVW-14	F-4J	USS *Enterprise* (CVAN-65)	NK 1xx	11 June 71–12 February 72
VF-143/CVW-14	F-4J	USS *Enterprise* (CVAN-65)	NK 1xx	12 September 72–12 June 73
VF-151 *Vigilantes*				
VF-151/CVW-15	F-4B	USS *Coral Sea* (CVA-43)	NL 1xx	7 December 64–1 November 65
VF-151/CVW-15	F-4B	USS *Constellation* (CVA-64)	NL 1xx	12 May 66–3 December 66
VF-151/CVW-15	F-4B	USS *Coral Sea* (CVA-43)	NL 1xx	26 July 67–6 April 68
VF-151/CVW-15	F-4B	USS *Coral Sea* (CVA-43)	NL 1xx	7 September 68–18 April 69
VF-151/CVW-15	F-4B	USS *Coral Sea* (CVA-43)	NL 1xx	23 September 69–1 July 70
VF-151/CVW-5	F-4B	USS *Midway* (CVA-41)	NF 2xx	16 April 71–6 November 71
VF-151/CVW-5	F-4B	USS *Midway* (CVA-41)	NF 2xx	10 April 72–3 March 73
VF-154 *Black Knights*				
VF-154/CVW-2	F-4B	USS *Coral Sea* (CVA-43)	NE 4xx	29 July 66–23 February 67
VF-154/CVW-2	F-4B	USS *Ranger* (CVA-61)	NE 4xx	4 November 67–25 May 68
VF-154/CVW-2	F-4J	USS *Ranger* (CVA-61)	NE 2xx	26 October 68–17 May 69
VF-154/CVW-2	F-4J	USS *Ranger* (CVA-61)	NE 2xx	14 October 69–1 June 70
VF-154/CVW-2	F-4J	USS *Ranger* (CVA-61)	NE 2xx	27 October 70–17 June 71
VF-154/CVW-2	F-4J	USS *Ranger* (CVA-61)	NE 1xx	16 November 72–22 June 73
VF-161 *Chargers*				
VF-161/CVW-15	F-4B	USS *Constellation* (CVA-64)	NL 2xx	12 May 66–3 December 66
VF-161/CVW-15	F-4B	USS *Coral Sea* (CVA-43)	NL 2xx	26 July 67–6 April 68
VF-161/CVW-15	F-4B	USS *Coral Sea* (CVA-43)	NL 2xx	7 September 68–18 April 69
VF-161/CVW-15	F-4B	USS *Coral Sea* (CVA-43)	NL 2xx	23 September 69–1 July 70
VF-161/CVW-5	F-4B	USS *Midway* (CVA-41)	NF 1xx	16 April 71–6 November 71
VF-161/CVW-5	F-4B	USS *Midway* (CVA-41)	NF 1xx	10 April 72–3 March 73
VF-213 *Black Lions*				
VF-213/CVW-11	F-4G/B	USS *Kitty Hawk* (CVA-63)	NH 1xx	19 October 65–13 June 66
VF-213/CVW-11	F-4B	USS *Kitty Hawk* (CVA-63)	NH 1xx	5 November 66–20 June 67
VF-213/CVW-11	F-4B	USS *Kitty Hawk* (CVA-63)	NH 1xx	18 November 67–28 June 68
VF-213/CVW-11	F-4B	USS *Kitty Hawk* (CVA-63)	NH 1xx	30 December 68–4 September 69
VF-213/CVW-11	F-4J	USS *Kitty Hawk* (CVA-63)	NH 1xx	6 November 70–17 July 71
VF-213/CVW-11	F-4J	USS *Kitty Hawk* (CVA-63)	NH 1xx	17 February 72–28 November 72
VMFA-333 *Shamrocks*				
VMFA-333/CVW-8	F-4J	USS *America* (CVA-66)	AJ 2xx	5 June 72–24 March 73

North American RA-5 Vigilante

Initially developed as the A3J-1 high-performance heavy attack aircraft to replace the A-3 Skywarrior, the Vigilante had first flown on 31 August 1958. The A3J-1 was delivered to VAH-7 in June 1961; by then, however, Polaris submarine-launched missiles had rendered this version (soon redesignated A-5As) obsolete as a nuclear bomber. The type was then successfully adapted as the RA-5C multi-sensor reconnaissance aircraft.

Although in clean configuration the Phantom II was faster than the Vigilante, in typical combat configuration RA-5Cs were faster as they flew without external tanks or armament whereas escorting F-4s carried a drop tank and missiles. Operating from the deck of the larger carriers throughout the war, eight Vigilante squadrons took heavy losses, twenty-seven RA-5Cs being lost either in combat or in operational accidents.

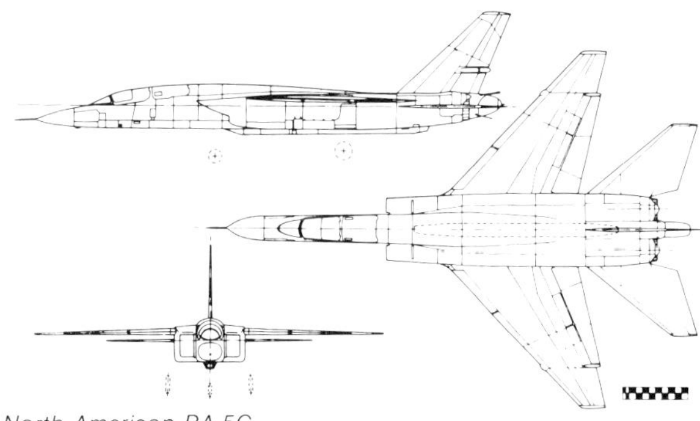

North American RA-5C

Below: While assigned to CVW-2, the Tigers of RVAH-1 deployed aboard USS Ranger *(CVA-61) for a cruise lasting from 27 October 1970 until 17 June 1971. During the war, the eight Reconnaissance Heavy Attack Squadrons which deployed to the Gulf of Tonkin lost fifteen Vigilantes to North Vietnamese AAA, three to SAMs, and nine in operational accidents. Although a little more than one out of every four RA-5Cs (fifty-five delivered as such, forty-three rebuilt from A-5As, and six rebuilt from A-5Bs) were lost during the war, Vigilantes had one of the lowest combat loss rates.* (Peter B Lewis)

RA-5 Vigilante Deployments

Squadron/Air Wing	*Aircraft*	*Carrier*	*Tail Code & Modex*	*Deployment Dates*
RVAH-1 *Tigers*				
RVAH-1/CVW-7	RA-5C	USS *Independence* (CVA-62)	AG 60x	10 May 65–13 December 65
RVAH-1/CVW-9	RA-5C	USS *Enterprise* (CVAN-65)	NG 10x	3 January 68–18 July 68
RVAH-1/CVW-2	RA-5C	USS *Ranger* (CVA-61)	NE 60x	27 October 70–17 June 71
RVAH-1/CVW-3	RA-5C	USS *Saratoga* (CV-60)	AC 6xx	11 April 72–13 February 73
RVAH-5 *Savage Sons*				
RVAH-5/CVW-9	RA-5C	USS *Ranger* (CVA-61)	NG 10x	5 August 64–6 May 65
RVAH-5/CVW-14	RA-5C	USS *Constellation* (CVA-64)	NK 12x	29 May 68–31 January 69
RVAH-5/CVW-2	RA-5C	USS *Ranger* (CVA-61)	NE 60x	14 October 69–1 June 70
RVAH-5/CVW-14	RA-5C	USS *Enterprise* (CVAN-65)	NK 60x	11 June 71–12 February 72
RVAH-5/CVW-2	RA-5C	USS *Ranger* (CVA-61)	NE 60x	16 November 72–22 June 73

Squadron/Air Wing	Aircraft	Carrier	Tail Code & Modex	Deployment Dates
RVAH-6 *Fleurs*				
RVAH-6/CVW-15	RA-5C	USS *Constellation* (CVA-64)	NL 70x	12 May 66–3 December 66
RVAH-6/CVW-2	RA-5C	USS *Ranger* (CVA-61)	NE 70x	4 November 67–25 May 68
RVAH-6/CVW-9	RA-5C	USS *Enterprise* (CVAN-65)	NG 60x	6 January 69–2 July 69
RVAH-6/CVW-11	RA-5C	USS *Kitty Hawk* (CVA-63)	NH 60x	6 November 70–17 July 71
RVAH-6/CVW-8	RA-5C	USS *America* (CVA-66)	AJ 60x	5 June 72–24 March 73
RVAH-7 *Peacemakers of the Fleet*				
RVAH-7/CVW-9	RA-5C	USS *Enterprise* (CVAN-65)	NG 10x	26 October 65–21 June 66
RVAH-7/CVW-9	RA-5C	USS *Enterprise* (CVAN-65)	NG 10x	19 November 66–6 July 67
RVAH-7/CVW-14	RA-5C	USS *Constellation* (CVA-64)	NK 60x	11 August 69–8 May 70
RVAH-7/CVW-11	RA-5C	USS *Kitty Hawk* (CVA-63)	NH 60x	17 February 72–28 November 72
RVAH-9 *Hoot Owls*				
RVAH-9/CVW-14	RA-5C	USS *Ranger* (CVA-61)	AC 9xx	10 December 65–25 August 66
RVAH-9/CVW-2	RA-5C	USS *Ranger* (CVA-61)	NE 60x	26 October 68–17 May 69
RVAH-11 *Checkertails*				
RVAH-11/CVW-17	RA-5C	USS *Forrestal* (CVA-59)	AA 60x	6 June 67–14 September 67
RVAH-11/CVW-11	RA-5C	USS *Kitty Hawk* (CVA-63)	NH 6xx	18 November 67–28 June 68
RVAH-11/CVW-11	RA-5C	USS *Kitty Hawk* (CVA-63)	NH 60x	30 December 68–4 September 69
RVAH-11/CVW-9	RA-5C	USS *Constellation* (CVA-64)	NG 60x	1 October 71–1 July 72
RVAH-12 *Speartips*				
RVAH-12/CVW-14	RA-5C	USS *Constellation* (CVA-64)	NK 12x	29 April 67–4 December 67
RVAH-12/CVW-9	RA-5C	USS *America* (CVA-66)	NG 60x	10 April 70–21 December 70
RVAH-12/CVW-9	RA-5C	USS *America* (CVA-66)	NG 60x	5 January 73–11 October 73
RVAH-13 *Bats*				
RVAH-13/CVW-11	RA-5C	USS *Kitty Hawk* (CVA-63)	NH 60x	19 October 65–13 June 66
RVAH-13/CVW-11	RA-5C	USS *Kitty Hawk* (CVA-63)	NH 60x	5 November 66–20 June 67
RVAH-13/CVW-6	RA-5C	USS *America* (CVA-66)	AE 60x	10 April 68–16 December 68
RVAH-13/CVW-14	RA-5C	USS *Enterprise* (CVAN-65)	NK 60x	12 September 72–12 June 73

Sikorsky SH-3 Sea King

Optimized initially for ASW operations and first flown on 11 March 1959, the twin-turboshaft engined Sea King later had the range of its activities increased when the SH-3G version was produced to replace the Kaman UH-2 in the utility-rescue role aboard carriers.

On 31 July 1964, the Navy had 159 SH-3As in service with ASW helicopter squadrons embarked aboard CVS carriers. In the Gulf of Tonkin, these squadrons not only flew ASW patrols but also combat SAR missions both at sea and inland, with their endurance being increased through the use of the HIFR (Hover-in-Flight Refueling) technique. In the SAR role they were joined by detachments from Helicopter Combat Support Squadron Seven flying SH-3As from attack carriers and smaller ships of Task Force 77. Later, HC-7 also flew HH-3As fitted with armament, armor, and additional fuel. In the utility-rescue role aboard attack carriers, SH-3As were first deployed by HC-1 in August 1969 aboard USS *Hancock* (CVA-19) and USS *Constellation* (CVA-64). The SH-3G version joined the fray in October 1970 aboard USS *Ranger* (CVA-61).

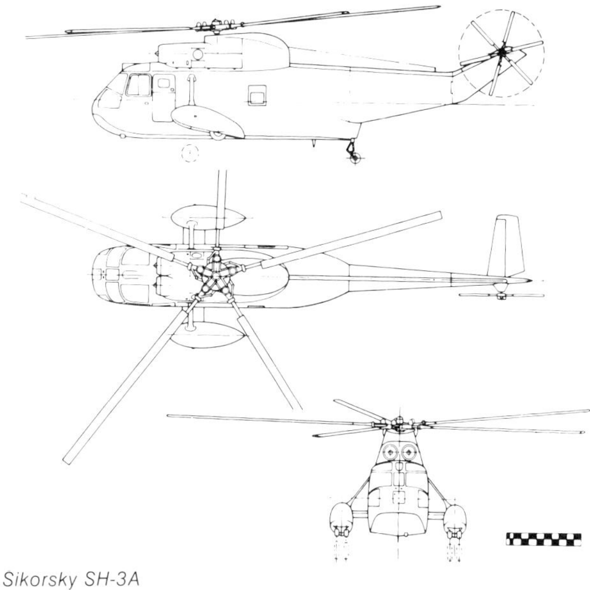

Sikorsky SH-3A

SH-3 Sea King Deployments

Squadron/Air Wing	Aircraft	Carrier	Tail Code & Modex	Deployment Dates
HC-1 *Pacific Fleet Angels*				
HC-1 Det 19/CVW-21	SH-3A	USS *Hancock* (CVA-19)	NP 00x	2 August 69–15 April 70
HC-1 Det 5/CVW-14	SH-3A	USS *Constellation* (CVA-64)	NK 00x	11 August 69–8 May 70
HC-1 Det 8/CVW-2	SH-3A	USS *Ranger* (CVA-61)	NE 00x	14 October 69–1 June 70
HC-1 Det 1/CVW-2	SH-3G	USS *Ranger* (CVA-61)	NE 00x	27 October 70–17 June 71
HC-1 Det 8/CVW-5	SH-3G	USS *Midway* (CVA-41)	NF 00x	16 April 71–6 November 71
HC-1 Det 4/CVW-14	SH-3G	USS *Enterprise* (CVAN-65)	NK 00x	11 June 71–12 February 72
HC-1 Det 3/CVW-9	SH-3G	USS *Constellation* (CVA-64)	NG 00x	1 October 71–1 July 72
HC-1 Det 6/CVW-15	SH-3G	USS *Coral Sea* (CVA-43)	NL 00x	12 November 71–17 July 72
HC-1 Det 7/CVW-21	SH-3G	USS *Hancock* (CVA-19)	NP 00x	7 January 72–3 October 72
HC-1 Det 1/CVW-11	SH-3G	USS *Kitty Hawk* (CVA-63)	NH 00x	17 February 72–28 November 72
HC-1 Det 2/CVW-5	SH-3G	USS *Midway* (CVA-41)	NF 00x	10 April 72–3 March 73
HC-1 Det 5/CVW-19	SH-3G	USS *Oriskany* (CVA-43)	NM 00x	5 June 72–30 March 73
HC-1 Det 4/CVW-2	SH-3G	USS *Ranger* (CVA-61)	NE 00x	16 November 72–22 June 73
HC-1 Det 6/CVW-15	SH-3G	USS *Coral Sea* (CVA-43)	NL 00x	9 March 73–8 November 73
HC-1 Det 3/CVW-21	SH-3G	USS *Hancock* (CVA-19)	NP 0xx	8 May 73–8 January 74

Left: Sikorsky modified one SH-3A to HH-3A standards and supplied nine conversion kits for installation by Navy personnel. In service with HC-7, HH-3As were normally operated without the TAT 102 minigun turrets and external tanks seen fitted on the prototype (Sikorsky Aircraft)

After deploying four times as a full SH-3A squadron aboard USS Kearsarge *(CVS-33), the Indians of HS-6 sent a detachment of SH-3Gs aboard USS* Constellation *(CVA-64) for the 1973 cruise.* (Peter B Lewis)

Squadron/Air Wing	Aircraft	Carrier	Tail Code & Modex	Deployment Dates
HC-2 *Fleet Angels*				
HC-2 Det 66/CVW-8	SH-3G	USS *America* (CVA-66)	AJ xx	5 June 72–24 March 73
HS-2 *Golden Falcons*				
HS-2/CVSG-57	SH-3A	USS *Hornet* (CVS-12)	NV 5x/6x	12 August 65–23 March 66
HS-2/CVSG-57	SH-3A	USS *Hornet* (CVS-12)	NV 5x/6x	27 March 67–28 October 67
HS-2/CVSG-57	SH-3A	USS *Hornet* (CVS-12)	NV 5x/6x	30 September 68–12 May 69
HS-2 Det 1/CVW-14	SH-3G	USS *Enterprise* (CVAN-65)	NK 00x	12 September 72–12 June 73
HS-4 *Black Knights*				
HS-4/CVSG-55	SH-3A	USS *Yorktown* (CVS-10)	NU 5x/6x	23 October 64–16 May 65
HS-4/CVSG-55	SH-3A	USS *Yorktown* (CVS-10)	NU 5x/6x	5 January 66–27 July 66
HS-4/CVSG-55	SH-3A	USS *Yorktown* (CVS-10)	NU 5x/6x	28 December 67–5 July 68
HS-6 *Indians*				
HS-6/CVSG-53	SH-3A	USS *Kearsarge* (CVS-33)	NS 5x/6x	19 June 64–16 December 64
HS-6/CVSG-53	SH-3A	USS *Kearsarge* (CVS-33)	NS 5x/6x	9 June 66–20 December 66
HS-6/CVSG-53	SH-3A	USS *Kearsarge* (CVS-33)	NS 5x/6x	17 August 67–6 April 68
HS-6/CVSG-53	SH-3A	USS *Kearsarge* (CVS-33)	NS 5x/6x	29 March 69–4 September 69
HS-6 Det 1/CVW-9	SH-3G	USS *Constellation* (CVA-64)	NG 00x	5 January 73–11 October 73
HS-7 *Shamrocks*				
HS-7/CVW-3	SH-3A/D	USS *Saratoga* (CV-60)	AC 00x	11 April 72–13 February 73
HS-8 *Eight Ballers*				
HS-8/CVSG-59	SH-3A	USS *Bennington* (CVS-20)	NT 5x/6x	22 March 65–7 October 65
HS-8/CVSG-59	SH-3A	USS *Bennington* (CVS-20)	NT 5x/6x	4 November 66–23 May 67
HS-8/CVSG-59	SH-3A	USS *Bennington* (CVS-20)	NT 5x/6x	1 May 68–9 November 68

With a top speed of only 319mph (513kmh), the A-1H Skyraider was the slowest fixed-wing aircraft flying combat sorties from TF 77 carriers. The EA-1F flying in a support role was even slower and, with a full complement of external ECM equipment, cruised at about 165 knots (306kmh). (US Navy by courtesy of Cloud 9 Photography)

***Table 10:* Aircraft Characteristics and Performance**

	A-1H	EA-1F	A-3B	A-4C	A-4F
Span, ft	50.0	50.0	72.5	27.5	27.5
(m)	*(15.24)*	*(15.24)*	*(22.10)*	*(8.38)*	*(8.38)*
Folded span, ft	23.9	24.0	49.4	—	—
(m)	*(7.28)*	*(7.32)*	*(15.06)*	—	—
Wing area, sq ft	400	400.3	812	260	260
(m²)	*(37.16)*	*(37.19)*	*(75.44)*	*(24.15)*	*(24.15)*
Length, ft	39.25	40.0	78.2	40.1	41.3
(m)	*(11.96)*	*(12.19)*	*(23.84)*	*(12.22)*	*(12.59)*
Height, ft	15.8	15.8	22.8	15.0	15.0
(m)	*(4.82)*	*(4.82)*	(6.95)	*(4.57)*	*(4.57)*
Empty weight, lb	12,072	12,097	39,620	9827	10,073
(kg)	*(5476)*	*(5487)*	*(17,791)*	*(4457)*	*(4569)*
Combat weight, lb	17,485	19,395	62,089	16,249	16,595
(kg)	*(7931)*	*(8797)*	*(28,163)*	*(7370)*	*(7527)*
Max. weight, lb	24,090	25,000	73,000	22,500	24,500
(kg)	*(10,925)*	*(11,340)*	*(33,110)*	*(10,205)*	*(11,115)*
Wing loading, lb/sq ft	43.7	48.5	76.5	62.5	63.8
(kg/m²)	*(213.4)*	*(236.5)*	*(373.3)*	*(305.2)*	*(311.7)*
Power loading, lb/hp	6.5	7.2	—	—	—
or lb/lb st	—	—	3.0	2.0	1.8
(kg/hp or kg/kg st)	*(2.9)*	*(3.3)*	*(3.0)*	*(2.0)*	*(1.8)*
Max speed at alt., mph/ft	342/15,400	308/17,400	585/35,000	657/4,000	672/3,000
(kmh/m)	*(550/4695)*	*(496/5305)*	*(941/10,670)*	*(1057/1220)*	*(1081/915)*
Max. speed at sea level, mph	319	289	640	655	672
(kmh)	*(513)*	*(465)*	*(1030)*	*(1054)*	*(1081)*
Cruising speed, mph	180	190	502	497	497
(kmh)	*(290)*	*(306)*	*(808)*	*(800)*	*(800)*
Max. rate of climb, ft/min	2850	2320	6510	7500	11,750
(m/sec)	*(14)*	*(12)*	*(33)*	*(38)*	*(60)*
Combat ceiling, ft	28,500	27,500	40,400	44,000	45,000
(m)	*(8685)*	*(8380)*	*(12,315)*	*(13,410)*	*(13,715)*
Normal range, miles	1315	1360	2850	825	1375
(km)	*(2115)*	*(2190)*	*(4585)*	*(1325)*	*(2210)*
Max. range, miles	3240	2315	3200	1860	2070
(km)	*(5215)*	*(3725)*	*(5150)*	*(2990)*	*(3360)*
Engine(s)	1 × R-3350-26WB	1 × R-3350-26WA	2 × J57-P-10	1 × J65-W-16A	1 × J52-P-8A
Max. thrust, lb	—	—	2 × 10,500	1 × 8300	1 × 9300
(kg)	—	—	*(1 × 4765)*	*(1 × 3765)*	*(1 × 4218)*
Take-off rating, hp	1 × 2700	1 × 2700	—	—	—
Guns	4 × 20mm	—	—	2 × 20mm	2 × 20mm
Air-to-air missiles	—	—	—	—	—
	—	—	—	—	—
Max. offensive load, lb	8000	—	12,800	8055	9195
(kg)	*(3630)*	—	*(5805)*	*(3655)*	*(4170)*

	A-6A	EA-6B	E-1B	E-2A	S-2E
Span, ft	53.0	53.0	72.3	80.6	72.6
(m)	*(16.15)*	*(16.15)*	*(22.04)*	*(24.57)*	*(22.12)*
Folded span, ft	25.3	25.8	30.4	29.3	27.3
(m)	*(7.72)*	*(7.86)*	*(9.27)*	*(8.93)*	*(8.32)*
Wing area, sq ft	529	529	506	700	496
(m^2)	*(49.14)*	*(49.14)*	*(47.01)*	*(65.03)*	*(46.08)*
Length, ft	54.8	59.8	45.3	56.3	43.5
(m)	*(16.69)*	*(18.23)*	*(13.82)*	*(17.16)*	*(13.26)*
Height, ft	16.2	16.3	16.8	18.3	16.6
(m)	*(4.93)*	*(4.95)*	*(5.13)*	*(5.58)*	*(5.06)*
Empty weight, lb	25,298	32,162	20,638	36,063	18,820
(kg)	*(11,475)*	*(14,588)*	*(9361)*	*(16,358)*	*(8537)*
Combat weight, lb	41,675	48,287	24,800	46,600	24,917
(kg)	*(18,903)*	*(21,903)*	*(11,249)*	*(21,137)*	*(11,302)*
Max. weight, lb	53,700	65,000	26,600	49,638	29,150
(kg)	*(24,355)*	*(29,485)*	*(12,065)*	*(22,515)*	*(13,220)*
Wing loading, lb/sq ft	78.8	91.3	49.0	66.6	50.2
(kg/m^2)	*(384.7)*	*(445.7)*	*(239.3)*	*(325.0)*	*(245.3)*
Power loading, lb/hp	—	—	8.13	5.75	8.17
or lb/lb st	2.45	2.16	—	—	—
(kg/hp or kg/kg st)	*(2.45)*	*(2.16)*	*(3.69)*	*(2.61)*	*(3.71)*
Max. speed at alt., mph/ft	555/35,900	665/5000	238/4000	374/12,500	265/5000
(kmh/m)	*(893/10,940)*	*(1070/1525)*	*(383/1220)*	*(602/3810)*	*(412/1525)*
Max. speed at sea level, mph	646	658	231	368	242
(kmh)	*(1039)*	*(1059)*	*(372)*	*(592)*	*(389)*
Cruising speed, mph	481	482	163	315	150
(kmh)	*(774)*	*(775)*	*(262)*	*(507)*	*(241)*
Max. rate of climb, ft/min	4850	11,360	1120	2385	1830
(m/sec)	*(25)*	*(58)*	*(6)*	*(12)*	*(9)*
Combat ceiling, ft	40,250	43,100	15,800	31,700	21,700
(m)	*(12,270)*	*(13,135)*	*(4815)*	*(9660)*	*(6615)*
Normal range, miles	1515	1625	1000	1850	1150
(km)	*(2440)*	*(2615)*	*(1610)*	*(2975)*	*(1850)*
Max. range, miles	3250	2020	1035	1905	1300
(km)	*(5230)*	*(3250)*	*(1665)*	*(3065)*	*(2090)*
Engine(s)	2 × J52-P-6A	2 × J52-P-408	2 × R-1820-82A	2 × T56-A-8	2 × R-1820-82A
Max. thrust, lb	2 × 8500	2 × 11,200	—	—	—
(kg)	*(2 × 3856)*	*(2 × 5080)*	—	—	—
Take-off rating, hp	—	—	2 × 1525	2 × 4050	2 × 1525
Guns	—	—	—	—	—
Air-to-air missiles	—	—	—	—	—
	—	—	—	—	—
Max. offensive load, lb	16,800	—	—	—	4906
(kg)	*(7620)*	—	—	—	*(2225)*

Left: The A-6A carried a heavier punch than any other aircraft operating from TF 77 carriers. The Sunday Punchers of VA-75 deployed to the Gulf of Tonkin aboard USS Saratoga *(CVA-60) in 1972-73. Earlier they had deployed aboard USS* Independence *(CVA-62), when in 1965 they had taken the* Intruder *for its combat debut, and aboard USS* Kitty Hawk *(CVA-63) in 1967-68.* (Peter B Lewis)

The F-8Js were modernized F-8Es with increased fuselage strength, increased wing fatigue life, larger horizontal tail, external fuel provisions, more powerful engine, incorporation of Sidewinder Extended Acquisition Mode (SEAM), pulse doppler mode added to the AN/APQ-94 radar, and Shoehorn ECM fit. (Peter B Lewis)

	A-7A	A-7E	F-8C	F-8J	RF-8A
Span, ft	38.7	38.7	35.7	35.7	35.7
(m)	*(11.80)*	*(11.80)*	*(10.87)*	*(10.87)*	*(10.87)*
Folded span, ft	23.7	23.7	22.5	22.5	22.5
(m)	*(7.21)*	*(7.21)*	*(6.86)*	*(6.86)*	*(6.86)*
Wing area, sq ft	375	375	375	375	375
(m^2)	*(34.84)*	*(34.84)*	*(34.84)*	*(34.84)*	*(34.84)*
Length, ft	46.1	46.1	54.3	54.5	54.5
(m)	*(14.04)*	*(14.04)*	*(16.54)*	*(16.61)*	*(16.61)*
Height, ft	16.0	16.1	15.8	15.8	15.8
(m)	*(4.88)*	*(4.91)*	*(4.80)*	*(4.80)*	*(4.80)*
Empty weight, lb	15,497	18,546	16,483	19,815	16,796
(kg)	*(7029)*	*(8412)*	*(7477)*	*(8988)*	*(7619)*
Combat weight, lb	27,856	28,731	24,475	26,793	23,752
(kg)	*(12,635)*	*(13,032)*	*(11,102)*	*(12,153)*	*(10,774)*
Max. weight, lb	34,500	40,450	27,938	35,000	27,822
(kg)	*(15,650)*	*(18,350)*	*(12,670)*	*(15,875)*	*(12,620)*
Wing loading, lb/sq ft	74.3	76.6	65.3	71.4	63.3
(kg/m^2)	*(362.7)*	*(374.1)*	*(318.7)*	*(348.8)*	*(309.2)*
Power loading, lb/hp	—	—	—	—	—
or lb/lb st	2.45	1.9	1.4	1.4	1.5
(kg/hp or kg/kg st)	*(2.45)*	*(1.9)*	*(1.4)*	*(1.4)*	*(1.5)*
Max. speed at alt., mph/ft	585/13,000	653/6000	1105/35,000	1151/36,090	984/35,000
(kmh/m)	*(941/3960)*	*(1051/1830)*	*(1778/10,670)*	*(1852/11,000)*	*(1583/10,670)*
Max. speed at sea level, mph	685	693	752	762	731
(kmh)	*(1102)*	*(1115)*	*(1210)*	*(1226)*	*(1176)*
Cruising speed, mph	478	470	570	556	570
(kmh)	*(769)*	*(756)*	*(917)*	*(895)*	*(917)*
Max. rate of climb, ft/min	5000	8630	25,400	22,300	10,500
(m/sec)	*(25)*	*(44)*	*(129)*	*(113)*	*(53)*
Combat ceiling, ft	41,500	37,910	52,500	51,000	51,800
(m)	*(12,650)*	*(11,555)*	*(16,000)*	*(15,545)*	*(15,790)*
Normal range, miles	1475	1265	1490	1375	2000
(km)	*(2375)*	*(2035)*	*(2400)*	*(2210)*	*(3220)*
Max. range, miles	3190	2860	1725	1600	2325
(km)	*(5135)*	*(4600)*	*(2775)*	*(2575)*	*(3740)*
Engine(s)	1 × TF-30-P-6	1 × TF41-A-2	1 × J57-P-6	1 × J57-P-420	1 × J57-P-4
Max. thrust lb	1 × 11,350	1 × 15,000	1 × 16,900	1 × 19,600	1 × 16,000
(kg)	*(1 × 5148)*	*(1 × 6804)*	*(1 × 7666)*	*(1 × 8890)*	*(1 × 7257)*
Guns	2 × 20mm	1 × 20mm	4 × 20mm	4 × 20mm	—
Air-to-air missiles	2 × AIM-9	2 × AIM-9	2 × AIM-9	4 × AIM-9	—
Max. offensive load, lb	13,500	13,500	—	2285	—
(kg)	*(6125)*	*(6125)*	—	*(1036)*	—

	F-4B	F-4J	RA-5C
Span, ft	38.4	38.4	53.0
(m)	*(11.70)*	*(11.70)*	*(16.15)*
Folded span, ft	27.6	27.6	42.3
(m)	*(8.41)*	*(8.41)*	*(12.89)*
Wing area, sq ft	530	530	753.7
(m²)	*(49.24)*	*(49.24)*	*(70.02)*
Length, ft	58.3	58.3	76.5
(m)	*(17.77)*	*(17.77)*	*(23.32)*
Height, ft	16.3	15.8	19.3
(m)	*(4.97)*	*(4.82)*	*(5.89)*
Empty weight, lb	27,897	30,778	37,498
(kg)	*(12,654)*	*(13,961)*	*(17,009)*
Combat weight, lb	38,505	41,673	55,617
(kg)	*(17,466)*	*(18,903)*	*(25,227)*
Max. weight, lb	55,950	56,000	79,590
(kg)	*(25,375)*	*(25,400)*	*(36,100)*
Wing loading, lb/sq ft	72.7	78.6	73.8
(kg/m²)	*(354.7)*	*(383.9)*	*(360.3)*
Power loading, lb/hp	—	—	—
or lb/lb st	1.13	1.17	1.64
(kg/hp or kg/kg st)	*(1.13)*	*(1.17)*	*(1.64)*
Max. speed at alt., mph/ft	1490/40,000	1428/36,090	1290/40,000
(kmh/m)	*(2397/12,190)*	*(2298/11,000)*	*(2075/12,190)*
Max. speed at sea level, mph	845	889	783
(kmh)	*(1360)*	*(1430)*	*(1260)*
Cruising speed, mph	580	564	567
(kmh)	*(933)*	*(907)*	*(912)*
Max. rate of climb, ft/min	40,800	41,250	27,900
(m/sec)	*(207)*	*(210)*	*(142)*
Combat ceiling, ft	56,850	54,700	48,400
(m)	*(17,325)*	*(16,675)*	*(14,750)*
Normal range, miles	1295	1275	2245
(km)	*(2085)*	*(2050)*	*(3610)*
Max. range, miles	2300	1955	3065
(km)	*(3700)*	*(3145)*	*(4930)*
Engine(s)	2 × J79-GE-8	2 × J79-GE-10	2 × J79-GE-8
Max. thrust, lb	2 × 17,000	2 × 17,859	2 × 17,000
(kg)	*(2 × 7710)*	*(2 × 8100)*	*(2 × 7710)*
Guns	—	—	—
Air-to-air missiles	4 × AIM-7	4 × AIM-7	—
	4 × AIM-9	4 × AIM-9	—
Max. offensive load, lb	12,000	12,000	—
(kg)	*(5440)*	*(5440)*	—

Left: In clean configuration, the F-4B was the fastest aircraft operating from TF 77 carriers. However, in typical combat configuration with missiles and one or more external tanks it was slower than the RA-5C which almost always flew in clean configuration. (By courtesy of Cloud 9 Photography)

Table 11: **Helicopter Characteristics and Performance**

	UH-2A	SH-3A
Rotor diameter, ft	44.0	62.0
(m)	*(13.41)*	*(18.90)*
Rotor disc area, sq ft	1519.8	3017.5
(m^2)	*(141.2)*	*(280.4)*
Length (rotors turning), ft	52.2	72.7
(m)	*(15.90)*	*(22.15)*
Height, ft	12.3	15.5
(m)	*(3.75)*	*(4.72)*
Empty weight, lb	6216	11,419
(kg)	*(2820)*	*(5180)*
Loaded weight, lb	10,680	18,044
(kg)	*(4844)*	*(8185)*
Rotor loading, lb/sq ft	7.0	6.0
(kg/m^2)	*(34.3)*	*(29.2)*
Power loading, lb/shp	8.5	7.2
(kg/shp)	*(3.9)*	*(3.3)*
Max. speed at sea level, mph	162	162
(kmh)	*(261)*	*(261)*
Cruising speed, mph	152	150
(kmh)	*(245)*	*(241)*
Max. rate of climb, ft/min	2100	1690
(m/sec)	*(11)*	*(9)*
Hovering ceiling OGE, ft	5100	8200
(m)	*(1555)*	*(2500)*
Normal range, miles	670	625
(km)	*(1080)*	*(1005)*
Engine(s)	1 × T58-GE-8B	2 × T58-GE-8B
Take-off rating, shp	1 × 1250	2 × 1250

To be able to respond more rapidly to Mayday calls, TF 77 regularly operated SAR helicopters from the decks of cruisers, frigates, and destroyers sailing close to the North Vietnamese coast. This UH-2A from HC-1 is seen operating from the helicopter deck on the stern of the guided missile frigate USS Mahan *(DLG-11).* (Kaman Aerospace)

Index